"Changing perspectives" in current scholarship on the Revolution of 1688 are beginning to revise the so-called "Whig view" which has been accepted for almost three hundred years. In an effort to advance this process of revision, this volume of novel and interdisciplinary essays offers new interpretations of the Revolution of 1688–89 and of the late Stuart and early Hanoverian world from an international and an English domestic perspective.

By employing some newly recovered or hitherto neglected material, and by dealing with little-explored issues from the perspectives of British, Dutch, and colonial American history, and of British political and religious history and theory, literature, law, and women's history, the contributors broaden the context in which the Revolution is usually placed and in doing so unite multiple disciplines. Several overriding conclusions emerge. The Revolution was more complex and subtle in process, ideology, settlement, and result than has been acknowledged previously. A lively print culture assured the circulation and importance of political and religious ideas. Radical as well as conservative ideas survived. The unfolding of the Revolution contained many contingent variables; there was nothing predictable or preordained about it. The events of 1688–89 comprised many revolutions that played out differently and were perceived differently from the vantage point of high or popular culture or in the contexts of England, Scotland, Ireland, France, and the American colonies.

The Revolution of 1688–1689

Allegory of the accession of William and Mary. Etching by Romeyn de Hooghe published by Carel Allard, 1689. The Banqueting House is depicted on the left; in the lower right Mary's ermine stole partially covers the portrait of one of her ancestors, William the Conqueror. The British Museum.

The Revolution of 1688–1689

Changing perspectives

Edited by Lois G. Schwoerer
Professor of History, The George Washington University

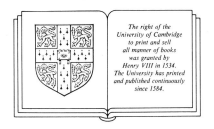

The right of the University of Cambridge to print and sell all manner of books was granted by Henry VIII in 1534. The University has printed and published continuously since 1584.

CAMBRIDGE UNIVERSITY PRESS
Cambridge
New York   Port Chester
Melbourne   Sydney

Published by the Press Syndicate of the University of Cambridge
The Pitt Building, Trumpington Street, Cambridge CB2 1RP
40 West 20th Street, New York, NY 10011–4211, USA
10 Stamford Road, Oakleigh, Victoria 3166, Australia

First published 1992

Printed in Great Britain at the University Press, Cambridge

A catalogue record for their book is available from the British Library

Library of Congress cataloguing in publication data
The Revolution of 1688–1689: changing perspectives/edited by Lois
G. Schwoerer.
    p.   cm.
Includes bibliographical references (p.   ) and index.
ISBN 0–521–39321–3 (hardback)
1. Great Britain – History – Revolution of 1688. I. Schwoerer,
Lois G.
DA452.R.49 1992
941.06′7 – dc20   90–26170 CIP

ISBN 0 521 393213 hardback

WV

This book is dedicated to

The Folger Institute Center for the History of British Political Thought,

Its Steering Committee, and

Its Spring 1989 seminar on the Glorious Revolution

Contents

Illustrations

Map

Figure

Contributors

Stephen B. Baxter is Kenan Professor of History at the University of North Carolina in Chapel Hill. Among his books are *The Development of the Treasury, 1660–1702* (Cambridge, Mass., Harvard University Press, 1957) and *William III* (London, Longman, Green, 1966). A Fellow of the Royal Historical Society, Baxter is the winner of two Guggenheim Fellowships. He has served as Clark Library Professor at the University of California, Los Angeles, and on the editorial board of the *Journal of Modern History*. At present he is on the editorial board of *Albion*.

J. M. Beattie is a University Professor at the University of Toronto. Author of *The English Court in the Reign of George I* (Cambridge University Press, 1967) and *Crime and the Courts in England, 1660–1800* (Princeton University Press, 1986), he is now working on criminal law and the administration of justice in London in the half century after the Revolution of 1688–89, and the history of the criminal trial in the eighteenth and nineteenth centuries.

Karl S. Bottigheimer teaches history at the State University of New York at Stony Brook, Long Island. He has written on the Cromwellian land settlement in Ireland – *English Money and Irish Land: the Adventurers in the Cromwellian Settlement* (Oxford, Clarendon Press, 1971) – and a short history of Ireland – *Ireland and the Irish* (New York, Columbia University Press, 1982). His current work deals with religious polarization and "The Failure of the Revolution in Ireland."

Gary S. De Krey teaches history at St. Olaf College, his Alma Mater. He has published *A Fractured Society: the Politics of London in the First Age of Party, 1688–1715* (Oxford, Clarendon Press and New York, Oxford University Press, 1985). An essay in the *Journal of Modern History* (1983) won the North American Conference on British Studies' Walter D. Love Prize for the best article published that year. Professor De Krey's research was supported by a 1987–88 grant from the National Endowment for the Humanities.

Jack P. Greene is Andrew W. Mellon Professor in the Humanities at the Johns Hopkins University. Long interested in metropolitan–colonial relations in the early modern British Empire, he has published *The Quest for Power: the Lower Houses of the Assembly in the Southern Royal Colonies, 1689–1776* (Chapel Hill,

University of North Carolina Press, 1963); *Great Britain and the American Colonies, 1606–1763* (Columbia, University of South Carolina Press, 1970); and *Peripheries and Center: Constitutional Development in the Extended Polities of the British Empire and the United States, 1607–1788* (Athens, Ga., University of Georgia Press, 1986).

K. H. D. Haley is Emeritus Professor of Modern History at the University of Sheffield. His extensive publications on Anglo-Dutch subjects in the seventeenth century include *William of Orange and the English Opposition, 1672–4* (Oxford, Clarendon Press, 1953); *The First Earl of Shaftesbury* (Oxford, Clarendon Press, 1968); *The Dutch in the Seventeenth Century* (Oxford, Clarendon Press, 1972); *An English Diplomat in the Low Countries: Sir William Temple and John de Witt, 1665–1672* (Oxford, Clarendon Press, 1986); and *The English and the Dutch* (London, George Philip, 1988). He was elected Fellow of the British Academy in 1987.

Bruce P. Lenman, reader in Modern History at St. Andrews, has written prize-winning works on *An Economic History of Modern Scotland* (London, B. T. Batsford, 1977), and *The Jacobite Risings in Britain* (London, Eyre Methuen, 1980). His other books include *The Jacobite Clans of the Great Glen* (London, Methuen, 1984) and *The Jacobite Cause* (Glasgow, Richard Drew in association with the National Trust for Scotland, 1986). A Fellow of the Royal Historical Society, Lenman has been a British Academy Fellow at the Newberry Library, a Council of Europe Research Fellow in Stockholm, and a John Carter Brown Library Fellow. In 1988–89 he was the James Pinckney Harrison Visiting Professor at the College of William and Mary. He is also a historian of the British Empire in India, and the author of some forty scholarly articles.

Howard Nenner teaches History at Smith College. His major study is *By Colour of Law: Legal Culture and Constitutional Politics in England, 1660–1689* (University of Chicago Press, 1977). He is currently completing a book on the English rule of monarchical succession from 1587 to 1714. A member of the executive committee of the North American Conference on British Studies and a member of the editorial board of the *American Journal of Legal History*, Nenner has been a seminar director at the Folger Institute Center for the History of British Political Thought, and a Fellow at the Washington University Center for the History of Freedom.

J. G. A. Pocock is the Harry C. Black Professor of History at the Johns Hopkins University. Since 1982 he has been chair of the Steering Committee of the Center for the History of British Political Thought, Folger Institute. His works include *The Ancient Constitution and the Feudal Law: a Study of English Historical Thought in the Seventeenth Century, A Reissue with a Retrospect* (Cambridge University Press, 1987); *Politics, Language and Time: Essays in Political Thought and History* (New York, Atheneum, 1971); *The Machiavellian Moment: Florentine Political Thought and the Atlantic Republican Tradition* (Princeton University Press, 1975); and *Virtue, Commerce, and History: Essays on Political Thought and History, Chiefly in the Eighteenth Century* (Cambridge University Press, 1985).

Lois Potter teaches English literature at the University of Leicester. Her publications include *A Preface to Milton* (London, Longman, 1971; 2nd edn 1986); an edition of books iii–iv of *Paradise Lost* (Cambridge University Press, 1976); an edition of *The True Tragicomedy Lately Acted at Court* (New York, Garland, 1983); *Twelfth Night: Text and Performance* (London, Macmillan, 1985); and *Secret Rites and Secret Writing: Royalist Literature, 1641–60* (Cambridge University Press, 1989). She was also General Editor of volumes i and iv of the *Reveles History of Drama in English* (London, Methuen, 1981, 1983). The author of many articles, she is now working on an edition of *The Two Noble Kinsmen* for the Arden Shakespeare.

John C. Rule is a Professor of History at The Ohio State University. He has been a fellow of the Folger Library and of the Henry E. Huntington Library and has served as associate editor of *French Historical Studies* and as co-president of the Society for French Historical Studies. He has edited and contributed to *Louis XIV and the Craft of Kingship* (Columbus, Ohio State University Press, 1970). His other publications include *Louis XIV* (Englewood Cliffs, N.J., Prentice-Hall, 1974), and *The Reign of Louis XIV* (Atlantic Highlands, N.J., Humanities Press, 1990). His book *Louis XIV: Bureaucratic King* is forthcoming.

Gordon J. Schochet is a Professor of Political Science at Rutgers University, and a member of the Steering Committee of the Folger Institute Center for the History of British Political Thought. Currently editing John Locke's unpublished writings on religious toleration and completing a book provisionally titled *John Locke and the Politics of Religious Toleration*, he is the author of *Patriarchalism and Political Thought: the Authoritarian Family and Political Speculation and Attitudes Especially in Seventeenth-Century England* (New York, Basic Books, 1975) and numerous articles, co-author of *Moral Development and Politics* (New York, Praeger, 1980), and editor of several volumes. Schochet is a former Fulbright Scholar and a National Endowment for the Humanities Senior Fellow. He was a Fellow at the Washington University Center for the History of Freedom.

Lois G. Schwoerer is a Professor of History at the George Washington University and a member of the Steering Committee of the Folger Institute Center for the History of British Political Thought. Her books are *"No Standing Armies!" The Antistanding Army Ideology in Seventeenth-Century England* (Baltimore and London, Johns Hopkins University Press, 1974), which won the Berkshire Conference of Women Historians' prize for the best book published by a woman historian in 1974; *The Declaration of Rights, 1689* (Baltimore and London, Johns Hopkins University Press, 1981), which received honorable mention in the John Ben Snow Prize competition (1981–82); and *Lady Rachel Russell: "One of the Best of Women"* (Baltimore and London, Johns Hopkins University Press, 1988). She has also published numerous articles, two of which have won prizes: the North American Conference on British Studies' Walter D. Love Prize in 1985, and the prize for the best paper presented at the Carolinas Symposium on British Studies in 1986. A Fellow of the Royal Historical Society, she was also a Fellow at the Washington University Center for the History of Freedom in 1987 and the Furness Lecturer in 1988 at Colorado State University. Formerly a Senior Fellow of the National Endowment for the Humanities and a Senior Fellow at the Folger Shakespeare Library, Schwoerer served as president of the North American Conference on British Studies from 1987 to 1989.

W. A. Speck is Professor of Modern History at the University of Leeds and has also been a visiting professor at the Universities of Iowa, Portland State, and Yale. His books include *Stability and Strife: England 1714 to 1760* (Cambridge, Mass., Harvard University Press, 1977); *The Butcher: the Duke of Cumberland and the Suppression of the 'Forty-five* (Oxford, Blackwell Press, 1981); *Society and Literature in England 1700–1760* (Atlantic Highlands, N.J., Humanities Press, 1983); and *Reluctant Revolutionaries: Englishmen and the Revolution of 1688* (Oxford University Press, 1988). He is currently working on a Concise History of Britain for Cambridge University Press.

Rachel J. Weil completed her Ph.D. in history at Princeton University in 1990 and is now teaching at Georgia State University. Her dissertation is entitled "'And Women Rule Over Them': Sexual Ideology and Political Propaganda in England, 1688–1714." She is co-editor with Carol Barash of a collection of primary sources, *Sex and the Social Order in England, 1660–1730*, forthcoming from Pandora Press.

Steven N. Zwicker is a Professor of English, Washington University, St. Louis. He has written on Marvell, Milton, Restoration politics and literature, and literary authority, including *Dryden's Political Poetry: the Typology of King and Nation* (Providence, Brown University Press, 1972); and *Politics and Language in Dryden's Poetry: the Arts of Disguise* (Princeton University Press, 1984). He is co-editor of *Politics of Discourse: the Literature and History of Seventeenth-Century England* (Berkeley, University of California Press, 1987), and has work forthcoming, including a Penguin *Selected Dryden*.

Acknowledgments

The contributors are as one in wanting to thank the many institutions and individuals who have made this volume possible. Above all, we are grateful to the George Washington University and the Folger Shakespeare Library for their co-sponsorship of an international and interdisciplinary conference entitled "The Glorious Revolution, 1688–89: Changing Perspectives," held in Washington, D.C., April 13–15, 1989, from which most of the essays printed in this volume were drawn. Dr. Stephen Joel Trachtenberg, President, the George Washington University, and Dr. Werner Gundersheimer, Director, Folger Shakespeare Library, wholeheartedly supported the project. Ms. Lu Kleppinger, Director of Conferences and Institutes, the George Washington University, managed the administrative side of the conference with the able assistance of Dr. Lena Cowan Orlin, Executive Director, Folger Institute. The conference and the publication project won the generous support of the National Endowment for the Humanities (an independent federal agency), the History Department of the George Washington University, and the Folger Institute Center for the History of British Political Thought. The conference alone enjoyed the patronage of several British, Dutch, and other American organizations, whose assistance it is a pleasure to acknowledge and thank. We are grateful to the British Embassy, Washington, D.C.: Ambassador Sir Anthony Acland and Lady Acland and Mr. James Daniel, then Cultural Attaché; and to the Royal Netherlands Embassy, Washington, D.C.: Ambassador and Mrs. John Fein and Mr. Robert Aarsee, Cultural Attaché, and his successor, Mr. Robert Sieben. Thanks go also to the British Academy, the British Council, Dr. Joel Lipkin, and the North American Conference of British Studies for their support of the conference. We also acknowledge the valuable insights offered by the conference audience and commentators, K. H. D. Haley, Cynthia Herrup, Carol Kay, J. G. A. Pocock, C. Clayton Roberts, and Lawrence Stone.

The illustrations in this book are reproduced with the kind permission of the British Museum, the Guildhall Library, City of London, the Henry E. Huntington Library, and the Ulster Folk and Transport Museum. We express warm appreciation to these institutions.

Individual contributors wish to record their special thanks, saying, again with one voice, that mistakes that may remain in their essays are their responsibility alone.

John Beattie is grateful for financial support to the Social Science and

Humanities Research Council of Canada and to the Ministry of the Solicitor General of Canada through its Contributions Grant to the Centre of Criminology at the University of Toronto. He also thanks Cynthia Herrup and John Langbein for their comments on an early draft of his essay.

Gary De Krey wishes to thank the following for their assistance with earlier drafts of his essay: Lois G. Schwoerer, Catherine Doherty De Krey, Cynthia Herrup, and Lawrence Stone. His research essay was made possible, in part, by a grant from the National Endowment for the Humanities.

Howard Nenner thanks Professor Clayton Roberts for his perceptive reading of his essay in draft form and for his several suggestions, which, he says, have made his paper better than it might otherwise have been.

Gordon Schochet notes that the research on which his essay is based was generously funded by the Fellowship and Research Divisions of the National Endowment for the Humanities as well as by the Center for the History of Freedom of Washington University, St. Louis, Missouri. He is delighted to record his gratitude to them and to Lois G. Schwoerer for permission to use her photocopy of Roger Morrice, "The Entr'ing Book." His special thanks go to Louise Haberman.

Lois G. Schwoerer wishes to thank the staff at the Folger Shakespeare Library for their ongoing kindnesses. She is grateful to the staff of the College of Arms and of Westminster Abbey for permission to work in their archives. She thanks Isabel W. Kenrick for help in locating and photocopying material in Great Britain and Linda Levy Peck and Barbara Taft for reading and commenting on an early draft.

William Speck wishes to thank the Henry E. Huntington Library for a Fellowship and the British Academy for a travel grant towards his visit to California in spring 1989, where the bulk of the research for his essay was completed. He is also indebted to Mary Geiter for an analysis of the sessions of the Privy Council in 1694.

Rachel Weil notes that early versions of her essay were presented at the Women's History Seminar at the Institute for Historical Research in London, the Princeton Graduate History Association Colloquium, and the Princeton–Rutgers Early Modern Women's History Group. She would like to thank Margaret Hunt, William Hunt, and Lael Sorenson for their sensitive and tough comments, and Eveline Cruikshanks for providing specific suggestions about the origins of the warming-pan story. Her deepest gratitude goes to Lawrence Stone, her dissertation advisor, and to Lois G. Schwoerer, who reviewed an early draft and made numerous useful suggestions for further research and revision.

Finally, the editor wishes to thank the appropriate authorities for permission to reproduce two articles: J. G. A. Pocock, "The Fourth English Civil War: Dissolution, Desertion and Alternative Histories in the Glorious Revolution," *Government and Opposition. A Journal of Comparative Politics*, 23 (1988), 151–66, and Steven Zwicker, "Representing the Revolution: Politics and High Culture in 1689," in Eveline Cruickshanks (ed.), *By Force or By*

Default? The Revolution of 1688–89 (Edinburgh, John Donald, 1989). She also expresses her deep gratitude to Louise Friend and Sarah Williams for providing expert and cheerful editorial assistance in copy-editing, indexing, and typing the manuscript.

Abbreviations and short titles

AAE	Archives des Affaires Etrangères, Paris
Add. Mss.	Additional Manuscripts (British Library)
BDBR	*Biographical Dictionary of British Radicals in the Seventeenth Century*, ed. Richard L. Greaves and Robert Zaller (3 vols., Brighton, Harvester Press, 1982–84)
BIHR	*Bulletin of the Institute of Historical Research*
BL	British Library
Bodl.	Bodleian Library
Burnet, *HOT*	Bishop Gilbert Burnet, *History of His Own Time* (6 vols., Oxford, 1832)
CA	College of Arms
CCJ	London Common Council Journal
CJ	*Journals of the House of Commons*
CLRO	Corporation of London Records Office
Cobbett, *Parlia. Hist.*	William Cobbett (ed.), *Parliamentary History of England* (36 vols., London, T.C. Hansard, 1806–20)
Cobbett, *Trials*	Thomas B. Howell (ed.), *Cobbett's Complete Collection of State Trials and Proceedings for High Treason* (34 vols., London, 1809–28)
CSPD	*Calendar of State Papers, Domestic Series*
Dalrymple, *Memoirs*	John Dalrymple, *Memoirs of Great Britain and Ireland From the Dissolution of the Last Parliament of Charles I Until the Sea-Battle Off La Hogue* (2 vols., London and Edinburgh, 1771–73)
DNB	*Dictionary of National Biography*, ed. Sir Leslie Stephen and Sir Sidney Lee (63 vols., Oxford University Press, 1885–1900)
DWL	Doctor Williams's Library, London
EHR	*English Historical Review*
Foxcroft, *Supplement*	H. C. Foxcroft (ed.), *A Supplement to Burnet's History of My Own Time* (Oxford, Clarendon Press, 1902)
FSL	Folger Shakespeare Library
Gibbs, *Complete Peerage*	Vicary Gibbs, H. A. Doubleday, Lord Howard de Waldon, and Geoffrey H. White (eds.), *The*

	Complete Peerage of England, Scotland, Ireland, Great Britain, and the United Kingdom, 2nd edn. (13 vols., London, St. Catherine's Press, 1910–40)
GL	Guildhall Library
Grey, *Debates*	Anchitell Grey, *Debates of the House of Commons, from the Year 1667 to the Year 1694* (10 vols., London, 1763)
HEHL	Henry E. Huntington Library
HJ	*Historical Journal*
HLRO	House of Lords Records Office
HMC	Historical Manuscripts Commission
HMSO	Her Majesty's Stationery Office
HOC	Basil Duke Henning (ed.), *The History of Parliament. The House of Commons, 1660–1690* (3 vols., London, Martin Secker and Warburg, 1983)
JMH	*Journal of Modern History*
LJ	*Journal of the House of Lords*
POAS	George deF. Lord (ed.), *Poems on Affairs of State* (7 vols., London and New Haven, Yale University Press, 1963–75)
PRO	Public Record Office
Rep.	Repertories of the Court of Aldermen
SP	State Papers, Public Record Office
SR	*Statutes of the Realm* (10 vols., London, 1810–22)
SRP	J. F. Larkin and P. L. Hughes (eds.), *Stuart Royal Proclamations* (2 vols., Oxford, Clarendon Press, 1973, 1983)

Introduction

Changing the perspectives on the Revolution of 1688–89 has been a long time in coming. For almost three hundred years, the so-called Whig view of the Glorious Revolution prevailed, virtually unchallenged. Historians, with but few exceptions, were content to perceive the context, political process, leadership, ideology, and consequences of the Revolution in much the same terms that Lord Macaulay laid out in his famous *History of England*, first published in the mid-nineteenth century.[1] Over the past twenty years, however, scholars have begun to revise that view by posing new questions and offering different interpretations. Recently this revived interest gained momentum because of celebrations of the tercentenary of the Revolution in Great Britain, the Netherlands, and the United States. For complex reasons associated with late twentieth-century politics, religion, and scholarship, those celebrations took different forms in the three countries, but whatever the proportion of ambivalence and enthusiasm in them, the public and scholarly attention focused on the Revolution was greater that at any time in its history.[2] Symposia and conferences – along with printed tee shirts and other memorabilia – abounded, the result being a harvest of publications which left no doubt that the old Whig consensus was in disarray.

The essays in this volume, themselves (with two exceptions) the fruit of an international celebratory conference held in Washington, D.C., in April 1989, offer novel and interdisciplinary interpretations of the Revolution of 1688–89 and the late Stuart and early Hanoverian world from both an international and an English domestic perspective. The goal animating the conference was – as it is of this collection – to broaden the context in which the Revolution is usually placed and to integrate multiple disciplines in doing so. Written by a distinguished group of scholars in British, Dutch, and colonial American history, and in British political and religious history and theory, literature, law, and women's history, the essays do not, of course, attempt to cover every issue – notably absent, for example, is systematic attention to Jacobitism, the subject of two recently published collections of papers[3] – but the present essays do variously ask fresh questions of traditional issues, deal with little explored topics, and employ some newly recovered or hitherto neglected

---

[1] Lord Macaulay, *History of England from the Accession of James II*, ed. C. H. Firth (6 vols., Oxford University Press, 1913–15).

[2] Lois G. Schwoerer, "Celebrating the Glorious Revolution, 1689–1989," *Albion* 20 (1990), 1–19.

[3] Eveline Cruickshanks (ed.), *By Force or By Default? The Revolution of 1688–89* (Edinburgh, John Donald, 1989); and Eveline Cruickshanks and Jeremy Black (eds.), *The Jacobite Challenge* (Edinburgh, John Donald, 1988).

I

material. They will contribute, it is hoped, towards the larger project of shaping a fuller and more accurate understanding of the Revolution of 1688–89.

The historiography of the Revolution of 1688–89, a subject in its own right not yet written,[4] forms an important part of the context within which the authors of these essays approached the subject. By the time they gathered in 1989, many new initiatives had already been taken that disputed the long-held conventional wisdom about the Revolution. Several features of that traditional view originated with historians who preceded Macaulay. The first history of the Revolution appeared within nine months of the revolutionary settlement[5] and was followed over the next hundred years by histories which were almost all "Court–Whig" in political orientation. Offering a political narrative of events in terms favorable to the victors, these early histories described the Revolution as "happy," "mighty," and "one of the greatest," and expressed awe that through the workings of Providence the nation's laws, liberties, and Protestant religion should have been rescued by a selfless Prince of Orange at the cost of so little violence.[6] Only a few historians, such as the Tory sympathizer James Ralph and the radical Catherine Macaulay, ventured to impugn the motivation and methods of Dutch William and his English supporters, Ralph asserting that "self-interest" explained the actions of both, and Macaulay censuring the English leaders for their moral turpitude, personal selfishness, and corruption of Parliament.[7]

Despite some adverse criticism, by the middle of the eighteenth century the events of 1688–89 were known as the "Glorious Revolution," and the epithet, with all its eulogistic connotations, was firmly embedded in the national consciousness. The first description of the events of 1688–89 as "The Glorious Revolution" seems to be a question of consuming interest to students, historians, and laymen alike. Before the term disappears entirely from the historical lexicon, a brief account may satisfy the curious. The word "glorious," meaning "entitled to renown," "splendid," and "magnificent," was much favored in 1688 and 1689 as a descriptive term for William and his undertaking. Its users intended to heap praise on the Revolution because the

---

[4] Articles on late Stuart scholarship have not reviewed the literature of the Revolution of 1688–89. See Stephen B. Baxter, "The Later Stuarts 1660–1714," in Richard Schlatter (ed.), *Recent Views on British History* (New Brunswick, N.J., Rutgers University Press, 1984), pp. 141–66; Stephen B. Baxter, "Recent Writings on William III," *JMH* 38 (1966), 256–66; Richard R. Johnson, "Politics Redefined: an Assessment of the Late Stuart Period of English History, 1660–1714," *William and Mary Quarterly*, 3rd series, 35 (1978) 691–732.

[5] *The History Of the Late Revolution in England, With the Causes & Means By which it was Accomplish'd. Together With the Settlement thereof under their most Serene Majesties King William and Queen Mary, by the Lords and Commons Assembled in this present Parliament* (London, 1689). Advertised in the *London Gazette*, November 14–18, 1689, no. 2506.

[6] *The History Of the Late Revolution in England*, p. 274; Abel Boyer, *The History Of King William The Third*. In three parts. (London, 1702–3), part II, p. 359; Boyer's comment is used verbatim by John Banks, *The History of the Life and Reign of William III. King of England, Prince of Orange, and Hereditary Stadtholder of the United Provinces* (London, 1744), p. 256. Also Laurence Eachard, *The History of England. From the First Entrance of Julius Caesar and the Romans, To the Conclusion of the Reign of King James the Second, And the Establishment of King William and Queen Mary Upon the Throne, in the year 1688* (3 vols., London, 1707–18), III, p. 956.

[7] James Ralph, *The History of England during the Reigns of King William, Queene Anne and King George I, with an introductory review of the reigns of the Royal Brothers, Charles and James, in which are to be found the seeds of the Revolution* (2 vols., London, 1744–46), I, pp. 997, 999, 1003, 1023–24, 1078. Catherine Macaulay, *Observations on a Pamphlet, entitled, Thoughts on the Cause of the present Discontents* (London, 1770), pp. 10–11.

settlement was achieved without significant bloodshed, represented the will of the people, and secured the nation's laws, religion, and liberties, which had been threatened by an absolutist Catholic monarch.[8]

The word "revolution," quite separately from the word "glorious," was also applied in 1688–89 to the revolutionary events. It carried more than one meaning, but not the modern one of a total overturning of social and economic structures as well as the political order.[9] Used in the sense derived from contemporary astronomy, which referred to the movement of heavenly bodies in a circle or ellipse as a "revolution," the word implied that the events had accomplished a return to past conditions rather than the creation of new ones. For example, John Locke described King William III as "our Great Restorer." The term also might convey the idea of upheaval and disruption. One tract writer, reaching for a laugh, made a joke about a fellow who, sensing that the world, as he put it, was being "turned upside down," asked to be buried face down, so that he would soon be the only person lying properly in his grave.[10] Less frequently, the word "revolution" also meant that a new irreversible political order had been achieved.[11]

To link these two words – "revolution" and "glorious" – was an act of propaganda that aimed to convey approval and approbation of what had happened in 1688–89. People who used the epithet revealed how myopic and narrow was their perspective, for obviously "Glorious Revolution" could apply only to England, not to Scotland or Ireland. Interestingly, it was not a historian who first described the events of 1688–89 as a "Glorious Revolution." The first person to do so (if the surviving record is accurate) was a Whig radical, John Hampden, Jr., in the fall of 1689 in testimony before a committee of the House of Lords. When that term appeared again it was in 1706 in sermons by Bishop Gilbert Burnet (a friend and confidant of King William and Queen Mary) and nonconformist preachers.[12] The first *historian* to conjoin the two words was Walter Harris, whose history was published in 1749.[13] For generations – right up to the late twentieth century – the term

---

[8] For example, Boyer, *History of King William The Third*, part II, p. 321; Dalrymple, *Memoirs*, II, Appendix, part II, p. A 2; *The History of the most Illustrious William, Prince of Orange* (London, 1688), p. A 2; and a sermon preached by Reverend John Tillotson, January 31, 1688/89: *A Sermon Preached at Lincolns-Inn Chappel, on the 31st of January, 1688. Being the Day Appointed for A Publick Thanksgiving To Almighty God For having made His Highness the Prince of Orange The Glorious Instrument of the Great Deliverance of This Kingdom from Popery & Arbitrary Power* (London, 1689), p. 29.

[9] For comments on the concept of revolution in seventeenth-century England, mostly at the time of the Civil War, see Perez Zagorin, *The Court and the Country* (London, Routledge and Kegan Paul, 1969), pp. 9–18 and studies noted there.

[10] *A Dialogue between Two Friends, a Jacobite and a Williamite, occasion'd by the Late Revolution of Affairs, and the Oath of Allegiance* (n.p., n.d., [1689]), p. 1.

[11] For example, BL, Add. Ms. 41,816, fol. 167, Daniel Petit to Earl of Middleton, September 7, 1688; HEHL, Hastings Mss., HA 7, Sir Edward Abney to Earl of Huntingdon, December 18, 1688; Sir James Montgomery, *Great Britain's Just Complaint*, in Sir Walter Scott (ed.), *A Collection of Scarce and Valuable Tracts, on the most Interesting And Entertaining Subjects: but chiefly such as relate to the History And Constitution of These Kingdoms. Selected From An Infinite Number In Print and Manuscript, In The Royal, Cotton, Sion, And Other Public, As Well As Private, Libraries; Particularly That Of The Late Lord Somers*, 13 vols. (2d edn. London, 1809–15), X, pp. 429–30.

[12] Eveline Cruickshanks (ed.), *By Force or By Default?* opposite frontispiece. And James R. Hertzler, "Who Dubbed It 'The Glorious Revolution?'" *Albion* 19 (1987), 579–85.

[13] Walter Harris, *The History of the Life and Reign of William-Henry, Prince of Nassau and Orange, Stadtholder of the United Provinces, King of England, Scotland, France and Ireland, etc.* (Dublin, 1749), Dedication.

remained the popular choice, although, as we shall see, historians prominently associated with the "old Whig" view disavowed it. Although it has
now fallen into disfavor, especially in Great Britain,[14] and is used in the
United States as a gambit to attract undergraduates (this writer suspects from
her own experience), the epithet "Glorious Revolution" remains the most
famous and most distinctive of the several descriptive terms that have been
attached to the Revolution.

It was not until the late eighteenth century that the question of the character of the Revolution – was it conservative or radical? – became an issue. The
matter was opened initially not by historians but by political commentators
who used the centenary of the Revolution as a centerpiece of their discussion
of the *French* Revolution and its applicability to British politics. On the one
hand, the radical Dissenting minister, Dr. Richard Price, and his friends in
the newly reconstituted Revolutionary Society, celebrated the one hundredth
birthday of the Revolution of 1688–89 with the intent of appealing to its
memory in support of reform measures in British society. In his well-known
sermon, *A Discourse On The Love Of Our Country*, delivered on November 4,
1788, William of Orange's birthday and the Society's annual meeting date,
Price described the Glorious Revolution as led by Whigs and as exemplifying
principles dear to him, whatever their actual relevance to the Revolution.
Among the principles he cherished were that all civil and political power is
derived from the people and that abuse of power justifies a people in resisting
a king and selecting another monarch. According to Price, the Revolution
accomplished substantial change and, even more importantly, laid the
foundations for reform to come.[15] On the other hand, Edmund Burke, in his
famous *Reflections on the Revolution in France*, printed in 1789 in response to
Price, emphatically denied every major point the latter had made, especially
that of the people's right to resist. Describing the Declaration of Rights (the
document that embodied the settlement of the Revolution) as "most wise,
sober, and considerate," and referring to it as a "statute" (which at law it was
not), Burke maintained that the settlement reinforced the principle of direct
hereditary succession – except for a slight deviation. Arguing in terms that
marked him as a believer in the idea of the ancient constitution (a myth of
enormous ideological importance created in the early seventeenth century
and definitively studied by J. G. A. Pocock),[16] Burke maintained that the
settlement had restored the nation's ancient "indisputable laws and
liberties," which he described as an "entailed inheritance, descended from the

---

[14] Only recently is this true. Up to 1983 it was British scholars, not American, who kept the term alive by using
it in the titles of books. See, for example, Maurice Ashley, *The Glorious Revolution of 1688* (New York, Scribner,
1967); John Childs, *The Army, James II and the Glorious Revolution* (Manchester University Press, 1980); Geoffrey
Holmes (ed.), *Britain After the Glorious Revolution 1689–1714* (London, Macmillan, St. Martin's Press, 1969); and
John Miller, *The Glorious Revolution*, Seminar Studies in History, ed. Roger Lockyer (London and New York,
Longman, 1983).

[15] *A Discourse On The Love Of Our Country. Delivered on Nov. 4, 1789, At The Meeting-House In The Old Jewry, To The
society For Commemorating The revolution In Great Britain* (London, 1790), pp. 29–30.

[16] J. G. A. Pocock, *The Ancient Constitution and the Feudal Law: a Study of English Historical Thought in the Seventeenth
Century, A Reissue with a Retrospect* (Cambridge University Press, 1987).

nation's forefathers." In no way did the Revolution change the prerogatives of the crown or the rights of the people; in no way did it justify further change. As Burke put it, the Revolution of 1688–89 was "revolution not made but prevented."[17] In an essay in this volume, J. G. A. Pocock has teased out the meaning of another of Burke's arresting remarks – that the Revolution was a just and necessary civil war – in ways that show that the comment exemplified Burke's basic perception of the Revolution.

Tom Paine, the radical, agreed with Burke that 1688–89 accomplished nothing of importance. He described the Bill of Rights (the statutory form of the Declaration of Rights) as the "bill of wrongs and insults," declared that the settlement was the work of a class-ridden Parliament, and maintained that the government it confirmed was for "courtiers, placemen, pensioners, borough-holders, and the leaders of the parties . . . It is a bad Constitution for at least ninety-nine parts of the nation out of a hundred."[18] However different their reasons, the concurrence of Burke and Paine in the late eighteenth century is much like the conservative historian J. C. D. Clark and the socialist politician Tony Benn agreeing on the Glorious Revolution in the late twentieth century, as they did in a radio broadcast commemorating the tercentenary.

The view that the Revolution of 1688–89 accomplished no significant change but only restored some rights long embedded in the nation's ancient constitution deeply influenced subsequent historians. Although not based on a thorough historical investigation – neither Burke's nor Paine's work was a history but a powerful polemic in a partisan exchange – this interpretation conformed with the prevailing conservatism, and historians, while differing in detail, followed it. Most important among them was Lord Macaulay, who more than anyone else determined how historians and the educated public understood the Revolution up to the middle of the twentieth century. Confining his attention largely to England and to constitutional and political issues, Macaulay painted the Revolution's leaders in black-and-white terms. Portraying King James II as a villain, the friend of Roman Catholicism, political absolutism, and French and papal power, and the enemy of Protestants, he depicted Prince William of Orange as a hero, a selfless champion of Protestantism, parliamentary government, and political freedoms, a "Deliverer" who, accepting the invitation of the nation's "Immortal Seven" (themselves selfless in their concerns), came to England only to rescue the nation's religion, laws, and liberties. Reluctantly accepting the crown, the prince agreed to the Declaration of Rights as a condition of his being made king and thereby entered into a contract with the people to uphold their rights. Macaulay characterized the Declaration of Rights as "equal in authority to any statute" and concluded that it imposed legal restrictions on the king. In language

---

[17] Edmund Burke, *Reflections on the Revolution in France*, ed. J. G. A. Pocock (Indianapolis and Cambridge, Cambridge University Press, 1987), pp. 14, 15, 16, 20, 27, 28, and 29.

[18] Quoted in E. P. Thompson, *The Making of the English Working Class* (New York and London, Pantheon Books, 1964), pp. 87, 92.

much the same as Burke's, Macaulay went on to say that, although "revolutionary," the Declaration of Rights did not change the law: "Not a single flower of the crown was touched. Not a single new right was given to the people. The whole English law, substantive and adjective, was ... almost exactly the same after the Revolution as before it." Exuding a sense of confidence and belief in "progress" characteristic of mid-nineteenth-century Britain, Macaulay also ascribed great significance to the long-term significance of the Revolution, declaring that it held "the germ ... of every good law" that followed and laid the foundation for what he regarded as Britain's democratic government.[19] For all his admiration of the Revolution, Macaulay specifically rejected the word "Glorious," selecting instead the word "preserving" as best embodying the event's nature.[20]

Macaulay's grand-nephew, George Macaulay Trevelyan, perpetuated this perspective in his *The English Revolution 1688–89*, published in London in 1938 to commemorate the two hundred and fiftieth anniversary of the event. As he saw it, the Declaration of Rights was "an agreed contract ... between Crown and people," a "condition" which William had to accept to win the crown. Although it limited royal authority, the document contained no new law.[21] Like Macaulay, Trevelyan also declined to eulogize the event as "glorious," saying that the word "sensible" was more apt.[22] Other historians interested in political and religious ideas contributed further important points to the conventional view. One was that the doctrines of divine-right monarchy and passive obedience were destroyed by the Revolution, and another that John Locke's *Two Treatises of Government*, printed in 1689, and suggesting that a dissolution of the government had occurred and justifying all that was done in terms of contract theory, exemplified the principles that had animated the revolutionary leaders.[23]

There, in brief, the "old Whig" view stood until the 1970s. Why did it take historians so long to reevaluate the traditional story and interpretation of the Revolution? One reason is surely the dead weight of nineteenth- and early twentieth-century histories which were so well researched and engagingly written that they seem to have intimidated scholars. Successive generations of historians, full of admiration for their predecessors (especially Macaulay), apparently felt that there was nothing more to be said. Then, for the months of the revolution itself, the sources are scattered and fragmentary, a situation that discouraged researchers, even as it showed the reality of upheaval. A further reason for the downplaying of the Revolution of 1688–89 was the enormous amount of attention paid over the past thirty years to the earlier

---

[19] Macaulay, *History of England*, III, pp. 1297, 1306–11.

[20] *Ibid.*, p. 131. In 1828 Macaulay wrote that the Revolution "was not, what it has often been called, a glorious revolution." See Lord Macaulay, *Critical and Historical Essays*, ed. Israel Gollancz (London, 1900), I, p. 211: a review of Henry Hallam's *The Constitutional History of England, from the Accession of Henry VII to the Death of George II*, which appeared in the *Edinburgh Review*, September 1828.

[21] George Macaulay Trevelyan, *The English Revolution 1688–89* (New York, Henry Holt, 1939), pp. 161–63.

[22] *Ibid.*, p. 1.

[23] J. C. D. Clark, *English Society 1688–1832: Ideology, Social Structure and Political Practice during the Ancien Régime* (Cambridge University Press, 1985), pp. 119–21.

Civil War. Scholars too well known and too numerous to name have implied or asserted that the real changes in English politics and society were achieved between 1640 and 1660, and that what happened in the second half of the century, which, of course, they did not study systematically, was nothing more than a kind of postscript. The result was that the Civil War took on the role of *the* English Revolution of the seventeenth century. Finally, there was no hope of change until scholars asked different questions and sought answers to them by a fresh look at existing sources and a renewed effort (which, in the event, met with some success) to uncover new material.[24] When that happened after World War II, when effort was made to add social, intellectual, and cultural matters to traditional political, religious, and constitutional ones, changing perspectives began to emerge.

In the 1950s a spark of renewed interest in the Revolution was ignited when an American historian, Lucile Pinkham, undertook to refocus the perspective on the Prince of Orange and to argue that he was no deliverer but a calculating conqueror who had engaged in a long-term conspiracy with self-interested Englishmen to seize the English crown for the purpose of gaining men and money for his war (largely a personal vendetta, Pinkham thought) against Louis XIV.[25] The result was a "respectable" revolution (Pinkham's epithet), which simply exchanged one king for another. Pinkham's work met with rebuff and her untimely death removed its most obvious defender, but she deserves credit for leading the way in systematically questioning received wisdom. After a pause, further heightening of interest in the late Stuart period and the Revolution occurred in the late 1960s[26] and gained steady momentum throughout the next two decades.

Over the past twenty years scholars, who may for convenience's sake be called "revisionists" (although they worked independently and formed no school), have rejected all but one tenet of "old Whig" history. Others, who may be called "neo-Whigs" (again for convenience's sake), but who themselves were in the process of revising the conventional view, have dissented from some revisionist conclusions. Among the issues that have undergone reassessment is the character of the two protagonists. In 1966 Stephen B. Baxter rescued Prince William of Orange from Pinkham's debunking and restored him to a hero's status, but he did so on grounds somewhat different from those of traditional scholarship. Placing the prince in an international setting, he portrayed him as a leader in the struggle for European liberty and toleration. Denying that William had engaged in a long-term conspiracy with English dissidents, Baxter argued that the prince's interest was principally

---

[24] For example, David Lewis Jones (ed.), *A Parliamentary History of the Glorious Revolution* (London, HMSO, 1988), reprints all the known sources of the Convention, including those recently recovered. Also Robert Beddard (ed.), *A Kingdom without a King: the Journal of the Provisional Government in the Revolution of 1688* (Oxford, Phaidon, 1988).

[25] Lucile Pinkham, *William III and the Respectable Revolution. The Part Played by William of Orange in the Revolution of 1688* (Cambridge, Mass., Harvard University Press, 1954).

[26] One of the most important was Geoffrey Holmes (ed.), *Britain after the Glorious Revolution, 1689–1714* (London, Macmillan; New York, St. Martin's Press, 1969).

dynastic, a concern to preserve his wife's and his own claim to the English crown. Baxter's portrait, erected on wide-ranging research in continental as well as English archives, and covering the reign from a political and diplomatic perspective, continues today to enjoy wide acceptance. It has prepared the way for the still unexplored question of William's psychological make-up and his willingness to take rash political and military gambles, and also for the topic of the culture of his court and reign which is opened by essays in this present volume.[27]

No comprehensive scholarly biography of James II has appeared since 1948, when F. C. Turner published his measured, but ultimately negative, verdict.[28] Thirty years later, from a study that focused on James's kingship, John Miller concluded that the king was genuinely devoted to the principle of religious toleration and insisted that he had no grand scheme for imposing absolutism in politics or religion.[29] Rejecting this rehabilitation of James II, William Speck maintained in his book, *Reluctant Revolutionaries*, that the King *did* harbor absolutist ambitions. Speck dismissed as "ultimately unconvincing" that all James wanted was toleration for his Catholic subjects.[30] A definitive study of James II from the perspective of his character, personality, political and religious principles and intentions remains to be written. When it is, a significant feature will surely be the nature of James's court and the relationship between the king, his ministers, and his Catholic friends and advisors.

The character of the Revolution is another matter in dispute. For such scholars as Jennifer Carter, J. C. D. Clark, H. T. Dickinson, J. R. Jones, J. P. Kenyon, Howard Nenner, and Gerald Straka, the constitutional results of the Revolution itself lack major importance.[31] In their view, conservative Tory and Whig elites collaborated to achieve minimal change in government – a change in the king – and deliberately avoided a change in the kingship. Accepting in this one instance an "old Whig" interpretation, revisionists regard the Declaration of Rights, which Robert J. Frankle showed in 1974 was a truncated version of an earlier more reformist draft, as nothing more than a reaffirmation of ancient rights.[32] The most extreme rejection of the Declaration of Rights came from Clark, a specialist in eighteenth-century British

---

[27] Stephen B. Baxter, *William III* (London, Longman, Green, 1966).

[28] F. C. Turner, *James II* (New York and London, Macmillan, 1948).

[29] John Miller, *James II. A Study in Kingship* (London, Wayland, 1977: reprinted Methuen, 1989).

[30] W. A. Speck, *Reluctant Revolutionaries: Englishmen and the Revolution of 1688* (Oxford and New York, Oxford University Press, 1988), p. 125.

[31] Jennifer Carter, "The Revolution and the Constitution," in Holmes (ed.), *Britain after the Glorious Revolution*, pp. 39–58; Clark, *English Society*; J. C. D. Clark, *Revolution and Rebellion: State and Society in England in the Seventeenth and Eighteenth Centuries* (Cambridge University Press, 1986); H. T. Dickinson, "The Eighteenth-Century Debate on the Sovereignty of Parliament," *Transactions of the Royal Historical Society*, 5th series, 26 (1976), 189–210; H. T. Dickinson, *Liberty and Property: Political Ideology in Eighteenth-Century Britain* (London, Weidenfeld and Nicolson, 1977); J. R. Jones, *The Revolution of 1688 in England* (London, Weidenfeld and Nicolson, 1972); J. P Kenyon, *Revolution Principles: the Politics of Party 1689–1720* (Cambridge University Press, 1977); Howard Nenner, "Constitutional Uncertainty and the Declaration of Rights," in Barbara C. Malament (ed.), *After the Reformation: Essays in Honor of J. H. Hexter* (Philadelphia, University of Pennsylvania Press, 1980), pp. 291–308; G. M. Straka, *Anglican Reaction to the Revolution of 1688* (Madison, University of Wisconsin Press, 1962); G. M. Straka, "The Final Phase of Divine Right Theory in England, 1688–1702," *EHR* 77 (1962), 638–58.

[32] Robert J. Frankle, "The Formulation of the Declaration of Rights," *HJ* 17 (1974), 265–79.

history, who invited some scholar to do for the Declaration of Rights what Sir Geoffrey Elton tried to do for the Apology of 1604: namely, strip it of all importance.[33] Confusion, hesitation, and theoretical conservatism, Nenner held, accompanied the crafting of the revolutionary settlement. Revisionists downplayed the role of radical ideas and disparaged the evidence of their presence. Instead, in sharp contrast to "old Whig" scholarship, Kenyon and Clark, for example, stressed the *survival* of the principles of divine right, hereditary monarchy, and passive resistance throughout society. Virtually untouched by the Revolution, the Church of England, the Anglican aristocracy, and the monarchy continued to dominate society until 1829–32, even as conservative ideas continued to enjoy a strong if discreet following. As Clayton Roberts and Jennifer Carter argued earlier, so John Brewer elaborated in his recent book, *Sinews of Power*, war and war finance, not the Revolution, account for whatever change took place in English politics and society.[34]

Other historians, however, were unable to accept all the points in this analysis. For "neo-Whigs" Corinne Weston and Janelle Greenberg and Lois G. Schwoerer, the Declaration of Rights and its statutory formulation the Bill of Rights did more than simply confirm ancient rights.[35] For Weston and Greenberg, stripping the king of the right to suspend and dispense with the law was a radical step that changed fundamentally the most important prerogative power the king possessed.

Schwoerer's study of the constitution history of each right claimed by the document showed that eight rights were not "undisputed" and "ancient." In her view, the decisions on the claims were not forced by legal logic, but involved political and ideological choices. In his recent book, Speck has accepted this reading. The Declaration of Rights, however, was not, as "old Whigs" thought, a condition that William had to accept to win the throne. Nor did it bear the force of law. Yet the document was treated in some ways, Schwoerer demonstrated, as if it were a law, and some contemporaries thought that it was. The Bill of Rights, however, despite the name – "Bill" – by which it is known, is a statute of the realm, and, of course, carries the force of law. On the basis of her study of the "rights" committees in the Convention, of evidence showing that some Tories attempted to sabotage the passage of the Declaration of Rights, and that Whigs, not Tories, managed the passage of the Bill of Rights, Schwoerer also dissented from the notion that the Tories were largely responsible for the Declaration of Rights. Tories and Whigs compromised on the settlement, with the principal leadership coming from Whigs.

---

[33] Clark, *Revolution and Rebellion*, p. 84.

[34] Carter, "The Revolution and the Constitution." Clayton Roberts, "The Constitutional Significance of the Financial Settlement of 1690," *HJ* 20 (1977), 59–76. Also Angus McInnes, "When was the English Revolution?" *History* 67 (1982), 377–92. John Brewer, *The Sinews of Power: War, Money and the English State, 1688–1783* (New York, Alfred A. Knopf, 1989).

[35] C. C. Weston and J. R. Greenberg, *Subjects and Sovereigns* (Cambridge University Press, 1981); and Lois G. Schwoerer, *The Declaration of Rights, 1689* (Baltimore and London, Johns Hopkins University Press, 1981).

Moreover, a calculated and intensive propaganda campaign, carried on by Prince William and his Dutch and English friends using mostly tracts, broadsides, prints, commemorative medals, and playing cards, testifies, she argued, to their recognition of the political power of non-elite social and political classes and calls into question the thesis that the Revolution was essentially a *coup d'état*, carried out by a very small number of people.[36]

Attempting to bridge the differences about the settlement between revisionists and neo-Whigs, Henry Horwitz underscored the importance of the radical decision to exclude Catholics from the succession to the throne. Agreeing that a "new conception of rulership" resulted from the Convention, Horwitz drew out a novel argument of some weight: namely the notion of monarchy as a public trust.[37] A topic that remains to be studied for the additional light it may shed on all these points is the role and political and religious ideology of the many sermons preached by Anglican and Dissenting clergy during the months of revolution.

Other scholars, Mark Goldie, Gary De Krey, Schwoerer, Thomas Slaughter, Weston, and Greenberg, variously uncovered evidence that showed the presence of radical ideas in both the press and the Convention and among middle- and lower-class groups in London, which latter point is further developed by De Krey in his essay in this volume.[38] By "radical," these historians generally meant not the radicalism of the Levellers, but rather views on the left-hand side of mainstream political thought which aimed to limit royal authority and transfer power to the king-in-parliament. With the exception of a tiny minority who flirted with republican notions, radicals wanted change in the relationship among the parts of government, not in its structure. They favored placing sovereignty in the king-in-parliament, but within that construct they privileged the parliament.

The "abdication" and "vacancy" resolution (which justified the removal of James II) also attracted scholarly attention. According to Slaughter, a radical political philosophy was embedded in the resolution and was retained, although the explicitly radical premises (which charged James II with violating the "fundamental laws," and "breaking the original contract") were removed as a result of compromise between Tories and Whigs. By analyzing the contemporary meaning of the words "abdication" and "contract," Slaughter undertook to show that Kenyon erred in insisting that the word "abdicate" implied a voluntary act on James's part, that the Convention had not engaged in resistance or deposed the king, and that contract theory was no part of the settlement, as later Whigs claimed. Slaughter argued that the word "abdicate" could mean depose *or* abandon voluntarily, that the former meaning was in the minds of contemporary leaders, and that the intellectual

---

[36] Lois G. Schwoerer, "Propaganda in the Revolution of 1688–89," *American Historical Review* 82 (1977), 843–74.

[37] Henry Horwitz, "1689 (and All That)," *Parliamentary History* 6 (1987), 23–32.

[38] Gary S. De Krey, *A Fractured Society: the Politics of London in the First Age of Party, 1688–1715* (Oxford, Clarendon Press, 1985); Mark Goldie, "The Roots of True Whiggism, 1688–1694," *History of Political Thought* 1 (1980), 195–236; Thomas P. Slaughter, "'Abdicate' and 'Contract' in the Glorious Revolution," *HJ* 24 (1981), 323–37; Thomas P. Slaughter, "'Abdicate' and 'Contract' Restored," *HJ* 28 (1985), 399–403.

context was more complex than granted. Miller came to Kenyon's defense and a spirited exchange with Slaughter over the contemporary meaning of words ensued.[39] Perhaps the critical point to emerge was that, as a contemporary explained, men chose the word "abdicate" because it could be made to bear different meanings.

That most radical of books, John Locke's *Two Treatises of Government*, did not play the role that earlier scholars assigned it. Peter Laslett demonstrated in 1967 that the *Two Treatises* were written in the early 1680s, at the time of the Exclusion Crisis, when Locke, Richard Ashcraft has argued in his *Revolutionary Politics and Locke's Two Treatises of Government*, was deeply (if circumspectly) involved in radical political activities. Ashcraft recently showed that Locke's ideas about contract, dissolution of government, and the right of the people to resist a tyrannical king, found reflection in tracts and pamphlets published by radical Whigs in the early 1680s. But, when *the Two Treatises* were published in the autumn of 1689, Martyn Thompson and Kenyon have argued, they furnished a *minority* view of the significance of the Revolution and for several decades were largely ignored. And it was not only Locke who made some eighteenth-century establishment Whigs uncomfortable. Central to Kenyon's thesis was the thought that, as he put it, "The Revolution of 1688 was as much an embarrassment to the Whigs as it was to the Tories."[40] Still, Lois G. Schwoerer has maintained that the evidence, as powerful as it is for the years *after* the Revolution, does not change the fact that *during* the weeks when the revolutionary settlement was under discussion Lockean ideas circulated and enjoyed some influence.[41]

Although the concept of the "ancient constitution" was beginning to weaken, most politically sentient persons were still wedded to this powerful myth. But even the ancient constitution has now been shown capable of supporting very radical ideas. In a stunning reinterpretation of the significance of the medieval sources of this myth – such as the *Modus Tenendi Parliamentum*, the *Mirror of Justice*, and *The Confessor's Laws* – Janelle Greenberg has found in these "innocuous" looking materials a radicalism that includes ideas of elective kingship, the contractual origins of government, the superiority of parliament to the king, and the right of the parliament to oppose and depose a ruler who violates that contract. Although usually characterized as conservative, in contrast to the rationalism of Locke, the ancient constitution also bore a radical face. Greenberg's analysis has enriched the ideological context within which the revolutionary settlement was crafted.[42]

Other contributions towards changing the perspectives on the Revolution

---

[39] See note 38, above; John Miller, "The Glorious Revolution: 'Contract' and 'Abdication' Reconsidered," *HJ* 25 (1982), 541–55.

[40] Kenyon, *Revolution Principles*, p. 200. Richard Ashcraft, *Revolutionary Politics and Locke's Two Treatises of Government* (Princeton University Press, 1986). Martyn P. Thompson, "The Reception of Locke's *Two Treatises of Government* 1690–1705," *Political Studies* 24 (1976), 184–91.

[41] Lois G. Schwoerer, "Locke and Lockean Ideas in the Glorious Revolution," *Journal of the History of Ideas* 51 (October–December 1990), 531–48.

[42] Janelle Greenberg, "The Confessor's Laws and the Radical Face of the Ancient Constitution," *EHR* 104 (1989) 611–37.

reflected the recent interest in the relationship between the provinces and the central government. Neither Andrew Coleby's *Central Government and the Localities: Hampshire 1629–1689* nor Anthony Fletcher's *Reform in the Provinces* was principally concerned with the Glorious Revolution, but both offered a different understanding of that event by showing the growing trend of central intervention in the affairs of the localities, a thesis questioned by Jack Greene in an essay in this volume. In effect, Coleby and Fletcher extended the point that J. R. Jones made in 1972 in his *The Revolution of 1688 in England*: namely, that the fear of displacement from local office, with consequent loss of status and influence resulting from the politics and practices of Charles II and James II, animated people against James II with about the same intensity as the fear of Catholicism. Jones's call to "municipalize" research has not really been heeded, but these two studies, added to David Hosford's book on the Revolution in the north, are steps towards that end.[43] In sum, in questioning "old Whig" perspectives, the studies of the past twenty years reinvigorated the topic of the Revolution of 1688–89 and showed that it was far from exhausted.

The authors of the essays in the present volume have undertaken further scholarly departures based upon new questions and material. They reached no "breakthrough" conclusions, nor did they achieve consensus on all points – in itself testimony to the complexity of an event that for so long seemed simple. But several significant insights emerged from both the conference discussion and the essays. Basic among them was that the Revolution was a multilayered event, more complex and subtle in process, ideology, settlement, and result than has been recognized. One reason for that was the powerful role played by the printing press, which poured out pamphlets, tracts, and plays about the issues. The fact of this lively print culture alone meant that the role of political and religious ideas was more important than sometimes granted. Theoretical discussion in debate and press was richer than understood. If conservative ideas survived, so too did radical ones, as the record of reprints of earlier tracts, some going back to the Civil War, proves. The memory of the Civil War was bright, as a powerful deterrent to radical action and to war, but paradoxically, it was also a source of radical ideas which were aired but did not prevail. The complexity of the moment was deepened by the fact that the political nation willingly accepted the pretense and fictions offered by leaders in justification of what they were doing. The notions of Providence and Necessity were the refuge of many troubled consciences. Because the sequence of events was compressed into a very short time – the entire process took no more than a year and the settlement of the crown three and a half weeks – chronology is peculiarly important. The unfolding of the

---

[43] Andrew Coleby, *Central Government and the Localities: Hampshire 1649–1689* (Cambridge University Press, 1987); Anthony Fletcher, *Reform in the Provinces: the Government of Stuart England* (New Haven, Conn., Yale University Press, 1986); David Hosford, *Nottingham, Nobles, and the North* (Hamden, Conn., published for the Conference on British Studies and Wittenberg University by Archon Books, 1976).

Revolution contained many contingent variables; there was nothing predictable or preordained about it. But perhaps the turning point, the most critical moment from which further developments depended, occurred in December with the meeting of the peers and those members of the House of Commons who had served in the parliaments of Charles II. Events in 1688–89 formed *many* revolutions that played out differently and were perceived differently from the vantage point of high or popular culture or in the contexts of England, Scotland, Ireland, France, and the American colonies.

It is not news that the Revolution had a continental dimension.[44] What K. H. D. Haley and John C. Rule newly stress is the degree to which continental decisions determined events, a perspective that underscores the element of contingency and the absence of predictability. In his discussion of the reasons why a Dutch consensus in support of William's invasion of England developed and the extent to which the Revolution satisfied the aspirations of those Dutchmen who favored the Prince's intervention, K. H. D. Haley argues that William's invasion could not have succeeded without the positive support of the Dutch. Maintaining that there was nothing automatic about that support – as late as the autumn of 1686 it was unthinkable – Haley shows that its emergence was due to William's propaganda, the presence of Huguenot refugees, Louis XIV's commercial policy, and above all, to the sense that if James II continued on the throne, Dutch national security would be at risk. In this reading William remains a "Deliverer," but of the national interests of the Netherlands rather than of England.

The French perspective offered by John C. Rule beautifully complements the view from the Netherlands. Basing his essay largely on the unexploited dispatches of Colbert de Croissy, sometime ambassador to England, and of Croissy's nephew, the Marquis de Seignelay, Rule argues that France was poised between two power blocs: one led by the emperor, the other by William of Orange. Rule chooses June 1688 as the moment of decision for France, when the army could have been mobilized. If Louis had followed Louvois's advice and invaded Cologne, then William could not have sailed when he did. Stressing that differences over foreign policy respecting both ends and means divided Louis XIV and rival factions on his council, Rule also focuses on the royal family's concern with domestic affairs, including the succession question. He demonstrates that as a consequence of French internal and foreign preoccupations, Prince William's possible options received little attention and the steps taken by France to promote other interests created a situation that facilitated the success of the prince's invasion of England. These two essays show the possibilities that await a thorough examination of the relationship between the continent and events in England and invite work on that topic with respect to Rome, Spain, the Holy Roman Empire and its states.

Fresh perspectives on the domestic dimensions of the Revolution in England are also offered in this collection. J. G. A. Pocock's almost playful essay

[44] John Carswell, *Descent on England: a Study of the English Revolution of 1688 and its European Background* (New York, J. Day, 1969).

inviting readers to consider a counterfactual approach to the Revolution in England within the context of Burkean dicta considers some central questions in ways that reorient approaches to the event. Postulating a Fourth Civil War in November and December 1688 (following 1642, 1648, 1651), Pocock provocatively helps us to see that civil war did – and did not – take place in England (!) and to understand the ideological significance of James's flight. In the wake of the king's departure, men constituting certain institutions of government actually filled the breach and anarchy was avoided. Although a minority of radicals argued otherwise, the majority of English leaders (and conservatives thereafter) were able to argue quite plausibly that neither they nor James II had caused a dissolution of government to occur. Pocock concludes his essay with the insight that the king's desertion "has irreversibly constitutionalized our perceptions of English history."

Another changing perspective in this collection is on the deception and pretense that informed the political process and settlement. That deception amounting to fraud occurred was clear to a contemporary, Abraham De la Pryme. Musing in his diary about the general prevalence and usefulness in "all kingdoms, revolutions, and nations" of "politick frauds," he remarked ruefully that without such fraud, "many a noble and excellent design would have perished in its birth."[45] Certainly this was the case with respect to a critically important issue in 1688–89 – the succession to the crown. Although "old Whig" historians (seconded by late twentieth-century revisionists) downplayed the violation of the principle of direct hereditary succession in the settlement, the fact remains that the principle *was* violated by bypassing the legitimate son of Catholic King James II and making Prince William and Princess Mary of Orange ostensibly joint regnant monarchs, but with executive power vested in William alone. The principle of direct hereditary succession gave way before the determination of the political establishment and the "people" to preclude a Catholic dynasty. By no stretch of law or reason was William a legitimate ruler – according to the principle of direct hereditary succession – but Mary *could* be regarded as legitimate *if* another pretense, the myth that James's baby was supposititious, were accepted as valid. As Rachel Weil's essay, one of the first to take the myth seriously, shows, English political leaders deluded themselves and others into accepting the crazy tale that the baby of James II and his second and catholic wife, Mary of Modena, had been brought into his mother's bed in a warming pan and hence was a fraud. The deception was of extraordinary importance, because it preserved in the line of succession to the throne Princess Mary, James's elder daughter by his first and then Protestant wife, Anne Hyde, and that of her sister Princess Anne, who later became Queen Anne. The myth worked to the advantage of everyone along the political spectrum who wanted to avoid a Catholic dynasty; hence Tories and Whigs alike embraced it, easing their

---

[45] *The Diary of Abraham De la Pryme, the Yorkshire Antiquary*, ed. (Charles Jackson), (Durham, Andrews, for the Surtees Society, 1870), p. 15. I thank Eveline Cruickshanks for calling my attention to this source.

consciences the while, at least during the weeks when a decision was being made.

Extending the point, Howard Nenner argues that pretense joined with pragmatism acted as stabilizers at a time of constitutional uncertainty and "missed opportunities" in the winter of 1688–89. His paper offers evidence of the confusion in people's minds as they struggled with the basic problem of how to render legitimate a settlement that was patently illegal according to strictly construed principles of divine-right monarchy and direct hereditary succession. Among the many arguments explored in debate and pamphlet to give legal standing to William's role, the most promising, Nenner declares, was the common-law principle that a husband was entitled to possess and administer his wife's estate. Hitherto neglected by historians, the "matrimonial crown" argument is further evidence of the ideological complexities that informed the contemporary justification of the revolutionary settlement.

Revolutionary leaders did not substitute one king for another, as is often said; rather, they created in the place of a James the dual monarchy of William and Mary, a constitutional arrangement unique in the nation's history. Pretense also clung to this aspect of the settlement. Although it was widely believed that Mary was truly a regnant queen, she was legally little more than a consort queen, for regal power was lodged solely in the hands of her husband. In recognition of this, the committee for the coronation ceremony, although at pains to give Mary marks of high status, crafted the ceremony, as the essay by Schwoerer shows, to convey to the knowledgeable observer that Mary's status was subordinate to her husband's. Because of her anomalous position, special regency bills had to be passed every time the king went off to war leaving Mary in charge of the government.

Why should there be deception about the constitutional status of the queen? Because the deception helped to win a consensus for the settlement. Tories especially – but also conservative Whigs – felt more comfortable in supporting a solution that placed monarchical power in the hands of two persons, one of whom was a legitimate heir to the throne – if, of course, another deception, that about the warming pan, were accepted! To pretend that Mary was a regnant queen was a concession won from William. William grudgingly agreed to share the crown with his wife, insisting that regal power remain in his hands. Mary, holding to contemporary views about the place of women in society, and having earlier assured her husband that if she should ever inherit the English throne she wanted him to rule in her stead, refused to go along with any arrangement that advanced her above her husband.

Mary's role in English politics is now, after much neglect, beginning to interest professional historians. Aiming to reassess the queen's contributions, William A. Speck is among the first scholars to judge Mary on her own terms and take her seriously. Although Mary ruled as regent at intervals totalling almost three years from 1690 to the end of 1694, when smallpox brought an untimely death at the age of thirty-two, historians have virtually ignored her.

Mary's own diffidence and self-deprecating attitude about her political abilities has been generally accepted at face value, clouding understanding of the
contributions she made. Drawing upon the unexploited Privy Council
records, as well as using poetry and eulogistic prose written at her death,
Speck shows that Mary played an important role as regnant queen.[46]

The larger question of the role women played in the Revolution has also
been the subject of recent work.[47] In the present volume, Rachel Weil uses her
essay on the warming-pan rumor to investigate the relationship between
gender ideology and political discourse. The rumor about the supposititious
baby was patriarchist in character and hence appealed to persons committed
to the principle of hereditary succession; but it also exposed the problem of
how to prove the paternity and legitimacy of an heir, a question peculiarly the
province of women. Hence it moved women into a central political issue as
participants and as legal witnesses, thereby opening a "space" for debate
about women's relationship to political power.

The significance of religion, seen from several perspectives, has a place in
almost all the papers. Gordon Schochet's essay recasts understanding of John
Locke's views on toleration by placing them in the wider context of the
debates on dissent in the 1680s, at the time of the Revolution, and in the early
1690s. Moving progressively from the mid-1660s towards advocacy of religious liberty for Protestant dissenters, Locke increasingly based his position
on the rights and entitlement of individuals, the personal and "private"
nature of religious belief, and the essential differences between church and
state. Locke's *Epistola de Tolerantia* provoked agitated response, especially from
Jonas Proest, whose important work scholars have ignored.

From another viewpoint, Stephen B. Baxter also underlines the importance
of religion. One theme of his essay is that the Revolution is a part of a
European-wide struggle over religion that reached back to the sixteenth-
century Reformation. He regards the Revolution as fundamentally conservative in nature. Insisting upon the complexity of the event (as did other
authors), he argues for a multidisciplinary approach to understanding the
society and culture of the era. His own focus is upon the court culture of the
new regime. Drawing upon iconography and the classical modes of discourse
that identified William of Orange with Hercules and Marcus Aurelius, he
relates court culture to Williamite politics.

Also joining iconographical and traditional materials, Lois G. Schwoerer
finds a fresh perspective in studying the coronation ceremony of April 11,
1689, and the new coronation oath required of William and Mary. Maintaining that the traditional outward forms of the ceremony concealed many new
features, she argues that the ceremony and the oath reflected the political and
religious convictions and partisan divisions and strengths of the principal

---

[46] Speck's paper extends and complements a recent article by Lois G. Schwoerer, whose purpose was to show
changes in the images of the queen from 1688 to 1695. See her "Images of Queen Mary II, 1689–1695," *Renaissance
Quarterly*, 42 (winter 1989), 717–48.
[47] Lois G. Schwoerer, "Women and the Glorious Revolution," *Albion* 18 (1986), 195–218.

leaders of the Revolution. Arguing that the new leaders looked to the coronation as a way of legitimating the Revolution and reassuring domestic and
foreign observers of the government's stability at a time of actual instability,
Schwoerer dissects the new oath (the first one to be formulated by a committee of the House of Commons), showing that in the section respecting law it
limited royal law powers in radical ways that reinforced the Declaration of
Rights, and that, in the section regarding religion, it revealed the prevailing
religious conservatism of Tories and mainstream Whigs, thereby hardening
divisions.

In another fresh departure, Gary De Krey reinforces historians who find a
radical component in the Revolution by insisting upon the presence of a
radical movement in London in 1688–89. Democratic and libertarian in
nature, but derived primarily from political circumstances in the city, this
urban radicalism, according to De Krey, reflected a tradition of civic ideology
that began in the 1640s and, contrary to some historians, continued
throughout the Restoration. De Krey demonstrates his thesis by delineating
the characteristics of London radicals, dissecting the vocabulary of political
debate in the Common Council, and analyzing the goals they hoped to achieve
from the Revolution. Although civic radicals were more pragmatic than they
had been in 1682–83 and more sober than their predecessors of the 1640s, their
draft statute for restoring civic government was a radical revival of the city's
constitution of 1649. De Krey maintains, therefore, that London should be
considered a revolutionary capital. Well aware, of course, of the disintegration
of radicalism in London politics, De Krey offers a provocative explanation for
that development that integrates religious, civic, commercial, and military
considerations. His essay opens new directions by giving a positive answer to
the question whether late seventeenth-century London radicals were
descended intellectually from earlier radicals. One general conclusion that
emerges from these several essays is that the ideology of the Revolution was
more complex and rich than is usually portrayed, that conservative and
radical ideas existed side by side, and that neither should be ignored.

The implications and consequences of the Revolution in Scotland and
Ireland, a much-neglected topic, engages the attention of two authors. It is, of
course, no news that the Revolution was different in Scotland and Ireland
from the Revolution in England. The challenge, adumbrated by the present
essays, is to integrate the history of the event in the three parts of the British
Isles, or, in other words, to adopt the perspective of *British* history. What is
needed is an approach that will deal with the interconnection between the
three nations. Picking up just one thread of the story, Bruce Lenman attempts
to explain the dearth of theoretical political debate in Scotland. One neglected
consideration that he brings forward is James's policy of repressing the publication of controversial works and of punishing seemingly innocuous actions
that implied criticism of his regime, practical steps that speak to the nature of
James's political philosophy. Finding some identities in the thought of John
Locke and the Reverend Gilbert Burnet, Lenman makes the interesting point

that both men were writing under the constraints of a rhetorical strategy imposed by James's actions. Reversing traditional interpretations, Lenman maintains that the ideas of Scottish leaders were largely conservative truisms, not radical notions at all. In fine, Lenman has discovered a prevailing consensus among Scottish commentators, including Jacobite leaders, that radical Catholicization and arbitrary government were unacceptable. He goes further, maintaining that the lack of polarization in Scottish political thought in 1690 (when militant Whigs actually cooperated with Jacobites) was an immediate reaction to King William III's effort to retain obnoxious features of the previous regime, another conclusion that speaks to the nature of the Revolution.

There was nothing "glorious" about the Revolution of 1688–89 in Ireland, as everyone knows. Arguing that James II's accession to the throne in 1685 reopened the question of land ownership in ways threatening to Protestants, Karl S. Bottigheimer links that issue to the even larger questions of the "failure of the Reformation" in Ireland and the remarkable, still not totally explained, survival of Catholicism. In 1688–89 and in 1690 Ireland was drawn close to the center of events in England because of the threat it posed to Protestant interests. The military victory at the Battle of the Boyne settled the questions of land and religion in favor of the Protestants and left a legacy in Ireland lasting to the present day. William III is no savior of imperiled Protestantism, but a destroyer of majoritarian Catholicism.

Bottigheimer's essay provokes several questions inviting further research. Among them is what influence news of Irish events had upon Prince William's decisions and calculations. Another is the patriot Jacobite rebellion in terms of the mythology and traditions it created. And a third is the extent of Irish Night panics in English provincial towns in 1688.[48] A crucial ingredient in the collapse of support for James II, antipopery was brutally exploited by William's friends. A little-known contemporary comment highlights the presence of anti-Catholic sentiments that are as intense and fanciful as any that developed ten years earlier at the time of the Popish Plot and Exclusion Crisis. "Strange" stories circulated about "instruments of torture" found in popish houses in all parts of the Kingdom; buried barrels of oil "to boyl hereticks in"; pincers, screws, and knives in a vault in Westminster to be used by James II to torment MPs who disagreed with him; and an underground stable where horses were kept in darkness and fed with human bodies to prepare them to "tear us to pieces." Spread by "supposititious [*sic*] letters, speeches, and such like," such rumors were designed "to irritate the people and encourage them to obey the revolution." Pertinent to the matter of integrating Irish history into accounts of the Revolution is the writer's remark that the most damaging of all rumors concerned the ravages of thousands of Irish whom King James had disbanded. That rumor began "in the south" and spread throughout so that "most people believed it." Disclaiming his own

---

[48] These points J. G. A. Pocock (and others) raised in discussion at the conference.

belief, De la Pryme described the rumors as "nothing but a politick alarm raised and set on foot by the king and council to see how the nation stood affected [*sic*] to their new king."[49]

Other essayists examine the question of the Revolution's implications and consequences from a cultural, legal, and literary perspective, rather than traditional constitutional, financial, or diplomatic viewpoints. The pivotal role of the Revolution in promoting changes in the criminal law and its administration over the next three or four decades is explored by J. M. Beattie in an essay that well illustrates the fresh approaches and questions historians are asking. Identifying three main developments – legislative activity resulting in important legal statutes, changes in the conduct of criminal trials by the intrusion of the central administration, and changes in the procedures respecting pardons – Beattie connects them with the conviction in parliament, courts, and central administration that criminal and social disorder required a firmer hand. In his view, this conviction was the indirect product of the Revolution, that is, the effect of warfare on patterns and perceptions of crime, the regularity of parliamentary sessions that provided opportunity for legislative initiatives, and the growth of a more powerful executive.

The interaction between politics and literature in the context of the Revolution is a new perspective developed with different results by Stephen Zwicker and Lois Potter. Noting the literary silence that enveloped the Revolution and denied it a hero, Zwicker uncovers the idioms available for imagining and representing the meaning of the event. Commenting on the apprehension and reluctance to praise the victors visible in panegyrics, he focuses on John Dryden's Jacobite drama, *Don Sebastian*, the revolution's only literary masterpiece, which praised the defeated James II rather than the triumphant William of Orange. The commercial success of the play provides seldom-used evidence of the nature of political values and commitment after the Revolution.

A different tack yielding different conclusion is taken by Lois Potter. Acknowledging that the sympathies of the legitimate theater remained with the defeated Stuarts, Potter shows, however, that Queen Mary II was more sympathetic to the theater than sometimes suggested and that the theater did offer plays, especially the musical spectacle, that were complimentary to the new monarchs. More to the point, Potter focuses on five heretofore neglected "pamplet plays" which expressed a view favorable to the new regime. Read aloud in coffee houses rather than performed, these staunchly anti-Catholic plays aimed to reach a wide audience by employing comedy and farce, scurrilous attacks on King James and Queen Mary of Modena, and caricatures of Irishmen and Frenchmen. By innuendo and direct remark, they also attempted to discredit James's literary supporters, Sir Roger L'Estrange and John Dryden. Together, Zwicker and Potter uncover an important dialectic between high and popular culture, and help to explain the generally passive

---

[49] *The Diary of Abraham De la Pryme*, p. 16.

reaction of high culture to the Revolution. Their work opens up the need to consider the literary response to the Revolution in continental states.

The Revolution of 1688–89 had a colonial dimension that is sometimes neglected by its historians or, at least, not integrated in their accounts. Jack Greene's essay avoids that myopia, developing a perpective that focuses on the interconnection between the colonies and the mother country. Taking issue with the currently received view that the Revolution and subsequent intercolonial wars helped to consolidate the authority of the British government over the colonies, Greene argues instead that, as a result of the Revolution of 1688–89, power devolved to the localities in the colonies, just as it did, he declares in another controversial assertion, in England, Wales, and Scotland. Colonists claimed that they shared in the Revolution's legacy, which they interpreted as a victory for the rights of Englishmen, including themselves, against oppressive royal officials, and which they translated into efforts to win written guarantees. Why the campaign for a consolidated empire was only modestly successful lies, according to Greene, in ideological aspirations and in the structure of governance in the empire. In a further controversial departure, Greene maintains that the colonies were not governed by force from London or even locally, but in accord with public opinion. The authorities, he believes, "used the [colonists] well," just as one of *Cato's Letters* advised.

The essays in this collection have not exhausted the questions that need to be explored for a complete understanding of the Revolution of 1688–89; but they do show the value of considering the Revolution of 1688–89 in an international context. They demonstrate that it is along the boundaries of more than one discipline that some of the most interesting answers to the nature of past cultures may be discovered. They make clear that there are no simple answers to what have long been obvious queries about the Revolution of 1688–89, or, to put it differently, the answers have changed over time – a salutary reminder that history is not only the mind of the historian but also the ideological context within which he or she is writing. In short, they show how perspectives may change when scholars from various disciplines together bring new questions and materials to the same topic.

1

The Dutch, the invasion of England, and the alliance of 1689

K. H. D. Haley

Prince William of Orange's invasion of England in 1688 was not the outcome of a simple personal decision. It could not have succeeded without the positive support, and not the mere acquiescence, of the States-General, the States or provincial assembly of Holland, and the city of Amsterdam. Although William was a rich man, he could certainly not have commanded the resources that he needed for an expedition which, it now turns out,[1] was much larger than was once supposed. The expedition was an immense logistical operation for its day, even if the size of William's army might seem small (not more than 15,000) by the side of the armies of Louis XIV. The prince needed the approval of the States-General (which the States of Holland and the city of Amsterdam could have obstructed) before he could leave the country, and he also needed their approval for the arrangements by which German prince-lings provided subsidized troops to take the place of his own during their absence.

If the expedition was costly – the Dutch were repaid 6 million guilders for the invasion of England, even though there was almost no fighting – it was also known by all to be extremely risky: there had been no hint of a successful invasion in three previous Anglo-Dutch wars. Not only would it be risky at any time, but William could not be spared from the continent until the normal season for operations on land was over, and in the unfavorable weather conditions of the autumn a naval expedition would be even riskier. When we think of the so-called "Protestant wind" which favored William and confined James's defending fleet to the Thames estuary, we ought also to remember the extremely un-Protestant wind which drove William's first attempt back to its starting-point at Hellevoetsluis. To make a second attempt in the month of November took great strength of character on William's part, and a third, or a long wait for the right conditions for D-day, would not have been possible.

Hopes that James II's sailors would not fight might or might not be

---

[1] See, for instance, Jonathan I. Israel, "The Dutch Republic and the Glorious Revolution of 1688/89 in England," in Charles Wilson and David Proctor (eds.), *1688: the Seaborne Alliance and Diplomatic Revolution* (Greenwich, National Maritime Museum, 1989), p. 33.

fulfilled; Monmouth's similar hopes of his former Guards in 1685 had come to nothing when the forces met. Even if an unopposed landing could be made, William's forces might be bogged down in an English civil war against numerically superior forces in which English support (which had failed Monmouth) was problematical. And finally, it could be regarded as certain that the expedition would lead to war, not only against James II, but against Louis XIV. In fact, only nine days after the landing at Torbay, Louis XIV declared war on the States-General.

William's expedition, therefore, was an expensive gamble which needed the backing of a consensus of the Dutch regent classes. It is the purpose of this essay to discuss the reasons why this remarkable consensus came about and the extent to which the results corresponded to the expectations of those Dutch regents who played an essential part in it.

The consensus was remarkable because only a year or two earlier it would have seemed quite unthinkable. In 1678 a peace party in the States of Holland, and in particular in the city of Amsterdam (which contained about one in every ten Dutchmen, and whose wealth supplied about one-quarter of the taxation) had brought about the Treaty of Nijmegen on terms and in a manner of which William disapproved: although, as we shall see, there are some reservations to be made here.[2] More important, in 1683–84 dissensions had been so bad that William had been totally frustrated in his endeavor to rescue Luxemburg from its seizure by Louis XIV. In his resentment against the conversations of some of the Amsterdammers with the French ambassador William had come near to attempting a kind of *coup* against them, so strengthening all the old regent fears of William's authoritarianism.[3] The tactics of the Ambassador D'Avaux were to play upon such quarrels, supporting the Amsterdam regents in particular against William's anti-French policies by threats suggesting that they were likely to lead to war, the dislocation of trade, and an unwelcome subordination to William. D'Avaux's memoirs[4] should be treated as an apologia for his eventual failure to prevent a Dutch consensus from emerging: he had numerous contacts in the States-General (including clerks who leaked the text of secret revolutions or the supposedly secret dispatches of Aernout van Citters, the ambassador in London), and also in the States of Holland and the town councils; he himself came to acknowledge that it was much more difficult to get the resolutions of the States of Holland than those of the States-General,[5] but he also had friends among the four burgomasters of Amsterdam who advised him what went on

---

[2] The classic accounts are in F. A. M. Mignet, *Négociations relatives à la succession d'Espagne sous Louis XIV* (4 vols., Paris, Imprimerie Royale, 1835–42), IV; and O. Klopp, *Der Fall des Hauses Stuart* (14 vols., Vienna, Braumüller, 1875–88), II. For more recent work, see the essays in J. A. H. Bots (ed.), *The Peace of Nijmegen, 1676–1678/9* (Amsterdam, APA-Holland University Press, 1980).

[3] G. H. Kurtz, *Willem III en Amsterdam, 1683–1685* (Utrecht, Kemink en Zoon, 1928).

[4] *Négociations de Monsieur le Comte d'Avaux en Hollande* (6 vols., Paris, Durand and Pissot, 1752–53). There is a further edition (Paris, 1754), differently paginated but with an apparently identical text. His dispatches (as opposed to his comments) are, however, best cited from the originals, which may be found in massive entry-books in PRO, FO 95, 571–74. These are, however, unpaginated, so that dispatches are referred to by date only (vol. 573 for 1687, vol. 574 for 1688).

[5] D'Avaux, January 21, 1687.

there. However, it is possible to wonder how selective and how slanted were the accounts he received of debates. He was not always so well informed as he supposed, and another serious handicap was that his instructions forbade him to talk to the "friends" and "creatures" of William of Orange, who in practice included all who shared the prince's view of foreign affairs, although, apart from five or six people, they could be dismissed as dependents "raised from the dust" by him. The result was that discussions of the international situation, other than William's alleged ambitions in England, were less and less reported as time went by.[6]

According to D'Avaux, as also to the Polish envoy in Amsterdam, Antoine Moreau,[7] religion was an important contributory factor (and one about which, by implication, he could do little) in the arousing of Dutch hostility to France, and by extension to James II of England. The influx of Huguenot refugees of all classes from French persecution made both Catholic monarchs unpopular. For Pierre Jurieu and other Calvinists, both Dutch and Huguenot, the Glorious Revolution was part of the divine plan for the triumph of God's people against oppression.[8] For the most part the Dutch regents may have been Arminian and Erasmian rather than Calvinist zealots, and they were not in any way responsible to a wider Dutch public, but equally they were not totally insulated from the views which were vociferously expressed, from the pulpit and in print, in a state where political and religious issues were freely discussed. And Walloons were not unimportant in Dutch society.

It is noteworthy that as early as 1681 D'Avaux reported that hitherto pro-French regents such as Willem van Haren, who had cooperated with the French at the Nijmegen peace congress in 1678, were alienated by reports of the sufferings of the Huguenots, and the ambassador feared the loss of the support of the two provinces, Friesland and Groningen, on which he relied for help in the States-General.[9] Such feelings could only be strengthened by the accession of James II and the Revocation of the Edict of Nantes in 1685. Many of the resulting fears of attempts to "ruin Dutch religion" were extremely wild, and wide of the mark; and yet it was not unreasonable for a Dutch politician to calculate that ultimately James II's Catholicizing policies in England would lead him to look to Louis for support, and that a dangerous power bloc would result. Yet in the last resort it seems impossible to believe that 1688 was intended to be a renewal of European religious wars, not least because both William and the regents consistently sought to play down anti-Catholic feelings in the Netherlands, both to guard against internal dissensions and because, if there was to be a struggle against Louis XIV, they would need the help of Catholic allies. The Emperor Leopold was known to be much under Jesuit influence, Madrid was no less Catholic than Vienna, and the Pope was counted on, not only to influence them, but to rule against the

---

[6] D'Avaux, *Négociations*, I, p. 2.   [7] BL, Add. Mss. 38493–5.

[8] For Jurieu, see F. R. J. Knetsch, *Pierre Jurieu, theoloog en politicus der refuge* (Kampen, Kok, 1967); and Elizabeth Labrousse, *Pierre Bayle* (The Hague, Nijhoff, 1963–64), chs. 7–9.

[9] D'Avaux, July 24, 1681 and *passim*, July–September 1681.

French candidate in the disputed election to the archbishopric of Cologne. For the Dutch regents 1688 was not exactly a religious crusade: there was no call for Dutch volunteers. The most that can be said is that the French persecution of Huguenots contributed to a pronounced antipathy amongst Dutch regents whose traditions were after all of tolerance. It was harder for D'Avaux to defend the idea of a Dutch partnership with the author of the Revocation and harder for his friends in the States of Holland to come forward.

If this was true of the place of God in men's calculations, it was also true of the place of Mammon.[10] In 1678 Louis had induced the peace party in the cities of Holland to make a separate treaty with France, thus leaving aside the other anti-French Confederates, by agreeing substantially to withdraw Colbert's protectionist tariff of 1667. Nine years later there seemed no further need for conciliatory measures of this kind. In September 1687 the news reached Rotterdam that Louis had prohibited the import of herring which was not cured with French salt, and this was generally interpreted as a deliberate blow against a profitable branch of Dutch trade. Worse followed when in November 1687 he substantially returned to the 1667 tariff, particularly as it applied to the cloth on which the Leiden textile industry depended, and much of which was exported by way of Amsterdam.[11] The results were extremely damaging, and, of course, lost nothing in the representations which merchants made to D'Avaux. Not only did they amount, according to one estimate, to a loss of one-quarter in the value of Dutch textile exports, but the manner in which it was done was extremely sharp and forceful, paying no heed to Dutch susceptibilities. A policy of intimidation seemed once again to be replacing one of conciliation; if the States-General would not toe the line, worse might follow. Complaints reached D'Avaux that the French were trying to ruin Dutch commerce as well as Dutch religion, and there was even wild talk that the Dutch could lose no more by fighting France. D'Avaux, again implicitly avoiding the responsibility for the breakdown of 1688, claimed to have wanted concessions.[12]

Yet, great as the acrimony undoubtedly was, it is very doubtful that it would by itself have led to war. The natural first step would have been counter-embargoes, as in 1669–71, and the Pensionary of Holland, Gaspar Fagel, and the city of Leiden were actively proposing these as late as August 1688.[13] It is true that these would have been viewed with mixed feelings by other towns whose trading interests lay elsewhere, but the same was true of war. The experience of 1672–78 showed that other branches of trade besides

---

[10] For a contrary view see Israel, "The Dutch Republic," pp. 36–38. Arguing that the motives for Dutch aggression were economic, Israel ignores altogether the disputes in the Rhineland and the wider international situation.

[11] See the table of French tariffs on imports from the Dutch Republic, 1664–1713, in Jonathan I. Israel, *Dutch Primacy in World Trade, 1585–1740* (Oxford, Clarendon Press, 1989), p. 288.

[12] See, for instance, D'Avaux, July 29, August 10, 21, September 2, 16, November 11, 1688, and *passim*.

[13] Cf. D'Avaux, August 21 and 27, September 16, 1688; William to Bentinck, August 25 in *Correspondentie van Willem III en van Hans Willem Bentinck, eersten graaf van Portland* ed. N. Japikse (5 vols., Nijhoff for Rijksgeschiedkundige Publicatien, 1927–37), part I, I, pp. 44–45.

that with France would suffer from war. In any case commercial complaints against France would not by themselves have won the support of allies, nor would they have justified, not merely a war against France, but invasion of England, without other considerations.

The fact was that since the Truce of Ratisbon in 1684 the international situation had become more threatening and more dangerous to the security of the Dutch state. The League of Augsburg of 1686 (to which the States-General were not a party) had no teeth and was unlikely to achieve anything while the Emperor Leopold was engaged in reconquering Hungary from the Turks, but it indicated a growing preoccupation with the defense of the Rhineland against French encroachment. Sooner or later the emperor would take up the defense of the Holy Roman Empire, and over the Palatinate and the Archbishopric of Cologne conflict was especially likely. In February 1688 the usual rumors were rife in Amsterdam that French troops were assembling on the frontiers of Germany, and that the objective would be the Palatinate.[14] There Louis might seek to enforce the claims of his sister-in-law the Duchess of Orleans, while Louis's interest in the key imperial fortress of Philippsburg on the Rhine was sufficiently obvious. If conceded, such claims would constitute a further continuation of the constant nibbling away of territory by France in the Spanish Netherlands, the seizure of Lorraine, Luxemburg, and Strasburg and other places as a result of the *chambres de réunion*. In spite of modern attempts to maintain the defensive nature of Louis XIV's policy, contemporaries would not have believed that these were Louis's last territorial claims in Europe. Farther north, long before the death of the Archbishop of Cologne on July 3, 1688, it was known that there would be a disputed election between the French protégé, Cardinal Wilhelm von Furstenberg, and Prince Joseph-Clement of Bavaria: for many years Archbishops of Cologne had also been Bishops of Liège, and the dying cleric was also Bishop of Münster and Bishop of Hildesheim.

The fact that the lands of Cologne and Liège had been used to facilitate the French attack of 1672, while the current Bishop of Münster had twice used his position immediately across the Dutch border to invade the republic in 1665 and 1672, alone made the disputed succession of concern to the Dutch. But there was a wider significance too. If the French dominated the Rhineland they might block the possibility of the emperor's coming again to the rescue of the Netherlands (Dutch and Spanish) as he had done in the war of 1672–78. If not earlier, the emperor's aid was likely to be needed when the childless and disease-ridden Charles II of Spain died and Louis XIV could be expected to claim the southern Netherlands with the rest of the Spanish succession, thus eliminating the buffer between France and the Dutch Republic and turning into reality the old bogey of France as a neighbor. But in the meantime there was the prospect of a European war arising from the Rhineland disputes, as the letters came in from Hendrik van Bilderbeke, the States-General's resident at Cologne.[15]

[14] Antoine, Moreau, BL, Add. Ms. 38494, fol. 37.   [15] Cf. D'Avaux, September 2, 1688.

From such a war the States-General could hardly remain aloof, and in such a war it appeared that, if nothing was done, England would be an ally of France. We now know that James II was preoccupied with his domestic policies, had no desire to be entangled in complications in Europe and was conscious of the unpopularity with his subjects which would result from close cooperation with France. But since the 1660s it had been axiomatic to Dutch politicians, whether to William or to De Witt and his successors in the States party, that James was not well disposed to the Dutch[16] and rather favored his Catholic cousin Louis XIV. The possibility that James (who was in his fifties) might soon be succeeded by his daughter Mary with her husband, William of Orange, was removed when, following rumors of the Queen's pregnancy in the concluding months of 1687, a healthy son was born to her and to James in June, 1688. The prospect of a permanent Catholic and francophile regime in England renewed memories of the trauma of 1672 when a joint French and English attack had brought the Dutch Republic to the verge of ruin. The French invasion which established Louis's armies in the heart of the Republic was in 1688 no more remote to Dutchmen than the end of the Vietnam war to Americans or the coming of Mrs. Thatcher to the leadership of the Tory party are to us now, and the enemy had been on Dutch territory.

It is easy to understand that this view of the international situation was being spread by William and those who thought like him, but less easy to appreciate that the same considerations were present to the minds of Amsterdammers and the former peace party, even to those who had opposed William in 1683–84. Amsterdammers too could remember that the French troops had reached the walls of Muiden, only nine miles away, before establishing themselves at Utrecht for eighteen months, and the villages of Bodegrave and Zwammerdam, where French atrocities figured largely in the propaganda of Dutch pamphleteers, were no more than thirty miles distant. These memories were not discussed with D'Avaux but were nonetheless potent. Moreover, it must not be imagined that the Amsterdammers were parochially minded merchants, concerned only with the immediate profits of trade. Probably the inhabitants of no other European city were better informed about international affairs. In addition to the security of the Dutch state they appreciated the importance of keeping Flanders, with the potentially rival port of Antwerp, out of French hands.

Such attitudes had shown themselves over a period of twenty years before the Revolution. An influential Amsterdam burgomaster, Coenraad van Beuningen, who served as ambassador both in Paris and in London, cooperated in the Triple Alliance of 1668 with England and Sweden, which restricted Louis's gains from the War of Devolution in the Spanish Netherlands. That alliance, incidentally, had been negotiated in only five days by a procedure not in accordance with normal constitutional practice, and might easily have been obstructed by Amsterdam and other cities had the need to

---

[16] See, for instance De Witt to van der Aa, August 4–14, 1670, *Brieven van De Witt*, ed. R. Fruin, G. W. Kernkamp, and N. Japikse (4 vols., Amsterdam, Müller, 1906–13), IV, pp. 79n.–80n.

prevent further Spanish losses not seemed paramount.[17] In the 1670s, in spite of the fact that Charles II had joined in attacking the Dutch in 1672, Van Beuningen looked to English participation in a coalition against Louis XIV, even favoring a joint ban on trade with France. The trouble was that England could not be depended on, primarily because king and parliament could not agree with each other on the policy to be pursued. After the withdrawal of the French from Dutch territory (except Maastricht) at the end of 1673 the continuing general war seemed increasingly futile, leading only to the loss of further Flemish towns at a burdensome cost while England now profited from its neutrality. Suspicions grew that William might use his army command to achieve his personal ambitions as his father had tried to do in 1650. It was when the great city of Ghent, only twenty-five miles from the Dutch border, fell into French hands early in 1678 and hopes of English support seemed likely to lead to nothing that the peace party in Amsterdam and other cities accepted the bait of French tariff concessions and insisted on peace even without the cooperation of their allies. But even then it is significant that they did not want peace at any price. When the French suddenly refused to evacuate those Flemish towns which they had promised to return to Spain until their Swedish allies were also satisfied, there were indignant protests. The French ambassadors at the Nijmegen peace congress were disconcerted to learn from the pensionary of Amsterdam that, irrespective of trading interests and the need for peace, even Amsterdam was prepared to fall in with England's proposal for an alliance and a continuation of the war should Louis not desist from his refusal to evacuate the towns.[18]

Louis XIV did desist and a Franco-Dutch treaty was hastily cobbled up at Nijmegen, but D'Avaux was conscious of the damage done to the peace party's trust in France, and the opinion of Sir William Temple, the English ambassador, was that an important factor in the signing of the treaty was the spreading of rumors that Charles II was not sincere in his professions of being ready to enter the war.[19] In the remainder of Charles II's reign even those like Van Beuningen who had hopes of bringing England into a defensive alliance had to give them up. It was against this background that William's ideas of going alone to the rescue of Luxemburg and maintaining large armed forces seemed hopelessly risky, futile, expensive, and likely only to serve his personal ambitions. William regarded objections to his attempts to raise more troops as merely obstructive and the conversations of some members of the *vroedschap* with D'Avaux as treasonable. In 1683 relations between William of Orange and the capital city of Amsterdam reached a low point.

Nevertheless, it is noteworthy that, after James II's accession to the English

[17] K. H. D. Haley, *An English Diplomat in the Low Countries: Sir William Temple and John de Witt, 1665–1672* (Oxford, Clarendon Press, 1986), pp. 170–72.

[18] Mignet, *Succession d'Espagne*, IV, pp. 604–5; Sir W. Temple, *Works* (4 vols., Edinburgh, 1754), I, pp. 360–64; M. A. M. Franken, *Coenraad Van Beuningen's Politieke en Diplomatieke Aktiviteiten in de jaren 1667–1684* (Groningen, Wolters, 1966), pp. 158–63; C. L. Grose, "The Anglo-Dutch Alliance of 1678," *EHR* 39 (1924), 349–72, 526–51; Bots, *Peace of Nijmegen*, pp. 145–56.

[19] D'Avaux, *Négociations*, I, p. 6; Temple, *Works*, I, pp. 364–66, 370–71, and IV, pp. 401–50.

throne only a few months later, the magistrates of Amsterdam connived at Monmouth's departure on his ill-fated expedition. After the rebellion's complete collapse at the battle of Sedgemoor, and as James's power and the strength of his army steadily grew to seem a probable support for Louis XIV's aggressions, there appeared more substance in the views William was putting forward. Enthusiasm for William did not necessarily grow at the same rate, but fears of Louis XIV warred with fears of William's authoritarianism and gradually grew stronger.

The pattern became one in which Amsterdam began by obstructing William's defense proposals, as with the annual Staet van Oorlog in 1687, but D'Avaux correctly foresaw they would in the end give way. D'Avaux put this down partly to the age of some of the stalwart old Republicans – Gilles Valckenier of Amsterdam died in 1680, while another leading republican, Adriaen Paets of Rotterdam, died in 1686. He still had acquaintances within the Amsterdam burgomasters, notably Johannes Hudde (aged sixty) and to a lesser extent Nicolaas Witsen, but he tended to dismiss them as "weak" and "timorous" (*craintif*) in the face of intimidation by William's friends, not realizing perhaps that along with their complaints about dangers to Dutch religion and commerce there was a more deep-seated change of attitude in progress. Jacob Hop, formerly pensionary of Amsterdam, who was sent on diplomatic missions in William's interests, was the son of a former strong opponent of the prince.

In October 1687 D'Avaux sought to solve a disputed case by means of threats to Amsterdam regents, and the four burgomasters sought to mollify him by inviting him to a dinner, following which Hudde, particularly, gave him assurances of their desire for good relations with France.[20] But there was little that was solid behind such professions, and as time went on D'Avaux put less and less faith in them.

Disputes on the Rhine were to be decided in 1688, but it rapidly became clearer that the key to the situation was in England. Already in July 1687 William had confided to the Amsterdammers what had taken place between James and Dijkvelt and between himself and the English ambassador over the Test Acts,[21] but it was not until the following summer that the process of taking them into his confidence went further.

For the Dutch, if not for William, the decisive fact seems to have been the birth of a Prince of Wales, on June 20, 1688 (according to the new calendar). The significance of the birth of a boy, rather than a girl or a still-born baby, was easily appreciated. Indeed, the "rabble" at Amsterdam demonstrated their feelings when the English consul sought to celebrate the news. They began to throw stones and to crowd up to the doors, and though the tumult was eventually stilled the authorities must have been uncomfortably reminded of what had happened to the De Witts in the earlier crisis of 1672.[22]

---

[20] D'Avaux, October 16, 1687.   [21] *Ibid.*, July 6, 1687.
[22] *Hollandsche Mercurius, 1688*, pp. 174–77, quoted by J. Wagenaar, *Vaderlandsche Historie* (21 vols., Amsterdam, Allart, 1790–96 edn), xv, p. 411.

D'Avaux tried to reassure his Amsterdam friends that Louis wanted peace, but he had to confess that he no longer had the same easy relations with them as he had once had. The preservation of peace was no longer their only motive, and they talked of risks from England after the birth of the Prince of Wales, and from Germany if the vacant bishoprics were occupied by clients of Louis XIV. He noted that they no longer paid the same attention to his representations.

In the same dispatch (July 6, 1688) D'Avaux reported that William's friend Dijkvelt had gone to Amsterdam. The process of sounding out burgomaster Nicolaas Witsen may have begun a little earlier before the prince's birth, but the news must have served to strengthen the old view that English support was indispensable for action against France, and the new argument that it could only be obtained by William's intervention in England, with the promise of English support. Appealed to for help from Amsterdam in the interests of freedom and religion (an allusion to the old revolt against Spain), Witsen agreed on the danger, but talked of trusting in Providence – and perhaps waiting until the following spring. However, he was sufficiently encouraging for Dijkvelt to invite him to an interview with the prince himself. After two days of consultation in the Hague, in which he received permission to consult his fellow-burgomasters Hudde and Cornelis Geelvinck, Witsen was more noncommittal than William had hoped but he was willing to give at least tacit consent to the provision of money for the preparations which the Amsterdam admiralty and others were making. Witsen may indeed have acted more positively than the impression left by his own account. There was opposition in the Amsterdam *vroedschap* to Witsen's previous consent to the provision of money for the raising of 9,000 sailors: it seems to have been on procedural grounds, but William and Witsen found means to evade the need to put the matter to a vote by using an existing fund. William had also cautiously asked that a fourth burgomaster, Jan Appelman, be not brought into the secret (though Appelman made no difficulty about his consent two months later) and no formal resolution for consent to the expedition was as yet put forward.[23]

By this time Vice-Admiral Herbert had arrived, bringing with him the famous invitation of the Seven, and it was an open secret that an invasion of England would not be a mere repetition of the Anglo-Dutch wars, but would be welcomed by a substantial proportion of the English population. By August 10 D'Avaux had been told by an Amsterdam friend that, according to "one of their principal burgomasters":

If any disorder took place over the affairs of Cologne or some other place, it would not be in their power to prevent the consequences, and . . . they would be carried away willy-nilly by the torrent . . . if they tried to open their mouths they would be reproached with throwing the Republic into its present state, and they would be asked if they wanted to

---

[23] J. F. Gebhard, Jr., *Het Leven van Mr Nicolaas Cornelisz Witsen 1641–1717* (2 vols., Utrecht, Provinciaal Utrechtsch Genootschap van Kunsten en Wetenschappen, Leeflang, 1881), i, pp. 318–27; Wagenaar, *Vaderlandsche Historie*, xv, pp. 424–31; D'Avaux, July 22, 27, 29, 1688.

come to an understanding with the enemy to see the annihilation of their religion and the destruction of their trade.

On August 21 he sent a special courier to Louis to make it plain that the expedition was to take place in the near future.

William retained his deep-rooted suspicion of the Amsterdammers, and was wary of "the timidity of some and the malice of others,"[24] but he was helped by the French themselves. Having declared publicly at the Hague that Louis was determined to maintain Cardinal von Furstenberg and the Cologne chapter in their rights and privileges, on September 9 he presented two memorials on Louis's tactless instructions, at this of all moments. The first declared that an attack on James would be treated by Louis as an act of hostility to himself, thus appearing to confirm the erroneous suspicion that Louis and James were in league against them. The second threatened the States-General with war if they interfered in the election to the archbishopric of Cologne. The two issues could not have been more closely linked.

The intimidation of course failed. D'Avaux still had his contacts in the town councils of Holland, and they provided him with their resolutions on the subjects of the proposed ban on French trade and the provision to be made for the security of the state. Rotterdam and Delft, for instance, unexpectedly favored a complete ban on French goods, and authorized their deputies to the States-General to concur in anything which might be thought necessary for the country's safety. There were no French hopes of Amsterdam: "those gentlemen were too weak, and the other towns too much embittered on matters of trade" for a vigorous opposition to be expected from the province of Holland. In general the small number who wanted peace dared not oppose the Prince of Orange unless (he hinted) they were fortified by a return to the tariff of 1678; the majority who wanted war were dismissed as "friends of the Prince of Orange" who were unscrupulously aiming at an invasion of England. There was no attempt in D'Avaux's *Négociations* to put it all in the context of Louis's activities over the previous twenty years.[25]

As soon as Louis had issued a manifesto against the emperor and it was clear that he was planning an attack on the imperial fortress of Philippsburg rather than an immediate attack on the republic, the proposed invasion was formally put before the towns, the provincial States, and the States-General for approval. Amongst the Amsterdammers there were some reservations about this belatedness, and the city opposed the ban on *all* French goods, but they agreed to the raising of more troops. There was no opposition in principle.[26] An emotional leave-taking from the States-General contrasted sharply with William's unpopularity in many quarters in 1683–84, though it should not be assumed that the cordiality was unanimous or permanent.

If this expensive gamble was successful in the short term in that it evicted

---

[24] Japikse (ed.), *Correspondentie, part* 1, 1, p. 57. But cf. *ibid., part* 1, 1, pp. 44–45.

[25] D'Avaux, September 2 and 16, 1688.

[26] D'Avaux, September 27, 1688; Gebhard, *Witsen,* 1, p. 330; Hudde's notes on the debate in the *vroedschap, ibid.,* 11, pp. 169–74.

James II from the English throne and installed a Dutchman and his wife in his place, the question remains whether, in the long term, Dutch hopes of the alliance which had at last been realized were fulfilled. In some respects the most important result was negative. The French danger to the Low Countries was staved off for a century. After a nine years' war of attrition the Peace of Ryswick of 1697 meant that the French advance had been held up, and though French troops in 1701 peacefully occupied the southern Netherlands after the death of Charles II of Spain, the allied victory at the battle of Ramillies in 1706 removed the possibility that the southern Netherlands would remain in the hands of Louis's grandson, Philip V; instead, they eventually became Austrian. At their insistence the Dutch at Ryswick secured the right to garrison a line of barrier fortresses on the frontier between the southern Netherlands and France, and they were promised an extended line in the first Barrier Treaty of 1709, when the Whigs needed to be sure that the States-General would remain in the War of the Spanish Succession. Although the barrier eventually gained was less extensive after the Tories had defaulted on their obligations in the Treaty of Utrecht,[27] it was considered an important military protection until the time of the revolutionary wars. For eighty years, indeed, with the exception of a brief period in 1744–48, the Low Countries enjoyed freedom from warfare. Even with that exception, there was a marked contrast with the previous 200 years between the time of Charles V and the Treaty of Utrecht, when war had been in progress there for most of the time. With the right to garrison the barrier fortresses there came also important commercial privileges, and above all the Treaty of Utrecht maintained the closure of the river Scheldt to foreign shipping, thus continuing to remove possible competition from Antwerp for the ports of the north.

Essentially, all this was attributable to the English alliance, and associated with it was Dutch support for the maintenance of the Protestant succession in Britain, so that a francophile Stuart should not come to power in London.[28] Dutch troops were called upon to assist as late as the time of the 1745 rebellion. The alternative for the Dutch would have been a policy of dependence on France, and the Dutch experience in the years 1780–83 and 1795–1813 suggests that the English connection was better for Dutch national security and prosperity.

Yet there was undoubtedly a price to be paid by the Dutch. The wars of 1689–97 and 1702–13 show the fleet once commanded by Michiel De Ruyter and Maarten and Cornelis Tromp increasingly subordinated to that of their former rivals at sea. The Anglo-Dutch treaty of 1689 (as a previous treaty of 1678 had projected) laid down that the English should provide five ships of the line for every three provided by the Dutch and consequently that the commander should be English; while on land there were to be five Dutch

[27] R. Geikie and I. A. Montgomery, *The Dutch Barrier, 1705–1719* (London, Cambridge University Press, 1930), esp. Appendix E.

[28] M. A. Thomson, "The Safeguarding of the Protestant Succession," in R. Hatton and J. S. Bromley (eds.), *William III and Louis XIV: Essays 1680–1720 by and for Mark A. Thomson* (Liverpool University Press, 1968), pp. 237–51.

regiments for every three English ones for the Low Countries.[29] Thus the main English effort was at sea and the main Dutch effort on land. This arrangement was suggested by the States-General themselves, and it was probably inevitable not only because of the 1678 precedent but because the Dutch were finding it increasingly difficult to provide ships equal in size and numbers to those of the English and the French. On the other hand, the land campaigns in the Low Countries were to be fought closer to their own borders and were vital as the war at sea scarcely was. William III was the natural allied commander in the estimation of others as well as himself, and the Dutch who would provide the core of his armies had much more military experience. William eventually selected Marlborough, as Princess Anne's favorite, to carry on his work, and it was Marlborough's military genius which completed the process of England's taking control of the war effort. The core of Marlborough's army, however, remained Dutch, at least until it was decimated at the battle of Malplaquet.

It is also undeniable that in proportion to population the Dutch contributed much more to the cost of these wars. Six million guilders were repaid to them for the cost of the 1688 expedition itself (though repayment for Dutch expenses in Ireland in 1690 took much longer). Those who backed William in 1688, though they foresaw that war would follow, could hardly have foreseen that the wars of 1689–97 and 1702–13 would require larger forces and be far more expensive than any previous war. Though the Dutch credit system was equal to them in the short run, the burden of debts was lasting and ultimately fell on taxation. There were Dutch grumbles that William's campaigns were fought in English interests (as there were English complaints that they were fought in Dutch interests). In the republic the grumbles were never as serious as they had been in 1677–78 or in 1683–84, for the need to resist Louis XIV was generally accepted. But the burden of taxation has been seen as a cause of Dutch economic decline.[30]

Again, Dutch merchant shipping and the fishing fleet suffered severely from the activities of the Dunkirk and Breton privateers during the war years. Trade to France, Spain, and the Levant never recovered its prewar position. In the longer term, the failure of the British to repeal the Navigation Acts as a condition of the alliance of 1689, in gratitude for vital Dutch help in 1688, was seen by some as a contributory factor in the Dutch failure to expand their commerce further in the eighteenth century.

Here we return to Nicolaas Witsen, whose backing had been sought by William in July 1688. As a burgomaster of Amsterdam, he was chosen to be one of the commissioners to negotiate in London in 1689, and much of what is known of the negotiations comes from him (though the original *Verbaal* of the

---

[29] G. N. Clark, *The Dutch Alliance and the War against Trade, 1688–1697* (Manchester University Press, 1923), pp. 37–43.

[30] J. Aalbers, "Holland's Financial Problems (1713–33) and the Wars against Louis XIV," in A. C. Duke and C. A. Tamse (eds.), *Britain and the Netherlands*, VI: *War and Society* (The Hague, Nijhoff, 1977), pp. 79–93; Charles Wilson, "Taxation and the Decline of Empires: an Unfashionable Theme," reprinted in Charles Wilson, *Economic History and the Historian* (London, Weidenfeld and Nicolson, 1969), pp. 114–27.

embassy is now lost). He found life in London boring; his English was imperfect; and he confessed, or boasted, that he was no courtier. But he was also no diplomat and he found the acquisition of diplomatic experience disillusioning. He was conscious, and surprised, that Dutchmen were not particularly popular in the ungrateful English capital. Instead of the allies falling into an immediate and ready agreement, there were differences of opinion, for instance on matters of naval command, and once more the old problem of Dutch trade with the enemy reared its head. Further, although Witsen never quarreled with the king, William's many preoccupations in the spring and summer of 1689 left little time for conversation. Witsen came to feel that he was in London largely for the sake of appearances, to show Englishmen that the city of Amsterdam he represented was in accord with William. When Witsen mentioned the Act of 1651 (curiously he did not refer to the more extensive later Navigation Acts of 1660 and 1663, which alone were legally valid), William only laughed and said that this was not the time to raise the matter.

To some who read this, it might appear that William, having received the backing of the regents when he needed it, now cared little for their interests. But he was surely right that there was no practical chance that the English parliament would repeal the Navigation Acts. William, who told Witsen that "seafarers do not understand politics," knew that in a time of preparation for war, such a proposal could only raise discord. In any case, there is no sign that the Amsterdam regents themselves set great store by a repeal at this particular moment. No such proposal was included in Witsen's instructions, and there were no counterconcessions which he was authorized to offer. As practical men, the regents knew that admission to trade with the American colonies would have been no more welcome to the English than the prospect of increased competition in the East Indies would have been to themselves.[31]

The extent to which Dutch trade suffered from the pressure of the Navigation Acts as a result of English "ingratitude" and failure to repeal them is not clear.[32] They were often laxly administered. They probably became most irksome in the middle of the eighteenth century. In the great boom in all transatlantic trade, Virginian tobacco and other products of the American plantations could only be transported to Holland by means of smuggling through Dutch West Indian islands or of reexport through London. In either case, the profits and the competitive position of the Dutch would also be reduced. The period in which Wagenaar wrote his multivolume and influential *Vaderlandsche Historie* (1749–59) was also one in which much regent opinion was soured following the revolution which, with English backing, had made William IV of Orange stadholder of all seven provinces in 1747. In 1756 Dutch neutrality in the Seven Years War once more raised awkward questions of the definition of contraband and "free ships, free goods" against

[31] Gebhard, *Witsen*, I, pp. 335–85; J. Scheltema, *Geschied en Letterkundige Mengelwerk* (6 vols., Amsterdam and Utrecht, van Terveen, 1817–36), III, part II, pp. 131–70; Wagenaar, *Vaderlandsche Historie*, XVI, pp. 40–42; Clark, *Dutch Alliance*, pp. 17–21, 24–28.   [32] It is not discussed in Israel, *Dutch Primacy*, ch. 9.

British privateers. Wagenaar used Witsen's account of what happened in London, with obvious implications.

In other ways, however, Dutch commercial and financial interests profited from the connection with England. They had always been trading partners as well as rivals, and at the end of the eighteenth century the Netherlands was still the principal market for English exports. C. Davenant put exports to Holland at £1,769,000 in 1700, rising to £2,417,000 in 1703.[33] Of this more than half was in cloth, and a large proportion came in the new trade in serges from the West Country by way of Exeter to Amsterdam. Traces of this trade can still be found in the "Dutch houses" at Topsham on the Exe.[34] In the early eighteenth century linens came in return from the bleaching greens at Haarlem. But of much more significance was the development as a direct consequence of the Revolution of a prosperous Anglo-Dutch community round the church of Austin Friars in London, where they took part in business partnerships, intermarried, and arranged for Dutch investment in the national debt. Dutch investment in the Bank of England alone (amounting to about 30 percent of bank stock in 1750) was to the advantage of the Dutch investor rather than to industrialists and other sections of the economy. It is true also that the Janssens, Vannecks, and the rest often settled in England rather than return to their native country.[35] It is no accident that Lloyds and the Stock Exchange have their tercentenaries shortly after that of the Revolution: the techniques of marine insurance and stock-jobbing both owe a debt to Amsterdam, where their regents had had their share in furthering the Dutch invasion.

It would be wrong to overestimate the cordiality of the feelings which the two peoples cherished for each other; the Anglo-Dutch alliance was essentially a matter of self-interest. But the invasion of 1688 was fundamentally to the advantage of the Dutchmen who planned and backed it. Of course, if the invasion had gone wrong the consequences would have been incalculable. On the other hand, what would the consequences have been, for both peoples, had a child been born to perpetuate the dynastic connection established when the English throne was offered to a Dutchman and his wife? By 1688, it probably seemed unlikely but not impossible (as a son had been for James II only twelve months earlier). Had William and Mary had a direct heir, both peoples might have celebrated the tercentenary of 1688 a little differently. Both human choices and chance have their part in the historical process.

---

[33] C. Davenant, *Political and Commercial Works* (5 vols., London, 1771), v, p. 403.

[34] W. G. Hoskins, *Industry, Trade and People in Exeter, 1688–1800* (Manchester University Press, 1935, reprinted University of Exeter Press, 1968).

[35] Charles Wilson, *Anglo-Dutch Commerce and Finance in the Eighteenth Century* (Cambridge University Press, 1941; repr. 1966); P. G. M. Dickson, *The Financial Revolution in England* (London, Macmillan, 1967), esp. pp. 28–62; see also G. Jackson, "Anglo-Dutch Trade, c. 1660–1760," in Wilson and Proctor (eds.), *1688: the Seaborne Alliance and Diplomatic Revolution*, pp. 75–78.

2

France caught between two balances: the dilemma of 1688

John C. Rule

It is the theme of this essay that France in the 1680s found itself perilously poised between two great power blocs: on the east a continental or European league, headed by a victorious emperor, Austria, Bavaria, Pope Innocent XI, and a scattering of allies. On the west a Maritime or Atlantic League, led by William of Orange and his Dutch political cohorts, and a scattering of German and Baltic princes. Poised, geographically, between them was the kingdom of France (see Map). The oscillation of these three great blocs: the aligning and realigning of leagues; the grouping, desertions and regrouping of allies; the *coups de force* or preemptive strikes drew Europe into a vortex of a great world war that took its name from the anti-French league signed at Augsburg in the summer of 1686. This essay further asserts that, given the diplomatic–military considerations of the summer of 1688, Louis XIV and his advisors had little choice but to order their troops into the mid region of the Rhine valley.

The balance of powers: in theory

In the parlance of international politics the term balance of power had become common coin by the end of the so-called Dutch War of the 1670s.[1] "The balancing" usually referred to a polarity between France and its confederates on one side and a shifting league of allies on the other. In the 1680s this polarity and the concomitant struggle for hegemony was replaced by the idea of a more intricate balance among the Great Powers: the emperor, his Danubian empire, allied German and Italian princes, and the Habsburg cousins in Spain; France and a third party – *tièrs parti*, as it was called – of

---

[1] For general accounts of the balance of power, theory and practice, see Ludwig Dehio, *The Precarious Balance: Four Centuries of the European Power Struggle* (New York, Knopf, 1962), ch. 2; Paul Kennedy, *The Rise and Fall of the Great Powers* (New York, Random House, 1987), pp. 102–3. Kennedy's is a more perceptive account than Dehio's; it should be noted, however, that Louis XIV did *not*, as Kennedy reports (p. 102), maintain an army of 200,000 men in peacetime. Although dealing with a slightly later period, there is the perceptive article by M. S. Anderson, "Eighteenth-century Theories of the Balance of Power," in Ragnhild Hatton and M. S. Anderson (eds.), *Studies in Diplomatic History* (London, Longman, 1970), pp. 183–98.

35

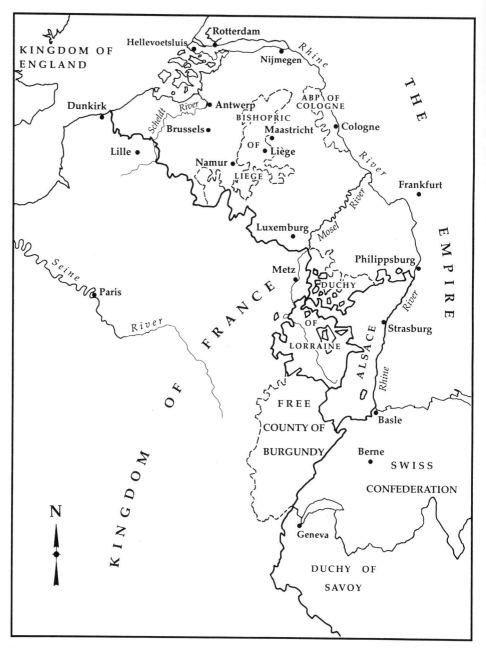

France and the Rhineland in 1688.

German and Baltic princes; and the Maritime bloc headed by the United Provinces of the Netherlands, and after 1688 England on the Atlantic rim. Out of the rivalries of these powers sprang, at the end of the century, the classic theory of the balance of powers.

As the idea of hegemony or universal monarchy withered during the world wars of 1688 to 1714, French statesmen spoke increasingly of "l'équilibre des Pouvoirs," "le repos de l'Europe," "le système de l'Europe," "le grand système," or the "Sûreté des Princes de l'Europe."[2] When the French ambassador to Spain, the Duc d'Harcourt, addressed a memorandum to the members of the Council of State in Madrid, he employed such phrases as "la conservation du 'repos' de l'Europe" and "la tranquillité pour l'Europe entière."[3] It was, he asserted, such a repose or balance that would ensure the maintenance and continuity of the Spanish monarchy.

In Italy the papal cardinal secretary of state (Cardinal Cibo) when writing to a nuncio invoked "il sistema degl'affari di Europa,"[4] with hardly a nod to the older concept of a "commune della Christianità."[5] And Henry St. John, Viscount Bolingbroke, explained to Simon Clement, the British minister in Vienna, "how great importance is . . . [this repose or equilibrium] not only to the Ballance of Power in Italy, and to the Liberties of that Country, but to the general system of Affaires in Europe."[6]

Balance grew within balance. Theories of regional repose appeared. The French ambassador to the Swiss, Comte du Luc, urged the French secretary of state, Colbert de Torcy, to help "rétablir par l'équilibre en Suisse" to insure peace for the area.[7] And the Abbé de Pomponne, ambassador to Venice, wrote to Louis XIV suggesting a "balance égale" between France and the empire in order to assure "le calme dans l'Italie."[8] Later in his embassy, when Pomponne addressed the Venetian senate, he warned their Serenities that they should cleave to the *anciennes maximes* of state: "amitié" with France and "l'appréhension de la trop grande puissance de l'Empereur,"[9] which would unbalance the equilibrium of Italy. On this point Pomponne's advice was echoed by the Tory statesman Bolingbroke, who believed "that Spain should not loose all footing there [in Italy] by wch means the house of Austria wou'd become not only Masters of Italy but have the See of Rome and the influence there."[10] And in a more ecumenical vein, the House of Commons at the end of the War of the League of Augsburg hastened to congratulate William III "for having restored to England the honour . . . of holding the Balance of Europe."[11]

[2] For phrases and expressions used by French statesmen to describe the balance of power, see Pierre Duparc (ed.), *Recueil des instructions aux ambassadeurs, Venise* (Paris, Centre National de Recherche Scientifique, 1958), XXVI, p. 127: Colbet de Torcy's *Instructions* to the Abbé de Pomponne; also Paris, AAE, Correspondance politique, Venise, CXLVII, fol. 42r.–v., May 15, 1706. AAE, Mémoirs et documents, France, CDXXIX, fol. 127, especially for the use of the phrase "*balance égale.*"

[3] Paris, Bibliothèque Nationale, Fonds français, Nouvelles Acquisitions 7488, fol. 26, Traduction du mémoire présenté au Roy d'Espagne par M^r Le Marquis d'Harcourt.

[4] Eugène Michaud, *Louis XIV et Innocent XI, d'après les correspondances diplomatiques inédites du ministère des affaires étrangères de France* (4 vols., Paris, G. Charpentier, 1882–83), IV, p. 64.

[5] Bruno Neveu (ed.), *Correspondance du nonce en France: Angelo Ranuzzi (1683–1689)* (2 vols., Ecole française de Rome, Université pontificale grégorienne, Rome, 1973), I, 220, Cardinal Ranuzzi to Secretary of State Cibo, July 30, 1683, Paris.

[6] BL, Add. Ms. 22,206, fol. 187r.   [7] AAE, Correspondance politique, Suisse, CCXLIX, fol. 5v.

[8] AAE, Correspondance politique, Venise, CXLVII, fol. 40r.–v.

[9] *Ibid.*, fols. 105–106v.   [10] BL, Add. Ms. 22,106, fols. 186–87.

[11] Andrew Lossky, "International Relations in Europe," in J. S. Bromley (ed.), *New Cambridge Modern History*, IV: *The Rise of Great Britain and Russia* (Cambridge University Press, 1970), p. 156.

English publicists of the 1680s were also quick to elaborate a balance-of-power theory. At the end of the Dutch War in 1679 the author of *Popery and Tyranny: the Present State of France*[12] spoke of the government of France as "an Absolute Monarchy, imposed upon the People by a standing, illegal, and oppressive Army." This tyranny, further sustained by "Machiavellian tricks," could be countered only by the vigilance of the European states. In *Discourses upon Modern Affaires of Europe*,[13] published in London the next year, the author was highly particularistic: "If the French be permitted to become masters of the Spanish Netherlands, and to possess *Ostend* and *Niewport*, then *England* will not only *not* have a footing on the Main, but all the Sea-Coast opposite to the whole body of it will be in the hands of the French, always Enemies to England." What the author advocated was a "New League" against France, with Ostend and Niewport in English hands.

By the end of the decade, as William and Mary were ascending the English throne, there appeared a spate of pamphlets on the balance of power. One such pamphlet elaborated *A View of the True Interest of the Several States since the Accession of their Present Majesties to the Imperial Crown of Great Britain.* "It is a Maxim of True Policy that whensoever any Prince is exalted too high, and becomes formidable to his Neighbours, the other Princes ought to enter into a League together, to pull him down, or at least to hinder him from growing greater."[14] The author praised Cardinal Richelieu and Louis XIII for having opposed the ambitions of the emperor, but saw the Triple Alliance of 1668 and the Dutch War as attempts to contain Louis XIV's overvaulting ambitions. In *The True Interests of the Princes of Europe in the Present State of Affairs*, also published in 1689, the author offers a highly sophisticated account of the "balance of Powers":

If we narrowly scan the great success of France, we shall find that they proceed less from the force of its government than from the feebleness of its Neighbours. The Kings of Spain and Sweden were children, the Emperor was possess'd by People whose fundamental Maxime is to sacrifice all Grandeurs in the World for their own Grandeur. *England* was in the hands of a weak Prince . . . Holland was enervated by its Divisions . . . [But] the case is now altered; in Europe two Houses [vie] . . . [and] the general Interest of other Princes is to hold those two Houses in equality . . . because [the victor would be too strong].[15]

The balance of power: in practice

In the world of practical international politics, a harbinger of the emerging balance of powers was the collapse in the early 1680s of the *tiers parti* or third party[16] of German and Baltic princes and principalities who had either sup-

---

[12] London, 1679, p. 1.   [13] London, 1680, p. 7.   [14] London, 1689, pp. 1ff.

[15] London, 1689, pp. 9–10; see also Lois G. Schwoerer, "Propaganda in the Revolution of 1688–89," *American Historical Review* 82 (1977), 843–74; see especially pp. 861–65 for references to Louis XIV and France.

[16] On the *tiers parti* (sometimes spelled "party"), see Janine Fayard, "Attempts to Build a 'Third Party' in North Germany, 1690–1694," in Ragnhild Hatton (ed.), *Louis XIV and Europe* (London, Macmillan, and Columbus, Ohio State University Press, 1976), pp. 213–40. Fayard reviews the decades previous to 1690. There is also an interesting account of France's payment of subsidies in the 1680s and 1690s.

ported France or remained neutral in the Dutch War. The flight from the French standard after the peace of Nijmegen (1679) was precipitated by a number of reasons: *inter alia*, the dread, as the English pamphlets showed, of French hegemony; mutual suspicion among allies; a lessening fear of the emperor and the Austrian Habsburgs; diplomatic successes of William of Orange and his partisans; the Pope's hostility to Louis XIV; the weakness of Spain.

Sweden was one of the first powers to desert the French: *la Suède perfide*, as one French diplomat derisively dismissed the so-called "Jewel of the Baltic." Sweden had as an ally been part of France's "Eastern Frontier," and at the cost of offending Brandenburg, the French had forced the allies at Nijmegen to restore the Swedish Empire. Charles XI, however, resented French patronage; and although he and many of his advisors continued to receive gifts and pensions from France, Charles entered into an economic and military agreement with the Dutch at the Treaty of the Hague in 1681. Amidst a flurry of anti-French feeling in Stockholm, followed by royal hesitations, Charles became a partner to the League of Augsburg in 1686, committing his country to an anti-French policy. In the early 1680s an opposite course of action was followed in Berlin, where the Elector Frederick-William Brandenburg, swayed by the need to swell his treasury and soothed by French promises of subsidies, espoused an alliance with Versailles. Appearances misled few statesmen, least of all the French, who discovered that their nominal ally, the Great Elector, had signed a defensive alliance with the United Provinces in 1685. What Versailles seems not to have known immediately was that Frederick-William, as practiced in perfidy as the Swedes, had also signed a treaty with the Emperor Leopold's representatives in March 1686. By this agreement the elector promised to send the emperor, if he was attacked, 8,000 troops – a sizeable force – for which he was paid 200,000 French livres or 66,666 thalers. The elector also promised to support the emperor's son at an imperial election and the Austrian Habsburg's claims to the Spanish succession. Publicly, Frederick-William, in a bid to gain sympathy from other Protestant princes, attacked Louis XIV for having revoked the Edict of Nantes. But it soon became clear to the French envoy, Comte de Rébenac, that Brandenburg had renounced the French cause more for material than for spiritual reasons. Nonetheless, whatever the motives, by 1687, two of the strongest military powers in northern Europe, Sweden and Brandenburg, had detached themselves from the French connection.[17]

During the early years of the 1680s Duke Ernst August of Hanover had also sought an accommodation with the emperor. His diplomatic aspirations were far less complicated than those of his powerful neighbors, Brandenburg and Sweden. He lusted after the electoral title, which would raise him in rank above his annoying relatives, the Dukes of Lüneburg-Wolfenbüttel. In 1682,

---

[17] For Sweden and Brandenburg, see F. L. Carsten (ed.), *New Cambridge Modern History*, v: *The Ascendancy of France, 1648–1688* (Cambridge University Press, 1961), chs. 22 and 23; and Michael Roberts, "Charles XI," in *Essays in Swedish History* (London, Weidenfeld and Nicolson, 1967), pp. 226–68.

as a gesture of solidarity and friendship, the duke sent Emperor Leopold 2 million crowns to support the imperial army in their struggle with the Turks. Ironically, some of the monies drawn from the ducal coffers had recently been augmented by an infusion of French subsidies. Thus, Louis XIV, however indirectly and however reluctantly, became one of the emperor's well-wishers.[18]

Louis XIV's government also lost a potential ally in the Neuburg family of Jülich-Berg and in 1685 of the Palatinate. The succession to the Palatinate was contested by France in the name of Louis XIV's sister-in-law, who was the former elector's sister and had claims to certain properties in the Palatinate. French lawyers saw an opportunity, they believed, to place the new rulers in Heidelberg on warning that they owed Versailles an accounting of these properties. When legal maneuvers failed to intimidate the new elector, Louis's ministers promised to drop the Orleanist claims altogether. But like Sweden, the Neuburgs resented French meddling and looked to the emperor for support.[19]

Although technically not included among the *tièrs parti*, England displayed an important characteristic of those princes of the third party: a willingness to accept French subsidies in exchange for a benevolent neutrality. At Louis XIV's court it may be said, without too much exaggeration, that England had the reputation for being a land of rebellions, regicides, and republicans; a country that had decapitated a divine-right monarch, restored a prince by parliamentary invitation, suffered popish plots, Rye House Plots, Monmouth rebellions, bloody assizes, and party dissensions. Indeed, the French often thought of England as a land of unstable rulers, unstable politicians, and unstable weather; on the latter point they have not changed their minds. Jonathan Swift characterized the period of the 1680s as being "an Heap of Conspiracies, Rebellions, Murders, Massacres, Revolutions, and Banishments."[20] And although Matthew Prior was not the King of Brobdingnag, he did complain that he had dined with a high French official who made "wise reflection on our Kingdom's being *le païs des révolutions*." "Newsmongers," Prior continued, "were all much in the same tone . . . and it was plainly the whisper in fashion throughout the whole court." "This is mighty whimsical,"[21] Prior lamented.

"Mighty whimsical" too, to the French observers, were early English politi-

---

[18] Ragnhild Hatton, *George I, Elector and King* (Cambridge, Mass., Harvard University Press, 1978), ch. 2, pp. 31–64, deals with the intricacies of the Brunswick–Lüneburg connection.

[19] Geoffrey Symcox, "Louis XIV and the Outbreak of the Nine Years War," in Hatton (ed.), *Louis XIV and Europe*, pp. 179–212, especially p. 186 for a discussion of the Neubergs. As a general survey Symcox's book is superb: the author's ability to create order out of the chaos of events leading to the autumn of 1688 is enviable. Where one might find some disagreement is over the tone of the essay. Symcox speaks, for example, of Louis XIV's "hypocritical Machiavellianism," and his "self-righteousness," etc. Most princes of the age suffered from these faults, not the least William III and Innocent XI.

[20] William Speck quotes from Jonathan Swift's *Gulliver's Travels*, in "Political Propaganda in Augustan England," in *Transactions of the Royal Historical Society*, 5th series, 22 (1972), 28.

[21] L. G. Wickham Legg, *Mathew Prior: a Study of His Public Career and Correspondence* (Cambridge University Press, 1921), p. 307.

cal parties, their names as incomprehensible as their creeds. An English royal official summed up the confusion: "the [English] nation was in a great ferment, most persons being distinguished by the opprobrious names of Whig (Exclusionist), and Tory (Loyalist); but there was a third sort of persons, who had the appellation of Trimmers, who . . . pretended great impartiality."[22] And when one recalls the foreign policy of Charles II and James II, it too appeared to France as "mighty whimsical." The French foreign minister of the 1680s, Colbert de Croissy, knew well the vagaries of English politics. He had served as French ambassador to England at the time of the signing of the Dover treaties and had been a plenipotentiary to the Congress of Nijmegen. He and Louis XIV could recall the second Peace of Westminster of 1674 that took England out of the Dutch War, to be followed in its exodus by the Archbishop–Elector of Cologne and the Prince–Bishop of Münster, hitherto staunch French allies. Croissy had early in the 1670s warned his brother, Jean-Baptiste Colbert, that "the [English] people are very susceptible to any calumnies that can be concocted aginst France." And later he wrote that "everything that is taking place in Parliament, Whitehall and London makes me see all too clearly that the Anglo-French alliance is like sailing against both wind and the tides."[23] Colbert had likewise denounced England's defection in 1674, claiming that they were increasing their trade with the Mediterranean and New World while France and the Dutch coalition stumbled on for three more years of bitter war.

And whimsical, too, was James II's policy toward France. An example of James's vagaries was his choice of ambassadors: the first, Sir William Trumbull, being the most obnoxious to the French, but only by a hair. Arrogant, more legalistic than the French, which was a difficult feat, and an ultra-Protestant at the time of the Revocation of the Edict of Nantes, Trumbull fussed, fumed, demanded special audiences with the king, and was finally, at Louis's request, recalled. Trumbull's mission, however abortive, symbolizes the basic unease that pervaded Anglo-French relations during James II's brief reign. Two incidents will illustrate the point: the first concerns the French occupation and administration of the principality of Orange; the second, ambassadorial privilege.

In 1685, not a month after Trumbull had arrived in France, William of Orange wrote to the English ambassador, begging him to employ "efficaciously" his good offices to further "my interests" in the ancestral lands of Orange, awarded to his house by treaty and inheritance. William "hoped for the powerful intercession of His Majesty" (James II) to help ameliorate conditions in "*ce povre paiis*" of Orange.[24] William's letter, though couched in polite and diplomatically vague terms, ignored proper diplomatic channels and might be construed as an affront both to the English secretary of state and

---

[22] Henry Horwitz, *Parliament, Policy and Politics in the Reign of William III* (Manchester University Press, 1977), p. 2.

[23] AAE, Correspondance politique, Angleterre, CIX, fol. 120.

[24] Ruth Clark, *Sir William Trumbull in Paris, 1685–1686* (Cambridge University Press, 1938), pp. 25–26.

to James II himself. Sir William, seemingly oblivious to the nuance of proto-
col, approached the French secretary of state, Colbert de Croissy, on William's behalf. Croissy, patient at first, observed that Louis XIV had written
to his ambassador in England, Paul Barillon d'Amoncourt, Marquis de Barillon, explaining his policy towards the principality of Orange. Then, becoming
increasingly irritated by Sir William's obtuseness, Croissy pointed out that
the king had "left quiet William's possessions so long as the prince had not
intruded in French affairs." But, "having opposed his most Christ^n Ma^{ty} so
openly" by plotting against him, Louis no longer saw fit to "keepe . . . ye same
measures" of friendship. Croissy informed Sir William quite bluntly that he
had spoken to the Dutch ambassador about William's "intrigues" and hoped
that that would be an end to it.[25] But it was not an end for Sir William, who
was, if nothing else, persistent. In the following months the complaints continued "sad and monotonous"; finally, Sir William reported: "It is to no
purpose to insist upon the Treaty of Nimeguen . . . for Monsr de Croissy says
that the King has now done all that he thought himself obliged to do in justice
and conscience for the salvation of the inhabitants of that town, and so the
business is at an end."[26] Indeed, Sir William continued to lodge protests; but
James II, after having questioned the French government and supported
William of Orange for a brief time, then dropped the issue. James's indifference was seen as hostility at William's court.

Trumbull also stirred up trouble between Louis XIV and James II over
diplomatic privilege. The privilege concerned the protection of the ambassador's French Protestant servants from arrest. They may be "set upon" here
in Paris, he complained to James II, or seized "as they go abroad with me,"
because the French authorities realize that "I acknowledge no Jurisdiction or
Tribunal but Y^r Maj^{ties}." Trumbull said he was certain that James "would
protect me in this known and undoubted Right."[27] James took the affair to
heart, saying that he "would not yield" to the French on ambassadorial
privilege. The English king spoke to the French ambassador Barillon "avec
tant de chaleur." Finally, after much prompting, Louis gave way on this case
and allowed Sir William to retain his servants. But such incidents led to
resentments in both countries. Just before Trumbull left Paris George Savile,
Marquis of Halifax, wrote to him concerning the Revocation of the Edict of
Nantes and the treatment of Protestants, saying that "I never understood that
God almighty was of that mind that one could not please him without being a
madman . . . Whatever [His Most Christian Majesty] thinketh fit to do to his
own subjects, he might have some regard for his poor allies."[28]

---

[25] *Ibid.*, pp. 31–32; also A. de Pontbriant, *Histoire de la principauté d'Orange* (Avignon, Seguin Frères, 1891),
p. 262, reviews the Longueville family claim to the principality of Orange and the historical argument, put
forward by the French government in the 1680s, that the principality had been wrongly awarded to the Châlons
family, pp. 233ff.

[26] Clark, *Trumbull*, pp. 64–65.

[27] *Ibid.*, p. 136; for the saga of the ambassador's servants, pp. 136–44.

[28] *Ibid.*, p. 106.

Three leaders

Amidst the uncertainties of the 1680s – the dissolution of the *tiers parti* and the gnawing realization of Stuart ineptitudes – three persons tilted the balance of power towards Austria: they were Max Emanuel of Bavaria, Pope Innocent XI, and William of Orange.

Until 1688 France had with a certain confidence felt that Bavaria would pursue a traditional policy of hostility to the emperor. The House of Wittelsbach, ultra-Catholic, a vigorous participant in the Thirty Years War, a major power in southern Germany, master of the Bavarian Imperial Circle, could challenge Habsburg primacy in the south and the west and aspire, perhaps, to the imperial crown. French envoys reported that Max Emanuel, who succeeded to the electoral dignity in 1679, personally disliked Leopold and even more his daughter, who had become Max's wife. Vain, prodigal, "as unsteady as a weathercock," addicted excessively to erotic entanglements with women other than his wife, Max seemed the perfect pawn for a clever minister or foreign envoys. But these men of state underestimated his pride in the princely house of Wittelsbach, his desire for military *gloire*, and, above all, the shrewdness with which he judged men's motives. His pride in family made him especially sensitive to the nomination of his brother, Joseph-Clement, to the "archepiscopal" throne of Cologne, a dignity the Wittelsbach house had held for over a century. Joseph-Clement's rival was a French nominee, Wilhelm Egon von Fürstenberg, Bishop of Strasburg, a man hated by many German princes. Soft-pedaling the Cologne affair and Fürstenberg's nomination, Louis XIV sent a special envoy, Hector, Marquis de Villars, to woo Max away from an imperial alliance. Like Max, Villars was vain, pursued personal *gloire*, and enjoyed his luxuries. As it happened, the French envoy became a confidant of Max and remained in Munich for nearly a year and a half (1687–88). The American scholar Richard Place has reviewed these events in Munich in a finely crafted article published in *The Journal of Modern History*.[29] There is no need to repeat the details which he lays out so skillfully; suffice to say that Max outplayed the French diplomats and turned for alliance to the emperor, who offered him the governorship of the Spanish Netherlands and support for his brother's candidacy to Cologne. In an age of *raison d'état*, political advantage outweighed personal sentiment.

Another statesman who supported Max's brother, Joseph-Clement, was Pope Innocent XI. If in 1688 Louis XIV and his councillors had been asked to name the enemy they most feared it would probably not have been Emperor Leopold nor William of Orange but Pope Innocent. An austere man, often unpleasant to his subordinates and rude to envoys, Innocent lived a monkish existence, seldom leaving the Vatican. Unlike his immediate pre-

[29] Richard Place, "Bavaria and the Collapse of Louis XIV's German Policy, 1687–1688," *JMH* 49 (1977), 369–93; also Richard Place's important article: "The Self-deception of the Strong: France on the Eve of the War of the League of Augsburg," *French Historical Studies* 6 (1970), 459–73. See also Andrew Lossky, "The General European Crisis of the 1680s," *European Studies Review* 10 (1980), 177–98, who questions the policies of the French government; he finds Louis XIV "a man foundering in the bog of his own contradictions" (p. 193).

decessors, he disliked the high baroque art that had made Rome famous in the age of Bernini and Borromini. He disliked the Turk and even more he disliked Louis XIV, who was dubbed by papal propagandists as "His Most Christian Turk at Versailles." The French reciprocated by calling Innocent "Pape Non," or in Italian "Papa Minga." In fact, Innocent was continuing an anti-French tradition that had been the policy of the Holy See since 1644, when Innocent X Giovanni Battista Pamphili, a client of the Spanish, drove the pro-French Barberini family (relatives of Pope Urban VIII) into an exile quite literally ultramontane, over the mountains to Paris. Innocent X's successors, Alexander VII Chigi and Clement X Altieri, had nurtured this anti-French policy; but it was late in the 1670s, during Innocent XI's early years, that the struggles had deepened and festered. The Pope and Louis XIV quarrelled over the expansion of the French king's regalian rights, over a resurgent Gallicanism, over attacks on Jansenist bishops and Louis's failure to support a crusade against the Turk.

These quarrels reached their denouement in 1687 and 1688. The immediate and apparent cause for disagreement was a struggle between France and the Papacy over the right of *franchises*, that is privileges and immunities, including the free transport (*franco*) of goods, within the quarter of the city of Rome immediate to the French embassy. In order better to regulate "the police" or administration of the city Innocent had abolished all franchises granted to foreign powers. Louis XIV resisted such an invasion of his rights of extraterritoriality first because he was generally suspicious of all Innocent's innovations, and secondly because he could employ these rights as a bargaining chip in negotiations touching on Gallican privileges and in the nomination to the Cologne see.[30]

Innocent then threatened to excommunicate anyone who upheld the right of franchise. In late summer of 1687 Louis personally selected Henri-Charles, Marquis de Lavardin, to succeed the recently deceased ambassador to the Holy See. Lavardin was a bluff soldier, veteran of the Dutch War, scion of a distinguished noble Breton family. When Lavardin entered Rome in November 1687 he rode at the head of seven hundred armed guards, who immediately swept the quarter for criminals and in doing so also seized several papal policemen. Pope Innocent replied to Louis's challenge by excommunicating his ambassador and laying an interdict on the church where he heard Christmas mass.[31]

In January of the fateful year 1688, Franco-papal relations drifted into open warfare. Word reached Versailles that the Pope had not only excommunicated the French ambassador but also the descendant of Saint-Louis, Louis XIV himself. Colbert de Croissy was so horrified by this news that, allegedly, he said that anyone who approached the king with such intelligence might well not survive the interview. The nuncio, Cardinal Angelo Maria Ranuzzi, already *persona non grata* at the French court, wisely, it is said, sent his personal

---

[30] See the detailed account of Jean Orcibal, *Louis XIV contre Innocent XI. Les Appels au futur concile de 1688 et l'opinion française* (Paris, J. Vrin, 1949), pp. 16–32.   [31] *Ibid.*, p. 10.

physician, Dr. Dominique Amonio, to inform the king of Innocent's condemnation. To the surprise of his advisors Louis listened attentively to the doctor, made him repeat his story, then enjoined those present to silence.[32]

There was not an open break between Louis and Rome at this time. The reason is evident: the Pope had not published his excommunication and Louis hoped, at the very least, that Innocent would not actively oppose Fürstenberg's election. When the elderly Maximilian-Henry of Bavaria, Elector of Cologne, died in June 1688, a contested election followed and the arbitration was given to a papal commission. At that time Louis and his council decided to send a secret mission to Rome. They chose as their emissary Jules-Louis Bolé, the Marquis de Chamlay.

The Marquis de Chamlay,[33] a confidant of the war minister, Louvois, was a great military strategist, known for his prudent planning, his measured judgment, and his honesty. Louvois had been displeased with Lavardin's appointment and hoped that Chamlay could bring sanity to the negotiations. Indeed the marquis did carry an olive branch decked with Louis's promise to recall the universally disliked Lavardin, to abandon his claims to the franchise, and to support Joseph-Clement's nomination as coadjutor to the see of Cologne.[34]

Innocent remained intractable and would not even receive Chamlay in audience. The impasse ended when Louis recalled Chamlay, issued a manifesto condemning the Pope's highhandedness, and sent troops to occupy Avignon and the Comtat. At the same time the French fleet at Toulon held itself ready to transport troops to the papal states for a possible invasion of Rome. Thus no French ships left the Mediterranean in the late summer of 1688 to form a viable counterweight to William of Orange's armada.

The third prince to challenge Louis XIV's policies in the 1680s was William of Orange, who was indefatigable in rallying the *tiers parti* to his cause. Although to many observers it may have seemed that William held the key to European politics, it did not appear so to the French court in 1688. Louis XIV and his advisors considered William the sinister puppet master of Protestantism: a "bad actor," an intriguer, a plotter, and ultimately a usurper, whose policies were as inconsistent as his personal life was erratic. The French court could recall but not forgive William's role in the rude seizure of their ambassador's letters to Versailles and the reading of those letters before the States-General, while adherents of William held the doors shut to two deputies from Amsterdam. The prince's conduct created a *scandale publique*, words that were anathema to Louis XIV. Moreover, the French court accused William not only of receiving English dissidents but of harboring

---

[32] *Ibid.*, p. 11, n. 45; see also Pierre Blet, *Les Assemblées du clergé et Louis XIV, 1670 à 1693* (Rome, 1972), and his excellent summary "Louis XIV et la Sainte Siège," in *XVII*e *Siècle* 31 (1979), 139–54. See also, for a general account of James II's relations with the Papacy, Bruno Neveu, "Jacques II, médiateur entre Louis XIV et Innocent XI," *Ecole française de Rome. Mélanges d'Archéologie et d'Histoire* 79 (1967), 101–64.

[33] Jean Hanoteau (ed.), *Recueil des instructions aux ambassadeurs et ministres de France depuis les traîtres de Westphalie jusqu'à la révolution française*, XVII: *Rome* II (*1688–1723*) (Paris, Félix Alcan, 1911), pp. xv, xvi, 1–24. Hanoteau also notes the crisis in the 1680s between the Jesuit order in France and Pope Innocent XI, which erupted over the appointment of a vicar general. Innocent's opposition to the Jesuit Order placed them strongly on Louis XIV's side. [34] *Ibid.*, pp. 3–4.

outright plotters against the English monarch's life. From London Ambassador Barillon wrote that James II deeply mistrusted his son-in-law and found himself "entièrement irréconciliable avec le prince d'Orange."[35]

The irony was that these two great practitioners of the princely craft, Louis and William, were strikingly similar to one another. Their very resemblance may have made them strangers. Both were deeply religious, although Louis's sister-in-law called the king's faith that of a babe in a nursery. Each was concerned with the salvation of his soul and each believed in Providence. For William, Providence was a predestined "high and sacred destiny," and for Louis it was the fulfillment of God's plan for his anointed servant. Both had a taste for personal and military *gloire*, though Voltaire says William made war like a soldier and Louis like a king.[36] Both were intensely loyal and generous to ministers and servants who had won their trust. Both were masters at masking emotion: of course, there were those who said that William had none. Both were followers of Machiavelli, exponents of *raison d'état*. Both were noted builders, gardeners, and hunters. And both were precise, hard-working rulers, princely bureaucrats.

There were differences, of course; largely personal, not public. For Louis the family was extremely important; he retreated at the end of the day to the apartments of Françoise d'Aubigné, Marquise de Maintenon, where he surrounded himself with his children and grandchildren and became a *père de famille*. This scene was removed from that of William, who had no children, disliked court functions, often retreated into himself. Louis had a finer aesthetic sense than William, learned in part from his mother and Cardinal Mazarin. He enjoyed the divertissements of the theatre, of opera, and ballet; he displayed a *sensibilité* that seemed lacking in the prince. Macaulay reflects that "letters and sciences meant little to William; the poems of Dryden and Boileau were unknown as were the [discoveries] . . . of Newton."[37]

Yet there is one tie beween the two that must not be forgotten: both were Europeans in the broadest sense of the word; both understood European politics and could read a map; both played midwife to the emergence of the classic balance of power.

Domestic challenges

In the early 1680s as Louis XIV and his court moved into their permanent home at Versailles, the king faced domestic challenges that had been post-

[35] Stephen B. Baxter, *William III* (London, Longman, Green, 1966), p. 429, n. 44. A recent assessment of the period is Ragnhild Hatton, "'1688' in Europees Perspectief," in L. J. van der Klooster, M. E. Tiethoff-Spliethoff, C. A. Tamse, and E. Elzenga (eds.), *Jaarboek 1988: Oranje-Nassau Museum* (The Hague, Oranje-Nassau Museum, 1988), pp. 5–27.

[36] Voltaire, *The Age of Louis XIV*, trans. Martyn P. Pollack, with a preface by F. C. Green (London, Dent, 1969), p. 181.

[37] Henriette Elizabeth Heimans, *Het Karacter van Willem III: Koning-Stadhouder. Proeve eener Psychografie* (Amsterdam, H. J. Paris, 1925), pp. 159–60. Heimans's work is an early example of psychobiography; still very useful, packed with examples drawn from nineteenth-century literature.

poned during the last years of the Dutch War. They concerned his private affairs, dynastic succession, problems of the Gallican church, and the completion of his bureaucratic capital at Versailles. During the 1680s Louis rather successfully met and, in his way, answered many of the challenges. When his wife died, he married Madame de Maintenon, who brought him domestic peace and wise counsel; when his mistress Madame de Montespan grew fat and too possessive, he exiled her to a villa; when his son came of age to marry in 1679–80, he selected as a wife for the younger Louis a Wittelsbach princess, who in the next few years presented a delighted father and grandfather with three healthy boys, thus securing the succession in the senior line of the Bourbon family. When the prelates of the Church of France demanded unity as reward for having financially supported the Dutch War, Louis encouraged a Declaration of Gallican Rights in the early 1680s; and when the church demanded purity, he revoked the Edict of Nantes.[38] And when his architects and artists solicited monies to complete Versailles and the attendant palaces of Marly and the Trianon, and Madame de Maintenon asked for a girls' school at St. Cyr, and Louvois requested a hospital for war veterans, the Invalides of Paris, Louis instructed his able controller-general of finances, Claude Le Peletier, to divert funds from other projects to support one of the largest building enterprises of the century.

But the strain on Louis's treasury was immense. In one year, 1686–87, the king spent nearly 14 million livres, on his palaces, hospital, and school. This expenditure represented nearly a twelfth of his budget. Other departments suffered. Naval expenditures remained about the same level during the 1680s: 7 million livres per annum until 1688, far below what was needed. Indeed, if in 1688 France had even wanted to send a fleet to Brittany and Rochefort on the Atlantic, they would have found it difficult, fiscally, to mount the operation. The army was reduced to 120,000 men on active duty, backed by 25,000 newly recruited militia, paid by local authorities:[39] not a sufficient armed force to meet the challenge of the Austrians, Sweden, and the German princes, let alone an augmented Dutch army. Supplies were dangerously low, as the French commanders in the Rhineland were to discover in 1688–89 when they quickly exhausted their reserves of gunpowder and shot. Chamlay and Sébastien le Preste de Vauban, Louis XIV's chief engineers, complained that fortifications were being neglected and that roads needed to be repaired. Demonstrably, Louis XIV's France was ill prepared for the war of 1688, especially a war on two fronts.

---

[38] This account is based in part on my essay "Louis XIV, roi–bureaucrate," in John C. Rule (ed.), *Louis XIV and the Craft of Kingship* (Columbus, Ohio State University Press, 1970), pp. 73–78. "Louvois saw the issue clearly: 'The Germans, henceforth, must be considered as our true enemies; they alone can do us great harm, *if they had an emperor who could mount a horse*'" (italics added). Thus was enunciated anew the old conception of France *inter teutonicos et latinos*. From Rule, *Louis XIV and the Craft*, pp. 77–78.

[39] André Corvisier, *Louvois* (Paris, Fayard, 1983), p. 330 for the "dépenses du roi" for war, which actually show little rise between 1683 and 1687–88; the great augmentation came after 1688.

The dilemma

Can we discern a thread of French policy in this heavily interwoven fabric of the 1680s? Yes, I believe we can if we accept that Louis XIV and his advisors were usually conservative (except in the first years of the Dutch War) and generally cautious in their diplomatic and military ventures. In his famous *tour d'horizon*,[40] written in the late 1660s for the edification of the dauphin, Louis saw nothing but weakness among his neighbors. There was no viable balance of power, nor for that matter, claims of hegemony, even from the French. The decade of the 1660s represented a pause, almost a hiatus, in diplomatic history. As the author of *The True Interests of the Princes of Europe* wrote in 1689, France proceeded in the 1660s "less from the force of its government than from the feebleness of its Neighbours."[41] But Louis and his advisors moved slowly and followed the traditional French policy of annexing lands from the old Burgundian inheritance, with its tangle of feudal, seigneurial, and judicial rights and privileges. Louis and his advisors constantly pressed their claims *de jure*: be they treaty concessions in Alsace, private law in Brabant, laws of dynastic inheritance in the Palatinate, feudal claims of homage in Flanders, or jurisdiction of the *parlement* of Paris in the same area, or treaty rights in Lorraine or family rights in Navarre. The list is long and often tedious. Following the siege and Truce of Luxemburg in 1684, Louis again wished to codify his gains by signing a treaty. His goal was in fact not realized until the treaties of 1697 and, more definitively, of 1714. In the meantime he resorted to rather less cautious strategies to hold his gains in the Burgundian legacy.[42]

The *tiers parti* of German princes having fallen apart, many of the treaties of neutrality violated, subsidies ignored both by the paymaster and the beneficiary, Louis XIV and Louvois resurrected in the summer of 1688 a policy that was later called "neutralization": the rapid, preemptive strike, known in the Mediterranean as the *razzia* and in French army circles as the *coup de force*, or a *coup accablé*. It is the rapidity of conquest, said the Marquis de Chamlay, "that will open the eyes of the Emperor and the Empire."[43]

The *coup accablé* had been employed previously by the French: in the Franch-Comté in 1668, and in the Dutch War at Ghent in 1678, at Strasburg in 1681 and again at the fortress of Luxemburg in 1684; and in the Mediterranean at Algiers and Genoa in the mid-1680s. By such a move both Chamlay and the great engineer Vauban thought France could make itself "absolute master of the Rhine," thus closing the *portes* or gates into France, the invasion routes used for centuries from the Port de Bourgogne (the Belfort gap) in the

---

[40] Paul Sonnino (ed.), *Louis XIV: Mémoires for the Instruction of the Dauphin* (New York, Free Press, 1970), pp. 26–28.

[41] London, 1689, pp. 9–10.

[42] Gaston Zeller, *L'Organisation défensive des frontières du Nord et de l'Est au XVIIᵉ siècle* (Nancy, Berger-Levrault, 1928), ch. 4; and Louis André, *Louis XIV et l'Europe* (Paris, Albin-Michel, 1950), pp. 120ff.

[43] Camille Rousset, *Histoire de Louvois et de son administration politique et militaire* (4 vols., Paris, Dédier et Cie, 1861–64), IV, pp. 160–61.

Vosges mountains, to bridgeheads at Strasburg and the key fortress of Philippsburg, to the Saar fortresses and the Moselle valley, which led towards the Rhine and cities of Bonn and Cologne. Louvois seemed obsessed by the dangers of invasion. Thus, when the old Elector of Cologne died in June 1688, the war minister strongly advised the king and his colleagues on the *Conseil d'en haut* to move troops at once into key fortresses from the Cologne area to Philippsburg. As Louvois wrote to the controller-general, Le Peletier:

I cannot prevent myself from telling you again that this thorny affair [of Cologne] is very harmful ... For the Prince of Bavaria [Joseph-Clement] to become Elector of Cologne and, apparently, Bishop of Liège or of Münster as well, as to be joined by the Duke of Jülich, the Elector of Palatine, the emperor and the Dutch, this appears to me to be a dangerous [conjuncture], ... particularly if the Spanish make the Elector of Bavaria governor of the Spanish Netherlands.[44]

But Louis XIV hesitated. He hoped the Chamlay mission to Rome would at least temper the Pope's decision on the Cologne affair and that the papal commission would accept a compromise. A vain and unrealistic hope. Louis believed, also, that the Elector of Bavaria might at the last minute declare himself neutral, especially if France would support his brother, Joseph-Clement, as Fürstenberg's coadjutor. Again a vain hope. When 15,000 troops of Brandenburg and Jülich-Berg began to move on Cologne and as an expeditionary force gathered in Bavaria, Louis XIV, meeting in council on August 22, 1688, ordered a preemptive strike against Philippsburg and other fortresses on the Rhine. This was done three months after the death of the Elector of Cologne. Apparently, there had been little or no discussion of William of Orange's designs on England in this "council of war." Croissy, indeed, believed James II to be so uncertain an ally that French offers of military aid might well be rejected.

The Marquis de Villars later summed up French policy: "In truth, the more I see the venomous hatred of the empire for us, the more I thank God for the design he had inspired in His Majesty to render himself master of the Rhine and place himself in a position where they can do no damage to us and we can do much to them."[45]

It would seem that Louis XIV's thoughts in the late summer of 1688 were concerned with a watch on the Rhine, not with the sailing of a Dutch armada.

Conclusion

One is reminded of the Dickensian phrase: it was the best of times, it was the worst of times; so was it for Louis XIV in the decade from 1679 to 1688. He celebrated the arrival of three grandsons; he married a sympathetic and

---

[44] John T. O'Connor, *Negotiator out of Season: the Career of Wilhelm Egon von Fürstenberg 1629 to 1704* (Athens, University of Georgia Press, 1978), p. 164.
[45] R. Place, "Louis XIV's German Policy," p. 391. See Charles Boutant, *L'Europe au Grand Tourant des années 1680, La Succession Palatine* (Paris, Société d'Édition d'Enseignement Supérieur, 1985), esp. pp. 827–41.

intelligent wife; he witnessed the completion of one of the world's great monuments, the palace of Versailles; he made peace with the Gallican Church, and even in foreign policy he witnessed triumphs in the Franche-Comté, Strasburg, and in a line of fortresses from the Saar valley to Dunkirk. And yet 1688 may be said to mark the nadir of his statecraft. Caught in a web of their own making, Louis XIV and his ministers found themselves confronted by two armed camps (camps that they had helped arm): one based on a Vienna–Munich axis, the other on The Hague (and soon, London). From these beginnings sprang the "Old Alliance" of Great Britain and the Austrian Habsburgs, broken only in 1756. Caught between these two camps, and the armed might of France, the neutrality of the German princes melted away.

For France the year 1688 was not 1660 nor even 1670. The feebleness of its neighbors had been replaced by the strength of alliances. In the 1680s Louis and his ministers encountered – to put a face on them – several determined enemies: Innocent XI, Emperor Leopold and his son-in-law, Max of Bavaria, and William of Orange. To be fair to the French statesmen, they seemed to have understood and coped with the antagonism between their king and the Gallican Church and the papacy, unremitting since 1644; likewise they developed defensive measures against the House of Habsburg: *l'ennemi traditionnel.* But though these statesmen recognized the weakness of James II, they seem – despite urgent warnings from the astute ambassador in The Hague, Jean-Antoine de Mesmes, Comte d'Avaux – to have underestimated the hostility and pertinacity of William of Orange and his political allies in the United Provinces and England. When confronted with the crisis of the summer of 1688 Louis's ministers strongly advised him to move his limited forces against the traditional enemy in Vienna and the new one in Munich rather than gamble with a strike that involved both friend and foe in the west. France thus inadvertently became midwife to the classic balance of power, centered in the early eighteenth century on three great blocs: the Anglo-Dutch, Bourbon, and Habsburg. Thomas Wentworth, Earl of Strafford, writing to Charles Talbot, Duke of Shrewsbury, from the Congress of Utrecht clearly enunciated the idea of that balance.

France mylord has ended with a Air of Frankness & Defference for the Queen, but yet I can't say the Negociations has been entirely carry'd on without Chicane on their Side. The Ballance of Power is what must secure the Wellfare of G. Brittⁿ. We shall leave France very great after this Peace, & a Possibility of Union with Spain may be destructive to Us & our Libertys, & in this case this mighty *Faith* they promise us, shou'd fail, & if we be attack'd, to whom can we call but the Empʳ & the Dutch. Wherefore I think we may still so end as to keep strict Alliance with them for our Mutual Security.[46]

The theory of preponderance or hegemony of one power was dead, not to be revived until the French Revolution and Napoleon, and then only briefly; and again in the twentieth century, and again with the Germanies. Thus 1688 is

[46] BL, Add. Ms. 22,221, fol. 124r., Earl of Strafford to the Duke of Shrewsbury, March 16, 1713 (NS), Utrecht.

not only momentous in the personal life of William of Orange and in the national life of England, but in the international life of Europe, for it marks the birth of a theory and practice of a power balance that has lasted until today.

3

The Fourth English Civil War: dissolution, desertion, and alternative histories in the Glorious Revolution

J. G. A. Pocock

Edmund Burke, reviewing in 1790 the events of 101–2 years previously, saw no objection to penning and printing the following remarkable words: "The Revolution of 1688 was obtained by a just war, in the only case in which any war, and much more a civil war, can be just. *Justa bella quibus necessaria*."[1] He cannot have meant that the revolution was "obtained," in the sense of "secured," by the wars in Europe which followed from 1688 to 1697, for he speaks of "civil war"; nor is it likely that he intended his words to refer to the war in Ireland which ended with the Treaty of Limerick. Burke's Irish perspectives might indeed lead to his viewing this as a civil war rather than a war of conquest, but the context which surrounds the words quoted makes it clear that he is thinking of the "Revolution of 1688" as an English political process and an English civil war. The "cashiering" or dethroning of a king – he is instructing readers of Richard Price's sermon to the Revolution Society – is not a legal or a constitutional process, which can form one of the normal procedures of an established civil society. It is, invariably and necessarily, an act of war, of armed rebellion and civil war. What occurred in 1688 occurred within the body politic of England, but not within any of its constitutional procedures or sanctions; it was a war, a civil war, and a *bellum necessarium*. A state of war in all three of these senses, and in the military sense as well, must therefore have obtained in England from the moment when William of Orange's invasion was recognized as impending and actual, and must have lasted in the military sense until there was no longer effective opposition to his arms – perhaps when James II took his first departure for France. In the juridical sense a state of war continued until it was determined that James had ceased to be king, and in the social and psychological sense (supposing Burke to be paying any attention to this) until there was no longer any effective force desiring his restoration by military means. We are now advised to consider the last of these moments to have been a long time coming. What is remarkable, however, is that Edmund Burke, a century later, should have

---

[1] Pending the completion of the current Oxford edition of Burke's writings, there is no standard edition of the *Reflections on the Revolution in France*. I may be permitted to cite my own (Indianapolis and Cambridge, Hackett, 1987), pp. 26–27.

52

declared the Revolution to have been obtained by a just and necessary civil war.

This is remarkable for both ideological and historical reasons. Burke, certainly, was concerned to insist that the British constitution contained no provision for deposing a king and no method of doing so; he therefore insisted that the Revolution had been justified by necessity and not by law, and had been an act of civil war, albeit a justified one. But this was a Tory argument, although one long since appropriated and annexed by Whig apologetics. With the more authentically Whig side of his political personality, Burke desired to maintain that the necessity which justified the Revolution had been the necessity of preserving the ancient constitution, and that the Revolution consequently had been carried out within the constitution and had had the effect of preserving and not subverting it. As a further consequence, his argument in 1790 strongly implied that there had occurred in 1688 nothing like the "dissolution of government" envisaged by radical Whigs, Lockeans, and commonwealthmen; certainly not one which had led to a reconstitution of government along lines including a right of "cashiering" kings. Yet, as we shall see, the concept of "dissolution" was hard to elaborate without an accompanying concept of "civil war," and it might be thought hard for Burke to contend that there had been "civil war" in 1688 while denying that there had been "dissolution." Because we think of Burke as propounding the historical continuity of English government, we are surprised to find him asserting a just and necessary civil war in 1688, the more so as the position that William III had asserted his rights to the crown by a just conquest had been angrily if not unambiguously repudiated by his accredited apologists.[2]

Burke's text is surprising for the further reason that it is a central fact of English history that there was indeed no civil war in 1688; no battle, that is to say, very little bloodshed, and no general relapse into a condition of epidemic armed violence such as had obtained in England between 1642 and 1646. The threat of a renewal of that condition had cost Charles I his head in 1649, had imperiled the life of Charles II in 1651, and had destroyed the political fortunes of Shaftesbury's Whigs in 1681. The English governing classes had gone to war with one another with the most agonized reluctance in 1642,[3] and their determination never to do so again, coupled with the grim knowledge that they might not be able to avoid it, is a cardinal fact of late Stuart politics. Hard as it may be to consider a non-event as a fact, it is therefore of crucial significance that James II ceased to be king and was replaced by William and Mary without the recurrence of English civil war in this sense; only because it did not recur are we able to look upon the Highland War which ended at Glencoe and the Irish War which ended at Limerick as marginal in their significance. That Burke should declare, in a context rendered English by its

[2] Mark Goldie, "Edmund Bohun and *Jus Gentium* in the Revolution Debate, 1689–93," *HJ* 20 (1977), 569–86.
[3] Anthony Fletcher, *The Outbreak of the English Civil War* (London, E. Arnold, 1981).

discursive structure, "the Revolution of 1688" to have been "ordained" by a "civil war" must arrest and challenge our attention.

To explain Burke's action in 1790 is one thing; to explain what happened in 1688 in the light of concepts available both to him in 1790 and to actors in 1688 is another. Burke, as we can now see, was obliged to represent the Revolution as both constitutional, in the sense that there had not occurred a dissolution of government and its replacement by a deposable or elective monarchy, and unconstitutional, in the sense that the constitution contained no regulated mechanism for the deposition of one king and his replacement by another. He therefore represented the revolution as an armed action, an act of state and of war – necessarily of civil war – but one justified and limited by the single imperative of preserving the ancient constitution against transgression from its own king. *Quod erat demonstrandum*; the Revolution had been both constitutional and a civil war, and neither James II nor a rebellious people had dissolved the constitution. But what – may we ask – of the actors in 1688 themselves? Had they seen themselves as engaged in civil war, or as emerging from it along the lines described by Burke?

To answer this question we must distinguish between two revolutions: one a violent *peripeteia* or reversal of worldly fortunes, which occurred in the months of November and December 1688 and culminated in the second flight of James and his refuge in France; the other a *ricorso* or *ridurre ai principi*, which occurred in the early months of 1689 and consisted in the attempt to discover and establish the principles on which James had ceased to be king and might be replaced as sovereign. It was the latter of these two which was recorded and remembered as "the Glorious Revolution," and though Burke writes "the Revolution of 1688 was obtained by a just war," it would have been possible to state that the Revolution of 1689 was "obtained" by the "just war" which occurred in 1688. We conflate the two processes, and date them by the year in which they began, because our attention is arrested by the dramatic overthrow of James II's personal rule; yet it was only the subsequent series of events occurring in 1689 which gave a constitutional meaning to those of 1688 and made possible such legal and historical formulae as that expressed by Burke.

If there was a just war or a civil war in England in these months, it occurred in November and December of 1688. By stating the problem in these terms, we of course relegate the Highland War and the Irish War to the Anglo-Gaelic frontiers, and imply that Highland and Irish Jacobites were not members of a shared polity and war with them was consequently not a civil war. It may well be considered misleading to do this. But "England" existed as a unified polity, and when Englishmen had fought one another in decades well remembered in 1688, they had described the experience, with fear and loathing, as one of civil war. It is therefore reasonable to suppose that Burke had English experience in mind when he wrote of 1688, and to ask whether there is meaning to his apparent statement that war and civil war then occurred, or alternatively, what he meant by making the statement in the teeth of the fact that civil war did not occur. Is there a sense in which it can be said that what occurred in 1688 was a war, whether or not just, civil, or necessary?

William of Orange, a powerful European prince, landed in the west of England at the head of an army in campaign order, composed of regiments of long-service professionals in historic transition from the status of *condottieri* to that of a national army. The King of England advanced to meet him with an army similarly organized and less heterogeneous in national composition; and for some time the two armies were in one another's presence, not indeed drawn up to offer or give battle, but in enough tactical contact to make battle an outcome it was reasonable to expect. But no battle occurred; the king became demoralized by the desertion to the prince of notable subjects, members of his own family and commanders at the head of his own troops, the latter finally deserting in such numbers that battle seemed no longer possible. He therefore fled in disguise to France, was intercepted and brought back, escaping a second time when political power and decision had passed into hands over which he had no control. The campaign of 1688 – "campaign" meaning an encounter between armies in the field or "campagne" – had no military solution, only a political and revolutionary one; by "revolution" would here be meant the dramatic collapse of a power structure and the overthrow of its head.

There had visibly existed, for a brief period, a state of war in England: an encounter between sovereign princes at the head of their armies. It had furthermore been a state of civil war, because the invading sovereign was making claims within the kingdom under its native law. He was claiming successive rights to the crown in the name of his wife, the Princess Mary, and – having been invited to do so by some powerful subjects – he was demanding a meeting of parliament to settle both the succession question and other grievances voiced by him and his supporters. William of Normandy in 1066, Henry of Bolingbroke in 1399, and Henry of Richmond in 1485 had invaded the kingdom in this way, claiming rights of their own and offering to redress the grievances of others, and on each occasion the crown had been violently transferred to another wearer. All these historic precedents were well known to the educated in 1688, but it was also well known that the condition of England in the seventeenth century differed from that in preceding ages. There was the great matter of the Protestant religion; and there had occurred the great civil war of the 1640s, recognized as radically unlike any baronial revolt of the Middle Ages. There were many Tories in 1688, but there were no revisionists.

What the Prince of Orange was doing was a legitimate use of war by a sovereign prince with an interest in the crown; the campaign of 1688 was a War of the English Succession. So far, the medieval precedents were valid; but the presence in the field of issues touching the religious and governmental structure of the realm of England transformed 1688 from another 1066 or 1399 to the possibility of another 1642. James II found himself at the head of his army in the heart of his own kingdom, facing not merely a prince come to challenge the succession but a rebellion of his own subjects, one which called into question his exercise of both his prerogative and the religion of the state. He ceased to be even another Richard II and found himself another Charles I; and the central fact of his father's reign had been civil war of a kind known to be unprecedented. It had been more than a rebellion by powerful subjects and their popular followings; it had divided the regional elites through whom the kingdom was ruled into factions, forced to fight each other much against their will along lines which raised fundamental, if equally unwelcome, issues of church and state. This was what the expression "civil war" meant to the English of 1688; it was not a conventional trope, but a bitterly remembered experience as close to them in time as World War II is to us; and it is, of course, in precisely this sense that civil war did not recur in 1688. The thing unheard of and unimaginable was that war could be levied within the kingdom, as it certainly was when William made his landing, without the consequences that had followed in 1642.

Civil war, in the sense all people remembered, did not follow, because the rate of civilian and military desertion to the prince broke the king's nerve, rendered it impossible for him to give battle, and precipitated his own desertion of his kingdom. Since we know that James II had alienated a great many of his natural supporters, and since we know that the desertions of Anne, Churchill, and others to the prince had been carefully planned in advance,[4] it is easy for us to regard the outcome as predetermined and the campaign of 1688 as nothing other than a political process interior to the elite, if one of an unusual kind.

Constitutionalist historians like to represent events as outcomes of a deep national consensus; revisionist historians like to reduce everything to triviality. Both have been tempted to depict the events at the close of 1688 as capable of ending only as they did, and as containing nothing which politics-as-usual cannot handle. But we also know that the English governing classes – and probably many beneath them – dreaded nothing so much as a resumption of civil war and the dissolution of government; and we know that – if only for this reason – many of them were deeply reluctant to see James deprived of his throne, and only with great difficulty and after many years were brought to consent to the consequences of the act. It makes sense to say that they would never have consented if James had not fled from his kingdom at the end of the year; but from the moment of using the conditional tense, we have begun to consider counterfactuals. There are obvious objections to doing so. History entails an infinite number of contingent variables, and for this reason our selection of countersuppositions is necessarily undisciplined. But counter-history is not the study of what would have happened, so much as of what might have happened; and the case for considering outcomes which did not occur, but which those engaged in the happenings knew might occur – or we

---

[4] W. A. Speck, "The Orangist Conspiracy against James II," *HJ* 30 (1987) 453–62.

with the benefit of hindsight see might have occurred – is that it enables us to understand better the problematics in which the actors were entangled. Any event in history is both what did occur and the non-occurrence of what might have happened; nobody knows this better than we who spend our lives within thinking distance of unthinkable possibilities, some of which happen from time to time.

It can therefore be valuable to play games: in this case, to invent scenarios which could have taken place if James II had been the man his father was. The thought of Charles I handling the situation which confronted his second son in November 1688 is one to be pursued *horrente capillo*. The first move would have been to offer battle; if James, who had led forces by land and sea, had given his regiments orders to fight, some might have obeyed him. The battle – perhaps on Salisbury Plain – should be thought of as the Unfought Edgehill. It had been by giving battle in October 1642, and exposing his own person in it, that Charles I had informed his subjects that they were in a state of civil war, for or against their king, and would have to go through with it; and though nobody quite knew who had won at Edgehill, it was the opinion of the historian of parliament that it was the king's cause which profited by the decisions the battle forced neutrals and hesitants to take.[5]

James II – the scenario continues – would not need to win at a second Edgehill; he might have survived defeat, thrown himself into Oxford, the historic citadel of royalist Anglicanism, set up his standard, and summoned his subjects to resist rebels and invaders in the name of church and king. Six of the Seven Bishops might have hastened to his side, and James would be back at the head of a Church of England militant, which might have forgotten Indulgence and supported him even now. The ensuing war would have been fought by professional armies of a kind unknown in 1642, but we need only suppose a winter of inaction followed by an inconclusive campaign in the Thames valley – with James as the pupil of Turenne he once was – to envisage Danby, Devonshire, and Delamere isolated in the north[6] and forced to choose between the roles of Newcastle and Fairfax.

There is no need to imagine another Cromwell. The scenario need include neither a Puritan resurgence nor a French intervention to make its point, which is that James might have acted in such a way as to force the English ruling classes to choose sides in a prolonged civil war. This must have been among the calculations of French statesmen hearing of the Prince of Orange's intention to set out for England. The resentment of the English, faced with such a challenge, would have been so intense as to be incalculable; but they might have responded, as they had before, with a massive *ralliement* to the cause of nonresistible monarchy. William's invasion had been a drawing of

---

[5] Thomas May, *The History of the Parliament of England which began November the third MDCXL. With a short and necessary view of some precedent yeares.* (London, 1647), book III (separately paginated), pp. 29–31.

[6] David H. Hosford, *Nottingham, Nobles and the North: Aspects of the Revolution of 1688* (Hamden, Conn., Archon Books, 1976).

the sword, and to that extent there was war in England; it was the Fourth Civil War, in the succession of 1642, 1648, and 1651, which might have happened and did not happen.

If the scenario is to continue, we must determine whether James is to wreck his chances once more by insisting on a Declaration of Indulgence and a policy of promoting Catholics. At this point the game becomes unplayable; there are too many options for us to choose between, and we look beyond the alternative possibilities of 1688 to a greater counterfactuality in English history. What would that history have been if the sons of Charles I had returned from exile as militant professors of the Church to which their father was a martyr? It remains extraordinary that they did not. In this scenario, the crisis of 1688 need not occur at all; but there is a 1688 counterfactual in which a defeated and imprisoned James II plays out the game to the last by insisting on his indispensability to any settlement, as Charles I did from 1646 to 1648. A psychobiographer at this point might be tempted to explain James's behavior in the history which really happened by suggesting that the prospect of imitating a father's martyrdom to a Church which the son deeply believed to be false might well make any man's nose begin to bleed uncontrollably. It may, of course, be replied that the English of 1689 were not about to repeat the regicide of forty years previously in any circumstances whatever. A more important reply might be that the exact nature of James II's Catholic devotion has not been much studied.[7]

None of these scenarios happened, none of them was going to happen, and it is futile to imagine in any detail how many of them might have happened. Description is thicker than fiction. But the value of examining the alternative possibilities of 1688 is to remind ourselves that there really was war in England that winter, according to the specifications of the *jus belli ac pacis*, and that it was civil war to the English engaged in it while it lasted. But because there was no battle there was no civil war like that of 1642, in which men all over England had been compelled to take up arms against one another; and it may be said that the Fourth English Civil War was over before it started. The fact that there both was and was not civil war furnished Edmund Burke with the opportunity, but also the necessity, of arguing as he did in 1790.

Now that we have established some propositions concerning what might have happened but did not, we can proceed to inspect what did happen in the light of what might have happened. The civil war which might have broken out would have been a war about sovereignty, like that of 1642, which had begun when a king departed from his parliament and had been fought to determine the terms on which he would be restored to it; fought, that is to say, with the primary intention of restoring sovereignty, but by the use of the sword involved in modifying its exercise. It would have raised questions about sovereignty far more momentous than even those entailed in declaring a king deposed and arranging for his succession. The First and Second Civil Wars

---

[7] See, however, John Miller, *James II: a Study in Kingship* (London, Wayland, 1977).

had destroyed both constitutionality and sovereignty in England, leaving it unclear where they resided in principle and a long and agonizing business to recover them in practice. In 1688 too, a king abandoned his capital, his parliament, and the seat of his administration; but he did not gather an army within the kingdom as an instrument to his return. The remaining legally constituted organs of government were able to gather without drawn swords in their hands, and make provisions for replacing him if he did not himself return (as they feared by now that he might). It was James's flight abroad, repeated after a first failure, that ensured the deepest belief of eighteenth-century Englishmen: less that the constitution limited sovereignty than that it contained sovereignty and was capable of renewing it. James in his own way testified to this principle by throwing the Great Seal into the Thames; his father would have kept it with him.

Not because James left his capital, but because he left his kingdom without setting up his standard within it – one can argue that it was impossible, but not that it was unthinkable, for him to do this – the proposition could be put forward that he had deserted his government, but that the "government" in the sense of "constitution" was not thereby dissolved. The difficulty next encountered was that of contending that he had thereby ceased to be king. On how this was achieved a great deal has been written; but this article is an exploration of counterfactuals, and from investigating the civil war which did not take place it will now proceed to investigate the dissolution of government that did not happen.

The phrase "a dissolution of government" has acquired, especially in the memory of historians, meanings derived from a certain way of reading John Locke's *Second Treatise of Government:* that is, we think of it as a juridical transaction, taking place in a universe of right and nature; a people has entrusted the "government" or regulation of their rights to others, and by verbal transference the term "government" has come to be used of these others and of the formal structures by which authority is distributed among them. But the "government" has failed in discharging the trust laid upon it, and in consequence the "government" is "dissolved"; the "power" to regulate and protect "reverts" to the "people," who are now entitled to renew "government" or not, in the same hands as before or not, according to the same formal structures of distribution or not, "as they list." Because the whole transaction takes place in "nature," where "rights" exist, it is thought that what the people are doing is natural, rightful, and as it were benign; they are not engaged in dissolving the ties that bind men in society.

But this was not how English people in 1688 necessarily employed the phrase "a dissolution of government," nor was it at all what John Locke had to say on the subject.[8] Dissolution of government had actually occurred in England

---

[8] This article may understate the extent to which Locke insists that the "appeal to heaven" is issued when the prince is already "at war" with his people, but insists that it is the people who judge whether such a state of war exists. John Locke, *Two Treatises of Government, Second Treatise,* ed. Peter Laslett (Cambridge University Press, 1988), p. 427, para. 242.

some forty years previously, and those who did not remember it had heard much about it from their elders. The phrase recalled an actual collapse and destruction of governing institutions; if we may use some of the titles of tracts of the times, it is "the confusions and revolutions of government," "the anarchy of a limited or mixed government," which should be allowed resonance.[9] "Dissolution of government" connoted a state of anarchy and anomy, in which right and liberty were uncertain because it was uncertain where the right to protect them lay or in what it was grounded. There had been revolutionaries – their memory was kept alive in such phrases as "the good old cause" – who had seen in this the opportunity of a better government or the millenarian need of none; but their memory was execrated by the governing classes and by those who obeyed their government, and unless one still shared such hopes, it was the fear, guilt, and insecurity of confusion and revolution that came readily to mind. Hobbesian politics were well entrenched in English historic memory, and the reign of Charles II had been a not un-Hobbesian scene; or we may cite the highly un-Hobbesian writings of James Harrington to the effect that "a people under deprivation of government" was "a living thing in pain and misery."[10] When power reverted to the people, it was not a revolutionary opportunity to renew nature and rights, but an agonizing obligation – almost impossible to perform without divine aid all too evidently withheld – to renew, not rights, but the structures of constituted and legitimized authority without which rights could not be ensured.

Dissolution of government, as the frontispiece to *Leviathan* makes clear, was the consequence of civil war; and civil war meant not only battles in the field, fighting in the lanes, soldiers quartered on the villagers, and families by the sword divided, but the actual collapse of legal government, because civil war was one thing which sovereignty could not contain. Civil war was a consequence of the drawing of the sword, and an alternative phrase for the drawing of the sword was the "appeal to heaven." When John Locke's "people" declare their government dissolved – it is only at their initiative that it can be so declared – they appeal to heaven; the phrase is repeatedly used. That is, they pronounce law and authority at an end, and submit themselves to divine judgment; but their God is a God of Battles, and all the literature of the 1640s – so much of which was reprinted in 1689 – together with the whole weight of English historic memory, pronounced that heaven responded to appeal by judgment delivered in the event of battle. The appeal to heaven was an appeal to civil war, and such a war would not be fought between the "people" on one side and the erstwhile "government" on the other. In civil war the "people" were by the sword divided; this was not something of which the seventeenth-century English needed to be reminded.

We are now sure that Locke wrote his *Second Treatise* somewhere between

---

[9] The former is the title of a tract by Anthony Ascham, the latter that of one by Sir Robert Filmer, both dated 1648.

[10] *A System of Politics*, ii, 18, repr. in J. G. A. Pocock (ed.), *The Political Works of James Harrington* (Cambridge and New York, Cambridge University Press, 1977), p. 838.

1680 and 1683; the later the more plausible, since writing it needs to be situated in the process of the Whigs' turning to desperate courses in the experience of defeat. There is no way of reading Locke's scenario of appeal to heaven, dissolution of government, and reversion of power to the people, except as a scenario of civil war. The appeal to heaven meant the drawing of the sword; the only alternative for us to imagine is some Tolstoyan or Gandhian process whereby the people dissolve government and revert to natural society by means of purely passive disobedience, and this was not available in an England where subjects possessed arms and were expected to use them. Shelley's *Men of England* could be written only when the people had been effectively disarmed, and the Revolution of 1688 was indeed a move in that direction. Legislation was already in force restricting the possession and use of weapons by the lower orders, and the gentry might have found it hard – as they would have been deeply unwilling – to arm their tenants for civil war in 1688 as they had in 1642. Perhaps this is why Richard, Lord Lumley, entered Oxford at the head of a body of clubmen. The importance of the bloodless campaign of 1688, however, is that the appeal to heaven did not occur and never did again. England and Scotland were to be both shocked and comforted by their disarmed condition in 1745.

This essay has been concerned with alternative histories and the possibilities of civil war, and the *Second Treatise* is richly illustrative of both. It was published in an England unrecognizably different from that in which it was written; and the difference is precisely that at the earlier date the *Treatise* called for an appeal to heaven which would result in civil war, whereas by the later the appeal had been made, the sword had been drawn, and civil war had not resulted. The events of November–December 1688 could not have been predicted at any moment before they occurred, and therefore it was not possible for the readers of the published *Treatise* to read the work as it had been written. The text and its readers – or rather Locke writing the *Treatise* and Locke sending it to the printer – existed, it is hardly too much to say, in histories which were alternative to one another. The difference, once again, is that between the civil war which many could remember and everyone foresee in 1681–83, and the civil war which everyone could see had been miraculously averted (for the present) in 1688–89. It is not the least of the myriad improbabilities of English history in the 1680s that one of Europe's great philosophers, who was a deeply political man, should have written a program for civil war and dissolution of government shortly after the shattering defeat of his party by the cry "forty-one is come again"; but it pales before the improbability that by the end of 1688 civil war should have begun and ended before it could begin. The actual history is far more improbable, and far less foreseeable, than any of the alternative scenarios we have considered. In history, the thought arises, we are often engaged in ensuring that the predictable does not happen and only the improbable does.

The Fourth English Civil War ended before it began – and in that sense was never a civil war at all – because desertions from the king's camp to his adversaries broke one sovereign's nerve and caused him to desert his kingdom. For this reason a dissolution of government did not occur, and no more did a reversion of power to the people. The constituted bodies of government were able to come together and provide for filling the space left vacant by James; though, because one of them – considering the Church to be such – was in a specially exposed position, they paid a heavy price in destabilizing for doing so. But it was possible to maintain – and the Church did not oppose maintaining – that the fabric of government had not been dissolved, though it had been preserved by actions for which it could not have made legal provision. In these circumstances, Locke's *Second Treatise,* which does envisage a dissolution of government, could be published and seem to reinforce the view that the Revolution of 1688 (of which it now became possible to speak) had been a legitimate process in English civil politics, and the sequence of appeal, dissolution, and reversion (of which the *Treatise* speaks) a legitimate process in natural politics.

The invention of the Glorious Revolution was now beginning. American historians habitually speak of the events of 1688–89 by that title, though British historians no longer do so, and it is amusing to suggest that they must be distinguishing it from some other revolution deserving a different epithet. Those who called the Revolution "glorious" in the centuries of Whig supremacy and Whig interpretation meant to suggest that it had preserved the constitution by constitutional means; even those like Burke, who insisted on the element of extraconstitutional necessity, did not deny the major premise of the assertion. John Locke, who used the phrase "our great restorer the present King William" in publishing his *Treatise of Government,* could claim to be upholding this complex of attitudes and was read as doing so; though the intention with which he published the text could not be identical with that with which he had written it. A civil war which may happen in a future is far removed from one which has not happened in a past. One meaning of "glorious" as applied to the Revolution of 1688 was "providential," and one meaning of "providential" was that civil war had providentially not happened. Locke could claim no credit for this, because he had argued for a dissolution of government; indeed, one of his purposes in publishing was to argue that "the present King William" owed his crown to "the consent of the people," the only lawful title to government, and another was to urge that the Convention should remain one and not become a parliament, with the implication that the government was in fact dissolved and a new one in process of construction. It is at this point that we can distinguish between "conservative" and "radical" interpretations of the revolution, and observe how the meaning of "dissolution of government" had altered in the wake of James II's desertion.

The original meaning of the term had been civil war, followed by the anarchy of not knowing where government lawfully resided; an experience so disturbing that the articulate classes dreaded nothing so much as its recurrence except what they meant by "popery." Only the dread of "popery" could lead them as far as some of them had gone in 1688: i.e., to the point of risking civil war and "dissolution" again. But a few there were who had welcomed, or at least embraced, the anarchy of 1647–49 as an opportunity to construct a better government; they had not experienced the "reversion of power to the people" as a dreadful obligation, so much as a revolutionary liberation. Some of these were still active in 1689 and had aims to pursue in a second dissolution and reversion; Locke knew some such men and may have shared their aims, though there is evidence suggesting that he had aims which were different. When he wrote the *Second Treatise* and envisaged civil war, he may have had aims which were worth pursuing at such a price, or he may have been so desperate that he thought nothing less could avert the evils he feared. When he published the *Treatises* and suggested that dissolution had occurred and should be pursued as still in effect, he may have had aims identical with those of the "good old cause men" like Wildman and Hampden, or aims which were different from theirs, extending perhaps no further than the proscription of his enemies called for in some of his papers.[11]

The question is not that of Locke's intentions, but of the context in which they were situated. Thanks to the flight of James II and the non-occurrence of the Fourth Civil War, the concepts "dissolution" and "anarchy" are now separable. The kingdom was settling itself under a new king, and it could be peaceably debated whether this king owed his crown to a dissolution of government and a reversion of power to the people, or – as Edmund Burke was to insist a century later – to the resolute decision of the governing classes that no such possibilities should be entertained for a moment. In the presence of an established "conservative" reading of the "Glorious Revolution," a "radical" alternative might be tolerated rather than repressed. Those who refused in 1689 to pay attention to Locke and others arguing that a dissolution had occurred may have entertained the conviction that if the "government" were declared "dissolved," civil war would not be long in following; they may even have feared the turbulence of the "lower orders." There is not a great deal of evidence on the point. What we do know is that there continued to be minority opinions averring either that a reversion of power to the people had occurred in 1688–89, or that it should have occurred. Edmund Burke confronted such an opinion in 1790, and informed those who held it that what they envisaged was in fact civil war: that such a civil war had both occurred in 1688 and not occurred.

We must dig deep in Burke's text to find him saying this, and we must dig deep in our own minds. In all probability, the members of the Revolution Society who heard Richard Price's sermon, and Richard Price himself, would have had to dig deep in their minds before realizing that they were debating the reality of civil war; they thought of revolution as a glorious, popular, and peaceful event, and it was this perception that Burke desired to contradict.

---

[11] James Farr and Clayton Roberts, "John Locke on the Glorious Revolution: a Rediscovered Document," *HJ* 28 (1985), 385–98; and Charles D. Tarlton, "'The Rulers now on Earth': Locke's *Two Treatises* and the Revolution of 1688," *HJ* 28 (1985), 279–98.

We may or may not agree with them. During 1989 the world held a series of apparently genuine Lockean revolutions in Eastern Europe, where peoples massively but peaceably withdrew their support from their governments and these in consequence dissolved. Against the glorious revolutions of Poland, East Germany, Hungary, and Czechoslovakia we ought to set the far more bloody and enigmatic events in Rumania – a revolution of a kind belonging to the world of Tacitus and Machiavelli rather than to that of Locke. But the effects on British and American minds of the original "Glorious Revolution" of 1688 – in the terms presented here of the instantaneous character of the Fourth English Civil War – have been to exile altogether the notion that civil war could have occurred in England after 1660. Even Monmouth's expedition and the battle of Sedgemoor count as a "rebellion," not a "civil war."

4

The politics of legitimacy: women and the warming-pan scandal

Rachel J. Weil

In 1703 an anonymous Jacobite writer made a subversive comparison between the events of 1688 and those of 1649. Speaking of the allegations that the son born to James II in 1688 was supposititious, he ridiculed the claims of skeptics that the birth of the Prince of Wales had not been well enough witnessed by offering a *reductio ad absurdum* of their position. "I cannot imagine what you would have," he wrote, "unless you would either have had ye Qn delivered, as her father-in-law [i.e. Charles I] was beheaded, at her Palace gate on a scaffold, or else have had her discharge all her Ladys of honour and persons of Quality and send for ye Good women out of St. James market to come to her labour."[1]

In a sense, these images of the queen's body being exposed to public view came uncomfortably close to the truth. The warming-pan scandal – so called because it was often alleged that a supposititious Prince of Wales had been smuggled into the queen's bedchamber in a warming pan as she pretended to give birth – became the subject of numerous rumors, pamphlets, and satirical lampoons in the summer and autumn of 1688.[2] These played an important role in the propaganda campaign and the politics of the Glorious Revolution,[3] and brought the physical details of the queen's pregnancy and labor into the public eye (plate 1). But did this public scrutiny of the queen's body constitute, as the Jacobite writer implied, a desecration of the dignity of monarchy, a breach of social hierarchy, and a metaphorical regicide? Or did it represent the triumph of the rule of law and of the principle of hereditary succession to kingdoms and property? Implicit in this question were the issues that lay at the heart of the debate over the birth of the Prince of Wales: Could the legitimacy or the authenticity of heirs be proven? Who had the authority to decide? How public or private should a royal birth be? The debate about the authenticity of the Prince of Wales was not simply about the royal succession

---

[1] BL, Add. Ms. 33,286, fol. 20.

[2] I shall use the phrase "warming-pan scandal" to refer to any story that the Prince of Wales was supposititious or spurious, whether it involves a warming pan or not. For one treatment of this affair, see J. P. Kenyon, "The Birth of the Old Pretender," *History Today* 13 (1963), 418–26.

[3] See Lois G. Schwoerer, "Propaganda in the Revolution of 1688–89," *American Historical Review* 82 (1977), 843–74.

Plate 1 An illustration of a broadside. This Dutch print depicts a room in a hospital and refers to the widespread rumor that the Prince of Wales was supposititious. James II's queen lies in bed, as if just delivered of a child. Nearby priests hold up their fingers in tokens of secrecy. A nurse plays with the baby, who carries a windmill to signify that his real father was a miller. By Romeyn de Hooghe, 1688. British Museum.

and the facts of who saw what in the queen's bedchamber, but about the status of childbirth as a political and social event.

We tend to think of seventeenth-century England as a society in which patriarchal structures and assumptions guaranteed the subordination of women in the family and their exclusion in affairs of state. The warming-pan affair, however, involved questions about the birth and legitimacy of children, questions about which women had been traditionally able to speak with more authority than men. For this reason, the debate about the authenticity of the Prince of Wales opened up an opportunity for women to speak out on a matter of political importance; it raised questions about the power that this privileged knowledge about legitimacy and childbirth gave to women to interfere with men's political and property rights; indeed the warming-pan scandal both reflected and shaped contemporary understanding of women's relationship to political life.

The announcement in January 1688 that the queen was pregnant touched off a crisis that had been brewing for years between James and his English Protestant subjects. If the child were to be a boy, he would take precedence in the line of succession to the throne over the staunchly Protestant Mary of Orange, James's elder daughter by his marriage to Anne Hyde. The queen's pregnancy raised the specter of a Catholic heir to the throne. It was at this moment, William Speck has argued, that the "Orangist conspiracy" was born[4] – and so was the warming-pan legend. Rumors of a fraud began to circulate almost immediately. Henry Hyde, Earl of Clarendon, noted on January 15 that "the Queen's great belly is everywhere ridiculed, as if scarce anybody believed it to be true."[5] Satirical lampoons on the royal pregnancy appeared by the beginning of March.[6] *Mr. Partridges Wonderful Predictions, Pro Anno 1688* predicted that "there is some bawdy Project on foot either about buying, selling, or procuring a Child, or Children, for some pious use," and that "some child [is to be] topt upon a Lawful Heir to cheat them out of their Right and Estate."[7]

Rumors about the possible fraudulence of the queen's pregnancy were also featured in the messages which Protestant politicians sent to the court of the Prince and Princess of Orange. William Cavendish, Earl of Devonshire, writing to William on March 13, reported ominously that "the Roman Catholics incline absolutely that it should be a son," and that "we expect great extremities."[8] The next day, Princess Anne wrote to her sister Mary that "Her [the queen's] being so positive it will be a son, and the principles of that religion being such, that they will stick at nothing . . . give some cause to fear there may be foul play intended." She drove the point home a week later, telling Mary that there was "much reason to believe it a false belly. For methinks, if it were not, there having been so many stories and jests made about it, she should, to convince the world, make either me, or some of my friends, feel her belly."[9] Anne's sentiments were echoed by Thomas Osborne, Earl of Danby, who wrote to William that "many of our ladies say that the Queen's great belly seems to grow faster than they have observed their own to do."[10] When the queen gave birth to a son on June 10, suspicions were already rife.

Gazettes and newsletters were "stuffed with nothing but rejoicings from Towns for the birth of the Prince,"[11] and the government spent £12,000 on fireworks to celebrate the happy event,[12] but rumors and lampoons continued

---

[4] See W. A. Speck, "The Orangist Conspiracy against James II," *HJ* 30 (1987), 453–62, for an argument about the timing of the rumors.

[5] Samuel W. Singer (ed.), *The Correspondence of Henry Hyde, Earl of Clarendon* (2 vols., London, Henry Colburn, 1828), II, p. 156.

[6] DWL, Roger Morrice, "Ent'ring Book, Being an Historical Register of Occurences from April, Anno, 1677 to April 1691" (4 vols.), II, p. 239, March 3, 1687/88.

[7] *Mr. Partridges Wonderful Predictions, Pro Anno 1688* [London, 1687/88], pp. 6, 13.

[8] Dalrymple, *Memoirs*, II, part I, pp. 218–19.

[9] *Ibid.*, II, part I, p. 300 (March 14, 1688); pp. 300–1 (March 20, 1688).

[10] Andrew Browning, *Thomas Osborne, Earl of Danby and Duke of Leeds, 1632–1712* (3 vols., Glasgow, Jackson, 1944–51), II, p. 120 (March 29, 1688).

[11] Narcissus Luttrell, *A Brief Historical Relation of State Affairs, from September 1678 to April 1714* (6 vols., Oxford University Press, 1857), I, p. 444 (June 18, 1688). See also pp. 448, 450, 452, 454.

[12] Roger Morrice, "Ent'ring Book," II, p. 284 (July 14, 1688).

to circulate. "People give themselves a great liberty in discoursing about the young Prince, with strange reflections on him, not fit to insert here," noted Narcissus Luttrell.[13] In a mock dialogue, the Prince of Wales's nurse told the papal nuncio, "O Lord, sir, now the whole kingdom laughs at the sham ... nay, the next Bartholemew fair they intend to have a droll called 'The Tragedy of Perkin Warbeck.'"[14] By October, the government decided to respond. The king called a meeting of the Privy Council on October 22, at which forty-two men and women gave depositions that they believed the Prince of Wales to be the king's son. These depositions were given quasi-legal status by being enrolled in court of Chancery, and were then printed by royal authority.[15] By this time, however, William's invasion of England was underway. Among other reasons for his actions, William's *Declaration of Reasons* cited "the just and visible grounds of suspicion" that "the Pretended Prince of Wales was not born by the Queen." He promised to refer to parliament "the enquiry into the birth of the pretended Prince of Wales, and of all things relating to it and the right of succession."[16]

How could William have believed that the birth was a fraud in spite of the testimony of forty-two people? The political force of incredulity is obvious: it provided him with an excuse to invade England in defense of the hereditary right of his wife. The importance of this as an excuse was emphasized in the "invitation" sent by the "immortal seven" on June 30, in which William was chided for having congratulated the king on the birth of his son:

we must presume to inform your highness that your compliment upon the birth of the child (which not one in a thousand believes to be the Queen's) hath done you some injury. The false imposing of that upon the Princess and the nation, being not only an infinite exasperation of the people's minds here, but being certainly one of the chief causes upon which the declaration of your entering the kingdom in a hostile manner must be founded on your part, although many other reasons are to be given on ours.[17]

William was also encouraged to make use of the rumors about the birth by his agent James Johnstone, who suggested that William secretly sponsor the publication of a pamphlet, purporting to be by a private citizen, which would air suspicions about the Prince of Wales's authenticity and call on the Prince of Orange to intervene.[18]

This evidence in turn raises the question of whether William and his allies

---

[13] Luttrell, *A Brief Historical Relation*, I, p. 449 [July 7, 1688].

[14] "The Sham Prince Expos'd. In a Dialogue between the Pope's Nuncio and bricklayer's Wife" (London, 1688).

[15] They were published as *The Several Declarations, Together with the Several Depositions made in Council on Monday, the 22nd of October, 1688. Concerning the Birth of the Prince of Wales* (London, [1688]).

[16] *The Declaration of his Highness William Henry, by the Grace of God Prince of Orange, &c. of the Reasons Inducing him to Appear in Armes in the Kingdom of England for Preserving of the Protestant Religion and for Restoring the Lawes and Liberties of England, Scotland, and Ireland.* (The Hague, Arnout Leers, 1688). The Declaration, dated September 30, 1688, was printed with a postscript dated October 24.

[17] *CSPD* 1688, no. 1236 (*SP* 8/1, pt. 2, fols. 224–27).

[18] See Lois G. Schwoerer, *The Declaration of Rights, 1689* (Baltimore and London, Johns Hopkins University Press, 1981), p. 107. The letter is reprinted in N. Japikse (ed.), *Correspondentie van Willem III en van Hans Willem Bentinck Het Archief van Welbeck Abbey* (2 vols., The Hague, Martinus Nijhoff, 1927–28), II, p. 603.

not only exploited existing rumors but also actually created and promoted them. Some Jacobites charged later that there was a premeditated plot by James's enemies to cast doubt on the queen's pregnancy even before she became pregnant. One writer quoted a letter from one "E.S." which contained information about a cabal of English gentlemen in Holland two years before the Revolution who "resolved not to attempt anything upon England, till they should hear of ye Queens being delivered of a son; and then to proceed upon yt point of its being a supposititious child." The same writer also recalled the remark made by Roger L'Estrange in *The Observator* after the birth of a daughter to Mary of Modena in 1682 that the Whigs had tried to cast suspicion on the then Duchess of York's pregnancy and only desisted when the child proved to be a girl. L'Estrange had prophesied that "the same flam shall . . . be trumpt up again upon the like occasion."[19] This evidence may suggest that there was a predisposition on the part of James's opponents to believe that Mary of Modena might fake a pregnancy. But as proof of a premeditated conspiracy, it should be taken with several grains of salt, as it comes from biased sources.

What is certain, however, is that from the early days of the queen's pregnancy, Protestant politicians played an important role, if not in creating the rumors, at least in creating the conditions under which it would be easy for other people to believe them. The role of Princess Anne was especially important in this respect. As already noted, Anne passed the rumors about the fraudulence of the queen's pregnancy to Mary as early as March. But, despite having given the impression in her letters that she had tried hard to find out if the pregnancy was real but had been rebuffed by the queen,[20] Anne did not remain on call to witness her stepmother's lying-in. When the queen gave birth on June 10 Anne was at Bath taking the waters for her health.

Anne's absence from the birth of the Prince of Wales lends (and lent) itself to some intriguing speculations. Writing to Mary on June 18, Anne expressed her "concern and vexation" that "I should be so unfortunate to be out of town when the Queen was brought to bed, for I shall never now be satisfied whether the child be true or false." She then, however, used this circumstance to cast suspicion on the queen for having misled the world about the date of her reckoning and "chosen" to give birth while Anne was away, "two days after she heard of my coming [back] to town [i.e., London]."[21] An early pamphlet about the warming-pan scandal developed this theme, charging that Anne had deliberately been sent away for fear that she would be a "vigilant observer."[22]

---

[19] BL, Add. Ms. 33,286, fols. 30v–31. The passage from L'Estrange is reprinted in Dalrymple, *Memoirs*, II, part I, p. 313.

[20] Dalrymple, *Memoirs*, II, part I, pp. 300–1 [March 14 and 20, 1688]. According to Margaret Dawson, a former gentlewoman of the bedchamber to Mary of Modena, Anne never expressed interest in examining her stepmother's belly or being admitted to her bedchamber. BL, Add. Ms. 26,657, "Deposition of Margaret Dawson, February 13, 1700/1."

[21] Dalrymple, *Memoirs*, II, part I, p. 303.

[22] *An Account of the Pretended Prince of Wales, and other Grievanses, That occasioned the Nobilities Inviting, and the Prince of Orange's Coming into England* (London, 1688), pp. 15–16. A more fully developed version of this pamphlet was

It is quite possible, of course, that Anne deliberately absented herself from the birth in order to avoid being called upon as a witness in case the pregnancy proved to be real, and to make it look as if the queen had tried to exclude her. Not surprisingly, this argument can be found in Jacobite literature: for example, James Montgomery suggested in *Great Britain's Just Complaint* (1692) that Anne had sought physicians who would advise her to go to Bath although her physicians in ordinary were against it.[23] This interpretation of Anne's behavior is also accepted by Anne's recent biographer, Edward Gregg.[24] Of course, we will never really know whether Anne deliberately stayed away or whether she genuinely did not expect the queen to be brought to bed so soon – although this in itself may be a tribute to her cleverness in covering her tracks. With or without premeditation, Anne found or put herself in the convenient position of not being able to confirm the authenticity of the birth.

Anne took further advantage of her own ignorance in a letter to her sister on July 24. Mary had presented Anne with a list of leading questions about the circumstances of the queen's pregnancy and lying-in. Anne responded to these with vague and inconclusive answers which, while they proved nothing, made it possible for Mary to believe that the authenticity of the Prince of Wales had not been sufficiently established.[25]

This was, of course, precisely the point. Anne's strategy, and that of other promoters of the warming-pan myth, was simply to give people a reason to believe what they wanted to believe. James Johnstone's letter of advice to William captured the essence of this technique. He did *not* say that a pamphlet about the Prince of Wales's birth would persuade neutral observers that the boy was supposititious. Rather, the goal was to preach to the converted: "Even those that beleeve that there is a trick put on the nation will be glad to know why they themselves thinck so, and those that only suspect the thing, will be glad to find reasons to determine them."[26] By keeping the burden of proof on those who said the birth was real, rather than on those who said it was false, promoters of the warming-pan myth were able to make every inconclusive detail look like a damning indictment.

The warming-pan myth was thus valuable and effective as one of the justifications for William's invasion in 1688. After the Convention met, however, it became inconvenient for William and his supporters for precisely the same reasons that it had previously been useful. As we have seen, the rumors about the false birth were effective only as long as their promoters had been able to insist that the birth had not been sufficiently proven to be real.

---

published under two other titles, *An Account of the Reasons of the Nobility and Gentry's Invitation Of His Highness the Prince of Orange into England. Being a Memorial from the English Protestants Concerning their Grievances. With a large Account of the Birth of the Prince of Wales* (London, 1688; Licensed and Entered According to Act of Parliament [which places its publication in 1689]) and *A Memorial From The English Protestants, For Their Highnesses the Prince and Princess of Orange* (n.p., n.d.).

[23] (James Montgomery), *Great Britain's Just Complaint* (London, 1692), p. 21.
[24] Edward Gregg, *Queen Anne* (London, Ark, 1984), pp. 53–58.
[25] Dalrymple, *Memoirs*, II, part I, pp. 305–10.   [26] Japikse (ed.), *Correspondentie*, II, p. 603.

Not even they, however, could prove that a fraud had occurred. Thus, during the debates in the Convention, Colonel John Birch, arguing that the settlement of the crown should not be based on the principle of hereditary succession, pointed out that "there's a Prince of Wales talked of; and if he be not so, you will never want a Prince of Wales."[27] Had the warming-pan story been used to justify the political settlement, there would always have been a pretender to the throne whose claims to be the real son of James II could not be disproved.

Furthermore, the warming-pan myth did not fit in with William's political ambitions. If William had indeed come to England to defend Mary's rights against those of the supposititious Prince of Wales, it seemed appropriate to put Mary on the throne as James II's legitimate heir. As Elinor James, a printer's widow turned prophetess, wrote in an open letter to the members of the Convention, "Nobody can condemn him [William] for looking after the right of his wife; but all the world will highly condemn you to give, or him to receive, the right of the King."[28] The author of *Reflections on the Present State of the Nation* argued that the immediate recognition of Mary as James's heir was the only way to "preserve ancient and hereditary monarchy" from "republican principles."[29] In the Convention the case for Mary was taken up by a small group led by Thomas Osborne, Earl of Danby.

The "Maryite" position, however, proved unacceptable to the Prince of Orange. In the wake of William's refusal to be his wife's "gentleman usher" and his threat to withdraw from England unless given the crown, the Convention decided to settle the crown jointly on William and Mary and to place in William's hands the sole administration of the kingdom.[30] For reasons of expediency, then, the warming-pan story was dropped as an official justification for the Revolution. Not surprisingly, the promised parliamentary inquiry into the birth of the Prince of Wales never materialized. As contractarian views of the Revolution became more accepted, the warming-pan story came to be seen as an embarrassment. As Sir John Dalrymple put it almost a hundred years later, "to defend the Revolution upon a pretended suppositious birth, is to affront it; it stands upon a much nobler foundation, the rights of human nature."[31]

Nonetheless, the truth or falsehood of the warming-pan story remained an important issue for many people. Queen Anne herself never lost interest. When her physician, David Hamilton, told her in 1712 that he believed "that the Pretender was not the real son of King James, with my arguments against it," the queen "received this with chearfulness, and by asking me several

---

[27] Grey, *Debates*, II, p. 59.

[28] Elinor James, untitled broadside beginning "My Lords, you cannot but be sensible . . ." [London, 1688].

[29] *Reflections on the Present State of the Nation*, printed in (Walter Scott [ed.]) *A Collection of Scarce and Valuable Tracts*, 2nd edn (13 vols., London, T. Cadell and W. Davies, 1809–15), x, pp. 203–4. This was also published as *Proposals Humbly Offer'd in Behalf of the Princess of Orange*.

[30] For accounts of parliamentary maneuvering on the question of succession, see Browning, *Thomas Osborne*, II, pp. 419–33; and Henry Horwitz, *Revolution Politicks: the Career of Daniel Finch, Second Earl of Nottingham 1647–1730* (Cambridge University Press, 1968), pp. 70–82.

[31] Dalrymple, II, part I, p. 313.

questions about the Thing."[32] The debate also remained alive in the popular press. In 1696, for example, William Fuller, the notorious informer, published *A Brief Discovery of the True Mother of the Pretended Prince of Wales*. The book was reissued in increasingly elaborate versions at least eight times between 1696 and 1702. Among the clergy, for whom questions of legitimacy were especially important, the warming-pan story remained the subject of passionate debate. William Lloyd, the Bishop of Worcester, devoted himself to finding new evidence that the Prince of Wales was supposititious, despite the fact that he had already argued in print that William had established his right to the throne by "conquest." In 1703, his evidence was summarized in a widely circulated manuscript, and found its way into Gilbert Burnet's version of the story as told in his *History of My Own Time*.[33] On the other side, a circle of nonjuring clergymen, including George Hickes and George Harbin, tried to refute Lloyd by interviewing some of the original witnesses to the birth. These nonjurors became active in September 1701 when the death of James II created a possibility that some nonjurors might be tempted to accept the warming-pan story in order to justify swearing allegiance to Anne. An extensive body of correspondence survives in which Hickes and Harbin strove to persuade a wavering comrade, Robert Jenkin, not to abandon the cause.[34] The warming-pan story was also kept alive through fears of a Jacobite invasion, and many of the earlier pamphlets were reprinted in 1715 and 1745. Altogether, between 1688 and 1745 over fifty works appeared which made significant reference to the birth of the Prince of Wales (plate 2).

The persistence of the warming-pan story suggests the tenacity of the doctrine of hereditary succession. It allowed those who could not accept William as the "elected" monarch at least to accept Mary as the hereditary one, and later provided a reason to swear allegiance to Anne rather than the Pretender.[35] On the other hand, the myth undermined the principle of hereditary succession by magnifying the problem that lay at the heart of it: how is one to know who the heir is? Ironically, the arguments made to prove that the Prince of Wales was a fraud bore a strong resemblance to arguments made almost ten years earlier during the Exclusion Crisis *against* hereditary succession by Whig opponents of James, then Duke of York and heir presumptive to his brother's throne. A review of these arguments allows us to understand why the warming-pan legend struck a responsive chord, and to underscore the issues that it raised.

One version of the Whig challenge to "patriarchalism" at the time of the Exclusion Crisis can be found in the work of Algernon Sidney. In his "Discourses Concerning Government" (not published until 1698), he argued that

---

[32] Philip Roberts (ed.), *The Diary of Sir David Hamilton 1709–1714* (Oxford, Clarendon Press, 1975), pp. 44–45.

[33] BL, Add. Ms. 32,096, "An Account of the Birth of the Pretended Prince of Wales, as it is Delivered by the Lord Bishop of Worcester"; Burnet, *HOT*, III, pp. 244–58.

[34] Bodl., Ms. Engl. Hist. b. 2; BL, Add. Ms. 33,286; and BL, Add. Ms. 32,096.

[35] Thus, J. C. D. Clark cites the persistence of the warming-pan legend as evidence of the continuity of patriarchalist political discourse in England: *English Society 1688–1832* (Cambridge University Press, 1985), pp. 126, 163.

Plate 2 A British broadside published about 1745 depicting the Young Pretender holding a warming pan. The cover is open to reveal a portrait of the Old Pretender, James Francis Edward Stuart – an obvious reference to the rumors about his birth in 1688. Copied from F. Chereau's print after a picture by Alexis Simeon Belle. British Museum.

the very concept of hereditary succession was flawed because of the many uncertainties surrounding marriage, legitimacy and the birth of children. He pointed out that bastards may be thought legitimate, and legitimate sons bastards, and that many marriages which had been thought legal had later been declared null. No people, said Sidney, had ever been "so careless of their most important Concernments, to leave them in such uncertainty, and simply to depend upon the humour of a man, or the faith of women, who besides their other Frailties have bin often accused of supposititious births."[36]

Sidney's point was that the succession of the crown should be determined by parliament. Other Whig opponents of the Duke of York, however, took the opposite approach. They upheld the doctrine of hereditary monarchy, but tried to manipulate the facts of the case in such a way as to make the Duke of Monmouth appear to be the legitimate heir. They did this by claiming to discover evidence that Charles II had been secretly married to Lucy Walter, the Duke of Monmouth's mother.[37] An even more interesting "legitimist" argument for Monmouth came from the legal reformer William Lawrence, who insisted that the existence of a formal marriage between Charles II and Lucy Walter was irrelevant.[38] He asserted that marriage was defined not by ceremony or contract but by the act of sexual union. It followed that Charles was by definition married to Lucy Walter by virtue of having impregnated her. All children, Lawrence argued, should be considered the legitimate children of their natural fathers and have a right to inherit from them. This led him to criticize the existing laws of legitimation which recognized the children of the wife to be the children of the husband. These laws, he argued, allowed women to pass off the children of their adulterous unions as their husbands' legitimate heirs. Women did this, moreover, with the cooperation of priests, who influenced succession by controlling the ceremonies which defined marriage.[39] This was, for Lawrence, evident in the infamous attempt of the Pope to prevent Henry VIII's divorce, and the efforts of the papists to deprive the Duke of Monmouth of his right to inherit the throne. As we shall see, Lawrence's work foreshadowed the rhetoric of the warming-pan tracts in important ways.

Whether they intended, like Sidney, to challenge the principle of hereditary succession, or like Lawrence to institute it in a more pure form, the Whig Exclusionists called attention to the fact that paternity and legitimacy were difficult to prove. In this context, it is not surprising that the warming-pan story would seem plausible and important. It touched on matters that, as far as pamphleteers on both sides of the question were concerned, should interest

---

[36] Algernon Sidney, *Discourses Concerning Government* (London, 1698), p. 340.

[37] See, for example, *A Letter to a Person of Honour Concerning the Kings Disavowing the Having been Married to the D. of M.'s Mother* [London, 1680]. See also (Robert Ferguson), *A Letter to a Person of Honour Concerning the Black Box* [London, 1680].

[38] (William Lawrence), *Marriage by the Moral Law of God Vindicated* (London, 1680) and *The Right of Primogeniture in Succession to the Kingdoms of England, Scotland, and Ireland* (London, 1681). Only the second book explicitly makes the case for Monmouth. On Lawrence's connection to the Whig Exclusionists, see O. W. Furley, "The Whig Exclusionists," *Cambridge Historical Journal* 13 (1957), 19–36, n. 21.

[39] Lawrence, *Marriage by the Moral Law*, pp. 72–75, 77.

any man hoping to pass his estate to his own legitimate heirs. The debate about the birth of the Prince of Wales was about who had the authority to determine matters relating to marriage, childbirth, or legitimacy. It was also a debate about the power and trustworthiness of women. As a result, it made women both the subjects and objects of political discourse.

At one level, the warming-pan affair created an opportunity for women to take part in political debate. It opened up a space where women's presumably superior knowledge about pregnancy and childbirth gave them the authority to speak on a matter of political importance. The roles of Princess Anne and Mary of Orange – roles which were available to them only because they were women – have already been discussed, and they clearly had the most to gain from the story. In addition, a number of women from a variety of social classes and occupations expressed opinions on both sides of the issue. These included the poet Aphra Behn and the midwife Elizabeth Cellier, who both hazarded predictions in print that the queen's child would be a boy;[40] the witnesses who gave depositions before the privy council; Lucy Armstrong, who approached the Earl of Nottingham in March 1689, with a story that the midwife had confessed the fraud to a woman of her acquaintance;[41] Isabella Wentworth and Margaret Dawson, who provided George Hickes and his circle of nonjurors with further evidence concerning the birth;[42] and Frances Shaftoe, who in 1708 published a narrative claiming that Sir Theophilus Oglethorpe was the true father of the Prince of Wales.[43]

But if the warming-pan affair put women in a privileged position to speak about political events, it also made them the objects of suspicion. Although the parallel was not exact, for the king and queen were charged in the warming-pan myth with conspiring *together* to foist a bastard baby on the nation, some writers tried to make the myth more convincing by citing cases of women who had feigned childbirth and appealing to male paranoia about wives foisting supposititious heirs upon unwitting husbands. One pamphlet cited an account of "a woman who pretended to be delivered in bed by a midwife, but the imposture was discovered afterwards by the said midwife and the true mother."[44] Robert Jenkin, the wavering nonjuror, reminded George Hickes that a supposititious birth had occurred "but a few years ago in a private family, unknown to the supposed father."[45] David Hamilton suggested that such events were common when he told Queen Anne, "I have been witness to the same imposition amongst persons of a farr, less Degree, and to answer a farr less design."[46]

[40] Aphra Behn, *A Congratulatory Poem to Her Most Sacred Majesty* (London, 1688); Elizabeth Cellier, *To Dr. —— An Answer to his Queries* [London, 1688].

[41] HMC, *Report on the Manuscripts of the late Allan George Finch* (4 vols., London, HMSO 1913–65), ii, pp. 195–96 (Lucy Armstrong to Nottingham, March 14, 1688/89).

[42] BL, Add. Ms. 26,657, "Deposition of Margaret Dawson, February 13, 1700/1"; BL, Add. Ms. 33,286, fols. 3–4, "Conference with the Lady Wentworth, April 22, 1702."

[43] *Mrs. Frances Shaftoe's Narrative* (London, 1707). Several versions followed.

[44] *A Compleat History of the Pretended Prince of Wales* (London, 1696), p. 12.

[45] Bodl., Ms. Eng. Hist. b. 2, fols. 188–89, Mr. Jenkins to George Hickes, 7 October 1701.

[46] *The Diary of Sir David Hamilton*, p. 45.

These apparently irrational fears about women's control over childbirth and legitimacy seemed realistic in part because they were linked to a long-standing tradition of anti-Catholic bigotry. William Lawrence's complaint about a conspiracy of women and priests altering the succession of kingdoms was often echoed in satirical literature. The Prince of Wales was frequently depicted as the son of a priest, in particular of the papal nuncio Ferdinand D'Adda, whose name lent itself to an incriminating pun. This image was convincing because of a widely held set of assumptions about the sexual ethics of the Catholic Church.[47] Significantly, Lawrence described the *English* laws concerning legitimacy as "popish vestiges" and satirized them in explicitly anti-Catholic terms as allowing for "the transubstantiation of the children of the wife into the children of the husband."[48] Similarly, in the warming-pan literature Catholicism was associated with a kind of monstrous motherhood that deprived men of their paternal rights. It was common, for example, for writers to take a jab at Mariolatry through an ironic identification of Mary of Modena's "miraculous" conception with that of the Virgin Mary. Sixteen-year-old Abraham De la Pryme, upon learning of the queen's pregnancy, wrote in his diary, "They say that the Virgin Mary has appear'd to her, and declair'd to her that the holy thing that shall be born of her shall be a son. They say likewise that the Pope has sent her the Virgin Mary's smok, and hallow'd bairn clothes."[49] *A Full Answer to the Depositions* (1689) employed almost identical imagery to the same point.[50]

The image of Mary of Modena as a pseudo-virgin, miraculously begetting heirs without the aid of a husband, was even more intimately associated with the Catholic Church in "The Tryumphs of Fire on the Stage of Water," a mock court masque written "in honour of the Mother of the P. of W." The "mother" turned out to be the Church herself; as the Jesuits said to James and Mary during the masque, "We've got a Prince, 'twas more than you could do." The image of the church as a mother was then rendered obscene. As the Jesuits put it:

> This Deity (for we ne're deal with other)
> Is fertile call'd, t'Imply a fruitful Mother;
> Around her naked sprawling infants cling,
> And at her feet are Hares engendering/ . . .
> This is the Nursing Mother, th'Infants we
> Who the true heires to all her Whoredoms be.[51]

Printed and unprinted propaganda thus invoked a rich set of associations among the pseudo-miracles of the Roman Church and the "miraculous" birth of the Prince of Wales, among Mary of Modena and the Church of Rome as apparent "mothers" who are really whores, and among the birth of the Prince

---

[47] For a lurid example of anti-Catholic sexual stereotypes, see (David Clarkson), *The Practical Divinity of the Papists Discovered to be Destructive of Christianity and Men's Souls* (London, 1676), especially pp. 337–60.

[48] Lawrence, *Marriage by the Moral Law of God*, p. 72.

[49] (Charles Jackson [ed.]), *The Diary of Abraham De la Pryme, the Yorkshire Antiquary* (Durham, Andrews, 1870), p. 11.

[50] *A Full Answer to the Depositions; and to all the Pretences and Arguments whatsoever, concerning the Birth of the Prince of Wales* (London, 1689), p. 4.   [51] Bodl., Ms. Rawlinson poetry 159, fols. 15–18.

of Wales, other fraudulent births, and Catholic sexual ethics in general. This created a strong emotional impact. The political usefulness of the warming-pan story, of course, made many English Protestants ready to accept it despite its unlikely character. But the appeal to male paranoia about paternity, especially when embedded in the familiar and powerful rhetoric of anti-Catholicism, made the story even more convincing.

In addition to casting suspicion on scheming wives and mothers, promoters of the warming-pan story tried to construct a standard by which births could be proven, and which this particular birth had failed to meet. Their attempts to do this raised the question of whether women could speak, and with what authority, about the birth of the Prince of Wales. *An Account of the Reasons of the Nobility and Gentry's Invitation* and *A Full Answer to the Depositions*, the two most important pieces of warming-pan propaganda published in 1688 and 1689, shared the conviction that births must be "public" and subject to strict standards of evidence. I shall briefly look at how the testimony of women as witnesses to the birth was treated in these tracts.

An Account focused on the question of who was present at the birth rather than on the details of what they saw. The argument was that the queen, once aware of the suspicions surrounding her pregnancy, should have taken steps to assure that the birth be properly witnessed and proved "beyond all possible contradiction." Her failure to do this itself violated the principles of "our English Laws" which "abhor any Entry upon the apparent legal Right of another," in this case the right of Princess Mary to her father's throne, "without sufficient Manifestation of their own greater or better Rights."[52]

This appeal to ancient principles of common law was a brilliant polemical stroke. It allowed the author to treat the allegedly supposititious birth as yet one more instance of James II's threats to the rights and liberties of Englishmen, and to cast himself as a defender of the unalterable principle of hereditary succession to the throne.[53] As legal scholarship, however, it left much to be desired. In an effort to define who was and was not a proper witness to the birth, the author invented or misused a number of legal precedents. When, for example, he claimed that common law "hath appointed twelve of the most able Neighbours to judg of all the Signs and Appearances of Fraud, and setting up Counterfeit Heirs,"[54] he may have had in mind a precedent in common law whereby, if a widow was suspected of feigning a pregnancy in order to procure a supposititious heir, the presumptive heir to the estate might obtain a writ of *de ventre inspiciendo*, entitling him to have the widow examined by matrons or midwives and to keep her under restraint until she was delivered.[55] However, the author of *An Account* stretched the precedent beyond recognition by applying it in a case where the husband was still alive. Equally dubious was his claim that it was the custom of all "civilized kingdoms" that royal births be witnessed by a host of dignitaries, including "the

---

[52] *An Account of the Reasons*, p. 11.   [53] *Ibid.* pp. 16–17.   [54] *Ibid.*, p. 21.
[55] For examples, see James Oldham, "The Origins of the Special Jury," *University of Chicago Law Review* 50 (1983), 137–213, especially 171–75. *A Full Answer* also cites this precedent.

Princes of the Blood, the chiefest Men of religion, and the greatest Nobles and Officers ... and the Ambassadors and Ministers of foreign Kingdoms."[56] The only precedent for who should be present at a royal birth which has surfaced contradicts this assertion: in the reign of Henry VII, only women were admitted to the queen's bedchamber.[57]

What is important for our purposes is that while the author of *An Account* was able to find reasons to exclude those who had been present at the birth on grounds that they were Roman Catholics, courtiers dependent on royal favor, persons not well known in the kingdom, and/or foreigners,[58] he never tried to exclude the female witnesses on grounds of their sex. On the contrary, in his elaborately constructed vision of who *should* have been present at the birth, women were given a significant role. Only women were qualified to witness with their own eyes the child emerge from the queen's body. These women were to be possessed of "sufficiency of knowledge and understanding in matters of Child-bearing, such as knew by experience all those works of nature"; they were to be matrons "whose gravity and sobriety were fit to attract some decent reverence from the men of like quality"; they should be aristocrats, so that they would "have more Audacity and Confidence to make such near Approaches to the Queen in her Travel and bringing forth, as are necessary."[59] The presence of men would give the birth its public character; that of women would guarantee its authenticity.

In theory, then, *An Account* acknowledged the authority of women. Its point was simply to show that instead of the noble Protestant matrons who should have witnessed the birth, the bedchamber had been filled with foreigners, papists, and courtiers.[60] *A Full Answer to the Depositions,* a work published in early 1689 in response to the Privy Council hearing, used a different tactic. Although the author never explicitly said that women were not sufficient witnesses to the birth of a child, he defined the nature of "proof" in such a way as to make the testimony that the women actually gave – including the noble Protestant matrons – look like insufficient evidence.

The differences between *An Account* and *A Full Answer* can be seen if we consider how they used the term "public." The birth, declared the author of *A Full Answer*, should have been "publick to extremity, but on the contrary it was private to a nicety."[61] The meaning of "public," however, was somewhat different from what it had been in the earlier tract. In *An Account,* a "public" birth meant one witnessed by the representative of the public. The author of *A Full Answer,* by contrast, never defined "publicness" in terms of a list of proper witnesses. Instead, he stressed the importance of legal and medical standards of evidence, especially physical details that could only be provided by doctors. Had man-midwives been present at the birth, they would not have been "so

---

[56] *An Account of the Reasons,* p. 11.

[57] (Society of Antiquaries of London), *A Collection of Ordinances and Regulations for the Government of the Royal Household, made in Divers Reigns* (London, 1790), p. 125.

[58] *An Account of the Reasons,* pp. 12, 14, 15.   [59] *Ibid.,* pp. 12, 13.

[60] In fact there were a number of Protestant women present, including Anne, Countess of Aran; Penelope, Countess of Peterborough; and Anne, Countess of Sunderland.   [61] *A Full Answer,* p. 9.

easily cheated as other men, nay, as Women, for being Doctors they could have distinguished the very Cries, whether true or Counterfeit."[62]

The author of *A Full Answer* thus used his faith in the medical verifiability of childbirth in order to expose what he saw as a crucial lack of detail in the depositions. His assumption was that "Child Births are obvious, and things the most capable of a plain Testimony and Explanation . . . of any humane Affair whatsoever."[63] The witnesses ought therefore to have given "incontrovertible proofs," if they had any, as to the authenticity of the birth. Needless to say, he found the testimony inadequate. For example, when Penelope, Countess of Peterborough, deposed that she saw the queen's belly "so as it could not be otherwise but that she was with Child," he pointed out that the countess had not said whether she saw the queen's belly clothed or naked. When Mrs. Mary Crane, a gentlewoman of the bedchamber to the queen dowager, stated that she had stayed with the queen after she was delivered and saw "all that was to be seen after the Birth of a Child," he complained that this phrase was "not well exprest," for Mrs. Crane had not specified whether the "all that was to be seen" had come out of the queen's body. He then interpreted this lack of detail in the witnesses' testimony as a sign of their acquiescence in the plot. The one exception to this method was his reading of the testimony of Thomas Witherly, a Protestant physician who deposed that he "was present in the Queen's bedchamber when the Prince of Wales was born." This time, the lack of specific detail was interpreted as Witherly's clever way of letting his audience know that he himself thought that the birth was a fraud but was afraid to say so in public.[64]

A Full Answer sought to discredit the testimony of forty-two witnesses by exploiting the gap that existed between what the deponents considered to be sufficient testimony and what the author led his readers to consider "incontrovertible proof." Most of the deponents seem to have thought it was enough to state their own belief. When Charlotte, Countess of Lichfield said that she was "sure she could not be deceived but that the Queen was with Child," or when Elizabeth Bromley said that she had "observed the Bigness of her Majesty's Belly, which could not be counterfeit," they were not being vague or evasive.[65] Rather, they were speaking with an authority that they thought due them by virtue of personal experience. They seem to have assumed that matrons familiar with pregnancy and childbirth did not need to give clinical details in order to claim to be "certain." The success of *A Full Answer* thus lay in the author's ability to define a standard of proof different from the one used by the witnesses.

---

[62] *Ibid.*, p. 7. The authority of doctors over midwives and women was further asserted in a gratuitous attack on Elizabeth Cellier, the "popish midwife," who was known not only for her political intrigues but also for her efforts to raise the professional status of midwives (p. 3). The author of *A Full Answer* also warned readers that "the wife's word, or [that of] only a profligate midwife," would not be considered sufficient evidence that a birth had occurred (p. 10). The pamphlet should be placed in the context of a professional struggle between midwives and "man-midwives" that lasted into the eighteenth century. See Jean Donnison, *Midwives and Medical Men: A History of Interpersonal Rivalries and Women's Rights* (London, Heinemann, and N. Y., Schocken, 1977; reptd. Historical Publications, London, 1988).   [63] *A Full Answer*, p. 13.
[64] *The Several Declarations*, pp. 8–9, 14, 35; *A Full Answer*, pp. 17, 19–20.   [65] *The Several Declarations*, pp. 17, 23.

It was precisely on the question of what constituted adequate evidence that the defenders of the Prince of Wales took issue with these and other pamphlets. They offered a critique of the entire business of "proving" the birth, pointing out that there was not "one subject in any of the three kingdoms that can prove his own birth so well as the Prince of Wales."[66] It was ridiculous to call this birth into question unless one was prepared to do the same for all others. This would, as the nonjuror Thomas Wagstaffe put it, "fill the world with confusion" and "at this rate make supposititious not only all princes, but all men in the world."[67] Similarly, George Hickes outlined the dire consequences that would follow if fathers were to disown their sons simply for lack of absolute certainty as to their birth or identity, and he asserted that "no suspicions or presumptions, how great soever, would defeat the title of a child owned by private parents."[68]

The defenders of the Prince of Wales thus dealt with the uncertainty at the heart of hereditary succession not by looking for better "proofs" of the prince's authenticity but, in effect, by accepting uncertainty as inevitable. In this they closely followed Robert Filmer, who, in response to Hobbes's claim that "it is not known who is the father to the son, but by the discovery of the mother," had argued that the social acknowledgment of parental identity was enough: "No child naturally or infallibly knows who are its true parents, yet he must obey those that in common reputation are so."[69]

In other words, the literal truth of the birth was not worth prying into. This attitude towards "evidence" gave supporters of the Prince of Wales a different attitude towards the testimony of women. Thomas Wagstaffe observed that there was "scarcely a woman in England, who ever had any children," who did not know that it was impossible to hide a baby in a warming pan! "Why should the Prince of Orange have so mean an opinion of us, that we would sit down and give up our faith to such pretences as every midwife and every woman can confute?"[70] Ultimately, however, if Jacobites and nonjurors did not subject women to scrutiny and suspicion it was not, or not only, out of a trust in female credibility but out of a trust in paternal instinct. It was impossible, they argued, for James to have done anything to disinherit his daughters, or any children that he might have in the future, in favor of a stranger. Paternal love was elevated to the status of a natural law: "Nature and the law which is copied from nature abhors" the thought that a father would prefer a "brat" to his own children.[71] Wagstaffe asked:

Will any man adopt an heir when he does not know but he may have one of his own? Much less will he pick up one from a dunghill to inherit the glory of his ancestors, when

---

[66] (George Hickes), *The Pretences of the Prince of Wales Examined and Rejected* [London, 1701?].

[67] Bodl., Ms. Engl. Hist. d. 1, pp. 3–4 (Thomas Wagstaffe), "Innocence Protected" [London, 1692?]. This pamphlet seems to exist only in manuscript.

[68] BL, Add. Ms. 33,286, fols. 11–12, Letter from Hickes to Robert Jenkin, September 22, 1701.

[69] Robert Filmer, *Observations Concerning the Original of Government* [1652], reprinted in Peter Laslett, *Patriarcha and other Political Works of Sir Robert Filmer* (Oxford, Basil Blackwell, 1949), p. 245.

[70] Wagstaffe, "Innocence Protected," p. 4.

[71] BL, Add. Ms. 33,286. This section is headed, "Out of a Ms. by Sir George Mackenzie."

his own loyns may afford him many branches to support it. Let all married men and women, who have any sense of children, consult your own bowels, and then let them believe this if they can.[72]

The faith of Jacobites and nonjurors in the testimony of women was thus grounded on an even greater faith in the power of men's paternal affections for their own children.

We must not, therefore, leap to the conclusion that the defenders of the Prince of Wales were also the champions of women. Rather, women had something to gain and something to lose on both sides of the warming-pan controversy. If the belief that the Prince of Wales was a fraud implied that some women are untrustworthy and might strive to alter the succession of estates and kingdoms, it also, if pushed to its logical conclusion, supported the claims of a woman, Mary of Orange, to the throne.[73] By contrast, supporters of the Prince of Wales upheld the trustworthiness of women, but also upheld the sanctity of men's paternal feelings. Given the complicated "sexual politics" of the warming-pan story, it is not surprising to find women on both sides of the debate.

This should lead us to ask larger questions about the gender dimension of political ideology in this period. Historians have customarily divided seventeenth-century political thought into two broad categories, "patriarchalist" and "contractarian." "Patriarchalism" has been used to denote the loose constellation of ideas associated with Robert Filmer: that the power of kings originated in the power of fathers over their families, that is God-given, that people owe absolute obedience to their rulers, and that monarchical power is inherited by primogeniture. By contrast, "contractarian" thought stressed the consensual and constructed character of political authority.[74] Many historians have also tended to link "patriarchalism" as a political discourse with "patriarchy" in the abstract sense of the subordination of women to men; and to assume, as a corollary, that "contract" ideology was conducive to more egalitarian sexual arrangements.[75] However, the debate about the authenticity of the Prince of Wales, which took place within a patriarchalist ideological framework, raises new questions about the status of women in patriarchalist thought. The debate gave some women a chance to speak publicly as women about a matter of political importance, while at the same

---

[72] Wagstaffe, "Innocence Protected," p. 4.

[73] For an example of a woman expressing Maryite sympathies, see Aphra Behn, *A Congratulatory Poem to her Sacred Majesty Queen Mary, upon her Arrival in England* (London, 1688).

[74] These are very loose categories. For a discussion of the different varieties of patriarchalist thought, and of what "contract theory" actually owed to patriarchalism, see Gordon J. Schochet, *Patriarchalism in Political Thought: the Authoritarian Family and Political Speculation and Attitudes Especially in Seventeenth Century England* (New York, Basic Books, 1975).

[75] For attempts to describe the relationship between political theory and the status of women, see, among others, Lawrence Stone, *The Family, Sex, and Marriage in England, 1500–1800* (New York, Harper and Row, 1977), especially pp. 239–44; Susan D. Amussen, *An Ordered Society: Gender and Class in Early Modern England* (Oxford, Basil Blackwell, 1988); Margaret J. M. Ezell, *The Patriarch's Wife: Literary Evidence and the History of the Family* (Chapel Hill, University of North Carolina Press, 1987); Lois G. Schwoerer, *Lady Rachel Russell: "One of the Best of Women"* (Baltimore and London, Johns Hopkins University Press, 1988); Mary L. Shanley, "Marriage Contract and Social Contract in Seventeenth Century English Political Thought," *Western Political Quarterly* 32 (1979), 79–91.

time calling women's expertise concerning legitimacy and childbirth into question. It underscored the fact that women had power to exert within a system of hereditary succession, but also raised anxieties about the fact that women had such power. This in turn suggests that "patriarchalism" as a mode of political discourse concerned with hereditary succession was not in itself inherently liberating or oppressive for women. Rather, it created a space for a debate about women's relationship to political power, without resolving it. This may help us to understand why some women (for example, Mary Astell) remained loyal to patriarchalist political ideology despite the possible feminist implications of contract theory; but it should also let us see the dangers as well as the opportunities that patriarchalism presented for women. A study of the warming-pan affair illustrates the power of political myths in the Revolution of 1688–89 and deepens our understanding of the complicated social and sexual meanings of political discourse in seventeenth-century England.

5

Pretense and pragmatism: the response to uncertainty in the succession crisis of 1689

Howard Nenner

On January 29, 1689, the slim hope that James II might remain nominally on his throne disappeared. The Lords, by a narrow margin of three votes, rejected the proposal for a regency, and with the death of that scheme came the anxious realization that an English commitment to hereditary monarchy might have died with it.[1] For the constitutionally scrupulous a second defense of the hereditary principle was to agree that James had renounced his right to the throne, that the infant Prince of Wales was a fraud, and that Mary, next in the line of succession, was legally their queen.[2] That, at least, would have made the pretense of a continuing hereditary monarchy more plausible. In the confused constitutional circumstances it was as "regular" a solution as there could possibly have been, but in the politics of the moment it was as impracticable to suppose that William would consent to being subordinated to his wife Mary as it had been to hope that James would consent to being reduced to the status of a nominal king. To most observers, therefore, it seemed certain that the Prince of Orange would in some way be elevated to the throne. To many that certainty also seemed appealing. The problem, then, was not whether William would make his way to the throne; rather, it was how he would get there. The crowning of the Dutchman might be the pragmatic solution to England's political needs, but it was not to be a simple solution. It depended upon the elaboration of constitutional pretense, and that in the end was a more complicated matter.

If the winds of a modest radicalism had prevailed, William's route to the throne would have been certainly less ambiguous and probably more direct. The men of the Convention, had they been bolder, could have seized the main chance and declared themselves to be a constituent assembly rather than

---

[1] HMC, *Twelfth Report* (London, HMSO, 1890), Appendix, part VI, p. 15; *LJ*, XIV, 110. For a discussion of slight discrepancies in various reports of the number of lords voting on each side of the regency issue see H. Horwitz, "Parliament and the Glorious Revolution," *BIHR* 47 (1974), 44, n. 3; Eveline Cruickshanks, D. Hayton, and C. Jones, "Divisions in the House of Lords on the Transfer of the Crown and Other Issues, 1689-94: Ten New Lists," *BIHR* 53 (1980), 59.

[2] This Maryite position had its strongest support from a small but influential group of peers led by the Earl of Danby. W. A. Speck, *Reluctant Revolutionaries: Englishmen and the Revolution of 1688* (Oxford University Press, 1988), p. 102; Burnet, *HOT*, III, pp. 387–93.

pretending to be only a slightly imperfect parliament. They might even have played the Lockean card of an appeal to heaven and a dissolution of government, instead of adopting the more comfortable fiction of a nation that had gone to the edge of the precipice but had resolutely stopped short of that last fatal step into the abyss. They would not have had to go so far as a renewed republicanism, which, after the experience of the Cromwellian Interregnum, scarcely anyone seemed to want. At a radical minimum they might have renounced hereditary monarchy, offered the crown to their new monarchs on the explicit condition that those monarchs accept the claims made in the Declaration of Rights, and then, in confident possession of their new status and powers, they might have easily admitted to having elected William and Mary as their king and queen. If this brand of radicalism which was clearly in evidence had prevailed, they might have done any or all of these things. In fact, they did none of them.

Whether these missed opportunities should be seen as the result of necessity or of deliberate calculation, as a failure of political nerve or as a vindication of constitutional intelligence, are issues that have been examined at length in other places. Overall, the case for the triumph of restraint over radicalism has been successfully made. Less settled, however, is whether the evidence is also persuasive of constitutional restraint having been more a consequence of temporizing and uncertainty than of a clear and consistent political vision.[3] Interestingly, similar questions can be asked about the succession. Did the placing of William and Mary jointly on the throne reflect a political consensus on the mutability of the hereditary principle, and a commitment to a new view of the right to be king? Did the men of the Convention mean to say or were they understood by the political nation to say that henceforth the crown was in the disposal of the people? To each of these questions the answer appears to be no. The eventual lesson of the Revolution would be that a hereditary claim to the throne was in all cases only a presumptive right; and, moreover, that the people and their representatives in parliament were empowered to counter that presumption when in their judgment it was in the interest of the nation to do so. But a lesson that would come clear over time was only imperfectly understood in 1688–89 and still a long way from being accepted. As late as 1688 the possible routes to the throne had not yet been fully and legibly mapped, and because to all but a few it was essential not to relinquish the principle of a heritable crown, the events of 1688–89 would serve to obscure the political and constitutional terrain even further.

To start with what is critical to our understanding and reasonably beyond

[3] Horwitz, "Parliament and the Glorious Revolution"; J. P. Kenyon, "The Revolution of 1688; Resistance and Contract," in Neil McKendrick (ed.), *Historical Perspectives: Studies in English Thought and Society in Honour of J. H. Plumb* (London, Europa Publications, 1974), p. 50; Kenyon, *Revolution Principles: The Politics of Party* (Cambridge University Press, 1977); Howard Nenner, *By Colour of Law* (University of Chicago Press, 1977); Nenner, "Constitutional Uncertainty and the Declaration of Rights," in Barbara C. Malament (ed.), *After the Revolution: Essays in Honor of J. H. Hexter* (Philadelphia, University of Pennsylvania Press, 1980), pp. 292–308 *passim*; Lois G. Schwoerer, *The Declaration of Rights, 1689* (Baltimore and London, Johns Hopkins University Press, 1981); Speck, *Reluctant Revolutionaries*; C. C. Weston and J. R. Greenberg, *Subjects and Sovereigns* (Cambridge University Press, 1981).

dispute, we should begin with the birth in June 1688 of James Francis Edward, the baby in the warming pan.[4] Despite the flood of rumor, there was no direct and credible evidence to support the allegations of fraud that accompanied his birth, and in other circumstances it is likely that those rumors would have been summarily dismissed. In this instance, however, there was too much at stake. That the king might be intent upon recatholicizing England was politically tolerable only so long as his efforts, even if successful, were certain to be short-lived. The political nation clung to that belief. It would remain discomfited but loyal in the confident expectation that with the death of its Catholic king the menace of his religion would be arrested and reversed. Yet, all that had changed on June 10, 1688. With the birth of the Prince of Wales, Mary had been instantly and automatically displaced by an heir apparent who was certain to be reared as a Catholic.

The result was ironically reminiscent of the reign of Henry VIII. For the second time in just over 150 years England was to experience a revolution that had as much to do with the politics of dynastic fertility as with the principles of government and religion. By the mid-1520s it had been realistically assumed that Catherine of Aragon would bring forth no further children, and by the mid-1680s the same, more in hope than in reason, was assumed of Mary of Modena. In the first case the assumption was right, in the second it was wrong; and in both cases a revolution ensued. If England embarked on its Protestant Revolution for want of a male heir, it began its Glorious Revolution because its queen had unexpectedly produced one. For as long as it was supposed that the Catholic James II would be succeeded on the throne by his Protestant daughter and heiress presumptive, Mary, it is at least probable that politically restive and disaffected Englishmen would have been prepared to bide their time. As James was the Catholic threat to England, Mary was its assured salvation.

There is much in this that is instructive about the English understanding of the succession. It tells us that in 1688 the English were so convinced of the workings of hereditary right that they believed nothing was likely to prevent the infant Prince of Wales from becoming the second in a theoretically unlimited line of Catholic kings. Yet, less than eight months after James Francis Edward's birth, his cousin William and his half-sister Mary were jointly offered the English throne in a manner readily suggestive of a new, or at least a newly revived, principle of succession. Although nothing on that point would be stated in the widely reported proceedings of February 13, it was more than reasonable to infer from the circumstances that the Prince and Princess of Orange had been elected to the monarchical estate rather than having received that estate as a matter of heritable right.

The result, however, was that the rule of succession, less the product of reason than of need, was not so much changed as it was confused. William and Mary neither asserted a hereditary right to the throne nor acknowledged that

---

[4] See Rachel Weil, "The Politics of Legitimacy: Women and the Warming-pan Scandal," in this volume.

they had received it as a gift of "parliament" or people. As a consequence, politicians and polemicists continued to cast about for the most satisfying rationalizations and justifications they could find for the change in the occupancy of the throne. The enterprise was highly successful. Nonjurors and Jacobites notwithstanding, the political nation accepted its new king and queen even though it could reach no easy agreement about the basis of their claim.[5]

As a practical matter, the avenues to the acceptance of William and Mary were as varied as they could be and as they had to be. The political nation began by embracing the warming-pan myth and then moved on to further flights of political imagination. The polemicists led the way, indulging in inventive constructions of Mary's hereditary right; assumptions about William's legal right to his wife's estate; fanciful interpretations of William as king by divine right; William as king by right of conquest; William as king *de facto*; and William and Mary as king and queen by right of election. Probably the best explanation of what had happened was offered by the Marquis of Halifax, who was to rationalize the settlement as a response to unique circumstances and hard necessity. The crown, he later insisted, "was only made elective *pro hac vice*, and then reverted to its hereditary channel again."[6] Yet even that, as all knew, was not quite accurate. Certainly, it was not all that had been done. The settlement, as it came to be made, not only abridged heredity for one more turn, by favoring the claim of the Princess Anne before any issue begotten by the king on a second or subsequent wife, it limited hereditary right permanently by forever excluding all Catholics from the throne.

William Sherlock, in *A Letter To A Member of the Convention*, wrote that if the Prince of Orange were to be made king, he would have nought "but a crazy title to the immediate possession of the crown."[7] Sherlock, of course, was using "crazy" in its archaic but still exact sense of "cracked" or "flawed"; but Sherlock, I think, went further than he needed to, not only because by 1690 he found his way to taking the oaths to William and Mary, but because in 1688–89 it was still uncertain how legally, constitutionally, politically, and practically, the presumption of hereditary right of the next in blood might be rebutted. William's title was "crazy" only if one were troubled by there being three other claimants, namely James's son and two daughters, who stood closer in line to the throne. It was not "crazy" if it could be allowed, as ultimately it was, that in some circumstances the line might legally be altered and that the presumption of strict hereditary right was only a presumption and as such could be overcome.

Not only could it be overcome, it had been overcome numerous times from

---

[5] The course for many was made easier by the adoption of a new oath of allegiance. In deference to those who were willing to acknowledge their new sovereigns as *de facto* rulers only, the reference in the oath to William and Mary as "rightful and lawful" monarchs, was judiciously omitted.

[6] Samuel Weller Singer (ed.), *The Correspondence of Henry Hyde, Earl of Clarendon, and of his Brother, Laurence Hyde, Earl of Rochester; with the Diary of Lord Clarendon from 1687 to 1690* (2 vols., London, H. Colburn, 1828), II, p. 261.

[7] (William Sherlock), *A Letter To A Member of the Convention* (London, 1688), p. 3.

the Norman Conquest through the Tudor victory at Bosworth. Still, it could be said in 1688 that for two hundred years there had been no interruption in the hereditary descent of the crown. Since Henry VII had broken the brief hold of the Yorkist kings in 1485, every monarch had come to the throne as next in the hereditary line. Even the abortive rule of the Protector Oliver bore striking witness to this constitutional continuity, as in 1660 Charles II came to the throne not in the first but in the twelfth year of his reign. Why then, even before the confounding effects of the Glorious Revolution were encountered, was the rule of succession in early 1689 so uncertain? The answer lies in the confusion wrought in the Tudor era by Henry VIII and his daughters, and in the next century by James I and his grandsons. Henry VIII tampered with the succession on more than one occasion during the last twenty years of his reign. The result at his death was a statute, his third Act of Succession, that did nothing to reverse either of his daughters' legislated illegitimacy, but which made both eligible to take the crown;[8] and a will, authorized by parliament, that attempted to exclude his Stuart descendants from reaching the throne. The compelling inference to be drawn from these maneuvers was that king-in-parliament or the king, acting on the authority of parliament, might override hereditary expectations, and might even violate the heart of the hereditary principle by making it possible for a bastard to succeed.

Elizabeth further confounded the issue. Whereas Mary Tudor had her first parliament restore her to legitimacy, Elizabeth, when she came to the throne, never bothered.[9] Did that mean that a bastard could inherit the throne? Did it mean that the corruption of the blood by illegitimacy was no different from corruption by treason, and that as the latter was cured by taking the throne, so too was the former? Did Elizabeth, in fact and in law, inherit the throne, or did she, like her sister and brother before her, take it by the authority of an Act of Parliament, her father's third Act of Succession? And if the answers to these questions are hard to come by, what are we to make of Elizabeth's second Treasons Act in 1571, wherein it was stated explicitly that parliament had the unqualified right to determine the succession?[10] Did Englishmen believe that to be true? And in the absence of parliament acting on that right, did the queen, on her deathbed, have the unilateral right to nominate her own successor, heredity and parliament be damned? Certainly there were many who thought that Elizabeth had chosen James VI of Scotland to be England's next monarch and, what is more, thought that she had a right to do so. Curiously, James did not think she had the right, nor did he think that queen-in-parliament had or could have the right to alter the succession; and certainly he did not believe that his great-great uncle Henry had the right in his will, with or without the authority of parliament, to deprive him, James, of his right to the English throne. James claimed his English crown on the basis

[8] 35 Hen. VIII, c. 1 (1544). *SR*, III, pp. 955–58.
[9] 1 Mar. St. 2. c. 1 (1533). *SR*, IV, part I, pp. 200–1.
[10] 13 Eliz., c. 1 (1571). *SR*, IV, part I, pp. 526–28.

of hereditary right alone, and both his council and first parliament were willing, without exception, to endorse his view.[11]

There is a case to be made for Tudor uncertainty having been corrected, or at least quieted, by Stuart consistency. Charles I and his sons all claimed their thrones by hereditary right. Still, the discourse of Exclusion between 1679 and 1681 was a persuasive reminder of critical issues that had never been resolved. Most important was the question of indefeasibility. It had been essential for James VI to buttress his claim to Elizabeth's throne with the argument that the descent of the crown ran not only in known channels but, at God's command, in fixed channels as well. In this construction of the rule of monarchical succession there were no choices to be made. There was only the nation's responsibility at the death of a monarch to recognize the next in blood as its lawful sovereign. No intervention of kings, parliaments, councils, or people could have any legal effect to the contrary. It was God's truth, it was the law's truth, and it was immutable truth. For that reason there were Tories in the three Exclusion parliaments who believed that a bill of Exclusion, even if it should make its way through both Houses and win the king's assent, would be null and void.[12] And because Exclusion failed, the Tory position could be read as having been vindicated. James, Duke of York, became king by hereditary right in 1685 and beat back the attempt of his bastard nephew, James, Duke of Monmouth, to unseat him. Had Monmouth's Rebellion succeeded, it is anyone's guess how he would have vindicated his right to the throne. He would have had several options: unalloyed hereditary right based on the pretense that his mother and Charles II had in fact been married; hereditary right based on his bastardy being cured by his taking the crown; a right of conquest based on his defeating James II; and a right of election based on "parliament" calling him to the throne.

Three and a half years after Monmouth's unsuccessful revolt, some of these questions were still waiting to be answered. And although the circumstances were different, the discourse had not been significantly changed. It was one of the ironies of an uncertain succession that the same men who, in political reality, elected William to his father-in-law's throne, did so in the more comfortable language of law and hereditary right. If it was the nation's responsibility merely to recognize and not to choose its sovereign, its representatives in the Convention would strain to persuade themselves that they were doing just that – and only that. It was not an easy task to accomplish, but in that political moment it was compelling to try. Admitting to the election of their monarchs, even in this seemingly unique instance, readily conjured images of the kingdom's descent into disorder and decay. David Hume, who, from the remove of the next century, understood the Whigs as much as he sympathized with the Tories, appreciated their common concern that "the election of one king was the precedent for the election of another;

---

[11] 1 Jac. I. c. 1 (1603). *SR*, IV, part II, pp. 1017–18.
[12] See, for example, the remarks of Sir Leoline Jenkins. Cobbett, *Parlia. Hist,* IV, p. 1191.

and the government, by that means, would either degenerate into a republic, or, what was worse, into a turbulent and seditious monarchy."[13]

The Earl of Nottingham, the Convention's voice of constitutional conscience, was intent upon making the hypocritical work of pretense even harder. If the throne is vacant, he said, "we must fill it either by our old laws, or by the humour of those that are to chuse."[14] Nottingham was exactly right, but wondrously, the Convention managed both to choose a king and at the same time to assure itself that it was proceeding "by our old laws." The aged and highly respected Whig lawyer, Serjeant Maynard, pointed the way. In an attempt to quiet Tory scruples he argued that the admission of an abandoned throne did not require a similar abandoning of the law. They would first need to recognize that the throne, through no doing of their own, had been left vacant, and "it will then," Maynard said, "come orderly in debate how it should, according to our law, be filled."[15] Maynard was making a promise that could not be kept, but in a time when self-delusion ran consistently ahead of reality, and credibility was no match for credulity, the hollowness of the promise hardly seemed to matter.

So to come full circle, the overriding constitutional problem of 1688–89 was not only how to rationalize James II off his throne, but how to rationalize William and Mary onto it. The settlement of the succession, according to the Declaration of Rights, was clear enough. William and Mary were declared king and queen "during their lives and the life of the survivor of them," with "the sole and full exercise of the regal power" in William alone. The remainder of the royal estate was to pass to the heirs of Mary's body, and should Mary die without surviving issue, the crown was to pass first to Anne and the heirs of her body. "And for default of such issue to the *heirs of the body* of the said Prince of Orange" (emphasis supplied). As to what would happen if William were to die without any direct descendant, the Declaration was curiously silent. A reasonable inference to be drawn was that the disposition of the crown would again revert to parliament, but nowhere in the settlement was there anything explicit to that effect.

Such evidence as there is points to the probable intention and certain effect of this silence. It was to enhance the appearance of hereditary succession and to preserve as much of the hereditary principle as was thought to be desirable. It had already been necessary to make two critical concessions to William. The prince insisted on being given nothing less than a life estate in the crown and he further demanded full and exclusive executive power. He was categori-

---

[13] David Hume, *The History of England*, repr. of 1778 edn (6 vols., Indianapolis, Liberty Classics, 1983), VI, pp. 524.

[14] *The Debate at Large, Between the House of Lords and the House of Commons, At the Free Conference, Held in the Painted Chamber, in the Session of the Convention, Anno 1688*, repr. of 1695 edn (Shannon, Irish University Press, 1972), p. 117.

[15] *Ibid.*, p. 111. This idea was echoed in the contemporary polemical literature. One such argument, advanced as being perfectly consistent with a commitment to hereditary monarchy, was that "it is very just and necessary, that in a dubious case, the body politick should determine themselves, whom to acknowledge as lawful successors." *A Political Conference between Aulicus, a Courtier; Demas, a Country-man; and Civicus, a Citizen: Clearing the Original of Civil Government, the Powers and Duties of Soveraigns and Subjects* (London, 1689), p. 41.

cally unwilling to share that power with Mary or to step down from the throne should Mary predecease him, telling a group of the leading peers on February 6 "that he would hold no power dependent upon the will of a woman."[16] William's conditions were met, but beyond those necessary accommodations Anne's hereditary rights were to be assured and to be placed before those of William's issue from any subsequent marriage. Yet as strikingly important as the provisions that were made, were those that were not. By providing no further than for the passing of the crown to the heirs of William's body, and for no contingent remainder beyond that, it was completely uncertain what principle of succession would apply in the event that Mary, Anne, and William were to die without surviving descendants. For some that may have been a discomfiting ambiguity. Not so for William, who, according to at least one account, found the ambiguity quite agreeable, "because it gave him an opportunity, through the uncertainty of the succession, to flatter whom he pleased with the hopes of it."[17]

This framing of the Declaration to prevent any of William's collateral heirs from coming to the throne was no accident or oversight. In 1689 William was the best of a necessary bargain. As could be supposed, there was no great joy at the prospect of a foreign king, still less at the possibility that as a widower he might take a second, and this time foreign, wife, and propagate a *line* of foreign kings. That much was understandable, but it still left a critical question: where, at the failure of the direct line, was the crown to go, this crown that the men of the Convention were all at great pains to protest would continue as a hereditary estate? The likely answer was that it was intended "to devolve," as Evelyn recorded in his diary for February 6, "to the parliament to choose as they think fit."[18] It is possible, moreover, that a resolution to this effect had been introduced in the Lords, only to be struck in deference to the Tories.[19] The Convention might contemplate and even anticipate the need to return to an elective crown, yet explicitly admitting to a reserved right of election was another matter entirely.

The result was silence and nothing else than a conspiracy of avoidance. With any luck the question would never have to be answered because it would never have to be addressed. Mary had conceived and miscarried twice in the late 1670s, and by 1689 it was rumored and assumed that she and William would be childless.[20] Anne, however, pregnant for the seventh time, was still in her fertile years and still more than likely to produce a surviving heir. As it happened, Stuart luck, like Tudor luck before it, turned bad, although it was

---

[16] Dalrymple, *Memoirs*, I, part I, p. 204.   [17] *Ibid.*, p. 209.

[18] E. S. de Beer (ed.), *The Diary of John Evelyn* (6 vols., Oxford University Press, 1955), IV, p. 621.

[19] Dalrymple states that the Lords resolved that in default of issue of William's body the crown would then pass "to the person that should be named in such manner as should be limited and regulated by act of parliament; and in default of such limitation, to the heirs of the Prince of Orange," and that these clauses were struck in the Commons partly to satisfy the prince and "partly because it removed the odium which attended the bringing his collateral heirs at all into view." *Memoirs*, I, part I, pp. 207, 209. There is, however, no record of this resolution in either the Lords or the Commons journals.

[20] As important as Mary's difficulties in carrying a child to term were the reports by mid-1679 that William was sterile. Stephen B. Baxter, *William III* (London, Longman, Green, 1966), p. 163.

not until 1700 and the death of the Duke of Gloucester, Anne's only surviving child, that the matter of an uncertain succession had once again to be faced.

The practical solution to the immediate problem of 1689 was prefigured in the advice of political pamphleteers. One suggested that in the interests of prudence and safety the crown and government be committed "to the next undoubted heir of the royal family, who is duly qualified,"[21] while another allowed that "sufficient respect" should be "shewn to the royal family, without rendring the nation unsecure."[22] That, in fact, was the course to be taken. Hewing as close to the precept of hereditary right as political necessity would allow, the Convention never lost sight of its fundamental task, the need to replace James II with an acceptable Protestant successor. The result was an array of argument that, while avoiding any admission of election, was shifting the focus from the rights of the Stuart dynasty to the needs of political society. Sir Robert Howard urged the Lords not to hold the Convention hostage to a strict and inviolable lineal succession. "When such difficulties are upon the nation," he said, "your lordships, I hope will give us leave to remember *salus populi est suprema lex*."[23] Maynard, citing the warrant of natural law, drew the same conclusion. He asserted that in "the law of nature . . . we have enough to justify us in what we are now a doing, to provide for our selves and the publick weal in such an exigency as this."[24] And Sir George Treby, moving from the comfortably abstract to the chillingly hypothetical, wondered whether anyone would object to tampering with hereditary succession if it had fallen out that Louis XIV was the next in line. He had no doubt in such a case, and supposed that no one else did either, that it would "be in the power of the states of this kingdom to devolve it upon another head."[25]

It is particularly significant that the Convention, conservative in so much of its discourse on the succession and straining at every turn for constitutional justification to deviate from the strict hereditary line, had little difficulty in deciding that the nation might bow to the necessity and henceforth exclude all Catholics from the throne.[26] It was clearly for necessity and in the language of necessity that the Commons resolved "that it hath been found, by experience, to be inconsistent with the safety and welfare of this Protestant kingdom, to be governed by a popish prince."[27] Some men pretended that the resolution could be understood as a statement of existing law, but in this instance words like "experience," "safety," and "welfare" pointed more to a pragmatic solution than they did to a legal one.[28]

[21] (Edward Stephens), *Important Questions of State, Law, Justice and Prudence, Both Civil and Religious, Upon the Late Revolutions And Present State of these Nations* (London, 1689), p. 10.
[22] *Political Conference*, p. 38.   [23] *Debate at Large*, p. 136.
[24] *Ibid.*, p. 157.   [25] *Ibid.*, p. 148.
[26] Henry Horwitz, "1689 (and All That)," *Parliamentary History* 6 (1987), 26. Speck regards "the agreement of both Houses to disinherit Catholic kings . . . [as] the single most radical act of the Convention." Speck, *Reluctant Revolutionaries*, p. 103.
[27] January 29, 1689: *CJ*, x, p. 15.
[28] See, for example, the remark of Sir Robert Howard "that it is inconsistent with our religion and our laws to have a papist rule over us." Cobbett, *Parlia. Hist.*, v, p. 98.

Appeals of pragmatism surfaced repeatedly during the several months of national political debate. It was asserted both in the Convention and in the press that the kingdom, if not in the first instance, then at least, as Gilbert Burnet pleaded, "in cases of extream necessity," was obliged to attend to its self-preservation.[29] For some that signaled a clear right of resistance. One polemicist held it to be an affront to "our reason, to think that our ancestors who made kings, were such fools or mad men, as not to reserve to themselves a power of turning them out if they endeavour'd to destroy them, or act[ed] contrary to those rules they had set them."[30] But one did not have to go that far, and most in fact did not. James II had eased the national burden of conscience by removing himself from England, so that instead of directing the argument of necessity to justifying rebellion, that argument could now be applied with greater comfort to the problem of settling the succession. The crown having already fallen, the major question was where it was to settle; and the answer, when it could not be provided by law, might be furnished by recourse to "reason of state [which] obligeth to lodge it where it may be most for the publick good."[31] A man, after all, was free to disinherit his eldest son if doing so was in the highest interest of preserving his family.[32] Why then should the nation not have the same right? The answer, once the argument was extended to a pragmatic – and even radical – conclusion, might be as the political opportunist Robert Ferguson would have had it, that the succession "is not to be governed by proximity of blood, but by weighing what is most expedient for the benefit of the community."[33]

In the end, the English did only what they believed to be minimally necessary for the preservation of their Protestant monarchy. Recourse to necessity did not come to mean the abandoning of heredity for a crown in the disposal of parliament – or so the political nation chose to pretend. At several turns the Convention was urged to exercise the power that was theirs to use and to declare accordingly for the principle of election. The best reason for making William their king, they were told, was that he had absolutely no claim to the crown except that which was conferred by the nation. As an elected monarch he would owe his crown not to right, but to the people who gave it to him.[34] That plea, however attractive to radical opinion, was rejected. The Convention chose instead to settle the crown on William and Mary with full power in William, and to justify that settlement in a compound of pretense and pragmatism. Mary, it would be argued, was simply not a sensible or practical choice for the throne. Given the present state of affairs, it

[29] (Gilbert Burnet), *An Enquiry into the Present State of Affairs: And in particular, Whether we owe Allegiance to the King in these Circumstances? And whether we are bound to Treat with Him, and call Him back again, or not?* (London, 1689), p. 12.

[30] *The Letter Which was sent to the Author of the Doctrine of Passive Obedience and Jure Divino Disproved, &c. Answered and Refuted* (London, 1689), p. 33.

[31] (Robert Ferguson), *A Brief Justification of the Prince of Orange's Descent Into England, and of the Kingdoms Late Recourse to Arms* (London, 1689), p. 34.

[32] *Letter to the Author of the Doctrine of Passive Obedience*, p. 14.

[33] Ferguson, *A Brief Justification*, p. 34.

[34] *Several Queries Relating to the present Proceedings in Parliament: More especially recommended to the Consideration of the Bishops* (London, 1689). p. 3.

was not "safe to trust the administration of affairs to a woman."[35] Also, Mary might be so consumed with the guilt of assuming her father's throne that she would be affected adversely by his unavoidable "entreaties and subtile insinuations." And finally, William would "not only [be] able to defend her and her kingdom from all the dangers that may happen, but also to take all the trouble which may occur in the administration of affairs off her hands, so that she will enjoy all the pleasure of being queen without any thing of trouble."[36]

It was not only to shield Mary from this disingenuous acknowledgment of the "thorny cares and next to insupportable toils that . . . are likely to attend the swaying of the English sceptre,"[37] that the princess's rights were subordinated to her husband's ambitions. William supposed that he too had rights in the matter. Some sought to persuade him that the absence of a Salic Law notwithstanding, his right was grounded in his being the nearest male in the hereditary line.[38] Years earlier, until he was disabused of the idea, he had even believed that the claims of both Mary and Anne were inferior to his own because their mother, Anne Hyde, had been born a commoner.[39] But the most promising ground for William, and that which lent some color of legal right to his having, as he maintained, "such a right as all the world knows to the succession of the crown,"[40] was the run of argument in support of his matrimonial standing.[41] The position at common law was that a man was entitled to the possession and administration of his wife's estate. Whether that rule could be applied to the monarchical estate, however, was uncertain. As one commentator observed, the "matrimonial crown is an unpathed way, it is not well known what it doth import."[42] Still, the Earl of Pembroke was prepared to argue, on recognizably tenuous historical authority, that Henry VII's title was in the right of his wife, Elizabeth of York;[43] and others were prepared to distinguish away the precedent of Philip of Spain's limited rights on the legally insubstantial ground that he married Mary Tudor only after she had become queen.[44]

Yet once again, if law was unavailable, legal pretense and political expediency would combine to meet the nation's needs. Furthermore, the

---

[35] *Ibid.*, p. 2. See also *Four Questions Debated* (London, 1689), p. 7. Another face of the same argument was that circumstances required "a vigorous and masculine administration, . . . a prince that is consummate in the art both of peace and war." *Reasons for Crowning the Prince and Princess of Orange King and Queen jointly: and for placing the Executive Power in the Prince alone* (London, 1689), p. 19.

[36] *Several Queries Relating to the present Proceedings in Parliament*, p. 2. See also *Reasons humbly offer'd, for placing his Highness the Prince of Orange, singly in the Throne during his life* (London, 1689), p. 18; Howard Nenner, "The Traces of Shame in England's Glorious Revolution," *History* 73 (1988), 238–47.

[37] Ferguson, *A Brief Justification*, p. 35.

[38] *A Discourse Concerning the Nature, Power, and Proper Effects of the Present Conventions in both Kingdoms Called by the Prince of Orange* (London, 1689), p. 18; *Four Questions Debated*, p. 7.

[39] Baxter, *William III*, pp. 129, 223–24.

[40] *The Declaration of His Highness William Henry, By the Grace of God, Prince of Orange, &c. of the Reasons inducing him to appear in Arms in the Kingdom of England, for preserving of the Protestant Religion, and for restoring the Laws and Liberties of England, Scotland, and Ireland* (London, 1688), p. 12.

[41] *Reasons for Crowning the Prince and Princess Jointly*, p. 19; *Political Conference*, pp. 41–42; *Four Questions Debated*, p. 7; *Proposals Humbly offered to the Lords and Commons in the present Convention, for Settling of the Government, &c* (London, 1689), p. 5; *Some Short Considerations Concerning the State of the Nation* (London, 1689), p. 7.

[42] *Political Conference*, p. 38.   [43] *Debate at Large*, p. 154.

[44] *Political Conference*, pp. 34–35; *A Discourse Concerning the Nature of the Present Conventions*, p. 15.

solution was happily advanced by Mary's proving to be a dutiful wife. She understood that it was "unsuitable and ungrateful," and "not to be expected, that so generous and warlike a prince . . . would suffer his wife to leave him or to become his sovereign,"[45] and that, in Burnet's words, "a titular kingship was no acceptable thing to a man."[46] This pointed the way to a practical resolution of the problem of succession in 1689. The political result, then, was clear even if the consistent denials of election and the twisted constructions of hereditary right were to leave a legacy of constitutional confusion in their wake.

[45] *Political Conference*, p. 34.

[46] Burnet, *HOT*, III, pp. 138–39. In a meeting of Burnet, Mary, and William that Burnet reported as having taken place in 1686, Mary told William that "she did not think that the husband was ever to be obedient to the wife: she promised him, he should always bear rule" (p. 139).

6

William III as Hercules: the political implications of court culture

Stephen B. Baxter

An anniversary is almost as good as a hanging for bringing a man's mind into focus. And a tercentenary is a particularly important anniversary. By the time an event is 300 years old it should be possible to discuss it without losing one's temper. Yet if something is only 300 years old, it can still be worth discussing. Such an event has, perhaps, reached the peak of middle age.

We must be careful, in celebrating important anniversaries such as that of the Glorious Revolution of 1688–89, to discuss them in their own terms rather than in ours. Ours is an age of the narrowest kind of specialization, which may be a working out in scholarship of the principles of the Industrial Revolution. But narrow specialization is not history. Many years ago, after I gave an early paper on William III, I was terrified to see Caroline Robbins bearing down on me in the corridor. She was in fact much too kind about the paper, but as she went off she said firmly, "Not my William III." Does each of us have our own William III? That would be a pity. Too much specialization involves both a failure of vision and a failure of scholarship, and until we become generalists again we shall not understand our own subject. It may help us if we try to take a look at William's own William III, and secondly at the view of him taken by his contemporaries.

Scholars write about worlds we do not live in and this puts added pressure on us to walk over the battlefields, visit the houses, and examine the artifacts that have been left behind. The fire at Hampton Court Palace was of course a tragedy. But it has been to a certain extent offset by the restoration of Het Loo, including the rediscovery of a basement room now identified as Queen Mary's confiture room. Are we faced here with a Protestant culinary tradition? If the queen sometimes made her own marmalade, which seems more likely now that we know the room in question to have been a confiture room and not a dairy, as was first thought, then we have a link with the court of Anne Boleyn, where marmalades made by the grandest ladies were in great demand.[1]

I am not about to propound a marmalade theory of history here. As it

---

[1] Eileen Harris, "Singing a Subterranean Song," *Country Life* 182 (1988), 250–52. Muriel St. Clare Byrne (ed.), *The Lisle Letters* (6 vols., University of Chicago Press, 1981), IV–VI.

95

happens, one of the few things we can be certain about in regard to the confiture room at Het Loo is that the queen never saw it. She may have commissioned it, to be sure; she may have looked over the plans with great care and attention. But she was never able to return to the Netherlands after the Revolution, and for her it remained a dream. A dream of the simple private life that someone in her position could not lead. Her husband's dreams were more ambitious, as we see when we look at the objects with which he surrounded himself. Some of the most beautiful of these were recently shown at the Cooper-Hewitt Museum in New York. The objects which were assembled for the "Courts and Colonies" exhibit were and are gorgeous. They have been recorded not only in a sumptuous catalogue but also in the October 13, 1988, issue of *Country Life*. Now even the most rural of country mice will be unable to ignore what William III thought of himself, which found expression in the objects he used every day, the houses and gardens he built as settings for his life, the propaganda which he was so careful and so astute in spreading across Europe for thirty years. In time, and with the assistance of a formidable group of Huguenot artists, he was able to make Louis XIV look unfashionable at home as he was fighting him to a draw on the battlefield. By the time the Nine Years War came to an end in 1697 English state beds were statelier than French ones, English gardens had winter plantings while French ones were left bare, English court silver was being produced in quantity and in styles of surpassing beauty while Louis XIV had had to melt down his plate as a contribution to the war effort. The Duchess of Orleans no longer recommended French clothing styles to her English friends, for the English were now setting the styles that French ladies copied.

The catalogue and the *Country Life* issue contain two important articles by Gervase Jackson-Stops, overlapping but not identical, which I would like to consider in their political implications.[2] Jackson-Stops posits the development of a court culture in the 1680s which he calls baroque. This is not the simple William and Mary style of the provinces and colonies, but a court style which included Tijou screens, Verrio staircases, state beds that might cost £470, solid silver suites of furniture, marquetry table tops, japanned or even boulle chests, and houses whose design was based ultimately on Nicolas Fouquet's great chateau Vaux-le-Vicomte. Only a very, very few individuals in England were capable of spending that kind of money or of understanding what it was all about. Among them were the Duke of Montagu at Boughton, the Duke of Somerset at Petworth, and William's secretary-at-war, William Blathwayt, at Dyrham Park. The private ends of these individuals in building, whatever they may have been, were usually satisfied by the construction of a single house. But William used the idiom of his generation for his own needs and,

---

[2] Gervase Jackson-Stops, "Courtiers and Craftsmen," *Country Life* 182 (1988), 200–9; "The Court Style in Britain," in Renier Baarsen, Jenny Greene, Leslie Geddes-Brown, and Clive Aslet (eds.), *Courts and Colonies: the William and Mary Style in Holland, England, and America* (New York, Cooper Hewitt Museum, distributed by University of Washington Press, 1988), pp. 36–61.

after purchasing the Huis ten Bosch, went on to build more of these houses than anyone else as settings for himself, the baroque hero-king. This court culture lasted down precisely to 1715, and was then replaced by a Palladianism which more accurately expressed the political realities of Georgian England.

What this baroque court culture tells art historians and ought to tell the rest of us is that personal monarchy survived the Revolution. In his own eyes, William was a Hercules, fighting to preserve Christianity from the monstrous forces of evil represented by Louis XIV (plate 3). In those days Hercules was an emblem of Christian fortitude, and also a figure of the warrior whose success brings peace and empire. But Hercules was also something of a house symbol of the family of Henry IV of France, a symbol adopted, for example, by the House of Savoy, which needed to demonstrate its place in the French line of succession. When William and the Savoyards used the Hercules figure they were among other things reminding people of their august origins. It would be unwise to forget that William was a great-grandson of Henry IV, just as it would be unwise to forget that Louis XIV was a great-grandson of Philip II. William was not merely Dutch William; like his cousin Eugene of Savoy he was also a French prince who had been deprived of his heritage by the Bourbon tyrant.

For the court of Henry IV, the Hercules emblem reflected the fact that their king was acknowledged supreme among Christian princes for his prowess in battle and political ability.[3] Hercules, the progenitor of the Houses of Navarre and Valois as well as Burgundy, was the sum of all virtues, a god of wisdom as well as physical strength. In classical mythology Hercules had not been very bright. His later intelligence came from his being identified with Hermes; but he was also identified with the Celtic god Ogmius, protector of Gallic peoples, the leader of armies and vanquisher of barbarians. The protector of church as well as state, the later Hercules is sometimes identified also with the Messiah by a reference to Isaiah xi: "righteousness shall be the girdle of his loins and faithfulness the girdle of his reins. The wolf also shall dwell with the lamb." It is interesting to note that in France the symbol of the Gallic Hercules faded away after 1605 and was scrapped on the assassination of Henry IV because of its antipapal connotations. But it does recur in the great Medici Cycle which the queen mother commissioned from Rubens in 1622. In the "Apotheosis of Henry IV," now in the Louvre, the hero is to be seen standing next that king.

The emblem of Hercules pointed out what should be evident to us all but is sometimes forgotten, namely that William was the only king of his generation other than John III Sobieski of Poland to lead his troops into battle. But there is much more to it than that. Both in 1672 and in 1688, he had led revolutions to restore legitimate government and the church. Success would bring peace and prosperity for the orthodox and toleration for the Dissenter, all in a

---

[3] Corrado Vivanti, "Henry IV, the Gallic Hercules," *Journal of the Warburg and Courtauld Institutes*, 30 (London, 1967), 176–97.

Christian and antipapal setting. It was not the most modest of messages, to be sure, and for that reason many Englishmen did not accept it, but it was not entirely inaccurate.

William's court culture, I would submit, is fundamentally humanist, continental, and sixteenth century in its thought patterns. Mary had a relatively easy time of it in justifying her conduct in the Revolution to herself. She might well argue that her church was in danger from James II, or that he was engaged in stealing her own inheritance. But William could only justify the Revolution to himself as the rescue of an oppressed people from slavery, a retelling in seventeenth-century costume of the great story of William the Silent and the struggle for Dutch freedom. As sovereign (of Orange) William III like his great-grandfather might lawfully intervene, especially if invited to do so, where subjects might not lawfully rebel. All this is in the *Apology* of William the Silent, as a great deal of contract theory is to be found in the *Abjuration* of 1581. Not all the artists involved in illustrating this theme were Protestant. Jean Tijou may have had a Catholic background; so had Rembrandt, for that matter, though his art is essentially Protestant. Antonio Verrio certainly was a Catholic, and would not paint for William III for some years after the Revolution. Fortunately, there were both Catholic and Protestant members of the Roettiers family, so that supplies of coins and medals never failed at the Mint, whoever was on the throne of England.

I would suggest that the Revolution of 1688, in the minds of those very few individuals who actually conducted it, was a war of religion, a throwback to the previous century. There were, of course, secular elements in the Revolution who wanted to establish what Dryden called a "Curtail'd Mungril Monarchy, half Commonwealth." But John Dryden had warned these people as early as 1681 that revolutions are hard to control:

suppose the business compassed, as they design'd it, how many, and how contradicting Interests are there to be satisfied! Every Sect of High Shooes would then be uppermost; and not one of them endure the toleration of another. And amongst them all, what will become of those fine Speculative Wits, who drew the Plan of this new Government, and who overthrew the old? For their comfort, the Saints will then account them Atheists, and discard them.[4]

To the fury of some Whigs, that is precisely what happened in England in the course of the year 1689.

If William thought of himself and wanted others to think of him as Hercules, as a great-grandson both of William the Silent and of Henry IV, and as the only legitimate grandson of Charles I, he managed to obtain recognition of many of his claims. He insisted, prudently as it turned out, on being king, and on being granted life tenure as king. He insisted on a great

---

[4] (John Dryden), *His Majesties Declaration Defended: In a Letter to a Friend Being An Answer To A Seditious Pamphlet, Called A Letter from a Person of Quality to his Friend: Concerning the Kings late Declaration touching the Reasons which moved him to Dissolve The Two Last Parliaments At Westminster and Oxford* (1681). The best modern edition, which I have used, is *The Works of John Dryden*, XVII: *Prose 1668–1691*, ed. Samuel Holt Monk (Berkeley, University of California Press, 1971), pp. 195–225. The quotations are from pp. 211–12.

war in alliance with the House of Austria, and won on that point too. This particular idea was not only not English, but neither Dutch nor Huguenot either. The concept for the Grand Alliance seems to have come to William from Franz von Lisola, the Habsburg diplomat.[5] It is the war that made the Revolution what it became in the long run, the occasion for the emergence of England as a great power for the first time since the death of Henry V in 1422. In the time of Elizabeth I and James I England had grown rich, rich enough to support a new culture that included the collecting of paintings and sculpture as well as books, the new art of the drama, and the courtly masque, powerful enough to lay the first foundation stones of empire. But the power that should have come from that wealth was for generations dissipated in faction. During the Interregnum the English appeared prematurely on the world stage only to sink back into relative obscurity during the Restoration. The reforms of Oliver had been unacceptable to most of the English simply because they came from Oliver, and in several cases good ideas had to be abandoned in 1660 because of their tainted source. 1660 demonstrated that the monarchy and the Church of England were still real elements in the power structure and that without them there was not much hope of achieving a satisfactory political equilibrium. A generation later the country was much richer and far more powerful. But the various power elites continued to be at loggerheads, and while that lasted England's true strength could not be deployed. Then in 1688 and 1689, to use the vulgar phrase, William got all his ducks in a row; and in that formation, they were very strong.

Jackson-Stops points out that the court style, as he calls it, begins with a few great country houses before the Revolution, sometime in the 1680s. By the same token, the new political and economic world of the eighteenth century has roots in the 1680s. Before about 1680 the empire did not amount to very much, and as late as 1688 England did 80 percent of its trade with Europe. But already the shift was beginning from the Thames valley and trade with the continent, towards the valley of the Severn, towards Bristol and Liverpool. Within a century England would do 80 percent of its trade outside Europe. Often this development is either forgotten or else conflated with the development of banking and the stock market in the 1690s, which is a mistake. The two went together, and they shared among other things a hatred of monopoly as well as a hatred of the Restoration monarchy, but they are two separate sets of events.

Already before 1688 England was probably better governed, in the technical sense, than almost any of the continental states. What was missing was a due concern for civil liberties, a due concern for the rights of private property, a due concern for the importance of Europe. By striking a bargain on these issues, the various elites were able to come together on a common program. The lawyers had been alienated since the packing of the bench by Charles II in roughly 1675. The younger generation of merchants, as Dr. De Krey has

---

[5] On this point, and some others, see my *William III* (London, Longman, Green, 1966).

pointed out in his fascinating book on London, had been opposed to the court for much the same time for their own reasons.[6] The Stop of the Exchequer in 1672, the collection of revenues in 1685 without parliamentary authority, the theft of the freeholds held by the dons of Magdalen, had been demonstrations of a frivolous attitude towards private property which must not be allowed to continue. Yet if the causes of the Revolution go back to, say, 1675, so do some of the solutions too. By then people were already talking of a marriage between William and Mary. By then people were already thinking of a solution which would involve increased authority for parliament and particularly for the House of Commons.

A few years ago there appeared a pleasant book with the title *The Reformation in Medieval Perspective.*[7] In history one should try to look forwards, not backwards. Most of the problems of English society were given a thorough airing in the debates of the three Exclusion Parliaments, and many of the solutions were proposed as well. At the time, the proposed solutions were rejected by the political nation as too radical, pipe dreams of Dryden's "fine speculative wits." But the most fascinating thing about the 1680s is that James II made the worst nightmares of Shaftesbury and Locke come true, and then that he tried to achieve his own goals through parliament. A suspending power was not enough for him; he insisted on the formal repeal of the Test Acts, and by doing so created a revolutionary situation.

Thus the demands for an extension of civil liberties, and for the extension of parliamentary authority, like the baroque court culture, have roots in the years before 1688 although their achievement comes afterwards. There were other strong elements of continuity in 1688 and in 1689. If several bishops became nonjurors, the majority cooperated. More important were the three great ladies, Mary herself, Anne, and the Queen Dowager Catherine of Braganza. Mary and Anne were central to the Revolution: without them there would not have been one in the first place, and without their daily continued support the Revolution would not have survived down to 1714. But it was more than convenient for all concerned that Queen Catherine, a Catholic, accepted the Revolution and went to call on William and Mary on the evening of February 13, the day they accepted the crown. Her complaisance made it easier to argue that William was the true heir of Charles II and that the interlude of James's reign was without significance. This was William the Restorer – not even Deliverer, much less Hercules.

William worked hard over the years to present himself as the immediate successor of Charles II. For this reason if no other he would have had no problem with the Hercules images in the two palaces of Charles II that we know much about, Windsor and Holyrood House. Charles II was no soldier and no hero; in those departments he needed all the help that propaganda

[6] Gary Stuart De Krey, *A Fractured Society: the Politics of London in the First Age of Party, 1688–1715* (Oxford, Clarendon Press, 1985).
[7] By Steven Ozment, *The Reformation in Medieval Perspective* (Chicago, Quadrangle Books, 1971).

could give him. But he was a grandson of Henry IV and thus entitled to use the family imagery as a cloak to cover his nakedness. After the Revolution this imagery ceased to be ridiculous.

In the years after 1689 the public found it easier to accept William as a great man, if not a Hercules, and Mary as the true queen. Thus the men of Enniskillen spoke in 1690 to William as to a hero: "our prospect was all black and dismal. Then it was that You, Sir, appear'd, like the Sun, to dispel those mists which had darken'd all our Sky. Your Declaration revived us from the very Grave, while it shew'd us a way only to stand by, and see the salvation of the Lord." Good Protestant theology, that, salvation without works. But their attitude towards Mary is quite different:

And what could we embrace with more delight, than to see the Crown, Madam, upon Your Royal Head, the next undoubted Heir to him who Abdicated it? Whose Virtues gave You as good a Title to the Election, as Your Blood to the Succession, in that Illustrious Line, which we Pray God may Reign over us till Time shall be no more.[8]

The difference is significant. William is the hero, a champion like Lohengrin. When he wins the fight he gets the girl, and may have whatever title he pleases; but Mary is Elsa, the Lady of Brabant. We must not carry this analogy too far, for in real life James Francis Edward was and remained an ugly duckling, not a swan.

The clergy were less restrained in their appreciation. To them William was David and James II Saul, from whom God had taken the government of Israel. In his sermon before the House of Commons on January 31, 1689, Gilbert Burnet made use of Psalm 144, not only alluding to William as David but also getting in a sly dig about the Prince of Wales: "Our Deliverer . . . delivered us from the hand of strange Children, whose Mouth speaketh Vanity, and whose Right Hand is a Right Hand of falsehood." The Psalm concludes with an appeal to the securing of property which was to be one chief blessing of the Revolution and Burnet called upon the Convention to assure "That our oxen may be strong to labour; that there be no breaking in, nor going out, nor complaining in our Streets, for happy is the people that is in such a Case, yea, and happy is the People whose God is the Lord."[9]

By the time of the Coronation, Burnet had moved on to Marcus Aurelius. Equating James II with Tiberius, Caligula, Nero, and Domitian, those "execrable monsters," he spoke of the revival of Roman happiness under Marcus Aurelius and demanded that the new king and queen demonstrate more than ordinary virtues if they were going to bring about a similar revival in England. But in the text of the sermon was another reference to David, and to his dying words:

[8] Andrew Hamilton, *A True Relation of the Actions of the Inniskilling-Men, from Their First Taking up of Arms in December, 1688 for the Defence of the Protestant Religion, and their Lives and Liberties* (London, 1690), pp. iv, ix.

[9] Gilbert Burnet, *A Sermon Preached before the House of Commons, On the 31st of January, 1688* (London, 1689), pp. 34–35. By his numbering it was Psalm 145.

> The God of Israel said,
> The Rock of Israel spake to me:
> He that ruleth over men, must be just,
> ruling in the fear of the Lord.
> And he shall be as the light of morning, when the Sun riseth;
> even a morning without clouds, as the tender grass
> Springing out of the earth by clear shining after rain.[10]

Already by the time of the Coronation there were people who felt that William was very far from being "like the light of morning at sunrise." Everyday living was a far cry from the ideals of the baroque court culture. It was difficult to get an audience; once an appointment had been obtained the audience was often unpleasant, for the king said little and granted less; petitions were not handled systematically; Bentinck was taking too many bribes, while William himself spent too much of his time in hunting.[11] The king himself remarked, "I can see that I am not made for this people, nor they for me." Soon the court was not full, a dangerous indication of society's displeasure, and it was not fun either. As the famous doggerel had it,

> The King thinks all.
> The Queen talks all.
> The Prince of Denmark drinks all.
> The Princess of Denmark eats all.
> The Lord Portland takes all.[12]

Nathaniel Johnston among others felt that the English had made a "dear bargain." For Johnston, King James had been a man of peace who promoted England's trade. The new government had to press men, and women too – to be made laundresses and nurses in order to fight the war. New and heavy taxes were a special burden, given "the perishing state" of the clothing trades, the mines, and the shoe industry. James's army, save for the three Tangier regiments, had been orderly. The men were all natives, the officers "younger brothers" suitably employed, rather than being "exposed to idleness, and all its vicious consequences. How many private Persons, unapt or unable to drive a Trade, were therein settled, in a Profession and Employment, which might maintain them competently, without danger of Gaols or Gallows?" William's army, on the other hand, was run by foreigners, including physicians who were better paid than English army doctors and yet did not prescribe good English medicines. The Presbyterians were the true victors of the Revolution, and we see Presbyterians or, worse, Erastians, getting all the promotions. James had been ruined for being too clement, too good to his enemies; but so long as this usurper held power, England could never be at peace. As Johnston put it:

---

[10] Gilbert Burnet, *A Sermon Preached at the Coronation of William III, and Mary II. King and Queen of England, ... France, and Ireland, Defenders of the Faith; In The Abby-Church of Westminster, April 11. 1689* (London, 1689), pp. 1, 6.

[11] *Journaal van Constantijn Huygens, den zoon, van 21 October 1688 tot 2 Sept. 1696* (2 vols., Utrecht, Kemink en zoon, 1876–77), II, p. 132.

[12] *Ibid.*, I, p. 126.

I am confounded, I must confess, with Horrour, to look onely back upon the Miseries we have hitherto felt; but when I consider that Pandora's box is but just open'd, and view a long Train of War, Famine, Want, Bloud, and Confusion, entailed upon us and our Posterity, as long as this Man, or any descended from him, shall possess the Throne, and see what a Gap is opened for every ambitious Person who can cajole the People to usurp it: These Considerations, I say, chill the Bloud in my Veins, and I cannot but lament my poor Countrie's Misfortunes with deepest Sighs and Groans.

The writer continued with an appeal to Englishmen not to keep up a

Government raised by Parricide and Usurpation, entered into by Violation of [William's] own Declaration, supported by the Overthrow of all our Laws Sacred and Civil, and the Perjury of the Nation. A Government under which we have suffered all hitherto related, to set up the Dutch, our Rivals, upon our Ruine, and from which we have gained nothing of what we aimed at, either as to the Establishment of our Religion, or our Property.[13]

During the spring and summer of 1689 there were increasing numbers of churchmen who would have agreed with Johnston, especially when it became clear that Presbyterianism would be established in Scotland. Over half the established clergy in that country lost their posts, and this, together with the Toleration Act and William's appointment of so many broad churchmen to high ecclesiastical office in England, infuriated the higher Anglicans. August of 1689 was probably the low point of the Revolution. Things were not going well at home, nor in Scotland, nor in Ireland. In his sermon Francis Carswell did what he could to cheer up those who attended the Berkshire assizes, held at Abingdon on August 6, and to shame those who had complained during the reign of James and were now complaining at the nature of their deliverance:

Thus when lately Rome threatned our Church with Idolatry,
France our nation with Slavery,
A corrupt pack'd Bench ready to decree it,
An Army encamp'd ready to enforce it,
A Prince resolute enough to attempt it,
Then all, as filled with Discontent, and sunk in Despair,
murmer out their Complaints, that their Religion is lost,
their Laws dispenc'd with and gone, the Government Arbitrary,
the Nation ruined, and themselves all undone; and cry out, *Help Lord, or else we perish.*

God heard and sent his Angel, and deliver'd us, and we are restor'd as at the first, and in the beginning, in so transcendent a manner, far beyond what in Reason we could wish or hope for, without effusion of Blood, or devastation of our Cities, that all must say, *It was the Lord's doing, and it is wonderful in our Eyes.*

And we being thus deliver'd, what is the meaning of all these lowings and bleatings in our Ears, discontents and murmerings, as tho' we design'd to confront Heaven, stubbornly to rebel against Providence, charge the most High with Injustice, and dare his Vengeance?

Tis just as if when God sent Samuel to tell Saul, that for his ill Government He had this day rent the Kingdom of Israel from him, and given it to David his Son-in-law, that was more righteous than himself, by whose hands He was resolv'd to save his people, and they had again reply'd, *We will not be saved after this manner,* by God's deposing the Father, and

---

[13] (Nathaniel Johnston), *The Dear Bargain. Or, A True Representation of the State of the English Nation under the Dutch* (London, 1689), pp. 4, 5, 7, 9, 24. He was, of course, a failed, or at least inactive, physician himself.

setting up his Son: *Save us by Saul in our own way, as best agrees with our humours, or save us not at all.*

How must this have provoked the holy One of Israel to have destroy'd until he had made an end, and their Land a desolation. Yet such as these may be found amongst us, as Fighters against God.[14]

If most Churchmen found it difficult to swallow the idea of William III as David, it was easier for them to agree with the idea of the Revolution as a restoration. August brought good news from Scotland, news at least better than before from Ireland, and the birth of the Duke of Gloucester. By the end of September, 1689, the Revolution was in fact established, though the seal would only be put on that establishment by the victory at the Boyne in July of 1690.

In contemporary perspective, then, the Revolution, whether it was a good thing as in the minds of Burnet and Carswell, or a bad thing as in the minds of Johnston and Dryden, was a religious and also an international event. One has only to leaf through the documents for 1689 in King William's Chest to see that it was a religious revolution, and as a religious revolution only a limited success; the plan for 1689 was to free the poor Protestants of the Cévennes. That portion of the Revolution failed. No contemporary ever denied the European character of the Revolution or its aftermath: William III and his Blue Guards, to say nothing of the taxes needed to support them, were far too visible ever to be forgotten.

A century later, commemorating the anniversary of the Revolution was complicated by attempts of the nonconformists to achieve a fuller degree of civil liberties. There was an increase in confessional strife in the later 1780s, and, at least at first, some nonconformist support for the French Revolution as that developed.[15] In England, at least, very few people found the prospect of democracy on the French model attractive; and where support appeared, in Scotland and in Ireland, it was suppressed.[16] It seems agreed that the reform movement of the 1780s aborted in large measure because of this English dislike for what the French were doing. For them, as for the men and women of the 1680s, there would have been no useful comparison between the two events. The English had got theirs right, the French had got theirs wrong, and that would have been that. There is a long, and I think not entirely erroneous, suspicion of general theories, both in English historical studies and in the field of English philosophy. And at least for the moment it might be well to think of the Revolution of 1688–89 as contemporaries spoke of it, *the* Revolution, a unique event.[17]

Half a century ago, when G. M. Trevelyan published his *The English*

[14] Francis Carswell, DD, *England's Restoration parallel'd in Judah's: or The Primitive Judge and Counsellor. In a Sermon Before The Honourable Judge at Abingdon Assizes, for the County of Berks. Aug. 6, 1689* (London, 1689), pp. 31–32.

[15] See John Money, *Experience and Identity: Birmingham and the West Midlands, 1760–1800* (Montreal, McGill–Queen's University Press, 1977).

[16] See, among others, Marianne Elliott, *Partners in Revolution: the United Irishmen and France* (New Haven, Yale University Press, 1982).

[17] Comparisons of 1789 with England 1640–60 seem more fruitful, at least to me, than comparisons with 1688–89.

Revolution 1688–1689[18] it was possible to write English history without many Scots, or Dutch, or women entering the picture. Trevelyan found little to say in that particular book about local history, or Shaftesbury, or crime, Ireland, or the colonies. Today his book still reads well, for Trevelyan was supreme as a prose stylist, but one finds errors even in the constitutional material which was for him the central theme. In these past fifty years we have learned a great many facts. But too many of us continue to write "central theme" histories, even when we write monographs. In a recent book, which is a good book, Gordon Rupp, in discussing *Religion in England 1688–1791*,[19] does not even mention the displacement of the Scottish clergy in 1689 as a factor in the disenchantment of English churchmen with the Revolution. And other experts, by concentrating on the purely English elements in the Revolution, give a slanted and two-dimensional picture of what actually went on. A more precise and richer picture than Trevelyan's, to be sure, but not a true one.

In the last half century much progress, and welcome progress, has been made in the fields of local history, social history, and political thought. There has been good work on the European character of the Revolution, and on the colonies to remind us of its world character. We pay more attention than we used to, to the women in history, and to the new field of women's history. Much work has been devoted to the buildings in which history was made, and to their decoration. Where we have failed, perhaps, has been in not putting these special studies together properly and in not putting them back into context. One way to do that is to pay more attention to William III and to his own view of himself. He may not have been a Hercules or a David, and he was certainly not a Christ figure; but he was, at least during his lifetime, the Revolution personified. From time to time the specialists get so caught up in their specialties that one might think the Revolution had consisted entirely of Locke, or of Dryden; but it should not be necessary to point out that neither of those was even present in any meaningful sense until the dangerous stage was all over. So long as he lived, William III was the Revolution as well as being the grand revolutionary. Perhaps his greatest contribution was in keeping revolution under control, as his greatest good fortune was that Anne chose to complete his work. In the end, of course, Shaftesbury and Locke won out. The Revolution after 1715, in its Palladian phase, was a very different thing from the Revolution in its early years. And by 1760 the wits had achieved their curtail'd mungril monarchy. But those changes are a function of the costs of the wars, and also a function of the extinction of the dynasty. Mary's death at the end of 1694, that of the Duke of Gloucester in 1700, and Anne's in 1714 even more perhaps than that of the king himself meant the end of baroque monarchy in England. But as William was fond of saying, he did not care how the world was like to go once he was out of it.

[18] Oxford University Press, 1938 and later editions.
[19] Oxford University Press, 1986.

7

The coronation of William and Mary, April 11, 1689

Lois G. Schwoerer

On Thursday, April 11, 1689, William and Mary, robed in crimson velvet and attended by spiritual and secular leaders, walked under a canopy of state along a cloth of blue from Westminster Hall to Westminster Abbey to be crowned king and queen of England.[1] There, at a moment of high solemnity in a ceremony whose traditional outward forms concealed many new features, they took a new coronation oath. The coronation ceremony and the oath offer a fresh and hitherto virtually unexplored perspective on the Glorious Revolution. Although the details of the ceremony have received exhaustive attention, and the oath has been the subject of comment in many constitutional and political histories, the political and ideological considerations involved in arranging the ceremony and devising the oath have largely escaped the attention of scholars.[2] In this essay I will argue that the coronation ceremony was self-consciously fashioned to look traditional, but that both it and the oath reflected the political and religious convictions and the partisan divisions and strengths of the principal leaders of the Revolution (plate 4).

The coronation of William and Mary was, of course, a ceremony that ancient custom required. Since the tenth century, a coronation ceremony and oath had officially and publicly solemnified the entry of every monarch upon his or her reign.[3] To be sure, every coronation ceremony is more or less a public spectacle that lifts the king and queen above all other subjects and invests the sovereign with the symbols of authority. But arguably the coronation of William and Mary, like those of Henry VII and Charles II, was especially important, for it symbolized the resolution of a severe crisis in church and state and gave the impression of unanimity and wholehearted support for the new regime. Further, the coronation in 1689 integrated the Dutch Calvinist king into the nation's dynastic tradition and its Anglican

---

[1] *An Exact Account of the Ceremonial at the Coronation Of Their Most Excellent Majesties King William and Queen Mary, The Eleventh Day of this Instant April, 1689* (published by Order of the Duke of Norfolk, Earl-marshal of England, London, 1689).

[2] For example, David Ogg, *England in the Reign of William III* (Oxford, Clarendon Press, 1955), pp. 235–39; Percy Ernst Schramm, *A History of the English Coronation*, trans. Leopold G. Wickham Legg (Oxford, Clarendon Press, 1937); William S. Holdsworth, *A History of English Law* (17 vols., London, Methuen, 1903–72), III, X, XIII.

[3] Schramm, *A History of the English Coronation*, pp. 1–26, *passim*.

Plate 4 Scene of the coronation of William and Mary in Westminster Abbey on April 11, 1689.
Engraving by Romeyn de Hooghe, 1689. The British Museum.

ritual. And more, it reinforced some aspects of the settlement embodied in the
Declaration of Rights which, as Prince and Princess of Orange, William and
Mary had accepted two months earlier, on February 13, when they were
proclaimed King and Queen of England.

The revolutionary settlement – a compromise between Tory and Whig
leaders carried out by a Convention, an irregularly elected body, whose status
and actions were, strictly speaking, illegal – did not meet with unanimous

favor. Indeed, publicly expressed opposition was immediate and continuing. On February 13, the very day of the proclamation, soldiers quartered in Cirencester prevented people from celebrating the event.[4] A week later an MP, commenting on the "ferment in the nation," remarked, "I think that the Clergy are out of their Wits"; if they had their way, "few or none of us" would be here. Echoing the point, another member declared, "I believe the black Coats and the red Coats to be the grievances of the Nation."[5] By the end of February Jacobite activity was so widespread that parliament temporarily suspended the *Habeas Corpus* Act, and in mid-March, responding to a serious crisis in the army, passed the first Mutiny Act.[6] On March 16, the same day the coronation was proclaimed, another proclamation branded as traitors anyone in arms against the new government and called upon "all" subjects to "Seize and Prosecute" them.[7] At the beginning of April, suspected papists and other disaffected persons were spreading sedition in London coffee houses.[8]

These tensions were aggravated by a host of issues. Among them were the still unresolved questions of the relationship between the Church of England and nonconformist groups and of how to adjust the oath of allegiance to ease the conscience of people who scrupled at violating their oath of allegiance previously taken to James II. Discord also attended the new king's foreign policy which was drawing the nation into war to defend the Netherlands and Protestantism from Catholic France and to protect England from James II, who, with French help, had landed troops in Ireland. The war required men and supplies and, above all, the money to pay for them, which, of course, meant higher taxes. Plans for the coronation, then, went forward within this broader context of disaffection with the political settlement, expectations still unrealized of a religious settlement, and the urgent needs generated by new international and military policies.[9]

For these reasons, it is a near certainty that the new government looked to the coronation to assist in legitimating the Revolution and reassuring domestic and foreign observers of the government's stability. The speed with which the Privy Council appointed a committee to consider the "time and manner of the coronation" suggests as much; they turned to that task on February 26, just three days after the Convention, in an effort to enhance its legal status, transformed itself by statute into the Convention parliament.[10]

---

[4] Anchitell Grey, *Debates in the House of Commons, from the Year 1667 to the Year 1694* (10 vols., London, 1763), IX, p. 110.

[5] *Ibid.*, pp. 98, 112; cf. p. 131.

[6] *Ibid.*, pp. 130–36. See Henry Horwitz, *Parliament, Policy and Politics in the Reign of William III* (Manchester University Press, 1977), p. 21; and C. Ellestad, "The Mutinies of 1689," *Journal of the Society for Army Historical Research* 53 (1975), 4–21.

[7] PRO, SP 45/13, no. 18. Also, BL, Ms. Loan 29/184, fols. 188, 196.

[8] *CSPD*, 1689–90, p. 53.

[9] See Horwitz, *Parliament, Policy and Politics in the Reign of William III*, ch. 2, for an overview of these months.

[10] PRO, Privy Council Register, PC 2/73, p. 19. Extracts from the Register are printed in J. Wickham Legg (ed.), *Three Coronation Orders*, Henry Bradshaw Society (London, Harrison 1900), XIX, Appendix 2. See also Lois G. Schwoerer, "The Transformation of the Convention into a Parliament," *Parliamentary History* 3 (1984), 57–76. The committee for the coronation included not only the earl-marshal, the Duke of Norfolk, the officer of the crown traditionally in charge of public ceremonies, but also the chief officers of the new regime, among them the Lord

So, too, does the decision, reached in mid-March, to hold the coronation on Thursday, April 11, thus allowing less than a month to complete what had become exceedingly complicated arrangements.[11] The result was frenzied activity. A flurry of orders went out from the committee of the Privy Council: to the Master of the Great Wardrobe (Ralph, Lord Montagu) for refurbishing or making new gowns, suits, gloves, and shoes; to the Master of the Jewel House (Sir Gilbert Talbot) for refitting the crowns and scepters and making a crown for Mary; to the King's Master of the Works (Christopher Wren) for erecting scaffolding and galleries in the Abbey; and to others to coordinate musicians and trumpeters, print admission tickets, spruce up the House of Lords, supply covered chamber pots, assign seventy-two people to their proper places in the procession and print that information, request the king to order the number and placement of guards to prevent disturbances, and so on and on.[12] Working under such constraints of time, people made mistakes. For example, an escutcheon was erected in the wrong place and had to be removed. Someone had forgotten to supply the king with coins for the first oblation, which created an awkward moment in the ceremony. On returning to Westminster Hall for the traditional banquet, the procession took a wrong turn. The banquet ran over time and the formalities of serving the second course were omitted. The Officers of Arms (or Heralds) complained bitterly that the committee failed to consult them and that no complete plan was presented, as in the past, "which gave [them] much trouble."[13]

For the new government to regard the coronation as a way to quiet tensions was consistent with King William's previous practices and policies. Processions, ceremonies, and the use of symbols of authority had been an important feature of politics during the months of revolution. To celebrate the proclamation of the new monarchs on February 13, the Convention Parliament arranged for a "presentation ceremony" in the Banqueting Hall, a procession preceding and another following the ceremony, and other public displays of approval.[14] Five days later, William used political symbols to underscore his

President, Thomas Osborne, Earl of Danby; the Lord Privy Seal, George Savile, Marquess of Halifax; the Lord Great Chamberlain, Robert Bertie, Earl of Lindsey; and the Lord Steward, William Cavendish, Earl of Devonshire.

[11] PRO, Lord Chamberlain's Papers, LC 2/13 (2), no. 1. The date was first fixed as April 12, but changed for unknown reasons to the 11th. The traditional coronation order (the *Liber regalis*, the fourth Latin recension, which was translated into English for the coronation of James I) called for the ceremony to be held on a Sunday or holy day; the 11th was neither, the choice underscoring, whether deliberately or not, the Protestantism of the new regime. See Legg (ed.), *Three Coronation Orders*, p. 133. Gibbs, *Complete Peerage*, II, Appendix F, gives the dates of accession and coronation of most monarchs from Richard II through George V. The lapse of time between the two dates ranges from 10 to 357 days.

[12] CA, Ms. Steer, no. 6, p. 20, no. 14, p. 53; PRO, LC 2/13 (2), nos. 2–6, 8, 10, 34; PRO, LC 428, fol. 4; BL, Harleian Ms. 6815, fols. 148r.–v; BL, Add. Ms. 6307, fols. 30r.–v; BL, Egerton Ms. 3350, XXVII, fols. 11–12v.

[13] CA, Ms. L 19, Ceremonials, p. 117; CA, Ceremonials Steer, no. 14, fol. 14; BL, Harleian Ms. 6815, fol. 152v. For the story of the coins, see *The Life of The Right Honourable and Right Reverend Dr. Henry Compton* (London, 1715), p. 49. The banquet was more than a meal; to contemporaries it symbolized an ancient way of ratifying compacts: *Reflection Upon the Late Great Revolution*, in *A Collection of State Tracts, Publish'd on Occasion of the Late Revolution in 1688. And during the Reign of King William III. To which is Prefix'd The History of the Dutch war in 1672. Translated from the French Copy printed at Paris in 1682. which was supprest at the Instance of the English Embassador, because of the Discoveries it made of the League betwixt the King of France and England for enslaving Europe, and Introducing the Popish Religion into These Kingdoms, and the United Provinces. With a Table of the several Tracts in this Volume, and an Alphabetical Index of Matters*, 3 vols. (London, 1705–6), I, p. 256.

[14] Lois G. Schwoerer, "The Glorious Revolution as Spectacle," in Stephen B. Baxter (ed.), *England's Rise to Greatness, 1660–1763* (Los Angeles, University of California Press, 1983), pp. 109–49.

authority and help achieve the swift introduction and passage of the Bill to make the Convention a legal parliament. Employing color and sound to attract attention, he came from Whitehall to the House of Lords by royal barge with kettledrums beating and trumpets blowing. Once in the Upper Chamber, he addressed the assembly seated on his throne, garbed in royal robes, and "adorned with His Regal crown and Ornaments," a moment memorialized in a picture by a Dutch engraver B. Stoopendahl (plate 5). William's appearance in his regal robes with the crown on his head violated custom and provoked adverse comment, but it also signaled his regal authority *before* the coronation ceremony.[15] William may have taken this step to counter the theory, appearing in manuscript, that the king had no authority until he took his coronation oath.[16] Yet his English advisors must have known that in 1608 judges in Calvin's case had resolved that the coronation was at law "but a royal ornament . . . [and] no part of the title" and that "there can be no interregnum."[17] Still, in William's case, there *had* been an interregnum; his reign dated not from the death of a predecessor, but from the proclamation of the settlement on February 13.[18] The gesture of crown-wearing apparently was significant to William, for he wore his crown a second time when he assented to the Bill for the new coronation oath on April 9, two days before the ceremony.[19]

The coronation ceremony also provided an opportunity for the king to reward his supporters and to win over men who were undecided. In other words, the coronation played a part in the patronage system of the new regime. Following a tradition established by Richard II, William granted eleven coronation peerages; for example, elevating Prince George of Denmark, the husband of the jealous and contentious Princess Anne, to a dukedom, rewarding Thomas Osborne, the Earl of Danby, with a marquisate, and making Henry Sidney a viscount. Particular effort was made to get the patent sealed for a viscountcy for Richard Lumley to enable him to "walk in that quality" in the coronation procession.[20]

At the same time, the court was at pains to reassure persons and corporations that claimed an ancient right to a role in the coronation proceedings that their rights, which carried fees and gifts, some substantial in value, would be honored.[21] The proclamation of the coronation, issued on March 16, included

---

[15] Schwoerer, "The Transformation of the Convention into a Parliament," p. 58. By the middle of the thirteenth century the king did not wear his crown when appearing in public on nonceremonial occasions. See Schramm, *The English Coronation*, pp. 59–61.

[16] BL, Hargreaves Ms. 497, fols. 20r.–v.   [17] Holdsworth, *A History of English Law*, III, p. 464.

[18] The statute book refers to "Statutes of King William and Queen Mary Made in the Session of Parliament, Begun to be holden at Westminster, on the Thirteenth Day of February," which was clearly a fiction.

[19] Legg (ed.), *Three Coronation Orders*, Appendix 4, p. 75.

[20] Gibbs, *Complete Peerage*, II, Appendix F, p. 653. *CSPD*, 1689–90, p. 51. In further gestures of good will towards Princess Anne, the committee assigned George a prominent place in the procession, ordered his train to be carried, and gave him precedence in paying homage to the new monarchs. CA, Ceremonials, Steer, no. 14, fol. 48v. PRO, C57/7, Coronation Roll. Edward Gregg, *Queen Anne* (London and Boston, Routledge and Kegan Paul, 1980), p. 72, must be mistaken to say that because of Anne's pregnancy she and George went incognito to the coronation.

[21] For the value of some fees: BL, Hargreaves Ms. 497, fols. 18–19; Francis Sandford, *The History of the Coronation of the Most High, Most Mighty, and Most Excellent Monarch, James II. By the Grace of God, King of England, Scotland, France and Ireland. Defender OF The Faith, And of His Royal Consort Queen Mary: Solemnized in the Collegiate Church of St. Peter in the City of Westminster, on Thursday the 23 of April* (London, 1687), pp. 126–85.

the announcement that the king had appointed an *ad hoc* Court of Claims (an ancient mechanism going back to the fourteenth century) to hear petitions on this subject.[22] Reflecting an earlier feudal relationship between king and great men, the rights included the unusual one of the Lord of Warsop Manor, whose role was to present the king with a right-hand glove and support his right arm while he held the scepter with the cross.[23] But one of the claims held important political implications: the city of London entered a claim to serve *both* the king and queen as chief butler, on grounds that anciently they had served the regnant monarch, the king, and now should serve the regnant monarchs, the king and queen.[24] The petition opened the questions of precedents (there were none), the nature of Mary's role, and what it would mean to the queen's position if the claim were denied. After lengthy debate, members of the court decided to grant the petition, thereby doubling the fees of the city, but preserving the fiction that the queen's power was equal to the king's.

A role in the coronation ceremonies was a sign of the individual's status and prestige and for some men was a coveted honor, but it also marked that individual as a champion of the new regime and provided visual testimony of his commitment. With that thought in mind, the Privy Council took steps to assure a good turn-out. The proclamation of the coronation also contained a threat. It charged everyone of "what Rank or quality Soever" who by "letters" directed to them, or by "reason of their Offices or Tenures or otherwise are to do any service" at the ceremony to perform that service "under peril," unless specifically excused.[25] Clearly, the government wanted to avoid the embarrassing absenteeism that had marred the February 13 "presentation ceremony," when only three bishops and 35–41 secular lords out of a possible 153 lords showed up.[26] Indeed, the government was more successful, for, although observers noticed absentees, in fact ten bishops and at least 81 secular lords were present at the coronation.[27]

The responsibility for arranging the ceremony (as distinct from the setting) was placed largely in the hands of Henry Compton, the Bishop of London and only cleric appointed to the Privy Council, who was added to the committee

---

[22] PRO, PC2/73 Privy Council, pp. 32–33; HLRO, Records of the Lord Great Chamberlain's Office, 10/2/1/20, 43, 44 (hereafter LGC). Gregory King, the current registrar of the College of Heralds, was asked to serve as registrar of the Court of Claims. The proclamation is reproduced in Legg, *Three Coronation Orders*, pp. 68–69. See Anne Sutton and P. W. Hammond (eds.), *The Coronation of Richard III. The Extant Documents* (Gloucester and New York, Alan Sutton and St. Martin's Press, 1983, 1984), pp. 245–53 for the early Court of Claims.

[23] CA, Ms. Steer, no. 6, p. 17. The Lord Great Chamberlain claimed the right, with the Lord Chamberlain, to dress the king in his shirt, undertrousers, breeches, and crimson silk stockings. HLRO, LGC, 10/2/1/37.

[24] CA, Ceremonials Steer, No. 9 R 21, no pagination. At Richard III's coronation, the city won the right to serve the consort queen: Sutton and Hammond (eds.), *The Coronation of Richard III*, p. 247.

[25] For the proclamation, see above, n. 22. For some excuses, *CSPD, 1689–90*, pp. 49, 55.

[26] Lois G. Schwoerer, *The Declaration of Rights, 1689* (Baltimore and London, Johns Hopkins University Press, 1981), p. 252.

[27] BL, Harleian Ms. 6815, fols. 170r.–v.; DWL, Roger Morrice, "Entr'ing Book, being an Historical Register of Occurrences from April, Anno, 1677 to April 1691," 4 vols., II, p. 530 (I have used a photocopy of the original [now in my possession] from the library of the late Douglas R. Lacey); CA, Ms. L 19. Ceremonials, p. 77; Andrew Browning (ed.), *Memoirs of Sir John Reresby* (Glasgow, Jackson, 1936), p. 571; S. W. Singer (ed.), *Correspondence of Henry Hyde, Earl of Clarendon, and of his Brother Laurence Hyde, Earl of Rochester* (2 vols., London, 1828), II, p. 269.

for the coronation on March 5.[28] The choice of Compton to serve on the planning committee presaged the decision to select him to officiate at the coronation service in the place of William Sancroft, Archbishop of Canterbury, who, after wrestling with his conscience, finally refused to participate.[29] The Archbishop of Canterbury had traditionally played the premier clerical role in the coronation service.[30] To deal with this departure from custom, authors of the statute that established the new coronation oath provided that the king – no mention is made of the queen – should appoint one of the archbishops or bishops "of this Realm of England" to administer the oath.[31] Although the surviving record is silent on the matter, William probably chose Compton, who had signed the invitation to him, because of his reputation for militant opposition to popery, and possibly because of Mary's affection for her former tutor.

Compton and the committee "stage-managed" the traditional ceremony (which had been modified in 1685 largely by Sancroft for the coronation of the Catholic James II)[32] to underscore within its ancient forms certain religious and political principles. One principle was the Protestant character of the new regime. Working from papers and books respecting James II's coronation,[33] Compton made several liturgical changes, some with political and religious overtones. Such a change was the reintroduction of the Anglican communion service, which had been omitted at James II's coronation because he was Catholic. Following the ancient precedent of Archbishop Egbert, Compton placed the coronation service in the middle of the Eucharist. Queen Mary was "very much against" the step, because she believed it was taken out of "worldly considerations" not religious ones, to underline the difference from her father. She also feared that she would be ill prepared to take communion because the coronation ceremony was so full of "pomp and vanity." All her life she blamed herself for doing so.[34]

The Bible was the most important symbol of Protestantism in the ceremony, and Compton significantly enlarged its role. One innovation was to place the Bible – a specially printed quarto-sized volume richly decorated

[28] PRO, PC 2/73, pp. 1, 27. Edward F. Carpenter, *The Protestant Bishop, being a Life of Henry Compton, 1631–1713, Bishop of London* (London and New York, Longman, Green, 1956).

[29] *The Auto-Biography of Simon Patrick, Bishop of Ely*, ed. J. H. Parker (Oxford, J. H. Parker 1839), pp. 139–40; Bodl., Tanner Ms., vol. 28, fols. 378, 380, 381. The summons to Sancroft to attend the coronation, dated March 21, 1689, still left open the archbishop's decision. Scholars debate whether Sancroft's commission, dated March 15, empowered suffragan bishops (of which Compton was one) to perform the coronation. The Archbishop of York attended the ceremony, but apparently was not considered as surrogate for Canterbury.

[30] By the early thirteenth century, the right of the Archbishop of Canterbury to crown the sovereign was established: Schramm, *A History of the English Coronation*, pp. 40–45.

[31] *SR*, VI, pp. 56–57. See the appendix to this chapter for the oath in 1685 and 1689 taken from E. Neville Williams, *The Eighteenth-Century Constitution 1688–1815: Documents and Commentary* (Cambridge University Press, 1960), pp. 36–39.

[32] Sandford, *The History of the Coronation of the Most High, Most Mighty, and Most Excellent Monarch, James II*. For changes in the ceremony for James II, see Legg (ed.), *Three Coronation Orders*, pp. xvi–xxx.

[33] An undated order from the earl-marshal appointed Gregory King to prepare a detailed account of James II's coronation: CA, Ms. vol. 4 Ceremonials, Steer, no. 6, p. 10. Compton asked Sancroft to send him his coronation papers: Bodl., Tanner Ms. 27, fol. 8. Sandford's printed account of James's coronation was also available.

[34] R. Doebner (ed.), *Memoirs of Mary Queen of England (1689–93) Together With Her Letters And Those of Kings James II. and William III. To The Electress, Sophia of Hanover* (London, Leipzig, Veit, and London, D. Nutt, 1886), p. 13.

with gold fringe and gold edging lace[35] – among the regalia and to present it to William and Mary in the ceremony in Westminster Hall that immediately preceded that in Westminster Abbey. Another was to carry the Bible in the procession to the Abbey, Compton himself displaying it before the people who lined the way.[36] In the Abbey service, Compton, continuing the practice followed by Elizabeth I, King Charles I, and James II, arranged for the monarchs to kiss the Bible after they had confirmed their oath at the altar with their hands on the Bible, gestures that replicated proceedings in ordinary law courts.[37] Their kissing the Bible, a symbol of a personal commitment to God's word, inspired de Hooghe to show Mary kissing the Bible in one of his coronation engravings (plate 6). Another innovation – called a "stroke of genius" by a later commentator[38] – was to present the Bible itself to the king and queen after they were crowned, the bishop admonishing them to make it "the Rule of [their] whole life and Government" and describing it as the "most valuable thing that this World affords."[39] Clearly, Compton thought it appropriate for the Bible to figure prominently in the coronation of a king who had come to England avowedly to rescue the nation's Protestant religion.

Another signal of the strong Protestant bent of the new government at this time was the choice of Dr. Gilbert Burnet (newly elevated to the Bishopric of Salisbury) to deliver the sermon. Burnet had long been identified with Whig leaders, especially Lord William Russell (who was executed as a traitor in 1683). Following the Rye House Plot, Burnet sought refuge in the Netherlands, where he became a self-styled advisor to the prince and a confidant of the princess. Returning to England with William, he had a role in the negotiations for the settlement. Taking as his text 2 Samuel xxiii. 3–4, which begins: "The God of Israel spake to me, He that ruleth over men must be just, ruling in the fear of God," Burnet exhorted the new king and queen to follow the Biblical injunction and "make the Law the Measure of their Will." Defining a just government as one consonant with the "principles of Reason," well exemplified in the reign of Marcus Aurelius, Burnet boldly linked his remarks to the current debate over religion by declaring that a just government did not intrude into "God's Immediate Province ... Mens Consciences."[40] The

[34] R. Doebner (ed.), *Memoirs of Mary Queen of England (1689–93) Together With Her Letters And Those of Kings James II. and William III. To The Electress, Sophia of Hanover* (London, Leipzig, Veit, and London, D. Nutt, 1886), p. 13.

[35] PRO, LC 2/13 (3), n.p.

[36] *An Exact Account of the Ceremonial*, p. 2. Legg (ed.), *Three Coronation Orders*, pp. 20, 94, 112. On her way to her coronation Queen Elizabeth I kissed and pressed to her bosom a richly bound Bible presented to her by a woman in white. David Cressy, "Books as Totems in Seventeenth-Century England and New England," *The Journal of Library History* 21 (1986), 97; *The Entire Ceremonies of the Coronation of His Majesty King Charles II. and her Majesty Queen Mary, Consort to James II* (London, 1761), Appendix, pp. 37–38.

[37] Cressy, "Books as Totems," p. 98. C. G. Bayne, "The Coronation of Queen Elizabeth," EHR 22, (1986) 670; Charles Wordsworth (ed.), *The Manner of the Coronation of King Charles The First of England At Westminster, 2 Feb., 1626*, Henry Bradshaw Liturgical Text Society (London, 1892), pp. lv, 24. Legg (ed.), *English Coronation Records*, p. 297.

[38] J. Perkins, *The Crowning of the Sovereign* (London, Methuen, 1937), pp. 89–90, quoted in Carpenter, *The Protestant Bishop*, p. 151.

[39] *An Exact Account of the Ceremonial*, p. 3. Legg (ed.), *Three Coronation Orders*, pp. 27–28. The Bible, now at the Hague, bears Mary's inscription, "This book was given to the King and I [*sic*] at our crownation." See *William and Mary 1689 Coronation & Royal Visits, 1989* (London, William and Mary Tercentenary Trust, 1989), p. 4.

[40] *A Sermon Preached at the Coronation of William III. and Mary II. King and Queen of England* (London, 1689), p. 9; cf. pp. 5, 7, 11, 13, 18.

Plate 6 Queen Mary kisses the Bible during the coronation ceremony. Engraving by Romeyn de Hooghe, 1689. The Henry E. Huntington Library, San Marino, California.

sermon, translated into Dutch, French, and German, was well received, John Locke, no special friend of Burnet, praising it.[41]

Further modifications to the traditional ceremony were required to reflect the nature of the dual monarchy, a constitutional innovation created to convey the impression of legitimacy and to satisfy the Tories. The committee for the coronation took the symbols of Mary's majesty seriously, querying whether she should walk under the canopy of state with the king and ordering the items in the regalia duplicated.[42] To distinguish her from a consort queen, who would have received the crown kneeling at the steps of the High Altar, a special coronation chair, "like unto St. Edwards Chaire," was ordered to be built.[43] Although Mary was widely seen as a regnant queen, the settlement had, in fact, lodged regal power in William alone. Thus, subtle gestures were devised to indicate that she was not her husband's equal. He was anointed first; the spurs were touched to his heel alone; the sword was girt about him alone; the armilla (or stole) was given to him alone; and he was crowned first.[44] These distinctions carried a significant message.

Compton and his committee also found ways in the ceremony to evoke the memory of Charles II: the order of the procession, it was said, followed that of Charles's coronation procession. Effigies of the king were on display in the Abbey; and final prayers mentioned by name the Dowager Queen Catherine.[45] Surely these gestures aimed to reinforce the legitimacy of the new regime and cultivate the good will of Tories.

Members of the House of Commons had no part in these arrangements, except for two requests, both reflecting their increased self-consciousness and the fact that parliament was in session (for the first time since 1485 at the time of a coronation) and hence many members were in town. One request was that General Frederick Schomberg provide foot soldiers to protect *them*[46] and the other that they be seated together in the Abbey in a place that would allow them to see clearly the unfolding ceremony. In response, the Privy council ordered Wren to erect a special gallery, which he constructed on the north side, facing the throne, and for the first time MPs were able to see the act of anointing.[47] In addition, the king sent members a message inviting them to

---

[41] E. S. de Beer (ed.), *The Correspondence of John Locke* (8 vols., Oxford, Clarendon Press, 1976–89), III, p. 611.

[42] BL, Egerton Ms. 3350, fol. 17; PRO, PC 2/73, p. 40.

[43] PRO, LC 2/13, p. 7. The chair, made of wood and rather crudely decorated, became the property of the Dean and Chapter of Westminster Abbey; over the years pupils at Westminster School carved their initials on it. Not used again since the coronation of 1689, the chair today is on display behind glass in the Abbey's Museum undercroft.

[44] Legg (ed.), *Three Coronation Orders*, pp. 5, 21–26, 79, 103. The decision not to gird Mary with the sword was deliberate, for a sword was originally ordered for the Queen "to be girt with." See PRO, LC 2/13, p. 3. The two precedent regnant queens, Mary I and Elizabeth I, received these marks of sovereignty. See Antonio Guaras, *Accession of Queen Mary*, ed. Richard Garnett (London, Laurence and Bullen 1892), p. 121; Bayne, "The Coronation of Queen Elizabeth," pp. 654, 669.

[45] BL, Harleian Ms. 6815, fol. 140 (for the procession); Westminster Abbey Muniment Room, WAM 51126; Legg (ed.), *Three Coronation Orders*, p. 34.   [46] *CJ*, x, p. 85.

[47] PRO, LC 2/13, p. 10. The Commons appointed a committee to confer with Wren about the accommodations: *CJ*, pp. 10, 82. See E. S. de Beer (ed.), *The Diary of John Evelyn* (6 vols., Oxford University Press, 1955), IV, 633, n. 1. BL, Add. Ms. 6307, fol. 31. *An Exact Account*, p. 3, asserted that the regal chairs were placed so as to make the monarchs "more Conspicuous" to MPs.

watch the coronation, to have special seats in Westminster Hall to observe the banquet, and to be his guest at a dinner later in the Exchequer Chamber. They also received the official coronation medal, in gold. But, as the king explained, it was "not so convenient for the House to bear any part in the ceremony itself."[48] The very fact that he went to the trouble to say anything like this is worthy of notice; contemporaries certainly commented on the courtesies extended to the Commons.[49]

At the same time that the coronation ritual was being revised, members of the House of Commons were drafting a new coronation oath. Before 1689, with only one exception – in 1308, when the barons imposed an oath on Edward II[50] – clergymen had assumed that responsibility. But in 1689 the Commons, without objection to their doing so (if the surviving record is complete), took on the task. This fact also reveals a change in their position.

It was predictable that the House of Commons would make some changes in the coronation oath, because in the Convention debates and in the press over the past several months men had indicated the need to do so. Interest in the coronation oath was not new: the oath had had a place in politics and political speculation for the entire century, and beyond. Medieval sources – especially the *Modus Tenendi Parliamentum*, the Mirror of Justice, and the works of Bracton, Fleta, and Sir John Fortescue – had discussed the nature of the oath. Medieval authors maintained that the oath bound the monarch to preserve the nation's customs and laws, and that if he failed to do so, he ceased to be king. The successive confirmation of Magna Carta and of the mythical Laws of King Edward the Confessor, reference to which had been in the coronation oath since 1308, supported this view. A section of the Confessor's Laws, the "Office of a King," explicitly conveyed the message that if a king ruled badly he deposed himself; the allegiance of the people was dissolved and they were empowered to elect another king. Also associated with King Edward was his sword, Curtana, mentioned in coronation records from the fourteenth century as a symbol of the primacy of law. A flat, square-tipped sword, Curtana was carried in the 1689 coronation procession, a visual reminder of Edward the Confessor.[51] The Confessor's Laws and other apocrypha – the *Modus* and the Mirror of Justice – were accepted as genuine by late Tudor and early Stuart scholars and legal authorities, and knowledge of them spread in manuscript and in printed accounts from the late sixteenth century onwards.[52]

---

[48] CJ, x, p. 82; *An Exact Account of the Ceremonial*, p. 3; de Beer, *Evelyn's Diary*, IV, p. 633; Browning (ed.), *Reresby's Memoirs*, pp. 571–72; CA, Ms. 19, Ceremonials, p. 88v.

[49] De Beer (ed.), *Evelyn's Diary*, IV, p. 633; Browning, *Memoirs of Reresby*, pp. 171–72.

[50] See Robert S. Hoyt, "The Coronation Oath of 1308," *EHR* 71 (1956), 370–83. See Hoyt's n. 2 for scholarship on this controversial oath.

[51] Arthur Taylor, *The Glory of Regality* (London, 1820), pp. 72, 74; Janelle Greenberg, "The Confessor's Laws and the Radical Face of the Ancient Constitution," *EHR* 104 (1989), 616, n. 4.

[52] The classic statement on the power of ancient texts is J. G. A. Pocock, *The Ancient Constitution and the Feudal Law: a Study of English Historical Thought in The Seventeenth Century. A Reissue with a Retrospect* (Cambridge University Press, 1987). For the importance of the Confessor's Laws, see Greenberg, "The Confessor's Laws," 617–18; for "Office of a King," 620, and n. 2 for circulation. Also, Corinne Weston, "'Holy Edward's Laws': the Cult of the

Throughout the seventeenth century the oath became embedded in political debate and treatises as the king and his critics argued over the nature of kingship. Representing a royal viewpoint, James I, in *The Trew Law Of Free Monarchies*, redefined the oath not as a contract between king and people, but as a promise to the people to rule "honourably" and argued that only God could decide if the promise were broken. Later, however, in his 1610 speech to parliament, James declared that in a settled state the coronation oath bound the king to observe the "fundamentall Lawes of his kingdom" and was a covenant as strong as "that paction which God made with Noe after the deluge."[53] Interest in the oath sharpened during the Civil Wars. Debate centered on the meaning of the Latin clause, *quas vulgus elegerit*, words that had appeared in the oath before the time of Charles I. To reaffirm the king's veto power over legislation, royalists declared in 1642 that *elegerit* meant "hath chosen," while anticourt writers, in an effort to deny the monarch the veto power, maintained that the word meant "will choose."[54] The clause figured in the 1644 trial of Archbishop William Laud, who was accused of removing the clause in the oath administered to King Charles I to enlarge royal power.[55] The climax of the issue in the early seventeenth century came at the treason trial of Charles I, who was charged with violating his coronation oath.[56] In *Eikon Basilike* (a collection of the king's prayers and essays purportedly written during his confinement), Charles denied that the "crown of England [is] bound by any coronation oath in a blind and brutish formality." Maintaining that he had fulfilled his oath by governing by the laws to which he had consented, he declared that a king need not accept laws contrary to his conscience.[57] Responding in *Eikonoklastes*, John Milton excoriated the king's position as the "mark of a tyrant." Arguing that the king was beneath law and parliament, Milton asserted that the coronation oath required the monarch to assent to laws passed by parliament.[58] Milton included a well-known story about the Emperor Trajan to highlight his account of the relationship of the king to law: Trajan, handing a sword to his general, said,

---

Confessor and the Ancient Constitution," in Gordon J. Schochet (ed.), *Restoration, Ideology, and Revolution*, Folger Institute Center for the History of British Political Thought, v (Washington, D. C., Folger Shakespeare Library, 1990), pp. 319–38.

[53] *The Trew Law Of Free Monarchies: Or The Reciprock And Mutual Duetie Betwixt A Free King, And His Naturall Subjects*, repr. in Charles H. McIlwain (ed.), *The Political Works of James I* (Cambridge, Mass., Harvard University Press, 1918), pp. 68, 309. The author of *Reflections upon the Opinions of some Modern Divines, concerning the Nature of Government in general, and that of England in particular*, in *State Tracts*, 1, 505 drew upon James's speech. The king's works were in the library of at least one member of the Convention, Sir Richard Temple. (See HEHL, Stowe Mss., Catalogue of Temple's Library, Stt. ci & 1, Box 2, 1641 to eighteenth century.)

[54] Corinne Weston and Janelle Greenberg, *Subjects and Sovereigns: the Grand Controversy over Legal Sovereignty in Stuart England* (Cambridge University Press, 1981), pp. 62, 64, 79–80, 292 n. 55.

[55] Wordsworth (ed.), *The Manner of the Coronation of King Charles The First*, pp. xl, lvii–lxv, examines the controversy over the validity of the charge brought by the then radical-thinking William Prynne.

[56] Don M. Wolfe (ed.), *Complete Prose Works of John Milton* (8 vols., New Haven, Yale University Press, 1953–82), iii, pp. 88–89. The charge is in J. G. Muddiman, *Trial of King Charles the First* (Edinburgh and London, 1928), pp. 78–79.

[57] Philip Knachel (ed), *Eikon Basilike: the Portraiture of His Sacred Majesty in His Solitudes and Sufferings*, published for the Folger Shakespeare Library (Ithaca, N.Y., Cornell University Press, 1966), p. 26. The papers were the work of both John Gauden, Bishop of Exeter, and the king: *ibid.*, pp. xxvi–xxxii.

[58] John Milton, *Eikonoklastes in Answer to a Book Intitl'd Eikon Basilake* (London, 1649), pp. 57–59, 235.

"Take this sword to use for me, if I reigne well, if not, to use against me."[59]

Other radical writers, such as Nathaniel Bacon, Philip Hunton, Philip Lawson, and John Sadler, stressed that the coronation oath obliged the king to observe the laws of King Edward and that the *quas vulgus elegerit* clause bound him to accept parliament's law.[60] Discussion on the clause disappeared at the Restoration, when the veto power was reaffirmed, but Sadler's *Rights of the Kingdom* was reprinted in 1682, and Bacon's *Historical Discourse*, Hunton's *A Treatise of Monarchy*, and Lawson's *Politica sacra & civilis* appeared in 1689 to reinforce the idea of a coronation oath as a contract between king and nation.

Only a decade before the Revolution, the Exclusion Crisis brought the coronation oath again into political debate. On the Tory side, Dr. Robert Brady, the historian, sought to deflate the importance of the oath. He argued that the oath implied that the laws were the king's and that the monarch promised only to grant and keep the laws preceding kings had granted to the community.[61] To the same end, a friend of the Duke of York was at pains to show why the oath did not necessarily bind a monarch.[62]

Whigs also discussed the oath. An anonymous critic of the Duke of York wrote privately to recommend changes in the oath to protect Protestantism. He suggested removing the reference to maintaining "ye Holy Church," because it smacked of catholicism, and substituting words such as "Defend and maintaine the Protestant Religion & the Government of the Church by Protestant Bishops." He also wanted to add some words "against the Pope's authority."[63] His suggestions were not far from what was done in 1689. The prospect of a Catholic king animated a tract writer to deny categorically that the Pope or bishop has the right to crown a monarch; rather, as the story of the biblical King David proves, the coronation of a king is from the people, who require the king to take an oath to govern according to the law.[64] Edward Cooke's (?) *Argumentum Antinormannicum*, printed in 1682, provided the most effective statement of Whig thought on the coronation oath and vivified it with a striking picture (plate 7). At the top of the picture, figures of soldiers depict William I's victory at the Battle of Hastings in 1066. In the middle sits William I, with the crown held above his head by an archbishop, while another archbishop holds a paper marked "The Coronation Oath." On the right, a woman, Britannia, extends to the king a scepter and a scroll marked "St. Edward's Laws." An accompanying text, exemplifying the concept of the ancient constitution, explains that after the people consented, William took the coronation oath, by which he vowed to rule with justice and to avoid "Absolute or Despotical Power." The king also promised "to observe and keep the Sacred laws of St. Edward."[65] *Argumentum Antinormannicum* was

[59] The story appeared in works by such men as Buchanan, Filmer, Grotius, and Ludlow. See Greenberg, "The Confessor's Laws," p. 616, n. 4; W. T. Allison (ed.), *Milton's Tenure of Kings and Magistrates*, Yale Studies in England, no. 40 (New Haven, Conn. Yale University Press, 1911), pp. 13–14, 90; Wolfe, *Complete Prose Works of John Milton*, III, 92.   [60] See Greenberg, "The Confessor's Laws," 618, 623, 624–28.
[61] Weston and Greenberg, *Subjects and Sovereigns*, pp. 217–18.
[62] BL, Add. Ms. 5540, fols. 45r.–v.   [63] BL, Add. Ms. 35,865, fol. 205.
[64] (William Lawrence), *The Marriage by The Morall Law of God Vindicated* (n.p., 1680), pp. 169–74.
[65] Edward Cooke (?), *Argumentum Antinormannicum* (London, 1682, repr. 1689), pp. A1–A2. The frontispiece appears in both editions.

Plate 7 Frontispiece from Edward Cooke (?), *Argumentum Antinormannicum* (London, 1682: repr. 1689). Folger Shakespeare Library. William I is depicted at the moment of receiving the English crown. A figure representing Britannia extends a scroll marked "St. Edward's Laws," which the text explains William I promises to observe.

reprinted in 1689 and was in the library of at least one member of the Convention.[66]

Tracts written at about the time of the Revolution also made essentially the same points, thereby providing an example of the ideological connections

---

[66] HEHL, Stowe Mss., Catalogue of Temple's Library, Stt. CI & I, Box 2, 1641 to eighteenth century.

across the century and reinforcing the ideas that appeared in the reprinted tracts. For example, employing the language of the ancient constitution, Daniel Whitby maintained that "the kings of England were kings by virtue of an Original Compact, made between them and the people ... by oaths that they took at their Coronation, to preserve to the people their ancient Rights and Liberties." A king who overturns the law "is no such King as our Constitution knows, or ever did admit of," he wrote.[67] Presenting the contrary view in terms like those King James I expressed in *The Trew Law Of Free Monarchies*, the "Jacobite" in a dialogue insisted that the coronation oath was between God and the king, not "between the King and the People," and is no "Compact or bargain with the People."[68]

Concern about the coronation oath also appeared in the debates of the Convention. A member of the House of Commons accused King James II of violating his coronation oath by trying to set aside the Test Act. Anxiety about the oath also animated members of the first "rights" committee, one of whom insisted that the "Coronation Oath should be inspected" to remove language suggestive of Catholicism.[69] The first list of rights – the Heads of Grievances – called for a review of the coronation oath.[70] The call did not appear in the Declaration of Rights, probably because it was clearly no ancient right, but it was heeded in arranging for the coronation.

In the meantime, the House of Lords was also drawn into considering the coronation oath. In discussing the "abdication and vacancy" resolution (the formula justifying the removal of the king), the peers sought legal advice on the words that James had broken "the original contract between king and people." The lords' nine lawyers found no help in their "books or cases," but William Petyt, drawing upon Saxon and Norman history, identified the original contract with the king's coronation oath. His definition met with approval, and, although that portion of the resolution was soon dropped, the Dutch ambassador reported interest in substituting "breaking the coronation oath" for "breaking the original contract." Petyt's definition had the advantage of sidestepping the notion that the government had dissolved and power had reverted to the people that was implied in the idea of "original contract." If the king violated his coronation oath, he ceased to be king, but his violation did not imply a dissolution of government.[71]

Against this background of expressed interest, the Commons appointed a committee on February 25 to inspect the coronation oath.[72] Among the thirty-

---

[67] *An Historical Account of Some Things Relating to the English Government and the conception which our Forefathers had of it,* in *State Tracts,* I, 590, 592. Another tract was Peter Allix, *An Examination of the Scruples of Those Who refuse to take the Oath of Allegiance* (London, Licensed April 16, 1689).

[68] *A Dialogue between Two Friends, A Jacobite and a Williamite, occasion'd; by the later Revolution of Affairs, and the Oath of Allegiance* in *State Tracts,* I, pp. 289, 290.

[69] John Somers, "Notes of Debate, January 28, January 29," in *Miscellaneous State Papers, from 1501 to 1726,* ed. Philip Yorke, second Earl of Hardwicke (2 vols., London, 1748), II, pp. 402, 415; BL, Add. Ms. 15,949, fol. 12v.

[70] The Heads of Grievances are conveniently found in Schwoerer, *The Declaration of Rights, 1689,* Appendix 2.

[71] HMC, *Twelfth Report, Appendix, Part VI. The Manuscripts of the House of Lords, 1689–1690* (London, HMSO, 1889), pp. 15–16; Pocock, *The Ancient Constitution,* pp. 229–31; Schwoerer, *The Declaration of Rights, 1689,* pp. 205–7.

[72] *CJ,* x, p. 35; Grey, *Debates,* IX, pp. 110–12.

nine members were Tories Sir Robert Seymour and Thomas Clarges, and Whigs Colonel John Birch and John Hampden, Jr. Sixteen members had served on the first "rights" committee, eleven on the second "rights" committee as well. These men took the oath seriously: one described it as the "very touch-stone and symbol of your Government"; another remarked that coronation oaths in the past were "no great matter," but this one was, for now the nation had a foreign king who might say he did not understand England's religion and laws.[73] The oath, then, was a salutary reminder that he was bound by law.

The committee rewrote two sections of the traditional oath, one relating to law, the other to religion, embodied the changes in a statute, and provided an explanatory preamble. The express aim was to provide an oath for "all Times to come." In the traditional oath, the king had promised to "grant and keep and ... confirm to ye people of England ye Laws and Customs to them granted by ye [preceding] Kings of England." In the 1689 version, the words "grant" and "granted" disappeared. Instead, the monarch took an oath to govern "the people of England and the dominions thereunto belonging, according to the statutes in parliament agreed on, and the laws and customs of the same." Three features of this language require comment. First is the assumption that the statutes, laws, and customs are not in the possession of the king, that he can neither grant not rescind them, and that he had no authority over law separate from his role in parliament. The language further implied the primacy of statutory law, ranking it ahead of custom or common law. This part of the oath was surely intended to reinforce the articles in the Declaration of Rights (which was not yet law) that denied the king the suspending power and also the dispensing power as recently practiced.

Second, the reference to "dominions" testified to the importance of England's recent economic and imperial activity. The oath claimed that the "dominions" – meaning the American colonies – belonged to England and extended the king's promise to them. Implicitly it discounted the possibility of conflict between the laws of England and of its dominions. And third, the new oath omitted any reference to the Laws of King Edward, a part of the English coronation oath since 1308 and, as shown, a prominent part of the discourse of the period. What explains the step? The preamble justified the omission on grounds that "the oath ... hath heretofore been framed in doubtful words and expressions" and "with relation to ancient laws and constitutions at this time unknowne." This admission reflected growing skepticism about man's ability to know the ancient past and about its value, were it known. In debate, Hampden had pointed out that the laws of Holy Edward were uncertain. "They were Capitularies, of which some are expired," he mused. Another MP made essentially the same point when he said, "There is a great difference betwixt what was anciently, and now."[74] Such an attitude testified to the

---

[73] Grey, *Debates,* IX, pp. 192, 193.
[74] *Ibid.,* pp. 122, 190.

decline in the Inns of Court, center for the study of the common law, and consequently to a weakening of the role of custom and precedent in political thought.[75] The concept of immemorialism did not disappear, but this portion of the oath reveals that its power was diminished.

Another change in language related to the king's administrative powers over law. Whereas the traditional oath had asked the king: "Will you to your power cause Law, Justice, and Discretion in Mercy and Truth to be executed in all your Judgements?" the 1689 oath dropped the word "Discretion" and "Truth." The omission of the word "Discretion" may have been intended to reinforce further the Declaration of Rights by suggesting that the king's personal discretion was limited, although the royal powers of pardon and veto were left untouched and remain a prerogative of the crown today. Why the word "truth" was omitted is unclear; perhaps because it was a word whose meaning was "doubtful," as the preamble had said.

No evidence of the debate on this section of the oath has survived, but we may infer that the committee had some difficulties, because apparently it "met several times, but could not come to a determination."[76] The attitude towards law implicit in it is one on which Whigs and Tories could agree. Yet the oath reflected more closely the views of Whigs than of Tories, some of whom in the 1680s had promoted or accepted the idea of the supremacy of the king over the law. Such lingering ideas may have delayed agreement.

Other parts of the oath dealing with religion also contained important changes. As critics had recommended, the words "ye Holy Church," with their Catholic overtones, were dropped. Further, the new oath asked monarchs: "Will you to the utmost of Your Power Maintain . . . the Protestant Reformed Religion Established by Law?" This language concealed sharp differences between Dissenting and Anglican aspirations and heated debates between Whigs and Tories, who, in the event, captured the vote of conservative Whigs.

Reformist Whigs wanted the words "as shall be established" to be substituted for "Established by Law," to signal the possibility of future change in religion. One Whig asserted, "I would have the church-doors made wider," while others warned of antagonizing Dissenters at home and abroad and provoking them against the new government.[77] Among Tories were men who wanted no change at all in the old wording of the oath. One Tory saw in the proposed words "shall be" a trick to bring in sectaries because "several persons call themselves of the Reformed Religion, as Quakers, Anabaptists, etc." Others worried that Presbyterians would take over the Anglican church. Still another recalled that during James II's reign, Dissenters had joined with Catholics to remove the Tests, and maintained that they deserved no quarter. But, in an effort to placate Dissenters, this member assured the House that the Church of England "from the Bishops downwards" favored comprehension and ease for tender consciences.[78]

---

[75] Pocock, *The Ancient Constitution*, pp. 240–41. [76] *CJ*, x, pp. 35, 61. Another member was added on March 22.
[77] Grey, *Debates*, IX, pp. 191, 192, 195, 197, 198.
[78] *Ibid.*, pp. 193, 194–95, 197, 198; cf. Morrice, "Entr'ing Book," II, p. 514.

An effort to reach a compromise by distinguishing between the doctrine and discipline of the church failed. The argument ran that the doctrine of the church was "by the Law of God," but that "Parliaments have changed many things in the Discipline of the Church."[79] But Anglican Tories were adamantly in favor of the words "Established by Law." Those words passed by 188 votes to 149 on March 25, and two attempts later to remove or change them were defeated.[80]

What explains this vote? Or to put it differently, what accounts for so marked a shift to the Tories? That shift, which underlay the vote, reflected disappointment in the Dutch king, anger over the war and higher taxes, and guilt over violating the oath of allegiance, the doctrine of direct hereditary succession, and the theory of nonresistance. Further, the vote revealed the strength of religious conservatism on all sides. The king's announcement that he supported repeal of the Test Act so that Dissenters could serve him in good conscience, and that he favored comprehension of all Reformed Churches alarmed Whigs as well as Tories. As Roger Morrice, a Presbyterian observer shrewdly remarked, "The House of Commons was stronger by 80 or 100 voices to reform things amiss in the State than in the Church."[81] Another observer echoed the point. Remarking in mid-March that the church party had a majority in both Houses, he wondered why "they knew their strength no sooner."[82]

William and Mary's coronation ceremony, with its outwardly traditional forms, presented the *illusion* of political legitimacy and stability. But the coronation of course solved none of the critical problems facing the nation, and it was, in fact, followed by increased partisan tensions. On the one hand, friends of the new government praised it, poets published pastorals and verse (some illustrated) about it, and engravers memorialized it in prints and medals.[83] Of the twenty-eight surviving medals, two directly reflect political themes embedded in the coronation ceremony. For example, one medal showed busts of William and Mary facing each other within two wreaths of rose and orange resting on a base consisting of a volume inscribed LEGES ANGLIAE, making a plain point. Also shown is an open book (perhaps symbolizing the Laws) surmounted by a cap of liberty, an ancient device going back to the Roman Republic and symbolizing a free man. Cornucopia on either side promise safety and plenty (plate 8).[84]

---

[79] Grey, *Debates*, IX, p. 193, cf. p. 195.
[80] *Ibid.*, IX, pp. 201–2.
[81] Morrice, "Entr'ing Book," II, pp. 505, 511, 534.
[82] BL, Add. Mss. 36, 707, fol. 62; cf. Browning (ed.), *Memoirs of Reresby*, p. 572.
[83] For example, *Court of England, Preparation for Coronation* (London, 1689), illustrated with a woodcut; *A Pastoral on the Coronation of William and Mary. Daphnis and Damon* (London, 1689); *Protestants Joy; or An Excellent new Song* (London, 1689), illustrated with a woodcut and sung to the tune of "Hail to the Myrtle Shades," the same tune used at the time of the proclamation. De Hooghe produced an iconographic history of the Coronation. De Beer (ed.), *Locke's Correspondence*, III, p. 597, for positive comment.
[84] Edward Hawkins (compiler) and August W. Franks and Herbert A. Grueber (eds.), *Medallic Illustrations of the History of Great Britain and Ireland to the Death of George II* (2 vols., London, British Museums Publications, 1885), I, p. 668, no. 39. The medal was struck in Holland and designed by R. Arondeaux. The other medal apropos of themes in the coronation shows William and Mary seated beneath a canopy of state, each with scepter and orb, with two bishops holding a crown over their heads. The legend reads: IDOLOLATRIA SERVITUTE. PROFLIGATIS. RELIGIONE. LEGIB. LIBERTAT. RESTITUTIS. (Idolatry and Slavery put to flight, Religion, the Laws, and Liberty restored), *ibid.*, no. 38. For a recent discussion of some medals, see Lois G. Schwoerer, "Images of Queen Mary II, 1689–95" *Renaissance Quarterly* 42 (1989), 717–48.

Plate 8 Coronation medal of William and Mary with an open Bible or book of laws. 1689. The British Museum.

On the other hand, feelings against the new government ran so high on the day of the coronation that a man was almost killed by soldiers for celebrating the event.[85] Dissenters declared that the oath "perpetuated and Riveted the Schisme" in religion.[86] Jacobites identified Mary with the Roman matron Tullia and interpreted the official coronation medal (plate 9), designed by John Hampden, Jr., to mean that Mary had dethroned her father. Vicious doggerel against the queen ran: "That you a father had you have forgot/ Or would have people think that he was not."[87] The coronation was not forgotten: in November 1689 a man named Ralph Grey, chaplain to Thomas Cartwright, Bishop of Chester, suspected of being a papist, turned Burnet's coronation sermon into a seditious paper and was fined and sentenced to stand in the pillory.[88]

Although coronation ceremonies and oaths are often regarded as sacrosanct and unchanging, William and Mary's coronation ceremony and oath reflec-

---

[85] *CSPD, 1689–90*, p. 61; cf. p. 257.   [86] Morrice, "Entr'ing Nook," II, p. 514; also p. 516.

[87] Quoted in Agnes Strickland, *Lives of the Queens of England* (8 vols., London, Longman, Green, Longman, and Roberts, 1860), VII, p. 215.

[88] *POAS*, v, 39–40.

Plate 9 The official coronation medal of William and Mary executed by John Roettier and designed by John Hampden, Jr. Jove (William) thunders against Phaethon (James II) and rescues the nation. But Jacobites saw the chariot as that of Tullia (Mary), the Roman matron who destroyed her father. 1689. The British Museum.

ted, in a significant degree, current political and religious ideologies and partisan strengths. Political and religious reasons motivated changes in the ceremony – to stress the Protestant character of the new regime and to show the limits of Mary's power. The seating of members of the House of Commons testified to their new status. The new coronation oath underscored the primacy of statutory law, reinforced the Declaration of Rights, and limited royal legal powers. Thus, the new oath supports the thesis that revolutionary leaders wanted a new kingship as well as a new king. The discussion of the new oath in parliament and press iterated points made by tracts (some reprinted in 1689) which had been published earlier in the Civil War, thereby illustrating ideological connections over the century and the resolution in 1689 of an important dispute about the relationship of the king to law. The oath also revealed the strength of the prevailing religious conservatism of Tories and mainstream Whigs and their distrust of dissent. The final formulation of the oath promoted divisions. There is irony, therefore, in the fact that *this* coronation should serve as the basis for all future coronations and, thereby, perpetuate the myth of the stability of the English monarchy.

Appendix

An act for establishing the coronation oath. [1689]

Whereas by the law and ancient usage of this realm, the Kings and Queens thereof have taken a solemn oath upon the evangelists at their respective coronations, to maintain the statutes, laws, and customs of the said realm, and all the people and inhabitants thereof, in their spiritual and civil rights and properties: but forasmuch as the oath itself on such occasion administered, hath heretofore been framed in doubtful words and expressions, with relation to ancient laws and constitutions at this time unknown: to the end thereof that one uniform oath may be in all times to come taken by the Kings and Queens of this realm, and to them respectively administered at the times of their and every of their coronation; may it please your majesties that it may be enacted: II: And be it enacted ... That the oath herein mentioned, and hereafter expressed, shall and may be administered to their most excellent majesties King William and Queen Mary, (whom God long perserve) at the time of their coronation in the presence of all persons that shall be there and there present at the solemnizing thereof, by the Archbishop of Canterbury, or the Archbishop of York, or either of them, or any other bishop of this realm, whom the King's majesty shall thereunto appoint, and who shall be hereby thereunto respectively authorized; which oath followeth and shall be administered in this manner; that is to say,

[As prescribed by the Coronation Order of James II [1685]]

Archbishop

Sir, will you grant and keep and by your Oath confirm to ye people of England ye Laws and Customs to them granted by ye Kings of England, your lawfull, and Religious predecessors; And namely ye Laws, Customs, and Franchises granted to ye Clergy by ye glorious King St. Edward, your predecessor; According to ye Laws of God, ye true profession of ye Gospel establish'd in this Kingdom, and agreeing to ye prerogative of ye Kings thereof, and ye ancient Customs of ye Realm?

King.

I grant, and promise to keep them.

Archbishop.

Sir, Will you keep peace, and godly Agreement entirely according to your power, to ye holy Church, ye Clergy and the people?

[As prescribed by the Coronation Oath Act [1689]]

The Archbishop or Bishop shall say.

III. Will you solemnly promise and swear to govern the people of this kingdom of England, and the dominions thereunto belonging, according to the statutes in parliament agreed on, and the laws and customs of the same?

The King and Queen shall say,

I solemnly promise to do so.

King.

I will Keep it.

Archbishop.

Sir, will you to your power cause Law, Justice, and Discretion in Mercy and Truth to be executed in all your judgements?

King.

I will.

Archbishop.

Sir, will you grant to hold, and keep ye rightfull customs, wch. ye commonaltie of this your Kingdom have? And will you defend, and uphold them, to the Honour of God, so much as in you lieth?

King.

I grant, and promise to do so.

Then shall follow ye petition, or Request of ye Bishops to ye King; to be read with a clear voice by one of them in ye name of ye Rest, standing by.

Bishop.

Our Lord, and King, We beseech you to pardon Us; and to grant, and preserve unto Us, and ye Churches committed to our Charge all Canonical privileges, and due Law and Justice: and yt. you will protect, and defend Us; as every good King in his Kingdom ought to be Protectour, and Defender of ye Bishops, and Churches under their government. The King answereth,

King.

With a willing and devout Heart I promise and grant You my Pardon; and that I will preserve, and maintein to you, and the Churches committed to your Charge all Canonical Privileges and due law and Justice. And that I will be your Protec-

Archbishop or Bishop.

Will you to your power cause law and justice in mercy to be executed in all your judgements?

King and Queen.

I will.

Archbishop or Bishop.

Will you to the utmost of your power maintain the laws of God, the true profession of the gospel, and the protestant reformed religion established by law? And will you preserve unto the bishops and clergy of this realm, and to the churches there committed to their charge, all such rights and privileges as by law do or shall appertain unto them, or any of them?

King and Queen.

All this I promise to do.

tour and Defender to my power by the
assistance of God; as every good King in
his Kingdom ought in Right to protect,
and defend the Bishops and Churches
under their government.

Then ye King . . . laying his Hand upon
ye Holdy Gospels, shall say,

After this, the King and Queen laying his
and her hand upon the holy gospels, shall
say,

King.

King and Queen.

The things wch. I have here before pro-
mis'd, I will perform and keep: so help
me God, and ye Contents of this Book.

The things which I have here before promised, I will perform and keep: so help
me God.

Then the King and Queen shall kiss the
book.

iv. And be it further enacted, that the said oath shall be in like manner
administered to every King or Queen that shall succeed to the imperial crown
of this realm, at their respective coronations, by one of the archbishops or
bishops of the realm of England, for the time being, to be thereunto appointed
by such King or Queen respectively, and in the presence of all persons that
shall be attending, assisting, or otherwise present at such their respective
coronations; any law, statute, or usage to the contrary notwithstanding.

8

William – and Mary?*

W. A. Speck

In the celebrated history of England, *1066 and All That*, by W. C. Sellar and R. J. Yeatman, chapter 28 is headed "Williamanmary. England ruled by an Orange." This essay seeks to discuss that proposition by examining the nature of the dual monarchy with a view to establishing, not whether it involved the rule of an Orange, but whether Mary deserves to be linked with William so closely as to make "Williamanmary" all one word.

The Bill of Rights made William and Mary joint rulers, but gave him sole exercise of the executive authority. Mary was quite happy with this arrangement whereby he, so to speak, wore the monarchical pants. "My opinion," she wrote in her *Memoirs*, "has ever been that women should not meddle in government."[1]

The king held the reins in his own hands through the first year of the dual monarchy. Inexperienced in the elaborate games of English politics, he made some ghastly initial mistakes. He had been persuaded that the Whig party was strong in England and that he had better go along with radical schemes to win their support. In fact, the Tories were still formidable. Had they not been let down badly by James II, who left them in the lurch when he fled to France, they might have retained the initiative throughout the Revolution. Even with their king in exile they managed to rally significant support for the idea of a regency. When this failed they fell in with the offer of the crown to James's daughter and son-in-law only on a *de facto* and not on a *de jure* basis. Many did not even do that, and refused to take the oaths to the new monarchs, becoming nonjurors. The nonjuring cause enlisted many Jacobites who were prepared to recall James as well as high-churchmen who could not in conscience violate their former oaths to him. The latter included several bishops and clergy of the Church of England, led by the Archbishop of Canterbury. Their stance stiffened resistance to the king's policy of cooperating with Whigs to the extent of offering some Dissenters bishoprics and even suggesting the repeal of the Test Act to allow some Protestant nonconformists to hold office under him, without having to take communion in the Church of

---

[1] R. Doebner (ed.), *Memoirs of Mary Queen of England(1689–93) Together With Her Letters And Those of Kings James II. and William III. To The Electress, Sophia of Hanover* (Leipzig, Veit, and London, D. Nutt, 1886), p. 23.

England. This maladroit move scuppered all chances of comprehending moderate Dissenters within the Anglican church, leaving them, along with other nonconformists, only the grudging concession of the Toleration Act, which specifically upheld the Test Act. By the end of 1689 William had created a great deal of bitterness and resentment amongst the Tories.

He learned something from these mistakes, becoming aware that Tories and high-churchmen were much more powerful than he had initially realized. Moreover, it seemed to him that they were natural supporters of monarchy. He suspected the Whigs, not only detecting a vein of republicanism in their ranks but also resenting their former advocacy of exclusion which, had it been successful, might well have seen the Duke of Monmouth on the throne and not him and his wife. In the winter of 1689–90, therefore, he turned towards the Tories, dissolved the Convention Parliament, and helped assure a Tory majority in the ensuing general election. How far this increased his own popularity, however, is to be doubted. It alienated a significant number of Whigs without necessarily securing the loyalty of Tories.

Mary's influence offset this disastrous start to the reign. Although she was supported more by Tories than by Whigs, she had supporters in both parties and, perhaps because she did not have to deal with them directly, made fewer enemies. William was well aware of this. He told the Marquis of Halifax in June 1689 that "if hee [i.e. William] left us, the Queen would governe us better."[2] According to Bishop Burnet, he came close to bringing this about:

> He thought he could not trust the tories, and he resolved he would not trust the whigs: so he fancied the tories would be true to the queen, and confide in her, though they would not in him. He therefore resolved to go over to Holland, and leave the government in the queen's hands . . . since he did not see how he could extricate himself out of the difficulties into which the animosities of parties had brought him: they pressed him vehemently to lay aside all such desperate resolutions . . . The debate was so warm, that many tears were shed: in conclusion, the king resolved to change his first design, into another better resolution, of going over in person, to put an end to the war in Ireland.[3]

William's decision to leave England in 1690 posed for the first time the problem of what arrangements should be made for the governing of the country in his absence. It seems that initially he was reluctant to leave Mary in charge at all, preferring to appoint a council which would simply report to her but be answerable to him. Thus he told Halifax that "there must be a Councell to governe in his absence, and that the Queen is not to meddle."[4] This suggests that his earlier threat to abdicate, leaving her in charge, was a deliberate bluff. In the event, however, an Act of Parliament was passed vesting the administration in Mary.

The Bill "for the exercise of the government by her Majesty during his Majesty's absence," commonly known as the Regency Bill, had its first reading in the House of Lords on Saturday, April 26. It had a quick and

---

[2] H. C. Foxcroft, *The Life and Letters of Sir George Savile Bart. First Marquis of Halifax* (2 vols., London, 1898), II, p. 222.

[3] Burnet, *HOT*, IV, p. 71.   [4] Foxcroft, *Halifax's Life and Letters*, II, p. 246.

apparently smooth passage through the Upper Chamber, being read again, committed and engrossed on Monday the 28th.[5]

When it came down to the Commons on April 30, however, it ran into choppy waters. It was debated that day, and in a committee of the whole House on May 1. So sensitive were the points at issue held to be that the debate was adjourned for five days. Even when it was resumed on May 5 further time had to be set aside for it on the 6th and it was not until the 7th that it was engrossed.

What caused such a protracted discussion after all had seemed to be plain sailing in the Lords? It was scarcely bad draftsmanship, although Sir Thomas Littleton did regret that their Lordships had not considered it better.[6] When passed with some amendments, the final Act was remarkably brief. In essence it simply stated that, notwithstanding the Bill of Rights, "whensoever and so often as it shall happen that his . . . Majesty shall be absent out of this realm of England it shall and may be lawful for the Queens Majesty to exercise and administer the regal power and government of the kingdom" (*SR*, vi, p. 170).

This apparently simple device ran into two difficulties, one constitutional, the other political. The constitutional problem was to decide what authority William still retained while he was out of the country. The political problem was that many politicians did not trust his wife to administer the government properly.

Constitutionally, the position was quite novel. The Revolution Settlement had created a unique dual monarchy for which there were no real precedents. Earlier examples of the arrangements made when monarchs left the realm were therefore irrelevant. As the Solicitor-General, John Somers, put it after rehearsing precedents, "This is a new case, and like none of those I have mentioned; and we are in a government not a year old." Serjeant John Maynard expressed it more forcefully: "The precedents . . . are like making a map of a country we have never seen." The Bill of Rights had vested the executive authority in the king alone to avoid any ambiguity. Now ambiguities were legion. Did the Regency Act terminate commissions which had been issued by the king and require the queen to issue new ones? Was William still king regnant or not? What if he and the queen gave conflicting orders? The Bill's initial silence on these points perplexed some MPs. "The more I have thought of this bill," confessed Sir William Pulteney, "the less I have understood it. I will not dispute what an act of parliament can do. It may make the moon shine for ought I know." Amendments to the Bill could take care of some of these problems. Thus it was clearly stated that the regency did not avoid or terminate any commissions. But the basic problem of how to give Mary executive power and yet not deprive William of his, or as Sir Thomas Lee put it, to "find out a way to invest the queen with the Regency as not to dispossess the king," was the ancient dilemma of how to have your cake and eat it too.

---

[5] 2 Wm & Mar c.6, *LJ*, xiv, pp. 475, 477.
[6] The debates can be followed in Cobbett, *Parlia. Hist.*, v, pp. 611–18, 622–35, see esp. pp. 615, 616, 617, 618, and 634.

The political difficulties exacerbated the constitutional problem. Sir Edward Norris put it very bluntly when he asked, "If the king should die in this expedition, and the queen be regent, what if, out of duty to her father, if he land, she should not oppose him?" It was only too apparent that some MPs, mainly Whigs, did not trust Mary. They wanted William to stay, and spun out the debate. Others, mainly Tory, saw no real problem. "The question is, Whether you will trust the government in the queen's hands or not at all?" stated Sir Edward Seymour. "When the king is gone, the government must be somewhere. Will you have it in other hands than the queen's? You have a good clause before you; there is no objection against it that is solid." All objections were removed by pointing out that "the king is resolved to trust the Queen." In his speech at the start of the session William had said that he "thought it most convenient to have the administration of the government in the hands of the queen during my absence." He had then asked the Houses to pass an Act to that effect. On May 7 they finally did so.

Although no mention is made in the Regency Act of a council, William appointed one to advise Mary. It consisted of nine of the principal ministers of state. He apparently gave her his opinion of them, for she wrote to him in July, "I thought you had given me wrong characters of men, but now I see they answer my expectation of being as little of a mind as of a body."[7] Their disagreements stemmed from the fact that five were Tories while four were Whigs, the result of William's preference for mixed ministries. Experience did not endear them to Mary, her own comments on each of them being negative. Of the President of the Council, Thomas Osborne, the Marquis of Carmarthen, although William had particularly recommended him to her, she wrote that he was "of a temper I can never like."[8] As Andrew Browning, the biographer of Carmarthen, commented, "When compared with what she has to say of the other members of her Council of Nine this brief comment might almost be described as effusive flattery."[9] Thus the Lord Steward, William Cavendish, the Earl of Devonshire, she found "weak and obstinate, made a mere tool by his party." The Lord Chamberlain, Charles Sackville, Earl of Dorset, was too lazy, and therefore of little use. Charles Mordaunt, Earl of Monmouth, and Thomas Herbert, Earl of Pembroke, were both "mad"; John Churchill, Earl of Marlborough, and Daniel Finch, Earl of Nottingham, untrustworthy; Sir John Lowther was "a very honest but weak man," while Edward Russell, though he "was recommended to me for sincerity, yet he had his faults."[10]

Mary was clearly not impressed by any of them. At first they were equally clearly not overimpressed with her abilities. She confessed to William that "as I do not know when I ought to speak and when not, I am as silent as can be."

---

[7] Dalrymple, *Memoirs*, II, part II, p. 143 (July 17, 1690).

[8] Doebner (ed.), *Memoirs*, p. 29.

[9] A. Browning, *Thomas Osborne, Earl of Danby and Duke of Leeds (1632–1712)* (3 vols., Glasgow, 1944–51), I, pp. 478–79.

[10] Doebner (ed.), *Memoirs*, pp. 29–30. Cf. "The Nine," *Poems on Affairs of State*, ed. W. J. Cameron (17 vols., New Haven, Conn., and London, Yale University Press, 1971), V, pp. 196–201.

"Every one sees how little I know of business," she further informed him, "and therefore believe will be apt to do as much as they can . . . I find they meet often at the Secretary's [Nottingham] office, and do not take much pains to give me an account."[11] They were to find, however, that they had underestimated her. Carmarthen, for instance, as Lord President, considered that he should have the prevailing influence. Browning regarded him as first minister in William's absence, while a Jacobite libeler claimed that "she's governed in Council by the marquis Carmarthen."[12]

In fact, she was very much her own woman. Perhaps realizing that Carmarthen, a Tory, was trying to monopolize her, which her trimming spouse would dislike, she made a deliberate point of cultivating the Whig Edward Russell. Finding Russell a little reluctant to approach her, she asked his celebrated relative, Lady Rachel Russell, to tell him she desired to speak to him. When they did finally converse, Mary "told him freely that I desired to see him sometimes, for being a stranger to business I was afraid of being too much led or persuaded by one party." When the Whigs tried to push their luck by offering the queen £200,000 if she would dissolve parliament, she dug in her heels and told Monmouth, the councillor who made the offer, that even if the whole Privy Council advised this step she would still have to consult the king about it.[13]

Mary's deference to William resolved the ambiguities raised in the debates about where ultimate authority really lay, which had not been satisfactorily taken care of by the Regency Act. An amendment stated that nothing in it should be taken or construed to exclude or debar the king from exercising the regal power, and that he could not be contradicted, but this would have been very difficult to implement in the event of serious disagreement between the joint rulers. In fact, the situation never arose because Mary was anxious to prevent it. "That which makes me in pain," she wrote to William, "is for fear what is done may not please you. I am sure it is my chief desire . . . as much as may be to act according to your mind."[14] She stuck by the resolution adopted at the first meeting of the nine that "all business that will admit delay must be sent to the king that his pleasure may be known."[15] Thus William, in the midst of a bloody campaign in Ireland, was asked to decide the most trivial issues. "It is requisite to know your pleasure about a lord Lieutenant for Leicestershire," wrote the Lord President. "My lord Fitzharding is dead and Colonel Berkeley succeeds to that title," the Secretary of State Nottingham informed William's secretary in Ireland. "The committee has recommended to her Majesty as you are desired to do to the king that he may be custos rotulorum of Sommersetshire."[16]

[11] Dalrymple, *Memoirs*, II, part II, pp. 119, 121 (June 24 and 26, 1690).
[12] Browning, *Danby*, I, pp. 478–79; *POAS*, v, p. 193.
[13] Dalrymple, *Memoirs*, , part II, pp. 122, 141 (June 26, July 15, 1690).
[14] *Ibid.*, p. 129 (July 3, 1690).
[15] HMC, *Report on the Manuscripts of Allan George Finch, esq. of Burley-on-the-Hill* (4 vols., London, HMSO, 1913–65), III, p. 378.
[16] Browning, *Danby*, II, p. 176; HMC, *Finch*, II, p. 303.

Mary's first stint as queen regnant was, however, a baptism by fire, for a crisis arose demanding immediate decisions which could not be deferred for the king's advice. The disastrous defeat of the fleet by the French at Beachy Head in June 1690 was attributed to the incompetence or even the treachery of the Admiral, Arthur Herbert, Earl of Torrington. Mary had to act to deal with an immediate emergency. She rose to the occasion. A newswriter noted: "Heaven seems to have sent us one of the most threatening junctures that England ever saw merely to set off with the greater lustre the wisdom magnanimity and justice of a princess who has made good some people's fears and other's hopes in deserving the character of another Queen Elizabeth."[17] Mary determined to dispense with Torrington's services and to clap him in the Tower to await the outcome of a judicial inquiry into his actions. Nottingham as Secretary communicated this decision to William, hoping he would approve it, since "however dangerous it may be to take a generall from the head of his army yet as this case is, tis more dangerous to leave him there; for 'twill be in his power to destroy the fleet, and few men here think he has the heart to save it."[18]

Fortunately, the immediate crisis was offset by William's victory over James II at the battle of the Boyne, which was fought the day before Beachy Head. Mary was relieved both that her husband had won and, despite Jacobite calumnies to the contrary, that her father had escaped unscathed. The notion that she hoped James would not survive the war in Ireland was quite preposterous. Mary's attitude towards her father was, to say the least, ambivalent. On the one hand, she had benefited from his misrule; yet, on the other hand, she felt guilty about her role in the Revolution. How she reconciled her conscience with the events of 1688 and 1689 is discussed below. But guilt continued to affect her until she discovered that James had actually encouraged a plot to assassinate her husband. Her relief when he survived the battle unscathed was genuine enough.

The question of replacing Torrington presented her with another problem which she had to cope with on the spot. Although it was referred to William, the advice he gave, to appoint a commission of Edward Russell and Sir Richard Haddock, was abortive. Russell declined the appointment, so Mary proposed that Haddock should serve with Sir John Ashby, a proposal which the cabinet, as the nine should be called, accepted after some dispute. Then the commissioners of the Admiralty were called in to be informed of the decision. One of them, Sir Thomas Lee, in Mary's words, "grew as pale as death and told me that the custom was that they used to recommend, and they were to answer for the persons, since they were to give them the commission, and did not know but they might be called to account in parliament."[19] Behind Lee's insistence on constitutional procedures Mary detected political animosity. Haddock was preferred by the Tory Earl of Nottingham and he,

---

[17] *Mercurius Reformatus or the New Observator*, 1 August 1690.
[18] HMC, *Finch*, III, p. 334.
[19] Dalrymple, *Memoirs*, II, part II, p. 147 (July 24, 1690).

Lee, was a Whig. It must be said that Lee was making a principled stand, since his family's interest was best served by falling into line with the royal command. That very summer his own son was seeking preferment in Ireland from the king.[20] Yet he was prepared to tell the queen that Haddock's commission "could not be." She replied, "Then the king had given away his own power, and could not make an admiral which the admiralty did not like; he answered, no, no more he can't." Fortunately for Mary, the cabinet backed her up. Even so, she had to accept a compromise, whereby Henry Killegrew was added to the commission to replace Torrington. Lee held out to the end, not signing the commission, though a majority of his colleagues on the Admiralty board signed it. Mary discovered the hard way that such things were done "by partiality and Faction." She was clearly bruised by the experience, writing to William, "When I see what folk do here, it grieves me too much, for Holland has really spoiled me in being kind to me; that they are so to you 'tis no wonder, I wish to God it was the same here."[21] Her first real experience as queen had been a searing one, and she was relieved when her husband returned to take over the reins. Yet she had shown mettle and spirit and that she was not to be pushed around by politicians.

By the time the king left England again in January 1691, this time for Holland, the previous year's experience of his absence in Ireland had established a routine for the running of the country in these circumstances. During his stay abroad, which, apart from a brief return in mid-April, lasted until October, the cabinet dealt with routine business while Mary coped with any crises. Unlike 1690, there was no emergency like Beachy Head. Indeed "the only thing of business" which she dealt with according to her *Memoirs* "was the filling the Bishoprics."[22] The bishoprics which had to be filled were those which had been occupied by the nonjurors. It is often claimed that William left all ecclesiastical appointments to his wife, but that is not so. He told Halifax in 1690 on the eve of his first departure, "The Queen shall give no bishoprics."[23] Those bishoprics which fell vacant due to deaths and translations were replaced by him; but the sensitive issue of depriving Archbishop William Sancroft and other nonjuring bishops he left to his wife. In close cooperation with Nottingham, she handled the situation admirably.[24] She chose John Tillotson as the new Archbishop of Canterbury. Tillotson was just the man to bring the Church of England through its gravest crisis following the Revolution. He had been one of the leading London divines in her father's reign who had played a key role in presenting a united Protestant front against Catholicism. His appointment was a sign of a surer hand at work

---

[20] HMC, *Finch*, iii, p. 304.   [21] Dalrymple, *Memoirs*, ii, part ii, pp. 162–63 (August 19, 1690).
[22] Doebner (ed.), *Memoirs*, p. 37.
[23] Foxcroft, *Halifax's Life and Letters*, ii, p. 251. Burnet claimed that "the king had left the matters of the church wholly in the queen's hands": *HOT*, iv, p. 211. But this seems to refer to the period after Tillotson's appointment. Possibly, William felt that she handled the replacement of the nonjurors so skillfully that she could be entrusted with ecclesiastical appointments thereafter. Even so, following the death of Tillotson in 1694, he translated Tenison to Canterbury when she would have preferred Stillingfleet; *ibid.*, p. 244. When he was in Ireland in 1690 the appointments of archdeacons and prebends were referred to him: HMC, *Finch*, iii, p. 325.
[24] G. V. Bennett, "William III and the Episcopate," in G. V. Bennett and J. D. Walsh (eds.) *Essays in Modern English Church History* (New York, Oxford University Press, 1966), pp. 104–31.

in Anglican affairs than William's bungling efforts in 1689. William Sherlock claimed that, "had it been put to the poll there had been vast odds on his side that he [Tillotson] would have been voted into the see of Canterbury."[25] Mary's choice of bishops to replace the other nonjurors was equally inspired. She was even prepared to risk offending William by promoting George Hooper to the deanery of Canterbury, for her husband had expressed his dislike of the new dean. The feeling was apparently mutual, for Hooper was alleged to have said of Mary that "if her husband retained his throne it would be by her skill and talents for governing."[26] These were recognized by both Houses of Parliament, which addressed her to thank her for her prudent care in the conduct of the government during William's absence when he returned.[27]

At the end of William's next absence abroad, however, Mary was actually criticized in parliament for her referral of matter to him. Although an address of thanks for her care of the country was passed *nem. con.* on November 11, 1692, on the 21st Sir Thomas Clarges gave his opinion that "the government here has been very loose; no act done here by the Queen but must first be sent beyond sea to have directions from foreign councils." Two days later Henry Mordaunt echoed Clarges when he expressed the wish that "she had dispatched more herself without sending abroad for orders."[28] What lay behind these criticisms is difficult to discern. They do not appear to have been partisan, since Clarges was a Tory and Mordaunt a Whig. Nor is it easy to determine what issues they might have had in mind, since our main source for the decisions taken in cabinet, the "minutes" recorded by individual members of it, dries up in 1692. Thus we know that there were 34 meetings of the nine in 1690, of which Mary attended 21, and 59 in 1691, of which she was present at 55. But we do not even know how often the cabinet met in 1692.[29] Our only source for its proceedings in 1692 is the correspondence of the Secretary, Lord Nottingham. One can deduce from it that Mary was less prepared than before to take independent decisions. Thus one can almost detect a note of exasperation in Nottingham's asking William to decide whether or not to give Lord Abercorn his late brother's title and estate. "It is a case so well deserving his Majesty's favour and compassion that the House of Commons had agreed to a particular clause on his behalfe, that the king might restore him both to the estate and honour," pointed out the Secretary, "and the cabinett councill thinks it very reasonable for the Queen to grant them; but her Majesty would take no resolution without the King."[30]

[25] William Sherlock, *A Sermon Preach'd at the Temple-Church, December 30. 1694. Upon the Sad Occasion of the Death of our Gracious Queen* (London, 1695), p. 17.

[26] Agnes Strickland, *Lives of the Queens of England* (8 vols., London, Longman, Green, Longman, and Roberts 1852), VII, pp. 316, 331.

[27] Both Houses addressed Mary to thank her for her care of the administration during William's absences in 1690, 1691, and 1692. *LJ*, XIV, pp. 519, 629; XV, p. 115: *CJ*, X, pp. 430, 541, 698. Significantly, neither House addressed her to that effect in 1693 and 1694.

[28] *The Parliamentary Diary of Narcissus Luttrell 1691–3*, ed. H. Horwitz (Oxford University Press, 1972), pp. 242, 251.

[29] Jennifer Carter, "Cabinet Records for the Reign of William III," *EHR* 78 (1963), 95–114.

[30] HMC, *Finch*, IV, p. 40.

It could be that the MPs who voiced the complaints were concerned at the handling of the decision to dispense with the services of Marlborough and to put him in the Tower. This move, which severely strained relationships in the royal family, created considerable tension in 1692. It also alarmed army and naval officers, who suspected that it was a prelude to a general purge. So seriously was this alarm felt to be, that Mary was moved to reassure naval officers of her faith in their loyalty. Lord Nottingham passed on a message to them "that she reposes an entire confidence in them all, and will never think that any brave English seaman will betray her or his country to the insolent tyranny of the French; and as it is their duty and their glory to defend the government, it shall be her part to reward their service."[31] This appeal inspired sixty-four naval officers to sign an address of loyalty, pledging to venture their lives in defense of her rights and the liberty and religion of England. They went on to win the battle of La Hogue and with it the command of the sea. Mary might have left more to William than she needed to have done in 1692, but, as this episode reveals, she could still rise to the occasion when it was required. The Lords congratulated her on her resolute government "by which the danger of an invasion was prevented and a glorious victory obtained at sea."[32]

The following year, however, produced friction between her and William. She noted in her *Memoirs* that her administration in 1693 "was all along unfortunate, and whereas other years the King had almost ever approved all was done, this year he disapproved almost everything."[33] The main reason was that Mary's attachment to the Tories was stronger than ever, while William began to move decisively towards the Whigs. In April the queen was godmother at the christening of the Tory Earl of Nottingham's fourteenth child.[34] Yet the previous month, before setting out for Holland, William had appointed the Whigs John Trenchard and John, Lord Somers, to the second Secretaryship of State and the Lord Keepership. The Whigs in the cabinet criticized Nottingham's conduct of naval affairs, particularly his alleged failure to protect a merchant fleet bound for Turkey which was attacked by the French. These attacks were distressing to Mary, who described Nottingham as "the man I found the most constant in serving the king his own way, and who was the only one who really took the most and greatest pains to do so." But when William returned to England he dispensed with Nottingham's services and offered his post to the Whig, Charles Talbot, Duke of Shrewsbury. "When I begin to reflect on this year," Mary noted at the end of

---

[31] *Ibid.*, pp. 141–42.
[32] *LJ*, xv, p. 115. Cf. the Commons address: "At a time when the greatest part of Europe was suffering the miserable effects of war, we, your Majesty's subjects under your auspicious reign, enjoyed the blessings of peace at home; and not only received a signal deliverance from a bold and cruel design formed and prosecuted for our destruction, but saw your Majesty's fleet return with so complete and glorious victory as is not to be equalled in any former age, and can never be forgotten by Posterity," *CJ*, x, p. 698.
[33] Doebner (ed.), *Memoirs*, p. 59.
[34] H. Horwitz, *Revolution Politicks: the Career of Daniel Finch, Second Earl of Nottingham* (Cambridge University Press, 1968), p. 141, n. 2.

1693, "I am almost frightened and dare hardly go on; for tis the year I have met with more troubles as to publick matters than any other."[35]

What she made of the further moves to the Whigs in 1694 can only be surmised, since her *Memoirs* stop abruptly with the end of 1693. It seems, though, that she played even less of a role as regent than ever. She continued to preside over the Privy Council, which met on average seven times a month. But she rarely attended cabinet meetings.[36] The major decision to have the fleet winter in the Mediterranean was taken entirely by the cabinet in consultation with the king.[37] On the eve of her death in December 1694, therefore, she was less involved in the actual administration than she had been in 1690. This made it easier for William to manage without her thereafter. Nevertheless, he had been abroad for two years and eight months in all since his first departure from England as king in June 1690, rather more than half the time. During those years Mary had played a crucial role in the development of a system of running the country with the first regularly absent monarch since the reign of Henry V.

Mary smoothed the path for William in other ways more crucial to the survival of the Revolution settlement than the exercise of executive authority. Had he been sole ruler from the start he would have been king of only half the nation, if that. Jacobitism, by no means a negligible force, would have become even more formidable. It was no coincidence that the most serious Jacobite plots against the regime took place after her death. By that time, however, the settlement was reasonably secure. Mary had reconciled many Tories to the dual monarchy because they could, if they chose to ignore her half-brother as supposititious, which many did, regard her as the next in line to the throne by hereditary right. As Aphra Behn put it in 1689:

> The murmuring world till now divided lay
> Vainly debating whom they shou'd obey
> Till you great Cesar's offspring blest our Isle
> The differing multitudes to reconcile.[38]

She also presented the more acceptable face of the dual monarchy. William, after all, was a Dutchman. The Dutch were disliked by the English, who had fought them three times since 1651. He made it quite clear that he preferred Holland and his fellow countrymen. Favorites like William Bentinck, the Earl of Portland, and Arnold van Keppel, Earl of Albemarle, were lavishly rewarded, which caused great resentment. Mary, by contrast, was English, and devoted to the Anglican church. Where her husband had the reputation of a rough soldier, arrogant, aloof, bad-tempered, cold, reserved, and taciturn by turns, she made the government seem gentler and more caring. People of all persuasions, except the overtly Jacobite, sang her praises. "I believe her

---

[35] Doebner (ed.), *Memoirs*, pp. 58–59.
[36] PRO, Privy Council Registers, PC2 73–76. Carter, "Cabinet Records," p. 105. Mary was instructed by William to hold no cabinet meetings at all. W. Coxe, *Private and Original Correspondence of Charles Talbot, Duke of Shrewsbury* (London, 1821), p. 34.   [37] *Ibid.*, pp. 66–69.
[38] Aphra Behn, *A Congratulatory Poem to her Sacred Majesty Queen Mary upon her Arrival in England* (1689).

the best woman in the world," admitted the Whig leader, Somers, to the House of Commons in 1690, "and she showed herself so since coming hither."[39] On her death there was a veritable competition amongst divines and poets to see who could laud her most to the skies. Burnet went over the top in his *Essay on the Memory of the Late Queen*: "She . . . was the glory of her sex, the darling of human nature and the wonder of all that knew her."[40] John Howe joined him: "Whosoever should behold the fabric she inhabited made up of pulchritude and stile, must conclude some very lovely and venerable inhabitant dwelt there."[41] As for the poets, as "an account of the poems on the death of the Queen" puts it:

> What bulky heaps of doleful rhyme I see!
> Sure all the world runs mad with elegy . . .
> Proud of whole sheets of tedious nothings full
> And like themselves emphatically dull.[42]

The author found the efforts by Thomas Durfey to cobble "a funeral Pindarique poem" particularly excruciating, a verdict with which one can but agree, given the following sample:

> That she
> Not only was Goddess of vertue, clemency
> Of Beauty; but, what's more, a patroness of poetry.[43]

Not that all poets were patronized by her: some Jacobite sentiments were expressed in verse. One in 1690 imagined her lying in bed by her impotent husband:

> At dead of night, after an evening ball
> In her own father's lodgings at Whitehall . . .
> When lo! the scene upon the sudden turns
> Her blood grows chill, the taper dimly burns
> A trembling seizes all her limbs with fear

The ghost of her mother, Anne Hyde, draws back the curtain and upbraids her daughter, saying:

> "Can quiet slumber ever close thine eyes?
> Or is thy conscience sunk too low to rise?
> From this same place was not thy aged Sire
> Compelled by midnight-summons to retire? . . .
> Had he been murdered, it had mercy shown
> 'Tis less to kill a king, than to dethrone."[44]

The dual monarchs had somehow to overcome the charge that they had both acted unnaturally in the Revolution, a charge summed up by none other than Tom Paine, who wrote, "The characters of William and Mary have

[39] Cobbett, *Parlia. Hist.*, v, p. 631.
[40] G. Burnet, *An Essay on the Memory of the Late Queen* (London, 1695), p. 96 [hereafter Burnet, *Essay*].
[41] J. Howe, *A Discourse Relating To the Much-lamented Death and Solemn Funeral Of Our Incomparable and most Gracious Queen Mary* (London, 1695), p. 34.
[42] *The Mourning Poets* (London, 1695), p. 11.
[43] T. Durfey, *Gloriana* (London, 1695), p. 7.
[44] *POAS*, v, pp. 298–99.

always appeared to me as detestable; the one seeking to destroy his uncle, and the other her father, to get possession of power themselves."[45]

Mary found the solution to this image problem in the concept of Providence. The notion that God had weighed her father in the balance and found him wanting and that she and her husband were the instruments to avenge divine wrath was psychologically crucial to reconcile her actions in the Revolution with her conscience. Otherwise it could scarcely be described as Glorious. As Burnet recorded, she was fully convinced "that God had conducted her by an immediate hand and that she was raised up to preserve that Religion which was then everywhere in its last Agonies."[46] Any setback to the Revolution was to be seen as a sign of God's displeasure not with the monarchs but with their subjects. This was the crucial message which Mary tried to put across. If the Jacobites were to succeed it would not be her fault or her husband's: it would be the nation's.

Not that this propaganda was a cynical ploy, for Mary clearly believed it herself. "I cannot tell if it should be his will to suffer you to come to harm for our sins," she wrote privately to William in Ireland, "for though God is able, yet many times he punishes the sins of a nation as it seems good in his sight."[47] The victory at the battle of the Boyne was a sign that Providence still smiled on their cause. But it could readily frown if the English mocked it by continuing in their sinful ways. What was needed to ensure the permanence of the Glorious Revolution was what has been called the Moral Revolution.[48]

The case for a moral revolution was spelled out clearly by William Lloyd, the Bishop of St. Asaph, in a sermon preached before the queen on January 30, 1692. As the occasion marked the anniversary of the execution of Charles I, the bishop would be expected to relate his theme to the political history of the age, and he did not disappoint his audience. Commenting on the immorality which prevailed after the restoration of Charles II, he made the following observations:

It was a riddle that any Government should suffer such things; till at last it appeared they were not only suffered but designed. The design of it was plainly this, to bring in Popery again. And that had certainly returned . . . if God had not wonderfully delivered us from it. It pleased God to give us a second Resurrection, more wonderful than the former . . . It was plainly the design of God by this turn to establish the Protestant Religion in these kingdoms. And in order to that, to unite us in that common design of driving out immorality and prophaneness out of this kingdom . . . That this is God's design he hath shown us particularly by giving us such princes as enjoin us to nothing but what they are patterns of themselves . . . But hath this good Providence of God the effect that he designs, and may justly expect at our hands? We are so far from it yet, that it is a shame to say what all men know. We are now, as to our morals, perhaps as bad as ever we were. I fear I said too much in saying perhaps. It is too true, it is notorious to all the world. There never was louder swearing, never more open drunkenness, never more impudent adultery, such

---

[45] T. Paine, *Rights of Man* (London, 1792), part II, p. 116 note.
[46] Burnet, *Essay*, p. 95.
[47] Dalrymple, *Memoirs*, II, part II, p. 130 (July 6, 1690).
[48] D. W. R. Bahlman, *The Moral Revolution of 1688* (New Haven, Conn., Yale University Press, 1957); see also G. M. Straka, "The Final Phase of Divine Right Theory in England, 1688–1702," *EHR* 77 (1962), 638–58.

daily robbing and killing not only in houses but in the open streets. And if this licentiousness should run on, what will it come to in time?[49]

Although the good bishop claimed that God had given the nation "such princes as enjoin us to nothing but what they are patterns of themselves," it was also notorious that only Mary could really claim to be a model of piety and virtue. One of the more impudent adulteries was that between the king and Elizabeth Villiers, which so distressed Mary. There were also rumors that he was a homosexual. A Jacobite ballad on the coronation, April 11, 1689, claimed:

> He is not qualified for his wife
> Because of the cruel midwife's knife
> Yet buggering of Benting doth please to the life
> A dainty fine King indeed.[50]

Although these rumors are usually dismissed as being politically motivated, they were clearly believed by courtiers. "Lady Albemarle they say must have all the court this winter," John Boscawen wrote from Kensington to Lady Yarburgh on October 30, 1701. "The king is almost as fond of her as he is of her lord, and those that know her say she is very well to be liked, so as lady Jersey must knock under."[51] Whatever the truth of such gossip, its very existence meant that William could scarcely set himself up as an example of moral purity.

There were similar attempts to castigate Mary as a libertine. Thus a Jacobite litany accused her, her sister Anne, and William of sexual misconduct:

> In a court full of vice may Shrewsbury lay Molly on
> Whilst Nanny enjoys her episcopal Stallion
> And Billy with Benting does play the Italian.[52]

However, the attempt to portray the court as "full of vice" failed because the projection of Mary as a moral exemplar was patently based on the reality. She was, claimed William Wake, "a Queen so virtuous that her very example was enough to convert a libertine and to reform an Age."[53] John Dennis outdid all the panegyrists in his poem *The Court of Death*, which imagines Discord advising Death to take Mary's life in order to unman her husband. Discord "could almost fear

---

[49] William Lloyd, Bishop of St. Asaph, *A Sermon Preached before the Queen at Whitehall* (London, 1692). One aspect of pious propaganda was the publication of sermons preached before the king and queen or before Mary alone. In the absence of a chronological catalogue of all published sermons in the period it is only possible to form an impression, but there appear to have been far more in the 1690s than in the reign of Charles II. Anglican sermons, of course, were not a feature of James II's propaganda. On the contrary, they tended to be preached against rather than before him.

[50] *POAS*, v, pp. 41–42.

[51] Borthwick Institute of Historical Research, York YM/CP/1.

[52] *POAS*, v, p. 221.

[53] W. Wake, *Of our Obligation To put our Trust in God, rather than in Men, and of the Advantages of it. In A Sermon Preached before the Honourable Society of Grayes-Inn: Upon the Occasion of the Death of our late Royal Sovereign Queen Mary.* (London, 1695), p. 17.

> That as one woman by her crime
> Involv'd succeeding Ages in her Fall
> And to thy boundless sway subjected all;
> So the immortal Graces of her mind
> Growing so fast should rise in time
>   To that Sublime degree
> As to restore all human kind
>   To immortality."[54]

Mary cultivated this image. She was the inspiration behind the Proclamations enforcing the laws against adultery, blasphemy, drunkenness, fornication, and, in some eyes worst of all, Sunday trading.[55] She responded sympathetically to the societies for the reformation of manners, personally altering the commissions of the peace for Middlesex and Westminster by her special command to appoint justices from among the societies' members.[56] She tried to suppress vice by fiat in the armies and fleets and even in the American colonies. "But it was no small grief to her," admitted Burnet, "to hear they were but too generally a reproach to the religion by which they were named (I do not say which they professed for many of them seem scarce to profess it)."[57] Whether or not there was a Glorious Revolution in America is debatable; that there was no moral revolution there seems clear. Mary tried to start one, however, by taking the initiative in founding the College at Williamsburg which bears her name and her husband's.

The result of all Mary's endeavors, according to the dissenters who presented William with an address of condolence on her death, was "that the Court, that is usually the centre of vanity and voluptuousness became virtuous by the impression of her example."[58] "So vertuous was her Court," claimed the author of *Albion's Tears*, "that angels there might undefiled resort."[59]

The consequence of Mary's reputation was that her death, so far from damaging the image of the crown, gave her supporters an unrivaled opportunity to counter Jacobite propaganda. The Jacobites, of course, tried to present the event as a judgment of God upon her. One pamphleteer even noted that she died in the same month that her father labored under an unnatural rebellion and about the same hour that he went from Faversham, while she was cut off in her prime – she was only thirty-two – according to the punishment threatened to breakers of the fifth commandment.[60] But the Jacobite mud did not stick. Mary's admirers turned the tables on the nation for its sins. "We have just cause to fear our sins have hastened her death," preached the Duke of Newcastle's chaplain.

---

[54] J. Dennis, *The Court of Death* (London, 1695), p. 19.

[55] *CSPD, 1690–91*, pp. 437–38.

[56] T. C. Curtis and W. A. Speck, "The Societies for the Reformation of Manners, a case study in the practice of moral reform," *Literature and History, a New Journal for the Humanities* 3, 45–64.   [57] Burnet, *Essay*, pp. 137–39.

[58] William Bates, *A Sermon Preached upon the much Lamented Death Of our Late Gracious Sovereign Queen Mary. To which is Added the Address of Condolance to His Majesty by the Dissenting Ministers* (London, 1695), p. 25.

[59] *Albion's tears on the death of her sacred Majesty Queen Mary* (London, 1695), p. 8.

[60] *A Defence of the Archbishop's sermon on the death of her late Majesty being a vindication of the late Queen, his present Majesty and the Government from the malicious aspersions cast upon them in two late pamphlets* (London, 1695), p. 1.

God in his goodness sent us such a princess as was both a patroness and example of goodness: a glass by which this crooked age might have rectified itself; and seeing he has waited divers years, and found no amendment, what was it but just to take the mirror from us? What should they do with a light who will not walk by it?[61]

"Natural causes had their share in this evil," conceded Thomas Tenison, acknowledging that Mary died of smallpox, "but it was the immorality, the sin of the nation which hastened it as a judgment."[62]

In a curious and almost macabre way Mary continued to sustain the state even after death. Her body was embalmed the day she died, a prudent precaution in view of the putrescent effects of smallpox.[63] It took from then, December 27, 1694, until February 21, 1695 to prepare for her lying in state, the arrangements for which cost over £50,000. She then lay in state until March 5 every day from noon until five o'clock (plate 10). Four ladies of honour stood about the corpse, being relieved by four others every half hour. One who attended described the scene:

Upon her head lyes the Crown, and over it a fine canopy; at her feet lyes the sword of State, the helmet and her arms upon a cushion, the banners and scutcheons hanging round; the State is very great, and more magnificent than can be exprest; all persons are admitted, without distinction.[64]

On March 5 she was buried with elaborate ceremony in Westminster Abbey. Sir Christopher Wren supervised the construction of a railed walk from the Banqueting House to the Abbey, the rails being covered in black cloth and the walkway with gravel. Along this the funeral procession made its way in a blinding snowstorm. For the first time in English history the coffin of a monarch was accompanied by both Houses of Parliament, since normally they were dissolved by the death of a king or queen regnant. There were those who argued that parliament should have been dissolved on Mary's death, but

---

[61] D. Pead, *A Practical Discourse Upon the Death Of Our Late Gracious Queen* (London, 1695), p. 19.

[62] T. Tenison, *A Sermon Preached at the Funeral Of Her late Majesty Queen Mary* (London, 1695), p. 20.

[63] For the gruesome effects of the disease on Mary's appearance see R. Gould, *A Poem Most humbly offered to the Memory Of Her late Sacred Majesty Queen Mary* (London, 1695), pp. 12–13.

Thou dost at once what Age is doing long
And harder treat the beauteous and the young
By other ills though w'are of life bereft
There's yet at least some humane likeness left
But when we do thy barbarous work behold
We know not if the dead were young or old.
From the detestable and loathsome sight
We turn our eyes and stiffen with affright . . .
By thee disguised so lies our sacred Queen
No more with joy and wonder to be seen:
A lazar scarce to her attendants known,
Her vernal hue and balmy sweetness gone.

Cf. *A Pindarick Ode on the death of the Queen*, by a young gentleman (London, 1695), p. 6.

Thick purple spots bedeck her heavenly face
But with such majesty with such a grace:
She look't so innocent and yet so bright,
Her Glory expell'd the darkness of the night.

[64] Narcissus Luttrell, *A Brief Historical Relation of State Affairs* (6 vols., Oxford University Press, 1857), III, pp. 420–21, 442.

Plate 10 Queen Mary lying in state. Mary's untimely death from smallpox in December 1694 grieved the king and the entire nation. Engraving by Romeyn de Hooghe, 1695. The Henry E. Huntington Library, San Marino, California.

they were overruled. This made Mary's funeral procession the largest ever held for an English monarch. It entered the Abbey to the solemn strains of Purcell's specially composed Funeral Anthem. The casket was laid under a black velvet canopy while the Archbishop of Canterbury preached a sermon, and then the casket was lowered into the tomb. Even then a wax effigy of the dead queen was placed on display in the Abbey. Mary's image was to be perpetuated beyond the grave, like that of a leader of a modern totalitarian state.[65]

Mary therefore played a crucial role in the business of selling the Revolution of 1688 as Glorious. She may have played second fiddle to her husband in matters of routine administration. But in the crucial concern of retaining support for the Revolution settlement she conducted the orchestra. In this respect Sellars and Yeatman were justified in depicting the dual monarchy as the reign of Williamanmary.

[65] For discussions of the theatrical aspects of Mary's funeral and those of other monarchs by Paul S. Fritz, see his "From 'Public' to 'Private': the Royal Funerals in England, 1500–1830," in J. Whaley (ed.), *Mirrors of Mortality: Studies in the Social History of Death* (London, Europa, 1981), pp. 61–79; and "The Trade in Death: the Royal Funerals in England, 1685–1830," *Eighteenth-Century Studies* 15 (1982), 291–316. Mary's was the last "public" royal funeral in England.

9

John Locke and religious toleration

Gordon J. Schochet

The "Act of Toleration," as it has been known since it was adopted as part of constitutional revision brought about by the Revolution of 1688–89, was the culmination of nearly forty years of struggle by non-Anglican Protestants for the legal entitlement to practice their religions without penalty. The Act ultimately undermined the Church of England by destroying its standing as the only lawful church. However, it did not weaken the relationship between church and state that had long obtained in England and did not grant full, political membership in English society to those who remained outside the established confession. Those changes were still more than a hundred years away. For John Locke, the Act's half-hearted and grudging toleration was insufficient, for it retained the unacceptable mixture of civil and religious affairs that were the hallmarks of an established church.

"The business of true religion," Locke wrote in his *Letter concerning Toleration*, has to do with "regulating men's lives in accordance with virtue and piety." It is not at all concerned with "outward pomp," "ecclesiastical dominion," or "force."[1] "The end of religious society . . . is the public worship of God, and, by that means, the gaining of eternal life."[2] Thus, it is

necessary above all to distinguish between the business of civil government and that of religion, and to mark the true bounds between the church and the commonwealth. If this is not done, no end can be put to the controversies between those who truly have or pretend to have at heart a concern on the one hand for the salvation of souls, and on the other for the safety of the commonwealth.[3]

A commonwealth, he said, is "a society of men constituted only for the preserving and advancing of their civil goods." "A church [on the other hand] seems to me to be a free society of men, joining together of their own accord

---

[1] John Locke, *Epistola de Tolerantia* (Gouda, 1689; written ca. 1685), trans. J. W. Gough from Locke, *Epistola de Tolerantia/A Letter on Toleration*, ed. J. W. Gough and Raymond Klibansky (Oxford University Press, 1968), p. 59. Cited throughout as Locke, *Epistola*.

The more familiar title, *Letter concerning Toleration*, was adopted by William Popple in his 1689 translation. Although it introduces some twentieth-century anachronisms, the Gough version is more faithful to Locke's original Latin text than Popple's and has the advantage of including the Latin on facing pages. It is the only other English translation. The Pepple version is conveniently available in a modern edition by James H. Tully (Indianapolis, Hackett, 1983).

[2] Locke, *Epistola*, p. 77. See also p. 103.

[3] *Ibid.*, p. 65.

for the public worship of God in such manner as they believe will be accept-able to the Deity for the salvation of their souls." The church, therefore,

> itself is absolutely separate and distinct from the commonwealth and civil affairs. The boundaries on both sides are fixed and immovable. He mixes heaven and earth together, things most remote and opposite, who confuses these two societies, which in their origin, their end, and their whole substance are utterly and completely different.[4]

While not unique, these were radical claims by the standards of late seven-teenth-century England, for Locke was implicitly calling for nothing less than the separation of the Anglican Church from the English state. Locke was certainly not direct in calling for this separation, but the implications of his words are clear. Not until he wrote a codicil to his will a few months before his death did he surrender his insistent refusal to acknowledge his authorship of the *Letter*. That denial and his continuing membership in the church may have been signs of Locke's appreciation of the radical nature of his argument. Throughout the 1690s he moved in Anglican circles that would have been closed to an enemy of the establishment and held governmental positions that he might have been denied had his true beliefs been known.

The aim of this essay is to consider Locke's views on the relationship of religion and politics in the context of Restoration England as well as that context itself, using "Locke and his times" to shed light on one another. By and large, my concerns are historical; I do not deal directly with the "transcendent" meaning of the *Epistola de Tolerantia* nor with its "contribu-tion" to the "development" of the idea and/or practice of religious liberty.

The essay makes three claims about the *Epistola*: first, that it was a political and not a religious tract, a characteristic that it shared with the prevailing manner of discussing the general question of toleration in late seventeenth-century England; second, that, despite its title, its subject matter was what we would call "religious liberty," not "toleration" and that in this respect the work differed considerably from most contemporary writings; and third, that its intended audience was the "ruling class" of England, the leaders of its government, established church, and society in general. The first of these claims is intended as a way of understanding both Locke and the discussions of religious dissidence to which his tract was a contribution. The second claim turns upon definitions and historical circumstances rather than upon textual analysis. The third explains why some of the arguments of the *Epistola* took the form they did.

The issue of religious "toleration" and the collateral issues by which it was surrounded were political in the period. Debates about the nature and content of religious belief and practice and about God's word and the meaning of Scripture – debates that were *internal* to religion – were either conspicuously absent or of secondary importance. The existence of an established church

---

[4] *Ibid.*, pp. 71, 85–87. Cf. John Locke, *Two Treatises of Government* (1690), ed. Peter Laslett (Cambridge University Press, 1960), part II, para. 2. The Aristotelian–functional differentiation of institutions and structures according to their ends or purposes was a cardinal element of Locke's philosophy and analytic method.

was sufficient to "politicize" what might otherwise have been a religious question, and the adoption of the Clarendon Code completed the process by making it a political offense to practice any religion other than Anglicanism.

I suggest below that resort to the terminology of "indifference" – or "*adiaphora*," as it was known in the early church – insured that the Church of England would fail to meet or deal with dissenters on their own grounds, that is, the nature of religious belief and practice. When nonconformists insisted that what the Church of England called "indifferent" – that is, religious practices about which God was allegedly silent and permissive – was, according to their consciences, "required" by God, they were not being recalcitrant but were manifesting the fact that the Anglican establishment had eliminated the possibility of discourse. They could hardly compromise on what they thought God had commanded, while the Church of England and its defenders in the House of Commons continued to maintain that since these were merely matters of indifference, they could be "imposed."

Recourse to the sanctity of "conscience" and pleas for its "liberty" fared no better, for conscience itself was a vague, potentially dangerous, and ultimately incoherent notion. In neither religion nor politics could conscience be an infallible guide: it was personal and irreducibly individual and it could err, as the conflicts among claims of conscience clearly showed. The troubles of the recent times, according to enemies of the nonconformists, were the confusion of the fact that consciences were materially and morally incoercible with a presumption of their sanctity and a consequent insistence upon *liberty* of conscience. In the period before 1688, this view was regarded by the Church of England as a dangerous doctrine that could not be admitted into the established Church; allowing those who preached it to remain outside the Church and unregulated would reintroduce the chaos of the Commonwealth and Protectorate period by permitting the spread of schismatic, heretical, and disloyal teachings that would mislead and corrupt the masses of the people. There was a saving factor, though, for conscience could be "informed" and "instructed" without being violated, and the "will" could be "engaged" while that instruction was taking place. It was a doctrine that had a respectable lineage in the Church of England, going back at least to Richard Hooker's injunctions to Puritans in his *Laws of Ecclesiastical Polity*. Incorporating the dissenters into the establishment was therefore to be desired, but if they refused to come along, they must be penalized – not for their erroneous consciences but for the threats they posed to the civil peace – and induced into submission.

Locke himself had taken this position as early as 1660–61 in his earliest political writings, a pair of tracts concerning the right of the magistrate to impose indifferent religious practices. He separated "a liberty of the jugdment" – which comprehended "the whole liberty of conscience" – from "a liberty of the will," which could "be removed without infringing the liberty of the conscience." Applying this distinction to indifferency, he insisted "that all the magistrate's laws, civil as well as ecclesiastical, those that concern divine worship as much as those that concern civil life, are just and valid, obliging men to act but not to judge; and, providing for both at the same time, unite a necessity of obedience with a liberty of conscience."[5]

He soon altered his views, and from 1667 on argued that indifferency was an inappropriate standard against which to evaluate the legitimate extent of magisterial power over religious practices.[6] Nonetheless, Locke remained constant in his insistence that from the perspective of the society at large, religion must be understood politically. While he had religious views that he expressed in other places, all his writings about "toleration" and related matters looked at the issues in terms of political consequences rather than religious validity. Seen from this perspective, the very point of the *Letter concerning Toleration* was to change the political perceptions of his audience. The tract was not concerned with whether this or that practice was indifferent or sinful, with the debate between trinitarians and socinians, or even with the requirements of salvation. The *Epistola* was about religion, rather than a part of it.

The term "religious liberty" was not widely used in seventeenth-century England, and the concept itself was infrequently employed. The prevailing vocabulary and conceptual apparatus, which Locke himself used, were those of "toleration." The modern view, strictly construed, distinguishes between *liberty* as a "right" or "entitlement" and *toleration* as a "grant" or "privilege." In seventeenth-century England, it was conceptually difficult to make this distinction, for liberty itself was only then emerging from a historic and legalistic framework in which it was conceived as a grant (and therefore a consequence of politics) into a conceptual context in which it could be understood as a right (and therefore prior to politics). Indeed, much of the political debate in the Stuart period was between these rival conceptions,[7] and the vocabulary and concept of rights themselves were relatively new and imperfectly understood in the seventeenth century.[8] Conceived as a grant, toleration thus presupposes a legitimate, granting agency that is empowered to bestow privileges – in this case, the king and/or the parliament, with the participation of the Church of England. Liberty, on the other hand, as an entitlement, is antagonistic to the notion of a grantor and is itself held up as a standard by which political agencies are to be judged.

[5] John Locke, "Second Tract on Government," in *Two Tracts on Government* (1660–61), ed. and trans. Philip Abrams (Cambridge University Press, 1967), pp. 238–39. Abrams cites Robert Sanderson, *De Obligatione Conscientiae, Praelectiones Decem* (London, 1660), bk. VI, paras. iv and v, and Jeremy Taylor, *The Liberty of Prophesying, Ductor Dubitantium* (London, 1648), bk. III, para. i, for parallel statements.

[6] See John Locke, "An Essay concerning Toleracon 1667," Bodl., Ms. Locke c. 28, fols. 21–32, esp. fol. 22r. A modernized and slightly incorrect version of the text was published by Carlo A. Viano in John Locke, *Scritti Editi e Inediti Sulla Tolleranza*, ed. and trans. with an introduction by Viano (Turin, Taylor Torino, 1961), pp. 81–105; the relevant passage can be found on p. 86.

[7] This, it seems to me, is precisely the point of J. G. A. Pocock's *The Ancient Constitution and the Feudal Law: a Study of English Historical Thought in the Seventeenth Century. A Reissue with a Retrospect* (Cambridge University Press, 1987). See also Howard Nenner, "Law, Liberty, and Property: a Retrospective View" in J. R. Jones (ed.), *Liberty Preserved* (Palo Alto, Stanford, 1992). Locke's *Two Treatises*, which argued that liberty is a natural right that is prior to the state, was a contribution to this debate.

[8] Richard Tuck, *Natural Rights Theories: the Origin and Development* (Cambridge University Press, 1979), is the central reference here, but my views obviously differ from his. See also Brian Tierney, "Tuck on Rights: Some Medieval Problems," *History of Political Thought* 4 (1983), 429–41, and the same author's "Origins of Natural Rights Language," *ibid.*, x (1982), 615–46.

Although our modern vocabulary of religious liberty and its conceptual trappings were not fully available to Locke, the *Epistola* was precisely about ending the ties between the English state and its established church and the consequent removal of all official, political distinctions that were based on religious beliefs and membership.

The vocabulary that was available to Locke was not quite appropriate or adequate.[9] He was forced to argue in terms that were set for him by the debate in which he was to engage. The key word in that debate was "toleration," which was ambiguously used in the sense of a granted privilege and as a "right" and "entitlement." It was the latter sense that Locke intended by "toleration," thereby extending the meaning of a prevailing set of concepts to cover something of which most of his auditors probably would not have approved.[10]

The claims of the *Epistola* were that religious diversity was ineliminable; that it would not be destructive of the social and political fabric; that the regulation of religious beliefs and practices *qua* religion was beyond the proper scope of civil magistracy; and that attempting to regulate it and impose practices and doctrines in pursuit of uniformity was dangerous and might provoke resistance. For "Man's first care should be of his soul, and he should do his utmost to maintain peace; though there are few who will think it peace where they see a desert made."[11] Behind this doctrine was an implicit appeal to religious liberty, to the notion that it is the "right" of people to have their own religious beliefs, perhaps as part of the "property" they enjoy as the natural rights of the *Two Treatises of Government*.[12]

The *Epistola de Tolerantia* is generally presumed to have been written four years before it was published – in 1685, on the heels of Monmouth's ill-fated rebellion[13] and when Locke himself was at work also on the *Essay concerning Human Understanding*.[14] Nothing is known about the precise circumstances of its composition – even the date is unconfirmed; the only source for it appears in an uncorroborated letter written in 1705 by the Dutch Remonstrant and

---

[9] The translator of the *Epistola*, William Popple, had called for "absolute liberty" in his Preface, a plea that Thomas Long, one of Locke's critics, called "a Jesuitical Plot." ([Thomas Long], *The Letter concerning Toleration Decipher'd and the Absurdity and Impiety of an Absolute Toleration Demonstrated* [London, 1689], p. 1. Locke ignored Long and did not reply to this attack.)

In the final analysis, Popple's was probably more extreme a claim than Locke wanted to make; it was a political liability as well. "Liberty of conscience" was another possibility, but Locke had specifically rejected it in the *Two Tracts* as an unsatisfactory basis for public policy. Conscience was best avoided altogether.

[10] Ironically, Locke thus made an important contribution to what has become the twentieth-century practice of using "toleration" as a synonym for religious liberty.

[11] Locke, *Epistola*, p. 131.

[12] As I have argued in "Toleration, Revolution, and Judgment in the Development of Locke's Political Thought," *Political Science* 40 (1988), esp. pp. 92–93.

[13] Which Locke supported and to which he made at least two financial contributions; see Richard Ashcraft, *Revolutionary Politics and Locke's "Two Treatises of Government"* (Princeton University Press, 1986), pp. 414, 424–25, 453, and 457–58; and Gordon J. Schochet, "Radical Politics and Ashcraft's Treatise on Locke," *Journal of the History of Ideas* 50 (1989), 495–96.

[14] Klibansky, Preface to Locke, *Epistola*, pp. xvi–xvii, suggests that Locke interrupted his work on the *Essay* – between books II and III – to write the *Epistola*. Maurice Cranston, *John Locke: a Biography* (London, Macmillian, 1957), p. 259, gives the year of composition as 1686, but without any references.

Locke's close associate, Philip van Limborch[15] – but the general subject was one that had long engaged Locke.

Of course, 1685 was an important year for anyone concerned about liberty – and especially religious liberty. The succession of James II in February, the failure of Monmouth and Argyll in June, and the Bloody Assizes that followed in its wake – to say nothing of Baron George Jeffreys's obvious hostility to dissenters in general and Presbyterians in particular – James's insistence upon installing Roman Catholic officers in the army and his eventual prorogation of parliament in November rather than confront its opposition to that policy, and his continuing political association with the French king all underscored what Andrew Marvell had contended in 1678, that "popery and arbitrary government" traveled hand-in-glove.[16] The Revocation of the Edict of Nantes on October 15, 1685, and the renewal of French persecution of Protestants – which, in fact, had begun several years earlier and was merely made official by the revocation – could only have aggravated the concerns of people like Locke and Limborch. So there is ample circumstantial reason to accept Limborch's date, but there is nothing in the *Epistola* as it was published to link it to any of the events of that year.

The original, Latin version of the *Letter – Epistola de Tolerantia –* was published anonymously in April 1689, in the Netherlands, where Locke had been living in political exile until February. Copies were sent to him almost immediately by Limborch, to whom he addressed the work[17] and who had supervised the printing of the first edition.[18] Locke received them in early June.[19] In the meantime, parliament had finally passed, and on May 24 – the twenty-seventh anniversary of Charles II's having accepted the Act of Uniformity – William had approved, the toleration Bill. Although Locke had no direct part in the passage of the Act, he closely followed the progress of the Bill.[20]

The English translation of the *Epistola*, prepared by the Unitarian William Popple – "without my privity," Locke declared[21] – was licensed on October 3

[15] On March 24, 1704/5, Limborch wrote to Lady Masham (the former Damaris Cudworth), in whose home Locke had died, that, known only to Limborch, Locke "wrote the famous letter concerning toleration to me" in the winter of 1685 while he was living in the home of Dr. Egbertus Veen (where he was hiding from English agents). Quoted in H. R. Fox Bourne, *The Life of John Locke* (2 vols., New York, Harper, 1876), II, p. 34, n. 1 (my translation).

[16] See, David Ogg, *England in the Reigns of James II and William III*, paperback edition (Oxford University Press, 1969), pp. 150–51, 161; J. R. Western, *Monarchy and Revolution: the English State in the 1680s* (London, Blanchford Press, 1972), pp. 138–39; and John Childs, *The Army, James II, and the Glorious Revolution* (New York, St. Martin's Press, 1980). The quotation is from the title of Andrew Marvell's *An Account of the Growth of Popery and Arbitrary Government in England* ("Printed at Amsterdam" [London, 1678]).

[17] For Limborch and Locke's relationship with him, see *The Correspondence of John Locke*, ed. E. S. de Beer (8 vols., Oxford, Clarendon Press, 1976–89), II, pp. 648–52 (a brief essay by de Beer entitled "Philippus van Limborch and the Remonstrants"); Mario Montouri, *John Locke on Toleration and the Unity of God* (Amsterdam, J. C. Gieben, 1983), pp. xvi–xix; and Cranston, *John Locke*, pp. 233–34 and ch. 18 *passim*. I have found Locke's copy of the work and am preparing a brief note on it.

[18] Limborch to Locke, April 15–25, 1690, in Locke, *Correspondence*, ed. de Beer, IV, p. 57 (letter 1283). All references to Locke's correspondence are to this edition.

[19] Locke to Limborch, June 6, 1689, *Ibid.*, III, pp. 633–34 (Letter 1147).

[20] There are several references to the Bill and to the general subject of toleration in the letters between Locke and Limborch during this period.

[21] In a codicil to his will dated September 15, 1704, Bodl., Ms. Locke b. 5, item 14, and now available in Locke,

of that year and was issued by the Whig publishers Awnsham and John Churchill, with whom Locke was associated for the rest of his life.[22] The *Letter* appeared during the opening session of a clerical commission appointed to revise the Prayer Book and immediately attracted the attention of Thomas Long, a High Church cleric and enemy of nonconformity, a prolific controversialist, and a member of the Convocation, who is generally unknown today.[23] The only other known response came from Jonas Proast, a rather less distinguished but better remembered critic.[24] Proast engaged Locke in a dispute that lasted until the philosopher's death in 1704, during which they exchanged five works, three by Proast, and two by Locke.[25]

Whatever the reason for publishing the *Epistola*, the English translation became a belated contribution to what was to become the toleration debates of 1688–89. These debates were themselves merely the latest installments in a controversy that had raged since the Restoration.[26] The return of the royal house of Stuart in 1660 brought to an end the relatively permissive sectarianism and religious freedom that had characterized the Protectorate. The accompanying reestablishment of the Church of England with its rituals and structures meant that England once again had a single, inclusive, national church. Even though Charles II promised to work for "a liberty to tender

---

Correspondence, VIII, pp. 419–27, at p. 426. In fact, Locke certainly knew Popple and had reported to Limborch as early as June 1689 that "some Englishman is just now at work in translating the pamphlet on Toleration." Locke to Limborch, June 6, 1689, in Locke, *Correspondence*, III, p. 634 (letter 1147). De Beer discusses Locke's relationship with Popple in Locke, *Correspondence*, III, p. 623, n. 2. On Popple himself, see Caroline Robbins, "Absolute Liberty: the Life and Thought of William Popple, 1638–1708," *William and Mary Quarterly*, 3rd series, 24 (1967), 190–233, reprinted in *Absolute Liberty: a Selection from the Articles and Papers of Caroline Robbins*, ed. Barbara Taft (Hamden,Conn., Archon Books, 1982), ch. 1.

[22] In fact, Locke had met Awnsham Churchill a year earlier in Rotterdam. See Cranston, *John Locke*, pp. 299 and 311 nn., and Locke, *Correspondence*, III, p. 475 (note by de Beer).

[23] Long is not noticed in the *Dictionary of National Biography* and is not mentioned by Klibansky or Gough. He has been described by one of Locke's bibliographers as a "fertile but rather unintelligent writer" (H. O. Christophersen, *A Bibliographic Introduction to the Study of John Locke*, Skrifter utgitt av Det Norske Videnskaps-Akademi i Oslo, II, no. 8 [Oslo, Jacob Dybwad, 1930], p. 16); Cranston dismisses him in a footnote (*John Locke*, p. 331, n. 2). He wrote more than thirty tracts in which he consistently attacked toleration, nonconformity, and the concessions the Church of England would have to make to achieve a reunion with Presbyterianism.

In the pamphlet against the *Epistola*, Long grouped the Presbyterians, Independents, Calvin, and Baxter with Locke as those who "would bring the whole Church and State to Confusion." *The Letter for Toleration Decipher'd*, p. 5. Long is not mentioned in Locke's library catalog. See John Harrison and Peter Laslett, *The Library of John Locke*, Oxford Bibliographic Society Publications, n.s., XIII (Oxford University Press, 1965).

It turns out that Long wrote the tract that has served as the principal source of information about the Convocation, the anonymous *Vox Cleri: or, The State of the Clergy concerning the Making of Alterations in the Established Liturgy* (London, 1690). Virtually every account of the Convocation is traceable to Long, a fact that has not been mentioned – and may not have been known – by commentators since the eighteenth century. See Gordon J. Schochet, "The Act of Toleration: Persecution, Non-conformity, and Religious Indifference," forthcoming in Dale Hoak and M. Feingold (eds.) *The World of William and Mary* (Berkeley and Los Angeles, University of California Press, 1992).

[24] Proast was chaplain of Queen's College, Oxford, and subsequently of All Souls'. He is discussed by A. A. Seaton, *The Theory of Toleration under the Later Stuarts* (Cambridge University Press, 1911), pp. 243 and 258–63; H. F. Russell Smith, *The Theory of Religious Liberty in the Reigns of Charles II and James II* (Cambridge University Press, 1911), p. 105; and Klibansky and Gough in Locke, *Epistola*, pp. xxii, 32, 33, 40, 44 and 46; and cited by Montouri, *Locke on Toleration*, pp. xxxi n. 1, xxxiii n. 4, xliv–xlvi, 143–45, and 164–65.

[25] See Christophersen, *Bibliographic Introduction*, pp. 16–19, for details.

[26] The following discussion draws upon Schochet, "The Act of Toleration." The best published account of toleration and comprehension in the period remains Roger Thomas, "Comprehension and Indulgence," in Geoffrey F. Nuttall and Owen Chadwick (eds.) *From Uniformity to Unity, 1662–1962* (London, Society for the Promotion of Christian Knowledge, 1962), ch. 4.

consciences" in his famous Breda Declaration,[27] the adoption of the Clarendon Code not only proscribed non-Anglican religious practices but called for the punishment of those who were caught engaging in them, thus at least *legally* bringing to a close the English Reformation.

Outside the official church there were now numbers of dissident Christians, who, in political terms, comprised three different groups: Roman Catholics, Presbyterians, and separatist or nonconforming Protestants. The Presbyterians wanted to be members of the established church but were kept out by their conscientious "scrupling" at some of the requirements of the Act of Uniformity and were reviled by many royalists and churchmen as king-killing revolutionaries. The separatists, especially the Independents (who were doctrinally akin to Presbyterians), the Baptists, Quakers, and members of other, smaller sects, intentionally separated themselves from the establishment because they did not accept the discipline of a national church or of ruling synods but organized themselves instead into loose confederations of "gathered congregations" (the Independents) or because of doctrinal differences.[28] The Catholics posed the greatest political difficulty. Many of them had been loyal to the restored king during his exile, and their cause was championed by Charles and later James (who eventually converted to Roman Catholicism), many of their political followers, and numbers of High Church Anglicans. Other Englishmen feared Catholics for their presumed loyalty to the Pope and dreaded the prospects of the loss of their Protestant religion and those parts of their estates that had formerly been church lands.

The issue, throughout the latter half of the seventeenth century, was what to do with these dissidents. Should the Presbyterians be "comprehended," that is, readmitted into the Church of England as they and their "liberal" Anglican supporters urged? If so, what liturgical and structural changes would be required? Conversely, what accommodations were the Presbyterians themselves willing to make? Should the remaining Protestants be "tolerated" and allowed to engage in their religious practices with impunity? Those questions were further compounded by the fact that those who intentionally separated from the Church of England increasingly asserted their "right" to exist and be tolerated. Was it possible to devise a toleration standard that would not include the Catholics? (Apart from the monarchy and, to a certain extent, the Quakers, there was little overt support for the toleration of Catholics.)

Further embedded in all this was a series of disputes about adiaphora and the legitimate extent of magisterial imposition in religious matters. There was little questioning of the proposition that the magistrate was not permitted to issue commands that were contrary to God's express will nor of the moral prohibition of his interfering with religious acts that were deemed "necess-

---

[27] The text is conveniently available in Andrew Browning (ed.), *English Historical Documents, 1660–1714* (London, Oxford University Press, 1954), doc. 1, pp. 57–58.

[28] The best recent account of the nonconforming Protestants in this period is Michael R. Watts, *The Dissenters: from the Reformation to the French Revolution* (Oxford University Press, 1978), esp. chs. 2 and 3.

ary."[29] Adiaphora were generally regarded by the church as legitimate objects of magisterial regulation. Those outside the Anglican establishment, on the other hand, often contended that indifferency signaled immunity from political imposition.

At another and more fundamental level there could be disagreement about the very assertion that something was an item of adiaphora and therefore optional. And so long as there was controversy at that stage, the contending parties would be arguing past each other, with one side engaging in political debate and the other in internal, religious disputation. Indifferency had divided the Church of England since the Reformation and was a major component of the religious debates on the eve of the Restoration. It was the subject of Locke's early essays[30] and, nominally, was the issue that kept Anglicans and Presbyterians apart and prevented their reunion after the Glorious Revolution. In the hands of the establishment, as Locke appreciated, the doctrine of adiaphora could be a powerful and – to Dissenters – dangerous weapon, for it provided the magistrate with a theoretical and allegedly divinely sanctioned justification for imposition and, when that failed, persecution. "Indeterminate things," he wrote, "however much they may be under the power of the civil magistrate, yet cannot upon that plea be introduced into sacred ritual and imposed upon religious assemblies, because in sacred worship they immediately cease to be indifferent."[31]

The period 1660–89 was marked by seemingly constant and endless debate about the political status of the various non-Anglicans and by attempts to replace the official policy of persecution with more moderate treatment. Comprehension and toleration schemes, usually in tandem, were regularly proposed in and to parliament, and were just as regularly rejected or mooted by the king's adjourning of the session.[32] One of the recurring goals of the Presbyterians, Independents, and their supporters was to devise a toleration measure that would not extend to Catholics. The usual formula was to retain the various penal statutes but to grant nonconforming Protestants "indulgences" from their operation. No such antipapist goal motivated Charles, and conflict over Roman Catholicism was among the issues that characterized his relations with parliament.

On March 15, 1672, Charles, apparently acting on the advice of the Earl of Shaftesbury, his Chancellor and Locke's patron, reissued a Declaration of

---

[29] To act contrary to God's commands is, of course, to sin, and the magistrate could hardly claim the power to order subjects to sin. In cases of conflict – when the magistrate and subjects disagreed about whether something was sinful – the doctrine of passive obedience permitted subjects to follow their consciences and to disobey the magistrate rather than God but required that they endure the civil penalties attached to their disobedience.

The only significant exception to this limitation was the doctrine of nonresistance, espoused by Sir Robert Filmer, Thomas Hobbes, and very few others. According to nonresistance theory, the sin was on the magistrate (or whoever the legitimate superior was who issued the order), who was answerable to God, rather than upon the subject, who was therefore obliged to act as commanded.

[30] The so-called *Two Tracts*, written in response to (Edward Bagshaw), *The Great Question concerning Things Indifferent in Religious Worship* (London, 1660). Abrams has provided a bibliography of indifferency literature, as an appendix to the *Two Tracts*, pp. 250–54.

[31] Locke, *Epistola*, p. 107.

[32] See John Spurr, "The Church of England, Comprehension and the Toleration Act of 1689," *EHR* 104 (1989), 927–46, for an excellent account of these proposals.

Indulgence. Ignoring traditional understandings of the suspending powers and specifically including Catholics, he declared it his "will and pleasure" that all ecclesiastical penalties "against whatsoever sort of nonconformists or recusants, be immediately *suspended*."[33] Because parliament had not been in session when the declaration was issued, there was no official response for nearly a year. During that time the indulgence was in force, and more than 1,500 dissenting ministers and chapels were licensed.[34] When it reconvened, the Commons criticized the declaration and launched a sharp attack on the suspending power itself, insisting that the king was "very much misinformed" about the nature of his prerogative rights, "since no such power was ever claimed, or exercised, by any of your maj.'s predecessors."[35]

Wisely refraining from escalating the developing constitutional struggle, Charles withdrew the declaration. He did not renounce his claim to a royal suspending power, but he did agree to the antipapist first Test Act, which was a direct response to the Declaration of Indulgence.[36] The Test Act drove Roman Catholics from office and effectively destroyed the current ministry. Of equal importance was the fact that the Act forced James – however tacitly – to acknowledge his conversion to Catholicism, for he refused to take the required religious test and shortly afterwards resigned as Lord High Admiral.

Some measure of the prevailing attitude towards liberty of conscience and toleration can be gathered from the railings of William Starkey, Rector of Pulham in Norfolk, who, in 1675, attacked the "two Idols set among our Brain-sick People."[37] Adopting what had become the standard, High Anglican (and Hobbesian) distinction between conscience and will[38] – and which Locke employed in his 1660–61 manuscripts on indifferency – Starkey ridiculed the nonconformists' pleas for liberty of conscience on the ground that consciences could not be coerced to begin with. "The Magistrates Sword and Power can reach only to *Goods*, or *Body*, or what is *external*," he wrote, "[and] can have no power of the conclusions of the Understanding, or resolutions of the Will, or any thing *internal*, which we must understand by *Conscience*." Force is "inconsistent with, and cannot be offered to *Conscience*." Laws and regulations that were necessary to the safety of society could be enforced without infringing upon people's consciences. Therefore, "to suspend *Penalties* is the ready way to make the Rulers undervalued and contemned; their *Laws* slighted and reproached; to cause the Offender to grow insecure, impudent

---

[33] Charles II, "His Majesty's Declaration to All His Loving Subjects" (1672), text from Browning, *Documents*, doc. 140, pp. 387 and 388; my emphasis. While the Declaration promised to license public places where Protestant nonconformists could meet for worship, Roman Catholics were restricted to "the exercise of their worship in their private houses only."

[34] Watts, *The Dissenters*, p. 248.

[35] Cobbett, *Parlia. Hist.*, IV, p. 551. See also R. A. Beddard, "The Restoration Church," in J. R. Jones (ed.), *The Restored Monarchy, 1660–1668* (London, Macmillan, 1979), p. 169.

[36] See Frank Bate, *The Declaration of Indulgence, 1672: a Study in the Rise of Organized Dissent* (London, University of Liverpool Press, 1908), for a detailed study.

[37] William Starkey, *An Apology for the Laws Ecclesiastical Established, that Command Our Publick Exercise in Religion* (London, 1675), p. A2.

[38] See Gordon J. Schochet, "Intending (Political) Obligation: Hobbes and the Voluntary Basis of Society," in Mary G. Dietz (ed.), *Thomas Hobbes and Political Theory* (Norman, University of Oklahoma Press, 1990), pp. 55–73; and Schochet, "Toleration, Revolution, and Judgment," esp. pp. 86–87.

and not ashamed; to make the heart of the Righteous *faint*, and the hands of the Weaker strengthened." Moreover, it would "involve the whole Nation confusedly to run into an Universal *Licentiousness,* upon hope of *Impunity.*"[39]

This was generally the way official attitudes would remain until 1687. That year, seeking to advance the causes of his fellow Roman Catholics,[40] James issued an indulgence proclamation that suspended the operation of the penal laws for Dissenters as well as Catholics. Constraining consciences in "matters of meer religion," James said, "has ever been directly contrary to our inclination, as we think it is to the interest of government, which it destroys by spoiling trade, depopulating countries, and discouraging strangers; and finally, that it never obtained the end for which it was employed . . . to reduce this kingdom to an exact conformity in religion."[41]

Fearing both the encouragements given to popery and the possibility that James might acquire the support of the Dissenters, moderate and high-churchmen alike were alarmed by the scheme. In fact, the king actively sought the support of nonconformists, and some Presbyterians then offered their public thanks,[42] throwing their lot in with the sectarians, thereby breaking from more conventional, nonseparating Presbyterianism.

The next year, with the apparent intention of forcing the cooperation of the church, the king reissued the declaration and ordered that it be read in all the parishes in the country.[43] Until that point, the church had been divided about the indulgence: moderates feared the use of the prerogative in support of papists, and high-churchmen objected to indulgence for nonconformists. The new order, however, was generally disliked and disobeyed and brought James and some of the leaders of the church into open conflict. The Archbishop of Canterbury, William Sancroft, otherwise a strong supporter of royal authority, and six of his fellow bishops petitioned the king to excuse their clergy from reading the declaration on the ground that it was based on the suspending powers and was therefore illegal.[44] Their petition to James was published

---

[39] Starkey, *Apology,* pp. 172–73, 181, and 185.

[40] According to a recent study, James believed that the religious reconciliation of everyone in England was possible. (John Miller, "James II and Toleration," in Eveline Cruickshanks [ed.] *By Force or Default? The Revolution of 1688–89* [Edinburgh, John Donald, 1989], pp. 8–27, esp. 18–19.) The threat of a return to Rome was not illusory. (See Lionel K. J. Glassey, *Politics and the Appointment of Justices of the Peace, 1675–1720* [Oxford University Press, 1979], pp. 66–99; and Geoffrey S. Holmes, "The Glorious Revolution and the Church of England," Friends of Lambeth Palace Library, *Annual Report* [1988], 13–28.)

[41] James II, "His Majesty's Gracious Declaration to All His Loving Subjects for Liberty of Conscience" (1687), reprinted in Browning, *Documents,* doc. 146, pp. 395–96.

[42] R. A. Beddard, "Vincent Alsop and the Emancipation of Restoration Dissent," *Journal of Ecclesiastical History* 24 (1973), 176–77. See also Thomas, "Comprehension and Indulgence," pp. 234–35. The "Address of Thanks from the Presbyterians of London" appeared in the *London Gazette* for April 28–May 2, 1687, and is reprinted in Browning, *Documents,* doc. 147, pp. 397–98.

[43] James II, "The King's Declaration for Liberty of Conscience," reprinted in Browning, *Documents,* doc. 149, p. 400. The reissue contained a new preamble and postscript.

[44] The power was effectively and finally removed in 1689 in the Bill of Rights. See Carolyn E. Edie, "Revolution and the Rule of Law: the End of the Dispensing Power, 1689," *Eighteenth-Century Studies* 10 (1977), 434–50; and Lois G. Schwoerer, *The Declaration of Rights, 1689* (Baltimore and London, Johns Hopkins University Press, 1981), esp. pp. 59–64.
   The precise words used by the Convention are:
(1) That the pretended power of suspending of Lawes or the execution of Lawes by Regall Authority without Consent of Parliament is illegal.

– although not by them – and they were charged with seditious libel. The famous trial *and acquittal* of the "Seven Bishops"[45] created a permanent political rift between James and the church but helped to establish an unprecedented cooperativeness between the church and the wing of the Presbyterian Dissenters led by Richard Baxter that had not supported the declaration. The short-term prospects for a genuine reunion of Anglicans and Presbyterians were probably better as a result of the declaration than they had been throughout the Restoration. But that was soon to change. Nonetheless, the declaration was among the important factors that led to the Revolution of 1688.

George Saville, Marquis of Halifax, was suspicious of the declaration and of James's having requested statements of appreciation. In a tract that was an extended love and marriage metaphor, Halifax asserted that "Thanks must be voluntary, not only unconstrained but unsolicited, else they are either trifles or snares . . . little less improper than love letters that were solicited by the lady to whom they are to be directed." The declaration, he said, was intended to advance the interests of Roman Catholics, not those of the Dissenters, and in a memorable and oft-quoted passage, Halifax warned the Protestant nonconformists, "You are therefore to be hugged now, only that you may be the better squeezed at another time."[46] Gilbert Burnet, writing from Amsterdam, declared that suspending laws was part of the "*Legislative Power*" which was so shared by the Lords and Commons "that no *Law* can be either *made, repealed,* or, which is all one, *suspended,* but by their Consent." In words that were worthy of Locke's "Second Treatise," he said that James's declaration amounted to "the placing this *Legislative Power* singly in the King, [which] is a subversion of this whole *Government* . . . being so contrary to the *Trust* that is given to the *Prince* who ought to execute it, [James's act] will put Men upon uneasie and dangerous Inquiries."[47]

The *Epistola de Tolerantia* apparently was not intended to be part of this debate, and it could hardly have been a response to the Act of Toleration. Not only was it written and published too early, but there is little in Locke's text[48] that can be linked to any specific or overt act or policy. On the whole, the work is too abstract and general to be applied to the Act of Toleration. Even though the inference of the argument was that the Act was inadequate, Locke

---

(2) That the pretended power of dispensing with lawes or the Execution of lawes by regall authority as it has been assumed and exercised of late is illegal.
(Text from Schwoerer, *Declaration*, p. 296.)

[45] See Roger Thomas, "The Seven Bishops and their Petition, 18 May 1688," *Journal of Ecclesiastical History* 11 (1966), 56–70; and G. V. Bennett, "The Seven Bishops: a Reconsideration," in Derek Baker (ed.), *Studies in Church History*, xv: *Religious Motivation: Biographical and Sociological Problems for the Church Historian*, Ecclesiastical History Society Publications (Oxford, Blackwell 1978), pp. 267–87.

[46] (George Savile, Marquess of Halifax), *A Latter to a Dissenter* (London, 1687) reprinted in his *Complete Works*, ed. J. P. Kenyon (Harmondsworth, Penguin, 1969), pp. 110 and 106.

[47] (Gilbert Burnet), *A Letter Containing Some Reflections on His Majesty's Declaration for Liberty of Conscience* (Amsterdam, 1687), reprinted in Burnet, *A Collection of Eighteen Papers Relating to the Affairs of Church & State During the Reign of King James the Second* (London, 1689), pp. 30–31.

[48] The Preface insisted, "It is neither Declarations of Indulgence, nor Acts of Comprehension, such as have yet been practiced or projected amongst us, that can do the work. The first will but palliate, the second increase our evil" (Locke, *Epistola*, Appendix, p. 164). But these were Popple's words, not Locke's.

himself was rather positive about it when writing to Limborch shortly after it was signed.[49]

But there is no need to link the *Epistola* to specific circumstances, for Locke had been writing about the relations between established religions and members of dissident sects for more than twenty-five years. It was the subject of his first major work as well as an issue to which he returned again and again throughout his life[50] and was the subject on which he was at work when he died. In one form or another, religious toleration constitutes the single strand that unites his entire intellectual and political career.

The detheologization of the rhetoric of religious dispute and its transformation into a relatively public, political discourse that had begun in Henry VIII's Reformation were pushed to a new level of intensity at the Restoration. The adoption of the Act of Toleration and the subsequent denial of comprehension in 1689 put an end to one aspect of that discourse and restored religious discussion to its status as internal conversation among members of the same church. As the threats of toleration and comprehension grew more serious during the reign of Charles II, exchanges between Anglicans and nonconformists about religion were ever more overtaken by political concerns. "Sin," "heresy," and "anti-Christ" were replaced by talk of order, peace, and stability; "schism" was displaced by disorder and anarchy;[51] "religious truth" gave place to liberty of conscience and debates about indifferency. The issue for the Church of England was not religious purity but uniformity; and behind that were power, place, and control. The Dissenters' claims were theologically irrelevant – and therefore quite beside the point – since what was at stake was all a matter of indifference.

As the Church of England structured it, the debate was political and external to religious belief; it was about the political significance of dissent. Accordingly, the church's rhetoric could seem to be gentle, for it was asking only that nonconformists stop their "quibbling" and go along with established practices.[52] For the Dissenters, however, the stakes were extremely high and reached the very meaning of their religious experiences and beliefs. Their importance was obscured by the church's rhetorical posturing, which required pointed and forceful responses that often made the rhetoric of nonconformity appear unreasonable and uncompromising, but there was no room for compromise where God's law was concerned. It was for this reason, in the end, that the demand for toleration as a matter of right

---

[49] See Locke to Limborch, June 6, 1689, Locke *Correspondence*, III, p. 633 (letter 1147).

[50] There are manuscripts that deal with toleration and the politics of religious dissidence among Locke's papers in Bodl. and PRO from 1667, 1671/72, 1679, and 1681–82. In addition, the topic was taken up in Book IV of the *Essay concerning Human Understanding*.

[51] Long charged that Locke wanted to introduce "a lawless Church." *Letter Decipher'd*, pp. 3 and 5.

[52] Edward Stillingfleet, *Irenicum. A Weapon-Salve for the Churches Wounds: or, The Divine Right of Particular Forms of Church-Government Discussed and Examined* (London, 1661), is a case in point. An uncompromising insistence that the church hierarchy was indifferent and therefore legitimately within the magistrate's domain, the work was written in a gentle, reasonable tone, which has led commentators to view it as a conciliatory tract about comprehension that leads to "latitudinarianism."

became the only possible option for the non-Presbyterians, who otherwise found themselves severely persecuted.

An established church is political by nature, unavoidably "politicizes" religion, and, in cases of conflict, substitutes politics for theology. Thus, the entire issue of toleration and comprehension was already and entirely political by 1688–89, and so it remained. The situation did not change materially with the accession of William and Mary. They apparently regarded Roman Catholics as *political* threats but were otherwise committed to as much *religious* freedom as was consistent with the existence of a single, dominant church. In 1687, in reply to an inquiry by an agent of King James's about their attitudes toward the English penal and test laws, William and Mary had said, "*That no Christian ought to be persecuted for his Conscience, or be ill used because he differs from the publick and established Religion.*" They endorsed repeal of the penal laws so long as "*those Laws remain in their full vigour by which the R. Catholics are shut out of both Houses of Parliament, and out of all publick Employments, Ecclesiastical, Civil, and Military.*"[53] In short, the future King and Queen of England opposed repeal of those parts of the Test Act that applied to Catholics and defended their position with the claim that merely keeping Roman Catholics from public employment did not persecute them "on account of their Consciences." It was "no more than a securing of the *Protestant Religion* from any Prejudices that it may receive from the *R. Catholics.*"[54]

On March 16, 1688/89, now King William addressed parliament about the need to fill "the vacancies that are in Offices and Places of trust, [as a result of] . . . this Revolution." Repeating the sentiments of his and Mary's earlier statement, he asked that provision be made "for the Admission of all Protestants that are willing and able to serve."[55]

The Tories immediately sprang into action. As Roger Morrice, the Presbyterian diarist, described it:

This passage . . . gave very great offence to the Toreys who have got all the military power both by Sea and Land, and are ready to get all the Civill power into their own hands, for they looke upon that passage, as if it signified that their designes were discovered, and that endeavours were used to prevent them, which if they should prove successfull it's probable they would be animadverted upon for engaging in them.

An angry group "mett at the Devill Tavern" that very night, Morrice continued, and resolved

that they would labour to obstruct the Bill for Comprehension and the Bill for Indulgence or Indemnity, or rather make them ineffectual to their ends, and then clamour upon the Dissenters as obstinate unreasonable and factious, and so endeavour to raise a new persecution against them and many other things of that nature, and in order thereunto hinder the alteration designed in many other Bills, and especially in the Corporation Bill for the Reformation of the State.[56]

[53] *A Letter Writ by Mijn Heer Fagel, Pensioner of Holland To Mr. James Stewart, Advocate Giving an Account of the Prince and Princess of Orange's Thoughts concerning the Repeal of the Test, and the Penal Laws* (Amsterdam, 1688), p. 1.
[54] *Ibid.*, p. 2.　　　　　　　　　　　　　　　　　[55] Cobbett, *Parlia. Hist.*, v, p. 184.
[56] DWL, Roger Morrice, "Ent'ring Book; Being an Historical Register of Occurrences from April, Anno 1677 to April 1691" (4 vols.), II, pp. 504–5, March 16, 1688/89.

The political motives for continuing to disable non-Anglicans that had been covered over by much of the Restoration debate finally came to the surface.

The gathering at the Devil Tavern proved to be a political success. Many of the Presbyterians still looked forward to reunion with the Church of England, but their aspirations waited upon comprehension, consideration of which was transferred by parliament to a future meeting of the convocation, where it ultimately died.[57] In the meantime, with other non-Catholic dissenters, they were brought under the Act of Indulgence, which was considerably narrower than either William's suggestion or James's prerogative indulgences had been. Nonconforming Protestants – including Quakers – were permitted to meet for worship behind unlocked doors without fear of penalty or official reprisal so long as they registered with local justices of the peace, took oaths (made declarations in the case of Quakers) professing their political allegiance and Christian beliefs, and continued to pay tithes. The penal laws were suspended but not repealed, and the civil disabilities of the Test and Corporation Acts remained in place,[58] leaving the political status of nonconformists as limited as it had been before the Glorious Revolution. It was precisely this sort of disability to which Locke objected in his *Letter concerning Toleration*, even though he did not directly address the provisions of the Act of Toleration.

Locke's contribution to the literary debate approached religion from the outside as an institution rather than internally in terms of the validity of its cognitive claims. He did not simply enter into a debate in conformity with structures that had been determined for him beforehand, for he had first taken up the whole issue of religious dissent in the *Two Tracts* in just these political and detheologized terms. While he was certainly sensitive to the substantive religious issues at stake, it was never part of his purpose to engage in theological disputation when he wrote on the question of religious dissidence.

From this perspective, the interpretation of the *Epistola* becomes relatively straightforward. The sharp distinction "between the business of civil government and that of religion"[59] – between regulating and protecting the public order, which was a matter of force and coercion, and the seeking of salvation, which rested upon faith and inner conviction – was central to Locke's premise that the magistrate had no title to meddle in ecclesiastical affairs. Magisterial "power consists wholly in compulsion," whereas "true and saving religion consists in the inward persuasion of the mind ... [which] cannot be compelled by outward force" and, in the final analysis, is a personal and individual matter. The magistrate is no more capable of saving others than is anyone else. "Neither the right nor the art of ruling carries with it the certain

---

[57] Henry Horwitz, *Revolution Politicks: the Career of Daniel Finch, Second Earl of Nottingham, 1647–1730* (Cambridge University Press, 1968), pp. 91–94 and 99–101; and the same author's *Parliament, Policy, and Politics in the Reign of William III* (Manchester University Press, 1977), pp. 28–31 and 37–40. The death of the comprehension proposal in Convocation in December 1689 is discussed in Schochet, "The Act of Toleration."

[58] An Act for Exempting Their Majesties' Protestant Subjects Dissenting from the Church of England from the Penalties of Certain Laws, 1 William and Mary, cap. 18 (1689), reprinted in Browning, *Documents*, doc. 151, pp. 400–2.

[59] Locke, *Epistola*, p. 65 (quoted in full at n. 3 above).

knowledge of other things, and least of all of true religion." And since the "way that leads to heaven is no better known to the magistrate than to private persons . . . I cannot safely follow him as my guide who may probably be as ignorant of the way as I am, and who certainly must be less concerned for my salvation than I am myself."[60]

Locke's having disposed of indifferency as a criterion of legitimate imposition did not commit him to a denial of all magisterial entitlement to regulate apparently religious matters. Although taking a practice into the confines of a church removed it from the category of indifferency, it did not follow that people should be permitted to do anything that was required by their religious beliefs. Locke used a different distinction to make this case:

> Of the doctrines of churches some are practical and some are speculative; and, though both consist in the knowledge of truth, yet these [i.e., speculative] terminate simply in the understanding, those [i.e., practical] in some way influence the will and manners. Speculative doctrines, therefore, and articles of faith (as they are called) which require only to be believed, cannot in any way be imposed on any church by civil law . . .
>
> Further, the magistrate ought not to forbid the holding or teaching of any speculative opinions in any church, because they have no bearing on the civil rights of his subjects.[61]

Practical opinions – or at least the behaviors based on them – did potentially bear on civil rights and could be regulated. The entire realm of the practical, however, was not subjected to magisterial oversight, only that part of it that violated the legitimate rules of civil society.

Members of religious groups did not escape their obligations as members of society because their religious commitments required them to act in ways that violated society's legitimate rules. The conceptual problem was how to determine what those rules were. Everyone was bound not to disturb the civil peace, the "common good," or the possessions and entitlements of others. Magistracy was instituted to protect the members of society from such disturbances, and those "ends . . . determine the magistrate's prerogative of making laws, that is the public good in worldly or earthly matters."[62]

The "public good" is an obviously vague category; what one person sees as the "public good" can seem hopelessly destructive and evil to another. Locke's reliance upon the concept here appears to have been an open-ended invitation to an interpretation that would have permitted that very imposition of religious uniformity that high-churchmen and their apologists claimed was necessary to prevent discord and strife.[63] Although his response was inconclusive and unsatisfactory, Locke was aware of this possibility. In what may have been a reference to the fines levied against nonconformists under the penal statutes, he said, "worldly things cannot therefore be taken away from this man and given to that at the magistrate's pleasure, nor can the private possessions of them among fellow-citizens be charged, even by a law, for a

---

[60] *Ibid.*, pp. 69, 95, and 97.   [61] *Ibid.*, p. 121.

[62] *Ibid.*, pp. 125 and 127. The "public good" was the same standard that was adopted in the *Two Treatises*; see, *inter alia*, II, paras. 131, 135, and 166.

[63] See, for instance, Edward Stillingfleet, *The Mischief of Separation, A Sermon Preached at the Guild-Hall Chappel, May 11. MDCLXXX. Being the First Sunday in Easter-Term, Before the Lord Mayor, &c.* (London, 1680), p. 58.

reason which in no way concerns the civil community, I mean for religion."
The magistrate's claim in such cases to be acting for the public good will also
fail:

As the private judgment of any particular person, if erroneous, by no means exempts him
from the obligation of the law, so the private judgment, as I may call it, of the magistrate
does not give him any new right of imposing laws upon his subjects, for this neither was
nor could be granted to him by the constitution of the commonwealth. Much less if the
magistrate does this to enrich and advance his satellites, the members of his sect, with the
spoils of others.[64]

Behind this was the conception of political power as a "trust" that was
central to the argument of the *Two Treatises*[65] and is a necessary presuppo-
sition of any doctrine of prerogative. The "people," as the conveyors of that
trust, were the ultimate earthly judges of whether it was being properly
exercised, and their final sanction was resistance. In this, the doctrine of the
Epistola was explicitly at one with that of the *Two Treatises*. "Just and moderate governments are everywhere quiet, everywhere safe," Locke wrote, "but
when men are oppressed by injustice and tyranny they are always
recalcitrant," and when they "groan under an unjust burden [they]
endeavour to shake off the yoke that galls their necks."[66] In the end, however,
it was "God alone" who would make the final judgment and "repay everyone
according to his deserts," for "there is no judge on earth between the legis-
lator and the people."[67] And when that impasse is reached and the people
must act against the magistrate in defense of their religions, it is not the
people who have caused the disturbance of the peace, but the magistrate who
has "mixed together two utterly different things, the church and the commonwealth." Can a magistrate who persists in interfering in a "matter . . .
which does not concern the civil law at all, but the conscience of each
individual and the salvation of his soul" expect anything other than

that these men, growing weary of the evils under which they labour, should in the end
persuade themselves that it is lawful to repel force with force, and to defend, with the arms
at their disposal, the rights which God and nature have granted them, and which are
forfeitable on account of crimes alone, not of religion?[68]

The *Epistola* was a call for the end of the Anglican establishment and a
demand that the Church of England take its rightful place alongside other
churches as "a free society of men, joining together of their own accord for the
public worship of God."[69] The insistence that the civil ruler had no authority
in ecclesiastical matters meant not only that the force and legitimacy of the
state could not be used to impose religious discipline but equally that no civil
advantage ought to accrue to any church or its members simply on religious
grounds. But that, apparently, was far more radical an argument than Locke

---

[64] Locke, *Epistola*, p. 129.
[65] Locke, *Two Treatises*, II, paras. 134, 139, 156, 171, 226–27, 231, 242, etc., and esp. 149, 210, 221–22, and 240.
[66] Locke, *Epistola*, p. 139. See also the passage from p. 131 quoted above at n. 11.
[67] *Ibid.*, p. 129; cf. *Two Treatises*, II, paras. 168, 176, and 241.
[68] Locke, *Epistola.*, p. 147. See also pp. 135–37 and *Two Treatises* II, para. 226.   [69] Locke, *Epistola*, p. 71.

wanted overtly to make. It was certainly an argument that would have found few supporters among those to whom he had written and had no place in the debates surrounding the adoption of the Act of Toleration. The issues of 1689 were toleration/indulgence and comprehension, not the utter separation of church and state, and certainly not the "absolute liberty" that Popple had demanded in the preface to his translation of the *Epistola*.[70] The repeal of the provisions of the Corporation and Test Acts that applied to Protestants would have gone a long way towards satisfying Locke's objectives, but even that was not on the cards in 1689.[71]

---

[70] See above, n. 9.

[71] The argument itself, of course, was picked up later and is recognizable as the basis of both Thomas Jefferson's sentiments in his *Notes on Virginia* and the religious freedoms guaranteed by the First Amendment to the United States Constitution. How much these views actually owed to Locke's "influence" remains an open question. However, the most recent scholarship has found considerable use of Locke in eighteenth-century America, contrary to what had been the prevailing Bailyn–Dunn–Pocock interpretation. See Steven M. Dworetz, *The Unvarnished Doctrine: Locke, Liberalism and the American Revolution* (Durham, N.C., Duke University Press, 1990), esp. chs. 3 and 5.

10

Representing the Revolution: politics and high culture in 1689

Steven N. Zwicker

On October 28, 1688, the Prince of Orange and 15,000 troops set sail for England. They were turned back by storms, but a successful expedition arrived at Torbay on November 5, the eighty-third anniversary of the Gunpowder Plot. So began a remarkable series of events whose provenance and meaning were contested from the moment of the prince's arrival. The character of William's intervention, the nature of James's retreat, the role of the Revolution in securing the Protestant faith and parliamentary freedom, all were vigorously debated in the Convention that met in January of 1689 and in the months and years following the coronation of William and Mary. The events of 1688–89 were regretted and denounced by those who remained loyal to James II; they also provided materials for constructing the story of the progressive foundation of political liberty, what we have come to know as the Whig interpretation of history. That story has come under revision and attack; historians are now as likely to argue the Revolution's conservative character; some suggest that the term "revolution" itself is a misnomer for the events of the late autumn and winter of 1688–89;[1] and one among them has recently argued the uninterrupted continuity of patriarchalism, deference, and divine-right ideology for the whole of the late seventeenth and eighteenth centuries.[2] However contested and revised, the events of 1688–89 – among them the first edition of Locke's *Two Treatises* and the creation of an English Bill of Rights – remain fixed as moments and texts of the highest importance in Anglo-American political history.

Yet if we look to the ways in which literary culture reflected and enacted the revolutionary moment we might be surprised by the indifference of the literary record to the fact of the Revolution. The standard histories of English literature, even studies of Augustan writing, hardly acknowledge the events of these months. And there is some justification for their silence. It is hard to

---

[1] See J. P. Kenyon, *Revolution Principles. The Politics of Party 1689–1720.* (Cambridge University Press, 1977), pp. 1–4; J. R. Jones, *Country and Court* (Cambridge, Mass., Harvard University Press, 1978), pp. 252–53. J. G. A. Pocock (ed.), *Three British Revolutions: 1641, 1688, 1776* (Princeton University Press, 1980), p. 13; and L. Stone in the Pocock volume, pp. 63–64; Gary Stuart De Krey, *A Fractured Society: the Politics of London in the First Age of Party, 1688–1715* (Oxford University Press, 1985), pp. 45–47.

[2] J. C. D. Clark, *English Society, 1688–1832* (Cambridge University Press, 1985), esp. section 3, "The Survival of the Dynastic Idiom," pp. 119–89.

165

think of a political crisis in this century so unremarked in literary form. The literary response to political change and crisis in this century is quite remarkable – Shakespeare meditating on the accession of James I in *Macbeth*;[3] Marvell worrying the relations between power and justice in 1649; Milton entering the whirlwind of national debate in 1659 with *The Ready and Easy Way*; or the subtleties and provocations of Exclusion displayed in *Venice Preserv'd* and *Absalom and Achitophel*. And we might well expect a literature of substantial energy and art to emerge in the months following William's intervention. But a reading of the cultural record produces few analogs to these masterpieces.

I want to speculate on the reasons for literary silence, partly for what that silence reveals of this Revolution and in part for what it suggests about the cultural absorption of 1688. Both issues will involve us in thinking about the character of the Revolution, its representation, and what effect the political habits of the Revolution – habits of obliqueness and innuendo – had on the literary imagination. In turn, I want to examine the Revolution through its only literary masterpiece, *Don Sebastian*; and retrospectively, I want to consider the shadow that this Revolution cast over one of the monuments of late seventeenth-century literature, the translation of Virgil that Dryden published in 1697. The aesthetic and popular success of *Don Sebastian* raises questions about the force and identity of Jacobite ideals and values in the midst of the Revolution; the *Virgil* allows us to consider the fate of heroic literature in a culture committed by 1697 to a European destiny and to a commercial revolution that for the next century and beyond fueled the creation of an empire.

On the eve of the Revolution and directly in its aftermath we might assume that the work of literature would have been obvious and extensive. The events of 1688 were in need of defense, interpretation, and celebration. An Horation ode on the landing at Torbay might have represented the complexity and anxiety of the moment, calibrated the fluidity of events, the possibilities of subversion, the moral and ethical consequences of political action, the dangers of resistance and passivity. Slightly more than a year before the Revolution we have an example of a literary text that does exactly this kind of work. Dryden's *The Hind and the Panther* expresses the very great sense of danger and instability that marked James's last year. What is communicated in this intricate and evasive work is the difficulty of achieving political credibility for a monarch much in need of credibility and explanation. A fair amount of its energy is expended in arguments for the rectitude and high-mindedness of the regime. But there are other facts about James's rule that the poem also suggests: the anxiety of those charged with its defense, the precariousness of its political and religious aims. Obliqueness and fear run through the poem, and its defensiveness conveys an idea of how significant must have been the resistance to James's monarchy by the middle of 1687.

---

[3] David Norbrook, "*Macbeth* and the Politics of Historiography," in Kevin Sharpe and Steven Zwicker (eds.), *Politics of Discourse* (Berkeley and Los Angeles, University of California Press, 1987), pp. 78–116.

The revolutionary enterprise found no such expression or exaltation. The only great literary text of the Revolution, and it comes almost a year after William's landing at Torbay, is a blank-verse tragedy that exalts the high courage and principles not of the leaders of the Revolution but of the monarch who had fled his country and was by then pawn and dependent of Louis XIV. Rather than a revolutionary text, Dryden's *Don Sebastian* embodies a reactionary creed; it argues not the high-mindedness of the Revolution but the terms in which its apologetics might be resisted; it celebrated not the preservation of liberties, but the cultural resources that could be summoned on behalf of a deposed and discredited regime.

Perhaps it was merely an accident of literary history that the former laureate should have been trapped in his Roman Catholicism and Jacobitism in 1689, that the greatest exponent and exemplar of high culture in the 1690s should have been an adherent of Stuart monarchy and Stuart policy; and that the closest student of his art, Alexander Pope, should also have been a Catholic and Jacobite, and in his first major work, *Windsor Forest*, should have identified himself as an acolyte of Stuart monarchy. Was it, however, solely chance that high culture should have been so firmly attached to Stuart monarchy, and that the Revolution should have been attacked in cultural terms as boorish, illiterate, and dull;[4] that William's first laureate was Thomas Shadwell, dunce of *Mac Flecknoe*; and the Williamite epic should have been Blackmore's *Prince Arthur* rather than Dryden's *Virgil*?

In fact, the bonds between the Stuart court and literary culture are deep and complex in this century.[5] Restoration panegyrists insistently linked the return of Stuart monarchy with the revival of arts and letters.[6] The patronage and production of high culture in the decades following the Restoration are impressive, not least so under James II. But it is to simplify the sources of that productivity to suggest that wit and luxury were the exclusive model, precondition, or main support of literary art. We should not forget that Milton's epics were products of the first years of the Restoration, or that Bunyan and Baxter could hardly have found the court a source of inspiration. Clearly, both patronage by, and resistance to, the court play significant roles in Restoration culture. The sudden disappearance of the center of that patronage with the flight of James II must have been a source of some consternation in 1688. Yet the patronage system itself not only continued – and often in the same hands – but new patrons emerged on the market together with a gathering force of patronage deployed for specifically political aims and purposes in the 1690s. The sudden flurry of new editions of Milton's works following the Revolution suggests the increasing role of recent politics in the formulation of literary canons.[7] But the Whiggish cooption of Milton

---

[4] The satiric verse in *POAS*, v: 1688–97, gives some idea of the reception of the Revolution.

[5] These links can be profitably studied at moments of crisis and celebration, as, for example, in the elegies lamenting the execution of Charles I and in the panegyrics on the restoration and coronation of Charles II.

[6] See, for example, the verse in *Britannia Rediviva* (Oxford, 1660); R. Brathwait, *To his Majesty on his Happy Arrival* (1660); or Waller's and Dryden's panegyrics.

[7] I have tried to deal with this topic in "Lines of Authority: Politics and Literary Culture in the Restoration," in Sharpe and Zwicker (eds.), *Politics of Discourse*, pp. 216–47; see also Stephen H. Daniel on Toland as biographer

argues more than a politicized canon; for republication, translation, and adaptation are more characteristic of the 1690s than is literary invention, a fact about the decade that returns us to the center of the problem: the literary silence surrounding the Revolution.

Not all, however, was silence. One of the most revealing texts of the Revolution is the set of debates engaged in by members of the Convention that settled the crown on William and Mary.[8] Those who have studied the language of the Convention have noted the detailed and careful exchanges surrounding the choice of words for describing James's absence and William's presence in England. The scrupling over language had an immediate and important political rationale. On the correct choice of words rested a cornerstone of the Revolution. For if the debates could satisfy the conscience of those who had sworn allegiance and passive obedience to James II, the Revolution might be swiftly secured. Hence, the careful deliberation over a vocabulary that would neutralize and pacify, that would suggest James's abandonment of the throne, its subsequent vacancy, and William's entry into England as an effort to secure and preserve parliamentary liberty. The deliberation was an effort at discovering a way of representing the Revolution that would cause the least disturbance to the civic fabric, that would raise the fewest qualms, legal scruples, and ethical anxieties. Such a discovery was made in the language of vacancy and abdication.[9] Of course, some regarded the debates as exercises in hypocrisy or self-delusion; but the efforts to fix a neutralizing vocabulary were in fact successful. The nation as a whole allowed the Revolution without hesitation. It helped, of course, that James had conducted an increasingly vigorous campaign to install his religion and co-religionists and secure that throne for Roman Catholicism in perpetuity, and the Revolution was, of course, accompanied by a flood of anti-Catholic propaganda.[10] But the linguistic activities of the Convention should not be underestimated in calculating the success of the Revolution.

What also needs to be remarked is that in the story which these debates tell not only do we find a neutralizing and pacifying vocabulary but also a language that suggests the remarkable passivity of the nation. This is a revolution not of heroic endeavor and godly militancy but of deep impassivity and retreat, not a civil insurrection but a revolution effected by conspiracy and secret invitation. William was blown across the Channel by a Protestant

---

and editor of Milton, *John Toland* (Kingston and Montreal, McGill University Press, 1984); and Bernard Sharratt, "The Appropriation of Milton," in Suheil Bushrui (ed.), *Essays and Studies*, n.s. vol. 35 (Atlantic Highlands, N.J., Humanities Press, for the English Association, 1982), pp. 30–44.

[8] The debates can be followed in Cobbett *Parlia. Hist.*, v, pp. 26–111. All the known sources for the debates in the Convention, including Lois G. Schwoerer's edition of "A Journal of the Convention at Westminster begun the 22 of January 1688/9," can be found in David Lewis Jones, *A Parliamentary History of the Glorious Revolution* (London, HMSO, 1988).

[9] See Thomas P. Slaughter, "'Abdicate' and 'Contract' in the Glorious Revolution," *HJ* 24 (1982), 323–37; John Miller, "The Glorious Revolution: 'Contract' and 'Abdication' reconsidered," *HJ* 25 (1982), 541–55; Slaughter, "'Abdicate' and 'Contract' Restored," *HJ* 28 (1985), 399–403.

[10] See, again, *POAS*, v, esp. pp. 19–36; and such volumes as *The Design of Enslaving England Discovered* (London, 1689); *London's Flames Reviv'd* (London, 1689); *Sidney Redivivus* (London, 1689); the verse panegyrics on William are filled with references to bigotry, superstition, and Egyptian slavery.

wind, the nation sat passively obedient (or disobedient, as the case may have been), and James withdrew from office.[11]

To cast the nation as victim at once of Jesuit machination and Protestant redemption clears the people of complicity both in Roman Catholic intrigue and Dutch usurpation. And the passivity is to be found not only in the debates but everywhere in the verse celebrating the deliverance. For the nation to have played a passive, if willing, role in the rescue means that some of the scrupling over passive obedience can be put to rest and that a *de facto* acceptance of William and Mary can be taken as the route of least political resistance. Passive obedience was a banner that flew high over the camp of nonjurors and Jacobites;[12] it was an idiom of considerable moral capital and authority. National passivity allowed the mysteries of Providence to wipe clear the crimes of rebellion and abjuration of oaths. So long as the Revolution was acquiesced in rather than effected, the politics of conspiracy and rebellion could be eased into the principle of happy deliverance. If we miss Old Testament ethical vigor and moral urgency in the language of this Protestant revolution, if we are surprised by the supineness of this foundation of liberty, we need to be aware that the Civil Wars remained part of the context of any constitutional change in the seventeenth century. It was after all James's father who had gone to the block, and some of those who had witnessed the execution would still have been alive in the Revolution.

If the Revolution of 1688 is glorious then in part because it is bloodless, cultural silence may have been one of the minor expenses incurred along the passive way. Not that the conventional effort is entirely absent, but it seems hampered, confused in its handling of themes, caught out for an idiom, a language of revolutionary exaltation, nervously suspended between claims of conscience and expediency. Of course, a respectable amount of verse was produced, although by comparison with the Restoration, a comparison that panegyrists tactfully avoid, the amount of celebratory verse is surprisingly small. And though the quality of writing is below even what we would expect for corporate and occasional exercises – university volumes from Oxford and Cambridge as well as showpieces by individual entrepreneurs – the panegyrics taken as a whole have an interesting story to tell about the engagement of high culture with this revolution. What comes immediately clear from the body of this verse is that both the character of the Revolution and the ways in which it was represented work against the creation of an heroic idiom for 1688. Not simply that the events of the Revolution were indeed bloodless, that the reigning monarch fled the country in fear, but also that the Revolution

---

[11] The "amazing concurrence of Providences, which have conspired to hatch and bring forth, and perfect this extraordinary Revolution," was a repeated theme in sermons and panegyrics on the Revolution; see Gilbert Burnet, *A Sermon Preached In the Chappel of St. James's, Before His Highness the Prince of Orange, the 23rd of December, 1688* (London, 1689); Simon Patrick, *A Sermon Preached At St. Paul's Covent Garden On the Day of Thanksgiving Jan. XXXI. 1688. For the great Deliverance of this Kingdom by the Means of his Highness the Prince of Orange From Popery and Arbitrary Power* (London, 1689); William Sherlock, *A Sermon Preached before the Right Honourable The Lord Mayor and Aldermen of The City of London, At Guild-Hall-Chappel, On Sunday, Nov. 4. 1688* (London, 1689); Simon Patrick, *A Sermon Preached In the Chappel of St. James's, Before His Highness the Prince of Orange, The 20th of January, 1688* (London, 1689).
[12] See Kenyon, *Revolution Principles*, chs. 5 and 6.

was hardly the result of a national effort. This revolution was deliverance from outside and above, a "providential revolution" effected by a foreign prince governing a former military and current commercial rival, stadholder of a nation that had effected a tremendous national humiliation in 1667. This prince was now chosen out by a mysterious Providence to spare a luckless people from the miseries of "popery and slavery"; a Dutchman was needed to rescue the virgin from the dragon's jaws.[13] Of course, the language of deliverance allows large sway for providential readings of this event, and sermon after sermon as well as nearly every panegyric celebrates the unpredictable and miraculous ways of Providence. And we need to allow that the conventions of panegyric include such elevation and agency; but this heavenly rescue was effected neither by a martial hero nor by a fearsome god. Zeal and enthusiasm were figures not welcome in this Protestant recovery; while miraculous, the Revolution was no leveling or overturning but a victory of piety and moderation.

From the central fact of national passivity and acquiescence there seems to be no escape. Nor perhaps was one wanted. Quite consistently in the panegyrics, the nation is depicted as confused, unhappy, reluctant, and recumbent. England lies wasted and dismal; justice has withdrawn, the laws lie broken and trampled, the nation is prey to insulting foes.[14] The rescue is effected, however, not by arms but by "looks."[15] This revolution is a triumph of virtue, its hero praised not for martial valor but for prudence, his breastplate stamped with "truth" and "love."[16] Although more than one of these pieces nervously acknowledges conquest and invasion, even usurpation, those disagreeable idioms are transformed, pacified, Europeanized.[17] Indeed, some of the offending vocabulary drifts from the point where it might most cogently or immediately be applied to quite different targets; the panegyrics tell us of "usurping France . . . invading English rights";[18] more than once, kingship by

[13] Cf. the satire, 'Mall in her Majesty," *POAS*, v, pp. 25–29.

[14] Rob. Symthies, "On the late Happy Revolution, A Pindarique Ode," *Musae Cantabrigienses* (Cambridge, 1689), sig. av.

[15] *Ibid.*, sig. a2v.:
The Land with dire confusion thus o'respread,
Call'd the Great Nassau to its aid,
The peacefull Warriour quickly came,
And struck it not, but look't it into Frame;
He came and took a pittying view,
The Conscious heap his meaning knew
And the unruly motions quickly drew
Into an Order regular and true.

[16] "A Panegyric upon their Majesties King William and Queen Mary," *Lux Occidentalis* (Oxford, 1689), p. 12.

[17] See, for example, John Herbert, "To the King," *Musae Cantabrigienses*, "Great Prince, what Glories do's Thy Name deserve?/ What Praise? who only Conquer'st to preserve," sig. b3v; or the reference in Rich. Stone's panegyric in *Musae Cantabrigienses*, c3r, to William's "kind Invasion"; or B. Cudworth's verse in *Musae Cantabrigienses*, c4v.:
No more the ancient Conquerour's splendid Name,
Shall fill alone the Glorious Rills of Fame;
Whose Arms, Revenge, or vain ambition lead,
And rais'd their bloody Trophies on the dead;
Your Pow'rfull Name the Mighty Work compleats,
And over willing minds an easier Conquest gets.

[18] Cf. Smythies, "On the late Happy Revolution," *Musae Cantabrigenses*, a2v; W. Bisset, "Great Heroe!" *Musae Cantabrigenses*, d2v.

blood and immutable divine right are elided for merit and *salus populi*.[19] One panegyrist mixes theories of kingship in order to account for, and give credibility to, William's unexpected and perhaps illegitimate presence in the kingdom:

> No dull Succession sanctifies his Right,
>   Nor conquest gain'd in Fight,
> But o're the Peoples minds, and there
> Does *Right Divine* triumphantly appear.
>   The mind, impassible and free,
> No pow'r can govern, but the deity,
> Howev'r o're Persons, and o're Fortunes, may
>   A bold Intruder sway;
> The *Right Divine* is by the people given,
> And 'tis their Suffrage speaks the mind of Heav'n.[20]

This odd mixture of providentialism, election, *jure divino*, and contract dismisses lineal descent and conquest only to rescue divine right from the language of contract and donation. What we have here is not an exercise in high-strung ambiguity and paradox but an irresolute and contradictory mixing of constitutional idioms. The lines, colored ever so slightly by a Miltonic rhetoric, suggest an absence of theory and a failure of idioms – heroic, legal, dynastic – by which one might indeed figure the meaning of the Revolution or the person of its hero.

Nor is it difficult to understand this reluctance to allow succession since the son-in-law and nephew displacing the father-in-law and uncle could hardly claim much protection from that model. Nor is the shyness over conquest hard to grasp. Conquest as a source of legitimacy carries a heavy price. What is worth observing about a number of these efforts is the very difficult and indeed contradictory circumstance into which the Revolution, and its consented-to representation, delivered those who would vindicate the event and its principal actors. Miraculous redemption and business as usual are difficult points of view to argue simultaneously. I have not touched on the very many references to William as savior of religion and the law, dwelling rather on the difficulties of model, office, and legitimating language because not only redemption but also continuity had to be addressed, and while the rhetoric of liberty and property is much and on occasion energetically deployed, the circumstance of the Revolution, the nature of William's entry, the very real as well as useful passivity of the nation, and the ambiguity of James's status created a troubled circumstance for a literature of heroism and high principles. It was a difficult task to adjudicate such a language in this revolution, but 1688 was not without parallels, analogs, and types that might explain the happy conquest.

It helped, of course, that the landing at Torbay took place on November 5,

---

[19] P. Sayve, "To the King," *Musae Cantabrigenses*, b2v.
[20] John Guy, *On the Happy Accession of Their Majesties King William and Queen Mary, To the Throne of England, &c. A Pindarique Ode* (1699), C2v-D1r.

and that 1688 was the hundredth anniversary of the English triumph over international Catholicism. The defeat of Marian persecution, Elizabeth's glorious reign, and the humiliation of the Spanish Armada are precursors and predictors of William's Protestant triumph. But the defeat of the Armada, the centerpiece of such analogs, had its own mildly subversive subtext. The year 1588 was an English triumph over threatened foreign invasion; 1688 was a triumphant foreign invasion and routing of an English monarch. Of course, the ironies of the analogy are partly hidden under the shadow of its more happy application, but they could hardly have been invisible in a literature that everywhere allows, indeed embraces, passivity. And the problem of claiming an English identity both for the Revolution and its resistance was, of course, a real difficulty. In fact, what seems to be at the center of the Revolution is absence: a throne that lies vacant; a king that has disappeared in the night; a people reluctant to act in defiance of, or on behalf of, William's entry. That set of circumstances – literal and metaphoric – suggests some of the difficulty of those who might have produced a heroic literature of the Revolution.

Let me sharpen the case slightly. The Revolution of 1688 might well be read as one of compromise and collusion. Rather than a trumpeting of high ideals, of a new social and political order, protection and retrenchment were its aims. This was a moment in the political culture when wary hestitation and cool distance marked much of the behavior of the political nation. Out of this circumstance, and more, out of disappointment, bitterness, and no little sense of irony came the literary masterpiece of the Revolution, *Don Sebastian*, a play whose aesthetic and popular success must raise questions about the force of Jacobite and nonjuring sentiments in the 1690s. The popular success of the play in 1689 is particularly puzzling, for the autumn of that year was a time when both the former laureate and his former master were under savage attack.

What then was the play articulating? For one thing, it is a feast of dramatic conventions and devices, of heroic rhetoric and high ideals, of double plots, concealed identities, hidden morals, interlocking rings, incestuous longings, and spurned honor. It is a play whose conventions Dryden knew well how to handle, and their somewhat nostalgic display in *Don Sebastian* must have provided a good deal of pleasure for those with a taste for heroic drama. But rather more was at stake for the former laureate than shuffling a familiar, if brilliant, hand of dramatic conventions. Dryden wanted very much to enter the public debate over the Revolution, and he wanted to enter it on his own ground, in forms of which he was a master, with conventions and codes whose meaning he might shape, with a language whose resonance he might control. *Don Sebastian* gave him a format that could provide not only artistic and financial rewards but also a means of vindicating his personal and political honor while minimizing the damage of his religious conversion and exposing the hypocrisy of the Revolution, the bankruptcy of its ideals, the hollowness of its slogans. In its own way, *Don Sebastian* is as steady and sharply directed a political argument as are the laureate's satires of the 1680s, but it is an argument conducted in so very different a set of circumstances that its very articulation has been denied and ignored in favor of what is read as timeless and universal in the work.[21] Needless to say, there is much that is timeless and universal in a play that announces a dramatic ancestry including Sophocles and Shakespeare. But we also need to recognize that the high ground of literary affiliation and literary history was itself a crucial vantage point for Dryden after 1688. There is some irony in the fact that the very success of *Don Sebastian* as timeless literary masterpiece argues Dryden's ability to cover the polemical with claims of high principles, to soften and universalize difficult particulars, to divert attention away from polemical values and political conclusions that were fixed in the revolutionary moment. But first and foremost *Don Sebastian* is a piece of very high culture indeed.

Tragedy is the genre of this play and it is so announced in bold letters that cross the title page. Under this rubric, we are invited to contemplate conquest, usurpation, betrayal, and retreat as the very stuff of high art. Tragedy not only elevates the materials of 1688 but lends to them a particular interpretation; for *Don Sebastian* centers on a hero flawed but majestic, whose fall was not a cowardly flight but a tragic inevitability, a reversal cruel and ironic but beyond comprehension and following from sins concealed in distant generations. Such tragedy cannot be averted, particularly in the realm of politics, and the pattern of conquest, betrayal, and retreat is lent tragic dignity by the play. Thus are the principles of the drama imagined and thus is the fate of the conquered portrayed. Altitude and dignity are in fact the argument not only of genre but also of the prefatory materials that accompanied the printed play.

Don Sebastian was dedicated to Philip, third Earl of Leicester. The dedication to Leicester allowed Dryden to do a number of interesting things; most obviously, the long and deep connections of that family with literature and patronage is itself a claim to aristocratic privilege and protection.[22] At one point in the dedication, Dryden poses as Spenser to Leicester's Sidney. But a more elaborate argument about politics and art is folded into the dedication, for not only were the Sidneys aristocratic patrons, they were a family with republican associations, nowhere more shockingly asserted than in the execution of Philip's brother Algernon for complicity in the Rye House Plot. The third Earl of Leicester had himself been a "zealous republican,"[23] and Leicester's younger brother, Henry, Earl of Romney, played a key role in the Glorious Revolution.[24] This dedication is, then, a claim to protection from a patron of Whiggish principles and republican lineage, and such patronage,

---

[21] See, especially, the commentary of Earl Miner in *The Works of John Dryden*, ed. Earl Miner, George R. Guffey, and Franklin B. Zimmerman (20 vols., Berkeley, Los Angeles, and London, University of California Press, 1976), xv, pp. 404–8.

[22] See *Ibid.*, pp. 408–9.

[23] See G. E. Cockayne's *The Complete Peerage*, ed. H. A. Doubleday and H. de Walden (12 vols., London, St. Catherine's Press, 1910–59), vii, pp. 556–57.

[24] The Earl of Romney was a five-guinea subscriber to Dryden's *Virgil*. He was given a particularly compromising plate for his subscription. See Steven N. Zwicker, *Politics and Language in Dryden's Poetry* (Princeton University Press, 1984), pp. 195–96.

dispensed without regard to party, not only allows a Jacobite to benefit from aristocratic largesse, it also articulates a whole system of moral, familial, and civic ties. Leicester's patronage is an example of the fullest meaning of charity and constancy, not despite Dryden's politics but because of them.

Perhaps because the dedication is laid at the feet of a republican aristocrat, Dryden can dare the arguments he indulges, nor could the principles of charity and constancy be faulted. Indeed, the high-minded display of such principles is steady throughout the play, and while such principles have not only a sustained moral but also a sharp polemical meaning, I need to allow that the application of such materials to personal and national politics in 1688 was not simple. Dryden was quite aware of the potential applications from the play and he both invites and shields the play from such. Part of the shield is to be found in the very complexity of materials within the play, the unsteady system of analogies and parallels, proximities and disparities, that defeats any simple allegorical arrangement and, in part, is meant to discourage historical applications.[25] This is, moreover, an important argument of the Preface, which suggests in other ways how generic issues insulate the play from too easy a political reading. Many poems and plays of this century are eager to appropriate the honorific of history, to marshall its qualities, to claim significance through veracity. But Dryden's argument in the Preface to *Don Sebastian* is quite the opposite: "As for the story or plot of the Tragedy, 'tis purely fiction; for I take it up where the History has laid it down . . . Declaring it to be fiction, I desire my Audience to think it no longer true, than while they are seeing it represented."[26] The intermixing of comic scenes, subplots, hidden identities, and delayed discoveries enlarges the scope of Dryden's claim that the play is pure fiction. And to those resources we must add the quite ostentatiously fictional element of the plot, the discovery of incest committed between hero and heroine. Whatever applications we might be invited to make from the play, no one was suggesting that incest was a crime either contemplated or committed by James II or William III. There might be a slight titillation in the fact that William III was both James's son-in-law and nephew, but the charge of incest is one of the few that was not leveled against William in the satiric literature of the 1690s, where just about every other natural and unnatural vice is charged to his person.

The Preface aims then to situate the play within the realms of romance, pathos, and tragedy; it shields the play against too quick an application – it would have us contemplate its politics philosophically as well as historically. And it has one additional and rather important argument to make about the character of the work: its lineage and its author's position within that lineage. Euripides and Sophocles, Lucan and Sallust, Shakespeare and Corneille – these are Dryden's models and peers. The exalted literary tradition and the lofty literary character of his work both insulate Dryden from some of the

---

[25] For a full discussion of parallel and analogy in *Don Sebastian*, see David Bywaters, "Dryden and the Revolution of 1688: Political Parallel in *Don Sebastian*," *Journal of English and German Philology* 85 (1986), 346–65.
[26] Miner (ed.), *The Works of John Dryden*, xv, p. 67.

dangers of a hostile political world and give him an authority to speak of its character and values. This may strike us as naive or wishful, but the very altitude of the work must have been part of its success in the 1690s. Both Dryden's prefatory writing and the highly wrought, self-conscious character of the play suggest that he knew quite well what the polemical values of altitude were, what protection they might offer, and what argumentative advantage they allowed. The invocation of high culture, even the explicit denial of historical accuracy and intent, offered a polemical advantage; it was one of the few that Dryden could easily claim after 1688.

Part of the polemical argument of *Don Sebastian* is, then, the connection between high culture and the values of the play: the meaning of principles, the nature of oaths, the quality of honor, the uncertainties of fate. The play also provides explicit political materials and arguments that it would harness to the loftiness of its enterprise; they not only suggest the abstract polemical situation of the work but also indicate very much how it is doing business with the claims made on behalf of the Revolution and its settlement. Dryden's handling of themes and plots, verbal and dramatic idioms is in fact an excellent guide to the polemics of the Revolution.

Any writer choosing the Portuguese king for his subject had by the late seventeenth century a wealth of histories and legends to sift among. The centerpiece of the histories was a sixteenth-century king of Portugal, a Catholic gallant who entertained fantasies of a glorious reign dedicated to military triumphs in the cause of his religion, a mystic and fanatic.[27] This history intersects Moroccan politics in the battle of Alcacerquivir, which closed an ill-fated campaign that Don Sebastian had conducted on behalf of a slighted heir to the Moroccan throne – but one incident in the saga of political and familial intrigue and treachery, fratricide, assassination, and rival claims to the throne. In fact, Moroccan history, the immediate background to Dryden's play, might itself be taken as an emblem of divided ruling houses, conquests, and usurpations. Don Sebastian's military crusade resulted in his own death and the decimation of the Portuguese army, a defeat followed by years of decline and domination by Spain, and the growth of the Sebastian legend, which held that the king had not died in battle but would one day return from exile to claim his throne.

It is not difficult to see what this history of political mayhem, Catholic chivalry, and Sebastianist hopes for an exiled prince might have offered Dryden in 1689. The parallels are so obvious that it may be surprising Dryden chose to dramatize the legend at all. Dryden may not have known of the political suppression of Massinger's Don Sebastian play in 1631,[28] but he must have been aware of the parallels to be drawn out of his subject in 1689, parallels which he, of course, orchestrates, complicates, and heightens himself. He must also have been aware of the danger of doing so, and we have

---

[27] For an excellent summary of the historical materials, see Miner (ed.), *The Works of John Dryden*, XV, pp. 391–92.
[28] *Ibid.*, p. 385.

seen some of the steps that he took both to excite the applications and to distance himself from them, to dehistoricize and neutralize the politics of the legend while allowing the obvious inferences to be drawn. He not only indulged these parallels and applications, he wove so complex a system of such parallels that their variety and number are slightly dizzying. If, for a moment, we take 1688 to be the center of *Don Sebastian*, we are offered parallels to English politics from both Moroccan and Portuguese history, and these are mixed and indulged in comic, satiric, and historical modes. What the multiplicity suggests is that revolution, usurpation, exile, and retreat are something like the inevitable conditions of politics, a conclusion amply illustrated in all the histories indulged and implied by the play. Self-knowledge, charity, and beneficence alone are beyond the reach of political revolution, which is, after all, simply an instrument of blind fate. A number of examples illustrate this pattern: Philip, Earl of Leicester, and his Roman counterpart, Pomponius Atticus; the former laureate and his Roman pattern, Cicero; the Don Sebastian of history and the Don Sebastian of Dryden's play, who closes the work with the renunciation and retreat; and of course James II, who is following such a pattern of retreat and piety at St. Germain. To abjure empire, to hold property and power in moral contempt, suggests the final example of piety and elevation: Christ of the Gospels. Dryden may not explicitly draw all the analogies, but the materials for constructing such a pattern and abstracting such a meaning from the play and its legends are obviously there. Given such a design, we can see how the dedication, Preface, and the play itself might be read as a thematically linked and continuous text pointing a repeated stoic moral, one quoted from Cicero and Virgil and expressed by the hero himself:

> The world was once too narrow for my mind,
> But one poor little nook will serve me now ...
> A Scepter's but play thing, and a Globe
> A bigger bounding Stone.

Politics is the prime example and inevitable stage of such instability: crowns and empires are slippery things; conquest and usurpation simply beget more such; once a rent is made in the fabric of bounds, oaths, and gratitude the state unravels. Political activism is clearly not Dryden's aim in *Don Sebastian*, but the consoling moral of endless fluctuation is repeatedly drawn in dramatic colloquy over such topics as title, empire, conquest, Providence, and fate. Although William and Mary have been crowned, James deposed, and his laureate dispossessed, the victory is but a momentary variation in the larger scheme of instability and change.

The histories that form the background to *Don Sebastian* provide both frame and consolation. The play itself engages more directly in polemical work, although we ought not to underestimate the polemical value in Dryden's handling of the large frame of providential histories. Providential rescue was a theme crucial to a revolution that argued the divine right of Providence as a handsome alternative to the divine right of kings. Dryden is careful to engage that theme at various moments in the play, so that we have both a general devaluation of the politics of Providence and a rather more specific refutaton of providential arguments applied to conquest and tyranny within the play itself. Indeed, rather than lift the play above the Revolution, such philosophical material situates *Don Sebastian* in the midst of that great political event, steadily engaging the themes, the principles, the banners, and the catchwords of the Revolution and its apologetics. The attack is aimed at the theory of the Revolution and its language, at the claims of necessity and high mindedness, at the character of its principles. *Don Sebastian* steadily inspects the rationale of the Glorious Revolution, the action of the rabble and its political and religious leaders, the slogans of popery and slavery, property and religion. Through comic scenes that slight the principles of the Revolution, through soliloquy that heightens nonjuring values, through a steady examination and deflation of such terms as title, slavery, conquest, tyranny, and sovereignty Dryden offers an alternative reading of the Revolution, its justification, its rhetoric, and its principal actors so that we might see 1688 not as the high-minded and selfless rescue of religion, property, and the law from the hands of a reckless and bigoted innovator but as an act of political betrayal motivated by greed, argued with lies, a revolution that everywhere revealed the cupidity, cowardice, and moral indifference of the nation.

The polemical engagement that I have been describing takes place in several ways. Most abstractly, the play spins out philosophical and moral principles: the universe is in flux, Providence is inscrutable, title is mere vanity; only an indifference to the things of this world can guarantee nobility of character and purity of soul. Less abstractly, the main characters in the play are allowed through language and circumstance to suggest, often in momentary, fleeting and almost always partial ways, the principal characters of the Revolution. The Moroccan shereef, a bloody tyrant, martial and heroic yet cruel and morally indifferent, flits in and out of focus as William III; the hapless, noble, and stoic hero, Don Sebastian, "Brave,/ pious, generous, great and liberal . . . no other could represent such suffering majesty," offers us an idealized James, a portrait that may strain credulity and is obviously intended as flattering suggestion rather than careful delineation; a virtuous princess loyal to her murdered father and brother's ghost, who upbraids the nephew of her father, a man who seized his throne, is obviously an inversion of Mary; and a set of secondary characters whose actions suggest momentary analogy with either the principal actors or the circumstances of the Revolution.[29]

Dryden also fits out the debates and exchanges in the play with a set of political idioms that were crucial to the Williamite representation of 1688. For example, playing out a scene in which real slaves are bought and sold at market, the drama literalizes the meaning and conditions of slavery in a manner intended to puncture and ridicule the political uses of that word. The

---

[29] See Bywaters, "Dryden and the Revolution of 1688," pp. 358–59.

steady cry of "popery and slavery" was crucial to the rhetoric of the Revolution. *Don Sebastian* insists that slavery is a word that has, first of all, a literal meaning and a political provenance; slavery is the direct result of conquest, and the Catholic slaves in this play are bought and sold at the whim of a conquering infidel. By literalizing the word and depicting slavery as the result of military conquest and by suggesting that conquest is indeed the condition of William's triumph, that retreat and retirement acknowledge such conquest, Dryden uses a set of political circumstances implacably to argue the meaning of national conquest: the people are now quite literally slaves of a conqueror, to be bought and sold at his whim. The scenes and colloquies that analyze slavery as language and condition have the effect first of all of insisting on root definitions and political preconditions. No one argued that James had taken the throne by conquest; many were troubled by the title of conqueror as it applied to William. This was in fact a crucial issue, and by linking conquest and slavery in both comic and serious scenes Dryden entered the debate, argued its language, and suggested that the most important political consequence of conquest was in fact slavery.

Scenes of mistaken identity, accidental appearance, and displaced lovers play out in a comic vein the rather portentous political and philosophical arguments of *Don Sebastian*. Fate itself, the comic scenes argue, is hardly a source for the authority or virtue of either action or agency. Thus the lottery scene early in the play, in which the fates of hero and heroine are supposedly decided, is a scene covered by whim and accident. That debunking of fate and fortune is then followed by repeated scenes of accidental and mistaken action and identity that alone seem to determine turns of plot and fortune. Arguments that based the Revolution on analogy with 1588 or likeness with other Protestant redemptions are engaged in specious polemic; justification by Providence is an argument made from whimsy dressed as legitimating divinity. Dryden also understood the power of images of mob rule and civil anarchy in treating of the Revolution. Both in scenes of high principle and in episodes of ridicule and burlesque, he derides the clergy and the mufti, who are seen alike as bent on profit and self-promotion, who willfully incite riot and tumult, who play on the greed of the multitude and the chimera of consensual politics to ride the crest of revolution to new heights of power and property. The repeated image of mob rule stalks the play as does the suggestion of a physics of revolution run towards chaos and destruction. Of course, the politics of fear were very well understood by publicists both for and against the Revolution, and indeed, those defending the Revolution had a rather more immediate arsenal of images with which to conjure rape, murder, and plunder. But figures of political tumult and social leveling were still forcefully to be deployed in 1688 and the evocation of the Revolution as "Chaos of Power, and privileg'd destruction" must have been potent in the months following the Revolution.[30] Once conquest and tumult were

---

[30] Miner (ed.), *The Works of John Dryden*, xv, p. 85.

embraced, the play argues, all stood in danger: "when Kings and Queens are to be discarded, what shou'd Knaves do any longer in the pack?"[31] The language neatly combines the figure of chance – politics as gaming – with the argument that revolutions, once begun, are difficult to control; all parties should have an interest in social stability. This revolution, the play argues, is a dangerous unhinging of social and political order.

Certainly, self-interest as an engine of the Revolution played an important role in the rhetoric of those who regretted 1688, and Dryden displays his mastery of the topic. In an extremely witty scene where the mufti excites opposition to tyranny and absolutism – the charges, of course, repeatedly hurled against James – he mingles self-interest, fantasies of a glorious national history, and religious hocus-pocus in order to rouse mob allegiance. The mufti's speech is riddled with ironies, nowhere more tellingly expressed than in the mufti's three Ps: "Self-Preservation, our Property, and our Prophet."[32] These are, of course, a debased and ridiculed version of the slogans of 1688; and while we can find the invocation of a people's right to self-defense in the contemporary pamphlet literature, not all those who embraced the Revolution were eager to raise the standard of self-preservation with its Hobbesian overtones, and Dryden repeatedly takes aim at this principle, contrasting self-preservation as low self-interest against the bonds of nature, family, and society. By fixing self-interest as the first principle of the Revolution, he aims to expose greed and cowardice as its driving force. As one of the characters who comically plays out the role of thief and principle of the new order admits: "Not very heroick; but self preservation is a point above Honor and Religion too."[33] This, from a character who cheats his father-in-law by stealing his daughter and using his property to found a new regime. The application to English politics is not simply obvious – it seems willfully so.

Indeed, the whole handling of property as a principle of the Revolution is extremely imaginative in the play. The topic allowed Dryden to debase the motives of the rabble as plunder and tumult and simultaneously to undercut the rhetoric of the revolutionary settlement. The steady reach in *Don Sebastian* is for the moral high ground, and nowhere does this reach allow Dryden more play than in his handling of property as a principal motive of the Revolution. Property addressed in various terms was indeed part of the apologetic rhetoric of 1688, but it was not a principal term, mainly, I think, because it was not indeed very heroic matter. Dryden sensed the vulnerability of the term and exploited its weakness as moral and social principle. This exploitation allowed him to arrange the political principles of the play so that property and self-interest and "our prophet Mohamet" vindicate 1688, and trust, loyalty, and the bonds of family and society suffer defeat. The old bonds of family and society are intended, of course, as a foil against which the poet can display the politics of plunder and property. If one might begin the argument that the Revolution was theft, and property its mainspring, then the authority of the

---

[31] *Ibid.*, p. 175.   [32] *Ibid.*, p. 173.   [33] *Ibid.*, p. 151.

entire action is undercut. From property springs the violation of familial bonds, social disorder, contempt for duty, trust, and gratitude; 1688 was a revolution driven by appetite, contemptuous of the polity, fixed in a brave new world of opportunism, craft, and greed.

Don Sebastian has, of course, more to argue than the hollowness of revolutionary principles and more ways of arguing that theme than I have suggested. What wants observing is how thoroughly the apologetics of the Revolution are engaged, how carefully structured, scene by scene, is this high drama of the Sebastian legend. The play was engaging in a contest for moral and cultural authority, and Dryden brought to that contest not only his gifts as a stylist of the heroic drama, a keen ear for political rhetoric, but also an understanding of how historical romance could be used to orchestrate a political argument. The matter of Don Sebastian allowed Dryden to indulge in a brilliant display of hints, allusions, and innuendo; it also allowed him to construct an allegory of moral principles, and in such a construction he is, of course, holding the winning hand. Honor and obligation, loyalty and gratitude, the spare soulfulness of Atticus and Cicero, these are the properties of a Jacobite position. Needless to say, such a conclusion did not altogether fit the public perception of either the Jacobite cause or of the playwright himself.

For whom did Dryden think he was writing this play in the summer and early autumn of 1689? He argues in the Preface that he was forced back to the stage by financial need; one could think of a number of topics, themes, and histories that might have offered more promise of wide popularity in 1689 than *Don Sebastian*. And yet what is most puzzling is not this apparent contradiction but the actual success of the play in 1689 and thereafter. This is not a play of opaque and occult politics; of course, an audience might always ignore or deny the applications, but the idioms of the Revolution are so clearly handled in *Don Sebastian* that it would have taken not simply a willing suspension of disbelief to ignore or elide the politics but an active denial of much of the language of the play to achieve an apolitical reading of *Don Sebastian*. It might well be that the philosophical materials of the play – and they are elegantly displayed in both dedication and text – are more immediate and attractive for us than are its politics. But for contemporaries the political currents would have been extremely difficult to ignore. That the politics of 1688 are provided with an overlay of philosophical meaning not only makes them more attractive but also deepens their argumentative coherence; philosophy gives the politics an altitude and a dignity that are in fact one of the principal polemical aims of the work.

To whom, then, could such a play have appealed? Could an audience, some of whose members had not simply accommodated the Revolution but embraced it, have been flattered by the portraits and arguments of *Don Sebastian*? What might they have seen in its exposition of revolutionary folly and greed, its condemnation of the new political morality, its debasement of the rhetoric of the Revolution? I have no certain answer to this puzzle, but we might think that the political and moral values that this play celebrates – gratitude, loyalty, honor, trust, beneficence – could not have been willingly abandoned by the nation in its rapid acquiescence to a convenient revolution. Although Dryden was in control of the action and language of his play, he could not entirely regulate its reception and understanding. One might well imagine an audience that both embraced the Revolution and proclaimed its allegiance to the values that this play honors. Dryden might hope to deny an audience this ground, but the embrace of paradoxes is not easy to regulate, nor can the playwright insist on scrupulous self-knowledge among his audience. The success of the play does not inevitably argue the acceptance of Dryden's polemical intentions; one might indeed embrace the principles of *Don Sebastian* while regretting the politics of its author and the misbehavior of James II. So eager was the political nation to deny the revolutionary character of 1688–89, so anxious was it to underscore the continuity with, indeed return to, ancient principles, to argue James as aberration, that it might go to the theater, witness a production of Dryden's play, and vigorously assent to the values of *Don Sebastian* without allowing the playwright's application of those principles. In fact, the success of *Don Sebastian* seems to me rather interesting evidence about the continuity of political values, or at least the moral and psychological advantages for Dryden's audience of professing such a continuity of values and forms.

Although the months following the flight of James and the installation of William and Mary were sufficiently fluid to allow for the ironies of Dryden's play and his audience's suspension of political disbelief, it would not have been surprising had the revolutionary settlement finally silenced Dryden. *Don Sebastian* turned out, however, to be not a valedictory work but the prologue to a remarkable decade for the former laureate; and while assassination plots, associations, and rumors of Jacobite invasion complicated the fabric of political culture throughout the 1690s, the revolutionary settlement did not remain suspended in ironies and suspicion. Running a literary shop on Jacobite and nonjuring sentiment proved more than adequate for the invention of *Don Sebastian*, but could it remain so after the battle of the Boyne, after William's European campaigns, and after the financial revolution that enabled William to prosecute the war against France? I want to reflect briefly on this issue by way of the literary masterpiece of the 1690s, Dryden's translation of the *Works of Virgil* (1697).

Dryden had hoped all his life for a circumstance in which to cultivate epic, and now opposition allowed him such an opening.[34] The analogy with Milton in the 1660s may take some edge off the strangeness of Dryden's coming to epic by way of Virgil in the 1690s, but the analogy should not too quickly deprive us of a sense of incongruity, the dissonance between the argument of epic and the circumstances of Virgil's translator. Dryden's own sense of their incommensurability was quite sharp: "What *Virgil* wrote in the vigour of his

[34] See H. T. Swedenberg, Jr., "Dryden's Obsessive Concern with the Heroic," in D. W. Patterson and A. B. Strauss (eds.), *Essays in English Literature of the Classical Period Presented to Dougald MacMillan* (Chapel Hill, University of North Carolina Press, 1967), pp. 12–26.

Age, in Plenty and at Ease, I have undertaken to *Translate* in my Declining Years: strugling with Wants, oppress'd with Sickness, curb'd in my Genius, lyable to be misconstrued in all I write."[35] We need to allow for the poet's familiar defensive gestures, but we should also honor their likelihood, the real as well as strategic distance between what Dryden saw of his own position and what he knew of Virgil's intimacy with the court of Augustus Caesar and with the project of empire. The potential uses of Virgil to celebrate William's consolidation of rule and success on the continent must have seemed too obvious to comment on, but the fate of Virgil in this decade was not to celebrate the investment in empire but to regret its coming. That the *Aeneid* could not wholly be made to obey this imperative must have been clear, perhaps to no one more than to Dryden, who had earlier assimilated Virgil to the imperial ambitions of Stuart restoration. But the force and poignancy of Dryden's translation came neither from its confidence in the triumphs of war nor from its complaint against invasion and conquest: rather, it came from the negotiation that Dryden had continuously to make between regret and ambition, between justice and fate. It is that negotiation that opened the space for literary culture in this decade.

If Dryden's translation of Virgil had been wholly the remnant of an age that was out, it would serve as a vivid emblem of Stuart court culture. But Dryden's Virgil was more than an act of Jacobite piety. Making an English Virgil in the 1690s allowed Dryden to regret "usurpation," but it also forced him to recast the invasion, to mediate his understanding of the revolution, to accommodate both himself and the events of 1688–89 to a larger frame. Perhaps with Marvell, Dryden understood Stuart demise in terms of a clear political calculus:

> Though justice against fate complain,
> And plead the ancient rights in vain;
> But those do hold or break
> As men are strong or weak.[36]

But what Marvell darkly acknowledges, Dryden heightens and celebrates in his rendering of Virgil's *fatum*. Translating Virgil enabled Dryden to express old principles but also to allow the mysteries of fate and the ambiguities of fortune their sway, to discover in the ample folds of Virgil's epic a way of coming to terms with past and present by acknowledging his regret over the unsteadiness of politics and by assimilating his ambitions not wholly to a political cause but to the immortality of verse.[37]

The Works of Virgil can also be seen to anticipate the circumstance of heroic literature in the years to come, when epic repeatedly took shelter in translation, nostalgia, and parody. There is indeed a prophetic irony in Virgil's celebration of imperial Rome turned against the foundations of British

---

[35] *The Poems of John Dryden*, ed. James Kinsley (4 vols., Oxford, Clarendon Press, 1958), III, p. 1424.
[36] *Andrew Marvell, the Complete Poems*, ed. E. S. Donno (Harmondsworth, Penguin, 1972), p. 56.
[37] On this theme in Dryden's late poetry, see David Bywaters, *Dryden in Revolutionary England* (Berkeley and Los Angeles, University of California Press, 1991.

Empire. Nor would that irony seem merely Jacobite regret, for Britain's age of military, commercial, and colonial triumph steadily resisted epic construction. Neither Dryden's Virgil nor Pope's Homer nor *The Dunciad* could be mistaken for imperial celebration. Perhaps *Robinson Crusoe*, that allegory of acquisition and empire, augurs a new day.

But the formulation of a new cultural order was accomplished neither in the midst of the Revolution nor in the years of William's rule. Comprehending the Revolution, charting its cultural implications, and untangling its rhetoric were difficult tasks, and it is not surprising that the Muses were reluctant to speak in 1688. They were, I think, uncertain of what to say and what forms to say it in. From that perspective, the silence surrounding the Revolution seems to have its own logic, as does the florescence of Jacobite culture in the years following James II's retreat.

The Glorious Revolution, we are told, ushered in the dullest decade in English literature; although this is not altogether just, it was a difficult decade for literary invention. Given the perplexity of values and events, the embarrassment and silence over the Revolution, it is not surprising that the greatest literary achievements of the 1690s should have been in translation. For the former laureate the Revolution no doubt provoked deep anxiety, a literal and figurative dislocation, but it also allowed a remarkably productive late phase, and elevation above or at least a bitter-sweet reconciliation with politics and empire:

> All, all, of a piece throughout;
> Thy Chase had a Beast in View;
> Thy Wars brought nothing about;
> The Lovers were all untrue.
>
> 'Tis well an Old Age is out,
> And time to begin a New.[38]

So Dryden wrote, in 1700, for the restaging of Beaumont and Fletcher's *The Pilgrim*. The lines glance back over the whole of Dryden's age to demystify the past; but with a clear and unregretting gaze they also acknowledge the future.

---

[38] Kinsley (ed.), *The Poems of John Dryden*, IV, p. 1765.

11

Politics and popular culture: the theatrical response to the Revolution

Lois Potter

A few months after the publication of Dryden's *Don Sebastian* in January 1690, an anonymous author published a play called *The Late Revolution, or the Happy Change*. It was prefaced by a sarcastic prologue addressed "To the Players":

> If e're this Play shou'd have the Grace
> To be beheld by your sweet Face,
> Take heed how you are to it civil,
> For, Sirs! believe me! 'tis the Devil.
> A *Williamitish* Piece all thro',
> With which you nothing have to do.
> *Sebastian* better does the trick,
> With Bobs and Innuendo's thick,
> Which Abdicated Laureat brings
> In praise of Abdicated Kings.
>
> (*The Late Revolution*, Prologue)

The implications are clear: the attitude of the established theater – and there had been only *one* legitimate theater since the merger of the two dramatic companies in 1682 – had been at best lukewarm with regard to the events of 1688–89. According to these verses, the players and their audience would have been utterly unsympathetic to a "Williamitish" piece, whereas they had happily tolerated the indirect political comments in *Don Sebastian*, the work of a known Catholic and Jacobite. The success of Dryden's play partly bears out this contention. So does its prologue: the marvellous wit and urbanity with which he turns his precarious situation into a joke would hardly have been possible even for Dryden if he had not expected a fair proportion of his audience to be on his side.

If actors and audience had at first been suspicious of the new government, it would hardly have been surprising. William and Mary were openly in favor of moral reform movements, which often had the theater among their targets.[1] William was never a theater-goer like his immediate predecessors. Pro-Williamite writers even made a virtue of his lack of interest in the arts: thus, Peter Motteux, in his *Gentleman's Journal* for February 1692, included a mock-

---

[1] Dudley W. R. Bahlman, "The Moral Revolution of 1688," *The Wallace Notestein Essays*, no. 2 (New Haven, Conn., Yale University Press, 1957, and Hamden, Conn., Archon Books, repr. 1968), pp. 15–16.

proclamation by Apollo, forbidding the publication of love verses during a time when William was fighting for the liberty of Europe, and urging writers to desist from satire during "this so just occasion of writing *Panegyricks*."[2]

It is often assumed that Mary's attitude to the theater resembled her husband's. In her *Memoirs* she mentions playgoing only once, and then only as a public gesture: she made a point of going to the theater in 1691, she claims, in order to show her confidence in the success of her husband's current campaign.[3] Another public-relations gesture backfired: in 1690 she ordered a special performance of Dryden's *The Spanish Friar*, a play which had been banned under James II, only to discover, to the delight of the audience, that one of the central characters was a queen who had deposed her own father.[4] This was not the only play which turned out to be awkwardly topical. *King Lear*, the archetypal story of two ungrateful daughters, had already acquired a new relevance in Nahum Tate's version (1681), where the old king survives but abdicates in favor of Cordelia and her husband. The parallel did not go unnoticed by the author of "The Female Parricide" (1689), whose comparison was explicit:

> But worse than cruel lustful Goneril, thou!
> She took but what her father did allow;
> But thou, more impious, robb'st thy father's brow.
> Him both of power and glory you disarm,
> Make him, by lies, the people's hate and scorn,
> Then turn him forth to perish in a storm.[5]

This comparison of Mary to Goneril may have been inspired by her first, unsuccessful, performance on her arrival in London, when she displayed so much cheerfulness as to make several spectators blame what they saw as her heartlessness towards her father.[6] As Bishop Gilbert Burnet explained, she was acting (in both senses) on the orders of William, who was anxious that they should seem completely in accord as to the justice of his invasion.[7] It is significant that *King Lear* was not performed during the reign of William and Mary.

But these facts give only one side of Mary's relationship with the theater. It needs also to be remembered that her mother, Anne Hyde, was said to have been a good amateur actress and that she herself played a leading role in the court masque *Calisto* (1675), for which she had been coached by the great actor Thomas Betterton and his wife.[8] As a queen, she continued to patronize

---

[2] *The Gentleman's Journal: or the Monthly Miscellany by Way of letter to a Gentleman in the Country, Consisting of News, History, Philosophy, Poetry, Musick, Translation, &c.* (ed. Peter Motteux), (printed and sold by R. Baldwin, February 1692), p. 7.

[3] R. Doebner (ed.), *Memoirs of Mary, Queen of England (1689–1693), Together With Her Letters And Those of Kings James II. and William III. To The Electress, Sophia of Hanover* (Leipzig, Veit, and London, D. Nutt, 1886), p. 36.

[4] John Loftis, *The Politics of Drama in Augustan England* (Oxford, Clarendon Press, 1963), pp. 22–23.

[5] *POAS*, v: 1688–97, William J. Cameron (ed.), (1971), p. 157.

[6] For example, *The Diary of John Evelyn*, ed. E. S. de Beer (6 vols., Oxford, Clarendon Press, 1955), IV, pp. 624–25.

[7] Gilbert Burnet, *History of the Reign of King James II* (Oxford, Clarendon Press, 1852), pp. 465–66.

[8] *The Letters of Elizabeth Queen of Bohemia*, compiled by L. M. Baker (London, Bodley Head, 1953), p. 286, quoted in Henri and Barbara Van der Zee, *William and Mary* (London, Macmillan, 1973; Harmondsworth, Penguin,

the theater, not only through command performances but also through financial gifts to dramatists of whom she approved, like the loyal Williamite, Peter Motteux – "doubtless," Motteux declared in the Preface to his *Beauty in Distress* (published 1698), because she hoped that he would "still keep to strict Morality, even in the circumstance of a melancholic Fortune." But, while the rewarding of morally edifying writers was certainly one of her declared aims, she also seems to have had a soft spot for plays with dashing heroes. According to Colley Cibber, whose acting career began just after the Revolution, she admired William Mountfort's performance as the rake hero in Aphra Behn's *The Rover* to the point where she was willing to disregard her disapproval of the play itself.[9]

Mountfort was a playwright as well as an actor. His *Successful Strangers*, performed about a month after *Don Sebastian* and published, like it, early in 1690, shows him coming out in favor of the Revolution well ahead of most of his contemporaries – a fact which may have had something to do with the queen's admiration for him. While this play is set in Spain, it contains a few allusions to recent events. They are cautious and conciliatory. For instance, a young Englishman who has just arrived in Seville is asked about the state of his country:

Ant[onio]. Troth Sir, 'tis in a fairer way then ever, the Prince and the People have faith in each other, and there's great hopes that *Brittain* will retreive [*sic*] its long lost glory.

(III, i, p. 27)

It is possible that the nonverbal aspects of the production may have made it less innocuous than this passage suggests. At one point there is a curious direction for a priest to cross "above the Stage" (II, p. 16), and it is easy to imagine how this silent appearance might have been used either for a general appeal to anticlerical feeling or for an attack on a particular priest, such as James's much-disliked confessor, father Edward Petre. At any rate, Mountfort says in his Preface that he received anonymous verses claiming that people were only laughing at his jokes, "Least those who dont, should be brought in for Treason" (sig. A3v).

The queen's fondness for Mountfort had a rather touching sequel, of which her *Memoirs* give only a brief hint. In 1693 Mary refers to the evidence of "so universal a corruption" in the behavior of the nobility at Lord Mohun's trial, "that we seem only prepared for vengeance."[10] It is not surprising that she had been following this scandalous trial with interest, since it concluded with the acquittal of Lord Mohun for the murder of Mountfort, killed in December 1692 during the lord's attempted abduction of an actress. It is clear that Mary's sympathies were with the talented actor–playwright rather than with the nobleman around whom his fellow peers had rallied.

1988), p. 20; Judith Milhous, *Thomas Betterton and the Management of Lincoln's Inn Fields 1695–1708* (Carbondale and Edwardsville, Southern Illinois University Press; London and Amsterdam, Feffer and Simons, 1979), p. 30.

[9] Colley Cibber, *An Apology for the Life of Mr. Colley Cibber. Written by Himself*, ed. Robert W. Lowe (2 vols., London, John C. Nimmo, 1889), I, p. 128.   [10] Doebner (ed.), *Memoirs of Mary*, p. 59.

If the queen's attitude to the theater was more sympathetic than is sometimes suggested, it must be admitted that the theater's attitude to her and her husband was at first cautiously noncommittal. Apart from the special case of Mountfort, it is hard to find much open enthusiasm for the Revolution in plays produced during the years immediately following it. Indeed, the most characteristic product of Williamite culture in the legitimate theater was the musical spectacle, more innocuous than drama, and more accessible to a royal spectator whose native language was not English. It was comparatively easy to turn such pieces into a compliment to the reigning monarchs, and it is likely that this happened more often than has so far been realized. Thus, Settle's and Purcell's *The Fairy Queen* (1692), an adaptation of *A Midsummer Night's Dream*, is notable for its softening of the quarrel between the fairy couple, so crucial to the original plot. Stressing instead the harmony between them, it includes a series of entertainments presented by Titania to Oberon on the occasion of his birthday and possibly intended as a compliment to the double reign. Works written after Mary's death generally make the most of the king's military success. Motteux's *Europe's Revels* (1697) depicts the representatives of various nations celebrating William's latest victories in a series of national dances. An adaptation of John Fletcher's *The Mad Lover* (1701) by Motteux and John Eccles features an interpolated masque and a "martial welcome" to the play's hero, Memnon, on his return from a successful conquest. It is clear that these spectacles were meant to be understood topically, and indeed, when the musical interlude was issued separately the printed text replaced Memnon's name with William's.[11]

However, these panegyrics also give some indication of the problems facing anyone who wished to deal with current events in the more realistic context of comedy. It is curious, for instance, that *Europe's Revels* includes no Dutch dancers to join such obvious stereotypes as the comic cowardly Irishman and the French Officer who unsuccessfully tries to court an English lady. The most embarrassing aspect of the Revolution, from the theatrical point of view, was the Dutch presence in England. The English tradition of dealing with foreigners in drama was simple: if they were meant to be sympathetic, the rule was to treat them as if they were English, making no distinction in their accent or vocabulary; unsympathetic or comic characters, on the other hand, were caricatured and made to speak an absurd dialect. The Dutch had once been fair objects for ridicule in, for instance, Aphra Behn's *The Dutch Lover* (1673), but they are invisible as far as the drama of the 1690s is concerned, though comic and villainous Frenchmen proliferate. Probably it would have been impossible to depict any Dutch character on stage without seeming to satirize the king. Thus, William and his court figure only in the international language of mythology and allegory – the language of high culture, but one which essentially spoke only to the converted. This is true even of Rowe's *Tamerlane*, the one serious play indisputably about William, to which I shall briefly return at the end of this essay.

[11] Peter Anthony Motteux and John Eccles, *Acis and Galatea* (1701); cf. pp. 4–5 of *The Martial Welcome* and *Mercurius Musicus* (January–February 1701), p. 1.

To find a genuinely popular Williamite drama, then, one must look outside the context of the legitimate theater with its inhibiting sense of decorum. It is certain that the theater of the fairgrounds was used for propaganda purposes, but as none of its plays survived one can deduce their nature only from such titles as that of the spectacle offered at May Fair in 1696: *King William's Happy Deliverance and Glorious Triumph over his Enemies or the Consultation of the Pope, Devil, French King and the Grand Turk, with the Whole Form of the Siege of Namur, and the Humours of a Renegade French-Man and Brandy Jean, with the Conceits of Scaramouch and Harlequin.*[12] However, the immediate post-Revolution years also saw the appearance of a number of pamphlets in the form of plays, clearly intended to resemble the products of popular culture. Many are called "tragi-comedies," a term which was also applied to satiric pamphlets in dramatic form in the 1640s,[13] and some of their subject matter is rather similar. Just as the satiric "tragicomedies" of the 1640s portrayed the parliamentary leaders as henpecked cuckolds, so the Williamites made James II the victim of a shrewish Mary of Modena. Ghost scenes, another favorite device of the Civil War tragicomedies, also recur in these plays. But, whereas the tragicomedies of the 1640s were mostly short pamphlets with little real theatrical quality, those of 1690 are virtually full length, with stage directions which suggest that some of the authors may have had performance in view, or at least wished to be thought of as writing for the stage. To some extent, they succeeded: Macaulay, one of the few historians to have read them, thought that one at least had been performed at Bartholomew Fair.[14] However, Sybil Rosenfeld's authoritative study, *The Theatre of the London Fairs*, insists that there is no evidence for this.[15] Quite apart from their explicitly political content, their depiction of contemporary events and real people, sometimes under their own names and sometimes under thin disguises, would have ruled them out for the licensed theater. It is more likely that the plays are closet dramas, perhaps intended for the coffee houses, where pamphlets were often circulated by being read aloud.[16]

The Late Revolution, from which I quoted at the start, is one of the earliest of seven anonymous pamphlet plays, all dating from 1690, which were advertised at a shilling apiece. Four deal with events of James's reign, one with the period immediately before it, and two with William's Irish campaign. All seven are probably due to the same publishers, John Dunton and Richard Baldwin, both of whom had been producing Whig propaganda since the early 1680s. Dunton, indeed, is credited with having created a whole

---

[12] Sybil Rosenfeld, *The Theatre of the London Fairs in the Eighteenth Century* (Cambridge University Press, 1960), p. 7.

[13] See Lois Potter, "True Tragicomedies of the English Civil War and Commonwealth," in Nancy Klein Maguire (ed.), *Renaissance Tragicomedy, Explorations in Genre and Politics* (New York, AMS Press, 1987), pp. 196, 205–8.

[14] T. B. Macaulay, *The History of England from the Accession of James II*, ed. T. F. Henderson (5 vols., Oxford University Press, 1931), III, p. 137.

[15] Rosenfeld, *The Theatre of the London Fairs*, pp. 6, 108.

[16] Lois G. Schwoerer, *The Declaration of Rights, 1689* (Baltimore and London, Johns Hopkins University Press, 1981), p. 157.

"Whig martyrology" by publishing emotional accounts – the work of a team of publishers and hack writers – of the sufferings of Protestants at the Bloody Assizes and after the Revocation of the Edict of Nantes.[17] Stephen Parks, in his study of Dunton's career, notes that Baldwin and Dunton advertised each others' works and used each others' imprints almost interchangeably as well as printing under other names which might have been fictitious.[18] All this suggests a concerted political effort, probably financed by English supporters of William.

The earliest plays in this group, *The Abdicated Prince*, *The Bloody Duke*, and *The Late Revolution*, seem to have been intended as a series. All were entered in the Term Catalogues of the Stationers' Company in May 1690, and probably appeared in the previous month, since *The Late Revolution* was advertised in the *London Gazette* for April 24–28.[19] They may have been issued to mark the first anniversary of the new reign. That either Baldwin or Dunton commissioned all three is clear from the fact that they were advertised collectively at the end of *The Bloody Duke*: "These *Three New Plays*, contain a full Account of the private Intrigues of the *Two Last Reigns*, and of all the most remarkable *Transactions* that have hapned [*sic*] since." In 1694 Dunton repeated the claim when he advertised the same three plays, along with *The Royal Voyage*, in *The Athenian Mercury* for September 29. By this time, *The Abdicated Prince* had gone into a second edition, the only one of the seven plays to achieve such a success. That the series was aiming at a wide readership is clear from the preface to *The Bloody Duke*, in which the author says that he intends to instruct "the meanest Protestant Christians," and depicts himself, with a mixture of modesty and anti-intellectualism, as "a Person of so unpolite a Stile" that he must be called a historian rather than an "Orator." *The Abdicated Prince* and *The Bloody Duke* are in fact by the same author, and they share a commentator character called Remarquo, equally "unpolite," whose function is to represent the views of the true Protestant Englishman. The scene of both plays is supposedly Hungary; the Catholics are called Pagans, the Protestants Christians.

The Bloody Duke tells of James's career during the last years of Charles II. Charles is Androgynes, a weak if good-natured ruler totally besotted with his mistresses. James (called Caligula) is seen planning the popish plot and the poisoning of his brother, with which the play ends. The author admits in the preface that he cannot prove this accusation, "yet the common Fame of it remaining amongst us" makes it allowable in "a work especially of this kind." The phrase suggests an interesting sense of the decorum of popular drama: hearsay and popular prejudice are evidently admissible here, as they would not be in a work with greater pretensions.

[17] Stephen Parks, *John Dunton and the English Book Trade, a Study of His Career with a Checklist of His Publications* (New York and London, Garland, 1976), pp. 38–40.

[18] Parks, *John Dunton*, pp. 198–99.

[19] Allardyce Nicoll, *A History of English Drama 1660–1900* (6 vols., Cambridge University Press, 1952–59), I, pp. 439–45, gives the dates at which these works were entered in the Term Catalogues of the Stationers' Company and those on which they were advertised in contemporary newspapers. I have also checked the latter myself.

The Abdicated Prince, though it deals with events taking place later than those in *The Bloody Duke*, was probably the earlier to be written. For one thing, the character corresponding to James II in this play is called Cullydada. This is in keeping with his more comic role, and it is easy to see why the author of *The Bloody Duke* would have felt obliged to change it when he moved from James's role as cuckold to his role as murderer. The main events of *The Abdicated Prince* are the Monmouth rebellion and the circumstances surrounding the birth of the Prince of Wales. "Common fame" had been equally busy with this episode. Although William had ordered, soon after his arrival in London, that no scurrilous libels should be published against the late queen or her newborn son,[20] such libels had been in circulation since the summer of 1688, possibly with his tacit approval; his widely circulated *Declaration* of that October had maintained that "not only we ourselves but all the good subjects of the kingdom do vehemently suspect that the pretended Prince of Wales was not borne by the Queen."[21] Thus, *The Abdicated Prince* was able to draw heavily on printed sources, some of them extremely scurrilous; the printer has even set some words and phrases in black-letter to indicate direct quotation from them.[22] The play shows how Mary of Modena attempts to get an heir first by committing adultery, then by feigning pregnancy and smuggling a newly born child into her room. In a particularly voyeuristic scene, Remarquo hides behind the hangings in the queen's chamber to spy on the supposed delivery, which includes the bringing in of the notorious warming pan (IV. ii, pp. 46–49). In the last act, Cullydada is haunted by the ghosts of Godfrey, Russell, Sidney, and Monmouth: as the latter is about to prophesy, the cock crows and a messenger enters with news of the invasion. The final scene of the play consists entirely of this stage direction, clearly unperformable:

Enter *Prince Lysander* [William], attended with the Nobility and Gentry of *Hungary*, and Guards in a magnificent manner, with Drums beating, Trumpets sounding, Colours flying, the People shouting, and the Guns round the great Tower firing; at which the Skies clear up, the Sun shines, and all the inchanted Pagan Mosques, Priests, Jebusites, Crosses, Beads, Quo Warranto's, Dispensators, Ecclesiastick Commissioners, &c., vanish in a Moment.   (p. 60)

As the imagery makes clear, Catholicism itself is seen as a stage spectacle, an illusion or enchantment, that vanishes in the light of day.

The Late Revolution also deals with events leading up to William's arrival in London. In other respects, it is rather different from the rest of the trilogy. For one thing, it claims on the title page to be the work of "a Person of Quality," and its author lives up to his description by writing in a more classical manner. Apart from Father Petre and the papal nuncio, most of the charac-

---

[20] *London Mercury*, January 7–10, 1689.
[21] Schwoerer, *The Declaration of Rights*, p. 115, also pp. 107, 111.
[22] For example, *A Full Answer to the Depositions: and to all other the Pretences and Arguments whatsoever, Concerning the Birth of the Prince of Wales* (printed for Simon Burges, London, 1689), which contains a number of the statements quoted in the play.

ters are anonymous, the equivalent to the messengers and chorus of classical drama. Of course, William and Mary never appear – decorum presumably prevents the depiction of either former or present rulers – but the author manages ingeniously to bring Princess Anne indirectly into the play. Having adopted the current belief that a plot to capture or murder the princess was the reason for her flight from London, he introduces an anonymous lady-in-waiting who quotes, at great length, the soliloquy supposedly uttered by Anne as she is torn between "mistaken Piety" towards her father and fears for her own safety (v. iv, p. 49). There is even a stage direction calling for the lady-in-waiting to cross the stage "with another in Disguise" (iv. vii, p. 52), obviously a subtle way of suggesting Anne's presence without directly stating it. The anonymity of the characters is important for another reason: it suggests the support for William among all classes of society. As the play draws to its close, we see one group of characters after another deciding to join his army; the implication is that England, after being divided for so long, has finally found a ruler it can trust.

The Royal Voyage belongs to the same period as the trilogy, but deals with present rather than past events. It was published in May–June 1690, just as William III was setting off on his Irish campaign, and its main function is clearly to stir up dislike of the Irish and their allies.[23] For this reason, it deals mainly with type-characters, mostly caricatured Irishmen and Frenchmen, with a few loyal Englishmen for contrast. Since the author announces that he intends to follow it with a second part, it is possible that *The Royal Flight* may have been meant for this purpose. The later play is, however, quite different in structure, perhaps because events took a more dramatic turn than even the author had dared to hope. William's victories in July, and his enthusiastic reception in London early in September, made it possible to ridicule James II even more harshly than in previous plays. *The Royal Flight* shows him to be a cowardly idiot, superstitiously dependent on priests and prophecies, asking his confessor to pimp for him, despised even by some of his own supporters. Told that the Queen of Heaven is on his side, he says that he would prefer Joan of Arc (ii. i, p. 13). After the battle of the Boyne and James's flight to France, the final scene shows his followers drawing their swords on one another. The main point of both these Irish plays is, of course, the contrast between the drunken, moronic Irish and the admirable qualities of English Protestants.

All the plays just mentioned can be seen as "popular" in the sense that they depict events in black-and-white terms and take advantage of widely shared prejudices, but at the same time their use of messenger speeches for many of the crucial events (like Monmouth's execution in *The Abdicated Prince* and the

---

[23] That the four plays already mentioned were the earliest to be published is confirmed by the fact that Gerard Langbaine mentions them, but not the others, in his *Account of the English Dramatick Poets*, published in Oxford in 1691. Langbaine seems to take them seriously as plays, and notes of *The Abdicated Prince*, "there needs no *Clavis*[,] the Persons, being obvious to all Intelligent Persons." (p. 525) His comments on the other three are similar. There is no doubt that if the other three plays had been available at the time he sent the book to press, he would have included them as well.

battle of the Boyne in *The Royal Flight*) suggests their dominance by a more refined kind of dramaturgy.

A more obviously "popular" play, in terms of its theatrical technique, is *The Banished Duke, or, the Tragedy of Infortunatus*, which dates from the autumn of 1690. It claims in its Prologue that it will depict events "more rare/ Than any *Show* that's been in *Smithfield-Fair*," and is more obviously like a fairground entertainment than its predecessors. Combining in one work everything from Monmouth's Rebellion to William's invasion, it is strongly, and traditionally, farcical, particularly in its treatment of James's court. The elderly Romanus (James) is the victim of his bad-tempered and unfaithful wife. Papissa not only claims to wear the breeches but pulls up her skirt to reveal that she is indeed wearing them (scarlet ones, to indicate her affiliation to the Whore of Babylon), then *"pulleth him by the Cravat and Perriwig"* (II. ii, p. 5). Later, when she is feigning pregnancy, she bursts in on the king's council, pulls a pillow out from under her dress, and throws it at them (II. ii, p. 17). The stage direction for the battle of Sedgemoor may perhaps have amateur performers in view, since it warns them not to be too ambitious: "three in a File (the Musket's lin'd with Pikes) may be enough to shew an Emblem of War, and demonstrate, to the curious Spectators, the result of a bloody Fight" (III. i, p. 28). There are also directions for the hanging of Infortunatus' (Monmouth's) supporters: "a Gibbet turneth out, like a crane, or yards [*sic*] Arm, with a great many men Hanging on't" (IV. ii, p. 40).

In its treatment of the warming-pan episode this play is more amusing than *The Abdicated Prince*. As the queen and her confessor play cards, symbolically putting the knave above the king of hearts, news is brought that she will have to feign birth pangs prematurely because six of the nine pregnant women kept for that purpose have just gone into labor. A series of midwives enter carrying babies in baskets, and there is an embarrassing moment when the first one brought in turns out to be a girl. Finally, having got rid of the increasingly suspicious courtiers, James and Judge George Jeffreys choose the fattest and fairest of the available candidates. As they hear the news of William's invasion, the queen ties the baby on Father Petre's back, and they all run out. Romanus is left pronouncing dire but useless threats against the rebels.

Although they do their best to represent themselves as the expression of the popular voice, it would be hard to call these plays genuinely popular. Both *The Banished Duke* and *The Abdicated Prince* are sympathetic to Monmouth's Rebellion, but only insofar as it was directed against James II. Their treatment of the duke's peasant supporters is comic rather than sympathetic; in *The Abdicated Prince* they have no names and are simply called "First of the Rabble" and so on. Even their pro-Williamite uprising in the last act is shown to be motivated by the desire to loot the homes of Catholics, and the author also shows his awareness that the Protestants have an ultimate advantage over the Catholics, even under James's reign, in being richer: "Wealth" is "the Sinews of all Power" (III. i, p. 33). *The Late Revolution* draws on popular superstition (in I. iii, citizens in the Royal Exchange see the scepter fall from the hand of a statue of Mary Tudor and take it for a good omen of the fall of popery), but after a London mob has attacked the papal nuncio and Father Petre two Protestant lords force the crowd to retire, announcing that the prince is displeased at their rudeness (v. viii).

What, then, is the purpose of this sustained exploitation of prejudice which the authors probably did not share, and a dramaturgy which they probably despised? Part of the answer may lie in the final play in the Baldwin–Dunton group (again, dating from some time in the autumn of 1690). Although it was also printed by Baldwin, *The Folly of Priest-Craft* is something of an anomaly; it is not "popular" in style, and not a short "tragicomedy" caricaturing real persons. It is a full-scale, sophisticated, well-constructed Restoration comedy, apparently set in the reign of James II, at a period when Catholicism was in the ascendant and there was still no sign of organized opposition to it. It never mentions William and Mary, nor indeed James himself. The author presents himself in the Prologue not as a political satirist but as a dramatist who wanted to write "Something that might deserve the name of New," replacing the predictable fops, bullies, and wits of earlier comedy with a new type, "the plotting Priest." The chief of these plotters, Father Politico, is a clerical Sir Politic Would-be. He is seen in the context of a well-contrasted set of colleagues: the dimwitted Irish Father MackDonnell, who can be counted on to ruin any plot; the fanatical Father Bigot, described as one who "might have been learned, honest, and wise, if his Religion had not made him a Dunce, a Knave, and a Fool" (I. i, p. 2); the greedy Father Cautious. The hero, Turnabout, flatters the various humors of this ill-assorted crowd in the hope of getting a lucrative place at court which will enable him to marry the wealthy but capricious Leucasia. However, one of Leucasia's humors is a loathing of priests. Turnabout's plot is thus counterpointed with her attempts to foil it by telling the priests what a hypocrite he really is. Ironically, her efforts actually help him, since the priests, taking Turnabout's overacted loyalty for granted, had been assuming that he would need no reward for his service. When Leucasia finally agrees to marry Turnabout, it is on condition that he break with them forever and prove his loyalty by making fools of them in public – which is what happens in the last scene.

Interestingly, the onstage audience for their humiliation includes a Roman Catholic peer, Lord Brittain, who has already been shown to be deeply patriotic and hence uneasy about his church's threat to traditional English liberties. The presence of such a character, and the absence of any reference to rebellion or invasion, indicates the basic moderation of the author. Turnabout himself, in the Epilogue, states a position which seems to be anticlerical rather than anti-Catholic:

> When Priests forsake the business of the State,
> And on the Duties of their Office wait,
> Expect the Issue of a prosperous fate.
> But when they steer the Helm, they hurry on

> A dismal Night of black confusion.
> Nature a wound in every part must feel,
> And her whole system with disorder reel.

As can be seen from a number of the satires collected in *Poems on Affairs of State*, anticlerical feeling (an important motif in *Don Sebastian*) was not confined to any one party.[24] In the play, the behavior of the priests is sometimes appalling: the greedy Father Cautious has a chest of ill-gotten gains, keeps a mistress disguised as a page, and is prepared to advise murder in a good cause. But their sheer absurdity makes the characters almost endearing at times. Father Politico, for example, comments on one of his disastrous plots that it "wants nothing but success to render it a Masterpiece for the best Politician in *Europe*" (v. iii, p. 56).

At the end, when Father Politico promises to treat the rest of the cast to supper and they in turn promise to say no more about what has happened, we are reminded of the conclusion of *Bartholomew Fair*. This ending, like the sympathetic treatment of Lord Brittain, suggests what was to be the main strategy of Williamite dramatists: to conciliate rather than to polarize opinion. There are other examples. Near the end of *The Late Revolution*, the crowd of people going to join William includes an old Cavalier and an old Parliamentarian who agree that they were fools to "knock out one another's little Brains" in the past. In 1693, Thomas Shadwell's *The Volunteers* would create the same myth of national unity by showing the reconciliation of an old Cavalier and an old Roundhead, and the range of characters, serious and comic, who have volunteered to fight under William.

However, there is a purpose behind the comic treatment: "You are made ridiculous," Turnabout tells Politico, "and your being ridiculous does make you impotent" (v. iv, p. 62). Williamite writers had reason to know the deadly power of ridicule when used by the other side, and the 1690s satires make frequent reference to notable writers in James's party. A striking feature of *The Bloody Duke* is its attack on Sir Roger L'Estrange, whose pro-government journal, *The Observator*, had attempted to defend James's policy from the point of view of an Anglican royalist. The play's intention is made clear on the title page, which gives as its epigraph a quotation from the *New Observator* (vol. II, no. 6): "*Justice requires an eternal mark of Infamy on the Perpetrators of certain Villanies of the last Reigne.*" L'Estrange's own words are turned against him not only here but in the play itself, where he appears under his *nom de plume*, Nobbs. He plays the frankly villainous role of a writer so obsessed with his own cleverness as to have lost all moral sense: thus, he is willing to write something to confute belief in the popish plot, but not until it has been generally accepted as true, "or else you must know it would not be worth my while to confute it" (II. i, p. 14); that a number of Catholics die in the meantime is no concern of his, and he even encourages them to hope for pardon so as to keep them from confessing at their executions (III. iii). What makes him most dangerous, however, is his wit. As he explains, his method is always to

[24] See POAS, V: 1688–97, Cameron (ed.), pp. 270–96.

espouse the *Court Cause* to be sure, *right or wrong*, and then do I, in a bantering sort of way, insinuate and introduce all the Arguments that the other side can possibly be suppos'd to bring, and by *ridiculing* some, and *waving* the rest, egad I leave them bustling and scratching their Heads to find out some new Matter.   (III. ii, p. 29)

This is a good description of L'Estrange's manner, but it also recalls Mr. Bayes, the famous caricature of Dryden in *The Rehearsal*, and indeed Nobbs at one point quotes "my brother *Bayes*," reciting a couplet from *Absolom and Achitophel* (III. ii, p. 28).

   This is as far as the Whig dramatists went in attacking Dryden, but implicit in all their plays is a sense of the need to come to terms with his powerful oppositional influence. Since the fall of James II was accompanied by that of his poet laureate, writers who were unsure how they felt about the first of these events could make up for it by unreservedly rejoicing in the second. Even *The Folly of Priest-Craft* (assuming that it is meant to take place in James's reign) gets in a somewhat anachronistic reference to "our cashier'd *Laureat*" (II. ii, p. 14). The Preface to *The Royal Voyage* compares the intended two-part play to Dryden's *Conquest of Granada*. Above all, as I indicated at the beginning of this essay, the success of *Don Sebastian* showed that the former laureate was still a powerful adversary. *The Late Revolution* takes up a position directly opposed to his, not only in manner (drawing on the popular rather than the tragic genre) but also in some of its imagery. Much of the effect of *Don Sebastian* derives from its Miltonic language, which associates the hero with the Satan of *Paradise Lost*, glamorous in ruin. When Sebastian has revealed his royal identity to his captors, his conqueror, deeply moved, describes his "suff'ring Majesty" as

a Sun

> Strug'ling in dark Eclipse, and shooting day
> On either side of the black orb that veil'd him.   (I. i. pp. 344–6)

This image ultimately derives from *Paradise Lost* ("Darkened so, yet shone/ Above them all th' Arch Angel" [I. 591–600]). In 1701 Rowe's *Tamerlane* was to invert the satanic imagery of *Don Sebastian* in the interest of an official Williamite drama, which was to be acted on the anniversary of the Revolution almost to the end of the eighteenth century.[25] But Rowe had been anticipated by the anonymous pamphleteers. In *The Late Revolution*, the citizens who act as a chorus also compare the satanic tyrant to the darkened sun. They do so, however, only in order to contrast this romantic picture with the sordid reality of James's behavior in his last days of rule:

> When tyrants act all thorough like themselves,
> They may deserve the name of glorious monsters;
> Something methinks of *Lucifer* shines thro 'em;
> A sort of *gloomy light*, that's great, tho' Devlish;
> But thus to yield and break, to fawn and truckle,

---

[25] See Charles Beecher Hogan, *The London Stage, 1776–1800* (Carbondale, Southern Illinois University Press, 1968), I, part V, p. cxlii. Lois Schwoerer has drawn my attention to a note in the *Morning Chronicle and London Advertiser*, November 5, 1788, expressing regret that *Tamerlane* was not performed in that year as in previous ones.

> Nay *crawl* to those whom they have lately injur'd,
> Beyond forgiveness both from God or Man,
> Does more indeed of *Scorn* than *pity* ask.   (ii. ii, p. 18)

This is why Whig writers attack the Stuart cause with the low humor of the popular tradition, in which the fallen man is always ridiculous, never an "archangel ruined." They borrowed the forms of "low culture" in order, first, to prove that the accession of William and Mary had been accepted by *all* classes of English society, and, second, to discredit Jacobite authors by opposing to their "wit" the plain common sense of the freedom-loving Englishman.

Appendix: dramatic works cited

(Place of publication is London unless otherwise stated.)

The Abdicated Prince: or the Adventures of Four Years. A Tragi-Comedy, As it was lately Acted at the Court at ALBA REGALIS, by several persons of Great Quality (printed for John Cartwright, 1690).

The Banished Duke: or, the Tragedy of Infortunatus. Acted at the Theatre Royal (printed for Richard Baldwin, 1690).

The Bloody Duke: or, the Adventures for a Crown, A Tragi-Comedy, As it was Acted at the COURT at ALBA REGALIS, By several persons of Great Quality. Written by the Author of the Abdicated Prince (printed for W. Bonny, 1690).

Dryden, John, "Don Sebastian," in Earl Miner, George R. Guffey, and Franklin B. Zimmerman (eds.), *The Works of John Dryden* (20 vols., Berkeley, Los Angeles, and London, University of California Press, 1976), xv.

The Folly of Priest-Craft. A Comedy. Scene, St. James's, or the Savoy (printed for Richard Baldwin, 1690).

The Late Revolution: or, the Happy Change. A Tragi-Comedy. As it was Acted throughout the English Dominions in the Year 1688. Written by a Person of Quality (printed for Richard Baldwin, 1690).

Motteux, Peter, *Beauty in Distress, a Tragedy* (1698).

Motteux, Peter, *Europe's Revels for the Peace, and his Majesties Happy Return. A Musical Interlude. Performed at the Theatre in Little Lincoln's-Inn-Fields, by His Majesties Servants. With a Panegyrical Poem Spoken There, on the same Occasion* (1697).

Motteux, Peter Anthony and John Eccles, *Acis and Galatea* (1701), (reprinted with *The Rape of Europe by Jupiter* [1694], Augustan Reprint Society, no. 208, introduction by Lucyle Hook [William Andrews Clark Memorial Library, University of California, Los Angeles] 1981).

Mountfort, William *The Plays of William Mountfort. Facsimile Reproductions with an Introduction by Paul W. Miller,* Scholars' Facsimiles and Reprints (New York, Delmar, 1977).

Rowe, Nicholas, *Tamerlane: A Tragedy. As it is Acted at the New Theater in Little Lincoln's-Inn-Fields. By his Majesty's Servants* (Jacob Tonson, 1702).

The Royal Flight; or, the Conquest of Ireland. A New Farce (printed for Richard Baldwin, 1690).

The Royal Voyage, or the Irish Expedition: a Tragicomedy, Acted in the Year 1689 and 90 (printed for Richard Baldwin, 1690).

12

Revolution *redivivus*: 1688–1689 and the radical tradition in seventeenth-century London politics

Gary S. De Krey

I

Discussions of major revolutions in the modern West frequently dwell upon the importance of popular movements of radical protest in revolutionary capitals. That the city of London could have generated a radical movement in the Revolution of 1688–89 is, however, a proposition of which many historians have been skeptical. Several considerations have encouraged this doubt about urban radicalism at the time of the Glorious Revolution. The concept of radicalism, derived from nineteenth-century political experience, is said to be anachronistic when applied to the entirely different political phenomena of the seventeenth century. Identifying radicalism with notions of social contract is unhelpful, we are told, because the pamphlet literature of 1688–89 reveals few efforts to legitimate the Revolution in such stark and novel terms. If we interpret radicalism as the ideology of a particular social group, objections are again raised. For instance, the urban poor of London are said to have been too politically unsophisticated and too economically marginal to subscribe to radical beliefs. Moreover, artisans and other ordinary people cannot easily be treated as a social audience for radical ideas because of evidence pointing to an upsurge of popular royalism in the 1680s. And where in London were the coercive crowds and the street politics so frequently associated with a revolutionary capital?[1]

These considerations to the contrary, this essay will suggest that London was home to a radical movement that culminated in 1688–89. London radicals

---

[1] J. C. D. Clark, *Revolution and Rebellion: State and Society in England in the Seventeenth and Eighteenth Centuries* (Cambridge University Press, 1986), pp. 97–103; J. P. Kenyon, "The Revolution of 1688: Resistance and Contract," in Neil McKendrick (ed.), *Historical Perspectives: Studies in English Thought and Society in Honour of J. H. Plumb* (London, Europa, 1974), pp. 43–69; Mark Goldie, "The Revolution of 1689 and the Structure of Political Argument," *Bulletin of Research in the Humanities* 83 (1980), 486, 490, 518–19; J. R. Jones, *The Revolution of 1688 in England* (London, Weidenfeld and Nicolson, 1972), p. 306; Tim Harris, *London Crowds in the Reign of Charles II: Propaganda and Politics from the Restoration until the Exclusion Crisis* (Cambridge University Press, 1987), esp. ch. 7.

I have advanced arguments about Restoration radicalism in two previous essays: Gary S. De Krey, "The London Whigs and the Exclusion Crisis Reconsidered," in A. L. Beier, David Cannadine, and James M. Rosenheim (eds.), *The First Modern Society; Essays in English History in Honour of Lawrence Stone* (Cambridge University Press, 1989), pp. 457–82; Gary S. De Krey, "London Radicals and Revolutionary Politics, 1675–83," in Tim Harris, Paul Seaward, and Mark Goldie (eds.), *The Politics of Religion in Restoration England* (Oxford, Basil Blackwell, 1990), pp. 133–62.

of the Glorious Revolution were the inheritors of a tradition of local radical expression that originated in the 1640s; and their political goals in 1689 reflected forty years of experience in articulating that tradition. However, this civic radical movement needs to be defined more narrowly than some historians have supposed. The views of London radicals were democratic and libertarian, but their views were more fundamentally derived from the local political circumstances and the history of the Corporation of London than from contractual or republican modes of thought. London radicals were democratic because they understood the Corporation as a civic polity designed to represent a socially diffuse citizenry. Also, London radicals were libertarian because they saw preservation of the historic rights of London citizens, to whom they believed the civic magistrates were responsible, as the *sine qua non* of London government. The radicalism of many London radicals, to be sure, was also influenced by religious considerations and by the constitutional experiences of the nation. However, local experiences were formative and critical in fashioning the seventeenth-century London radical tradition: a civic institutional matrix of wards and guilds, of Common Council and of Common Hall, provided an essential academy of political learning for many citizens. Nurtured in this common school of political participation, radical Londoners of different social ranks became committed to the same democratic and libertarian understanding of the Corporation. Of course, not all London Whigs were also radical; but London Whigs who were radical were often civic radicals by definition and English Whigs by extension.

I have elsewhere examined the attempted internal revolution in the city that followed the parliamentary events of 1689, and I need here to recapitulate briefly what I have said.[2] The leaders of the London Whigs seized the initiative in both the Court of Aldermen and the Court of Common Council during the Glorious Revolution. Once in power, the civic Whig leaders became increasingly concerned about the status of the charter of the Corporation of London. Declared forfeit in the Court of King's Bench in 1683, the charter had been restored just prior to the Revolution through the prerogative of a now-deposed monarch. These city Whigs desired not only to have this restoration confirmed through parliamentary approval but also to clarify many disputed procedures of civic government. They drafted a statute for this purpose and submitted it to the House of Commons.

The London Whigs' draft statute was a remarkable document that contemplated democratic departures from the recent past.[3] (See figure 1.) The indirect election of the lord mayor, for instance, which had involved a combination of electoral choice by the guildsmen in Common Hall and of aldermanic vetting, was to be replaced by direct Common Hall election. Similarly,

[2] Gary S. De Krey, "Political Radicalism in London after the Glorious Revolution," *JMH* 55 (1983), 591–600; Gary S. De Krey, *A Fractured Society: the Politics of London in the First Age of Party* (Oxford, Clarendon Press, and New York, Oxford University Press, 1985), pp. 49–55.
[3] CLRO, CCJ 51, fols. 33–36. Also see CLRO, Misc. Ms. 141.10 and GL, Ms. 5099.

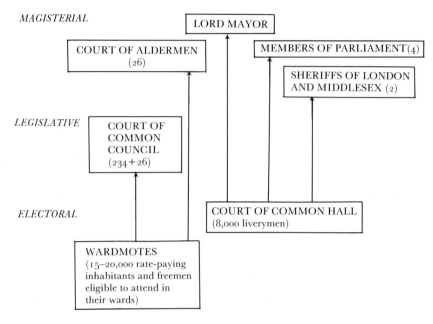

Figure 1 Institutions and personnel of the Corporation of London Governance. The major electoral processes within the Corporation are indicated by arrows.

The liverymen were those freemen whose status and incomes had prompted their selection for the livery of their guilds.

Common councilmen were directly chosen by the wardmotes, and MPs were directly chosen by Common Hall. Elections of aldermen and of the lord mayor were indirect, with the Court of Aldermen choosing from nominees forwarded, respectively, by a wardmote or by Common Hall. The lord mayor's claim of a right to nominate one of the sheriffs prior to the shrieval election was contested vigorously by radical liverymen.

The twenty-six aldermen sat as a separate and distinct body in the Court of Common Council.

the intervention of the lord mayor in Common Hall shrieval elections through prior nomination of one candidate was to be replaced by direct Common Hall election of both sheriffs. This radical draft also emancipated the Court of Common Council from all magisterial encroachments upon its legislative autonomy. The London Whigs' program for civic democracy not surprisingly fell foul of a parliamentary leadership that had successfully balanced revolution with constitutional compromise. Though considered by the House of Commons, the measure was not approved by parliament.[4]

But when and why did the London Whigs of 1688–89 become attached to these internal reforms for the Corporation? Why do the origins of their program support a characterization of many of them as radical? To answer these questions, I intend to describe and to interpret the radical tradition in seventeenth-century London politics, a tradition that connected London events in 1689 to London events in 1649. Moreover, I will suggest that London was a revolutionary capital in the 1680s because this decade saw a critical joining of

---

[4] Grey, *Debates*, x, pp. 43–45, 54–61.

civic issues that were derived from 1649 and that had undermined the Restoration settlement of the city long before 1689. Indeed, the Glorious Revolution in London was a watershed in a forty-year debate over civic government, and many radical Londoners had awaited this Revolution as an opportunity to revive and to perfect the accomplishments of another Revolution.

II

A democratic restructuring of the city's constitution had accompanied the establishment of a commonwealth in England in 1649. Accomplished through a statute of the Rump Parliament, this restructuring followed the election of a majority of political independents to the Common Council.[5] Like the London Whigs' draft statute of 1690, the act of 1649 made the city's government more popular by stripping the lord mayor and aldermen of some powers and by enhancing the authority of the common councilmen as spokesmen for the citizenry. It required the lord mayor to summon Common Council if requested to do so by any ten common councilmen. It denied him authority to dissolve Common Council without the consent of the majority. It denied the lord mayor and aldermen any veto over the actions of Common Council.[6]

The Rump's statute did not, however, provide a radical answer to every question in civic government that had been disputed during the 1640s. Between 1649 and 1651, several additional radical motions were debated in Common Council. Some of these were implemented and others were not. For instance, the common councilmen asserted their right to the appointments of many civic officers; and they deprived the lord mayor and sheriffs of much income from the sale of offices.[7] The common councilmen considered the termination of life tenure for aldermen; and they debated proposals for a more democratic mode of electing the lord mayor, the sheriffs, and the city MPs. All of this they did as the "representative" of the city and in order to "vindicate the just rights and privileges" of the citizens.[8]

Those who supported, initiated, or implemented these changes are best conceived as a coalition of religious and political radicals. Encompassing the entire spectrum of citizens who had, in 1647–48, supported the army against the king and conservative MPs and magistrates, these London radicals included parochial independents and separatists of both Congregational and Baptist tendencies. Best known among their leaders were Praise God Barbone; Colonels Owen Rowe and Robert Tichborne, the regicide merchants;

---

[5] CLRO, CCJ 40, fols. 312–13; C. H. Firth and R. S. Rait (eds.), *Acts and Ordinances of the Interregnum* (3 vols., London, HMSO, 1911), III, pp. cxi–xii.

[6] London politics in 1648–49 are examined in James Farnell, "The Politics of the City of London (1649–1657)," Ph.D. thesis, University of Chicago, 1963; James Farnell, "The Usurpation of Honest London Householders: Barebone's Parliament," *EHR* 82 (1967), 24–46; Ian Gentles, "The Struggle for London in the Second Civil War," *HJ* 26 (1983), 277–305.

[7] CLRO, CCJ 41, fols. 4, 8, 12–14, 28, 39, 63; Farnell, "Usurpation," 30–32.

[8] CLRO, CCJ 41, fols. 7, 35–36, 39–40, 65; Farnell, "Usurpation," 33–37.

and Slingsby Bethel, whose involvement in London politics continued beyond the Revolution of 1688–89.[9]

This brief sketch of civic radicalism under the Commonwealth is open to at least two objections. The first is that the political extremism of civic figures like Barbone and Bethel falls so far short of that of the Levellers and Diggers as to preclude use of the terms radical and radicalism. If political efforts to turn "the world upside down"[10] are considered, can the concept of radicalism legitimately be applied to these narrower disputes about the Common Council, the Common Hall, and the aldermanic veto?

This objection rests upon a misconception about urban radicalism and the Levellers. We know that many of the London supporters of the Leveller authors arose from among the separatists and, to a lesser extent, the religious independents.[11] Why was this the case? Was it solely because of the originality with which John Lilburne and William Walwyn and other Leveller thinkers handled the ideas of social contract and secular republicanism? Or, was it also because Lilburne and Walwyn were Londoners, had been deeply involved in London reform from the early 1640s, and had first gained prominence by attacking the civic, commercial, and religious monopolies that offended so many citizens? If we want to understand the social and political roots of the Levellers, we need to start with the local vocabulary of political debate in London. We do need to talk about the Common Council, the Common Hall, and the aldermanic veto. Around these civic institutions and procedures, radical perspectives first emerged in the 1640s.[12] The Leveller authors re-focused these perspectives upon national and universal issues, but the Levellers did not exhaust civic radical views. The history of Civil-War radicalism in London does not end with the collapse of the Leveller movement because that movement was, in the context of London politics, only one application of civic radical thought.

A second objection to the argument is that this Commonwealth coalition of civic radicals was but a temporary alliance of cautious reformers and bona fide revolutionaries. David Underdown, for instance, describes the religious independents of London as moderates interested only in "limited, rational reform," unlike the religious separatists, whose genuine radicalism had been displayed in their support for the Levellers.[13] Moreover, the separatists have been described as the true civic radicals because some of them wished to democratize the guilds and to replace the electoral Common Hall of liverymen with a more representative electoral assembly chosen by all the freemen.[14]

[9] For biographies of these individuals, see *BDBR*.

[10] Christopher Hill, *The World Turned Upside Down: Radical Ideas during the English Revolution* (New York, Viking Press, 1972).

[11] Murray Tolmie, *The Triumph of the Saints: the Separate Churches of London 1616–1649* (Cambridge University Press, 1977), pp. 144–50.

[12] See, for instance, the perspectives of John Bellamie, *A Plea for the Commonalty of London* (London, 1645); (John Lilburne), *London's Liberty in Chains Discovered* (London, 1646); (John Price), *A Moderate Reply to the Citie-Remonstrance* (London, 1646).

[13] David Underdown, *Pride's Purge: Politics in the Puritan Revolution* (London, Allen and Unwin, 1985), p. 325.

[14] *Ibid.*, p. 326–27; Farnell, "Politics of the City of London," 175–85; Margaret James, *Social Problems and Policy during the Puritan Revolution 1640–1660* (London, Routledge and Kegan Paul, 1966), pp. 193–223.

The radical civic coalition of 1648–49 did indeed begin to fragment after the revolution of 1649. However, the disagreements among London radicals arose over *how* the citizens of London ought to be represented in the Corporation rather than *whether* they ought to be represented. These disagreements occurred between those radicals who saw the primary purpose of the civic revolution as the legislative emancipation of a representative Common Council and other radicals who were also interested in achieving greater social and electoral equality in the guilds and the wards.[15] However, this radical division, comparable to similar divisions in other revolutions, emerged most clearly after 1649. Even then, any systematic identifications of religious independency with constitutional moderation in the city, or of religious separatism with constitutional radicalism, frequently fail the test of personal example.[16] And, to a certain extent, a significant expansion in the size of the livery of many guilds, which made the Common Hall electorate larger and more representative, eased this quarrel in the 1650s.[17]

To summarize the argument to this point, then: the objectives of the radical London Whigs of 1689 showed the influence of the city's 1649 revolution. And, the London radicals of 1689 followed in the footsteps of previous radicals, who had disagreed among themselves about how the London citizens might best be represented in the civic constitution.

III

The history of radical ideas and radical persons in London between the Restoration and the Glorious Revolution is undeservedly obscure. The development of two arguments will penetrate this obscurity. Firstly, a revival of civic radicalism in the Corporation preceded the emergence of the Exclusion-era London Whigs. Secondly, civic radicalism was central, rather than peripheral, to the urban Whig party of the 1680s.

A return of radical persons to Corporation politics is noticeable from the end of the 1660s, coinciding with the agitation of urban nonconformists against parliamentary adoption of the second Conventicle Act. Independents, Baptists, *and* Presbyterians in some eighty weekly meetings defied that Act through their public worship. As younger Presbyterian clergy abandoned the idea of comprehension in favor of the idea of toleration, the old city coalition of religious radicals grew larger; and the Corporation saw a political reassertion of dissent directed by Commonwealth and Protectorate veterans.[18] Before 1669, for instance, dissenting representation upon the Restoration Common Council was nominal; but one out of six common councilmen chosen in 1669 can be identified as nonconformists. Efforts to secure the selection of dissent-

---

[15] See, for instance, *London's Liberties; or a Learned Argument of Law & Reason* [London, 1650].
[16] Tolmie, *The Triumph of the Saints*, pp. 187, 236, and elsewhere.
[17] I am indebted to Dr. Eveline Cruickshanks for this point.
[18] BL, Add. Ms, 36,916 (Aston Papers, xvi), fol. 183; SP 29/293/28, 29/293/233, 29/294/36, 29/294/178; *CSPD 1671*, pp. 560–61, 568–70; *CSPD 1671–72*, pp. 27–29.

ing magistrates also intensified in 1669; and by 1672, almost one-quarter of the aldermen were also nonconformists.[19]

Best known amongst the old saints who now renewed their civic credentials were William Kiffin, the Baptist merchant–preacher, and Slingsby Bethel. Returned by ward electors as an aldermanic choice in 1669, Kiffin was rejected by the Court of Aldermen; and in 1670 he was elected sheriff, although he chose not to serve. Bethel, a promoter of conventicles, was also a ward aldermanic nominee vetoed by the sitting aldermen, as was Henry Brandreth, onetime associate of the Leveller William Walwyn and a radical spokesman on the 1650 Common Council.[20] Edward Bushell, an independent in the 1650s, also led stubborn jurors in acquitting leading Quakers of holding an unlawful assembly. Fined and imprisoned for his conduct, Bushell was vindicated in the 1670 case bearing his name, a case which also established the immunity of juries from judicial fines.[21]

As Dissenters with radical antecedents regained prominence in the city, radical civic postures and ideas resurfaced. In 1669, when the London Dissenters sought to extend the tenure of a sympathetic lord mayor, they were accused of "fomenting popular notions" and of seeking to "overturn all" through constitutional innovation.[22] During the third Dutch War a polarization developed in civic politics between royalist aldermen and opposition common councilmen. Again disputed were the extent of Common Council's autonomy, the roles of the aldermen and common councilmen in legislation, and the place of mayoral preference in shrieval elections and the appointment of civic officers.[23] Recognition that these disputes revived fundamental issues of an earlier civic revolution was explicit. Opposition Common Council spokesmen claimed in 1675 that the magistrates had "invaded" rights guaranteed "by the charters and Magna Carta." And the lord mayor warned the ministry that "the designe of this faction is to take the Sole Power of Government into the hands of the Commons."[24]

In 1676 the Commonwealth London heritage was fused with new Country concerns in a dramatic rearticulation of radical civic ideology. The central figure in this restatement was Francis Jenks, a linendraper, who interrupted the Midsummer's Common Hall to demand a meeting of Common Council so that the Corporation might petition the crown for a new parliament. Jenks's

---

[19] BL, Stowe Ms. 186, fols. 5–9, surveys the aldermanic bench as of 1672 (reprinted in *The Gentleman's Magazine*, 39 (1769), 515–17; BL, Add. Ms. 36,916, fol. 197; De Krey, "London Whigs Reconsidered," pp. 463–64.

[20] SP 29/289/126; BL, Add. Ms. 36,916, fols. 186, 190; HMC 51, *Manuscripts of F. W. Leyborne-Popham* (Norwich, HMSO, 1899), p. 166; *BDBR* on Brandreth; Tolmie, pp. 114–15; Farnell, "Usurpation," pp. 35, 46; Alfred B. Beaven, *The Aldermen of the City of London temp. Henry III–1908* (2 vols., London, Eden Fisher, 1908–13), I, pp. 247–48.

[21] SP 29/291/207; *CSPD 1671*, pp. 385–86; HMC *Leyborne-Popham*, p. 167; Thomas Andrew Green, *Verdict According to Conscience; Perspectives on the English Criminal Trial Jury 1200–1800* (University of Chicago Press, 1985), ch. 6.

[22] BL, Stowe Ms. 186, fol. 5; SP 29/251/186: *A Few Sober Queries upon the late Proclamation, for enforcing the Laws against Conventicles, &c.* (London, 1668); *CSPD 1668–69*, pp. 419–20, 616.

[23] CLRO Aldermanic Repertory 76, fol. 62; Repertory 78, fol. 213; Rep. 79, fols. 267, 377, 405–8; CLRO CCJ 47, fols. 206, 216, 275; *CSPD 1671–72*, p. 40; *CSPD 1673*, p. 557; *Letters Addressed from London to Sir Joseph Williamson*, ed. W. D. Christie (2 vols., Westminster, Camden Society, new series, vols. VIII–IX, 1874), II, p. 55.

[24] BL, M/863/11, Coventry Mss. (Papers of the Marquess of Bath at Longleat House), XVI, fols. 9–11, 21–22.

speech and the accompanying printed vindications of it asserted the power of Common Hall over both Common Council and the aldermen. For Jenks, the source of Common Hall's institutional supremacy was its representative nature: the 8,000 liverymen acted in city politics on behalf of and "instead of the whole body of the freemen," who were the ultimate authority within the Corporation. According to Jenks, the Common Hall had the power to undo magisterial error and to defend the independence of the common councilmen against overbearing magistrates.[25]

This reformulation of civic radical ideas transcended the old disagreements about representation in the Corporation that had divided Commonwealth radicals against one another. The continuing enlargement of the livery since the 1650s facilitated Jenks's redefinition of the liverymen, whom Lilburne had identified with monopoly,[26] as the representatives of the people. The explanation of Common Hall supremacy provided by the London radicals was, moreover, an answer to contemporary questions about the origins of legitimate political authority. Couched in civic language, this answer clearly was local and historical rather than national or universal, as in the thought of John Locke, but it was generated by radicals and Dissenters involved in a broader political world. For example, Jenks was the son-in-law of the Leveller theorist Walwyn, and he therefore had one foot in the radical city past. But because he was also a client of the Duke of Buckingham, Jenks had another foot in the Country camp.[27] The ideas of civic radicals like Jenks might be applied to national politics in a republican manner; but these ideas were native to a political environment that more encouraged libertarianism than republicanism. The first London Whigs were the inheritors of this rich, local radical creed. How they perpetuated the radical civic tradition in the revolutionary politics of the 1680s I need now to clarify.

IV

I will sketch three arguments to illustrate the radicalism of the Exclusion-era London Whigs, each of which also bears upon the character of the urban Whigs at the time of the Glorious Revolution. Firstly, Whig political beliefs were expressed in the particular radical vocabulary of Commonwealth civic experience rather than in the broader vocabulary of social contract and secular republicanism. Secondly, because these libertarian ideas appealed to dissenting Whigs from many occupational and social backgrounds, London

---

[25] Guildhall Library, Ms. 3589: Parliamentary proceedings temp. car. II AD 1676–1678, fols. 6–7; *CSPD 1676–77*, pp. 180, 253–56, 193–94; Cobbett, *Trials*, VI, pp. 1189–1208; *An Account of the Proceedings at Guild-Hall, London, At the Tolke-Moot, [sic] or Common-Hall, Held 24th. of June 1676. Relating to the Cities Petitioning His Majesty for a new Parliament* [1676]; De Krey, "London Radicals," pp. 138–40.

[26] John Lilburne, *A Postscript* [to *Londons Liberty in Chains Discovered*] (London, 1646), pp. 40–41.

[27] For the identification of Jenks as son-in-law of Walwyn, see De Krey, "London Radicals," pp. 157–58, n. 26. For the connection between Jenks and Buckingham, see *CSPD 1676–77*, p. 564; *CSPD 1677–78*, p. 22; Cobbett, *Trials*, VI, p. 1208; K. H. D. Haley, *The First Earl of Shaftesbury* (Oxford, Clarendon Press, 1968), pp. 409–12, 416, 425, 440.

radicalism reflected a vertical division of civic society rather than a horizontal division. Thirdly, their radical heritage enabled some London Whigs to complete a political odyssey from constitutional opposition to extraconstitutional resistance and finally to revolutionary conspiracy and action. By 1682–83, the ministry rightly feared that some London Whigs were again intent upon making their city a revolutionary capital.

The political strategies of the London Whigs during the Exclusion Crisis repeatedly reflected Commonwealth civic precedents and perspectives. For instance, the two city Exclusion petitions of 1680–81 were launched in popular manners that violated the governing assumptions of royalist magistrates. One petition was initiated in Common Hall; the other was launched in an extraordinary meeting of Common Council summoned by popular demand.[28] Moreover, when Whig common councilmen challenged the aldermanic veto, they were not raising a narrow jurisdictional question. They were instead challenging the entire oligarchic philosophy of government that had replaced the consensual and participatory assumptions of Commonwealth civic government. The evidence for this statement is found in the Whig common councilmen's demands for full legislative autonomy, for cognizance of city petitions, for oversight of their own agenda, and for a free choice in the selection of many Corporation officers.[29]

The best measure of the radicalism of the early London Whigs is their transcendence of the old radical disagreement about the relative authority of the representative Common Council and the liveried Common Hall electorate. To quote both a leading Whig alderman and the city's Whig recorder, neither a radical "mechanick," Common Hall was "the supreme authority in London" and "the greatest of all lawful Assemblies in the Kingdom."[30] Following Francis Jenks, these London Whig spokesmen believed both that Common Council owed its creation to Common Hall and that Common Hall itself was an embodiment of the civic supremacy of the freemen. They derived the authority of Common Hall historically from the "old folkmoot" of the city and functionally from the vicarious participation of the freemen in the electoral actions of the liverymen.[31] And again, although these assumptions might be applied in a republican manner to national politics, they were not intrinsically republican.

Who in the city expressed these views in purposeful political behavior? Who were the London radicals of the 1680s, and what do their lives reveal about the sociology of London radicalism in a decade of revolution? The later

---

[28] CLRO, CCJ 49, fols. 170–71; *CSPD 1679–80*, pp. 579, 581; *CSPD 1680–81*, p. 131; *CSPD 1682*, p. 610; HMC 14th Report, Appendix, part IV: *The Manuscripts of Lord Kenyon* (London, HMSO, 1894), p. 125; D. F. Allen, "The Crown and the Corporation of London in the Exclusion Crisis, 1678–81," unpublished Ph.D. thesis, Cambridge University, 1977, p. 135; De Krey, "London Radicals," p. 144.

[29] See, for instance, D.N., *A Letter from an Old Common-Council-Man to one of the New Common-Council* [London, 1682].

[30] *Some Account of the Proceedings At Guild-Hall, London, On Saturday the 24th. of June being Midsummer-day, 1682* (London, 1682); *CSPD 1682*, p. 417.

[31] *The Lord Mayor of London's Vindication* (London, 1682), p. 5; *The Priviledg and Right of the Free-men of London* (London, 1682), p. 6. For a broader discussion, see De Krey, "London Whigs Reconsidered," pp. 470–75.

Table 12.1 *1680 realty assessments of London radical core group and of London Common Councilmen (1680–83)*[32]

	Radicals (%)	Common Councilmen (%)
£84 or more	30	7
£66–84	11	8
£50–66	20	16
£36–50	19	21
£20–36	14	32
£20 or less	7	15

careers of old Interregnum separatists like Kiffin and Bethel intersected with the history of the first London Whigs, as did the careers of Cromwellian officers like Henry Danvers, John Manley, and John Wildman. By the 1680s, however, these Commonwealth veterans were the doyens of a movement dominated by a younger generation in its civic prime. A radical core group of about one hundred citizens has been identified to portray the social character of early civic Whig radicalism. These Londoners are those Whigs whose 1680s' careers suggest the strongest adherence to the civic-libertarian creed. Many of them were also active during and after the Glorious Revolution.[33]

The data tabulated in table 12.1 point to the astonishing appeal of radical principles to some individuals of high social standing. The 1680 assessments show this core group of radicals to have included a greater proportion of well-to-do people than a comparable group of 400 citizens, both Whig and Tory, who served on Common Council.

The survey of occupations in table 12.2 also points to the radicalism of some truly wealthy citizens of the early 1680s. Furthermore, the similarity between the occupational profiles of 1680s' London radicals and post-Revolution London Whig common councilmen is striking. The core radicals of the 1680s were engaged in the same assortment of occupations as Whig Common Council recruits of the 1690s. This resemblance points to important continuities in the social ethos of the urban Whigs before and after the Revolution. Moreover, the heterogeneous assortment of occupations suggests the wide

[32] CLRO, Assessments Boxes for 1680 Parliamentary Aid; Arthur G. Smith, "London and the Crown, 1681–1685," unpublished Ph.D. thesis, Universtiy of Wisconsin, 1967, p. 24.

[33] This core group of city radicals has been selected from a larger group of some 400 persons believed to have been radicals and known to have been active in London in the 1670s and 1680s. Criteria for inclusion in the core group are: (1) evidence of outspoken Whig principles in a Corporation context that suggests both radicalism and political leadership; (2) an indication of radicalism in at least one other source. Examples of sources employed for the first criterion are: SP 29/417/277 ("List of 59 leading Whigs" [1683?]); SP 29/419/165, 168, 138 (petitions in favor of Whig candidates after the 1682 shrieval election); SP 29/425/43 (lists of Londoners to be disarmed at the time of the Rye House plot); BL, Add. Ms. 34,362, fols. 4–15 ("The Citty Painter" [1676?], a satirical poem identifying the friends and supporters of Francis Jenks); GL, Ms. 507 no. 21 (Sir John Moore papers: lists of those charged and convicted for the 1682 city "riot"). Many sources have been employed for the second criterion, including the names of persons apprehended or suspected in the Rye House plot (*CSPD, 1683* [*Jan.–June*]; *CSPD 1683* [*July–Sept.*]) and the names of Londoners arrested at the time of Monmouth's Rebellion (CLRO, Lieutenancy Court Minute Books).

Table 12.2 *Occupations of London radical core group and of subsequent new Whig Common Councilmen (1695–1703)*[34]

	Radicals (%)	Whig Common Councilmen (%)
Overseas merchants and gentry	33	34
Professional services	19	11
Domestic wholesale and retail trades	19	19
Victualling trades	15	17
Manufacturing and industrial trades	14	19

social appeal of radical principles. The civic radical cause brought together tradesmen like Peter Essington and Josiah Keeling (the original Rye House plot informant), shopkeepers like Francis Jenks and John Brett, and merchant princes like William Ashurst and Thomas Pilkington.

To suggest, therefore, that the radical Whig movement of the Exclusion era had primary appeal to any one urban social audience is misleading. The strength of London radicalism in the decade of the Revolution lay rather in its ideological mobilization of Dissenters and Whigs from many backgrounds. The London Whigs were not a popular movement that reflected any horizontal division of class. They were instead a popular movement that cut a vertical division through London society, integrating citizens from different walks of life.

Civic radicalism was nevertheless intimately associated with a particular social milieu. Radical Whigs lived throughout the Corporation, but half the radical core group resided in the city interior (see table 12.3). At the heart of the city's retail trade and shopkeeping, the inner-city wards contained a population that was considerably wealthier, on a per capita basis, than was the case elsewhere in the Corporation. These wards had also bred much of the assertive puritanism of the 1620s and 1630s and much of the urban radicalism of the 1640s and 1650s. Moreover, the civic overrepresentation of these wards, which returned almost half the common councilmen, ensured that opinion trends within the "shopocracy" quickly influenced Corporation counsels.[35] The inner city, then, was the seed-bed of civic radicalism in the 1680s, but it was not the entire garden. Committed radicals of many social backgrounds resided in the middle-city wards; and the wards without the walls provided

[34] The occupations of 1680s' radicals have been derived from numerous sources, but especially from descriptions of them in the appropriate volumes of the CSPD. For occupations of 1690s' Whig Common Councilmen and for this classification of occupations, see De Krey, "Political Radicalism," p. 608 and n. 70.

[35] De Krey, *A Fractured Society*, p. 113; Bernard Bailyn, *The New England Merchants in the Seventeenth Century* (New York, Harper and Row, 1964), pp. 36–38.

Table 12.3 *Residences of London radicals by geographical sectors of the Corporation*[36]

	Radicals' residences (%)	Distribution of urban rate-payers (%)
Inner-city wards	49	27
Middle-city wards	24	36
Wards without the walls	27	37

invaluable urban organizers like Charles Bateman, a Cripplegate barber–surgeon, and Jonathan Cantrell, a Spitalfields glover.

How far beyond constitutional opposition were these radical Londoners prepared to push their popular principles? Many radical London Whigs engaged both in extraconstitutional resistance and in revolutionary conspiracy before the Glorious Revolution. "Monster" petitions, pope-burnings, and constitutional role-playing in Common Hall were all part of the original Whig political repertoire. The London Whigs were especially successful in marshalling the people in the streets, although the London Tories also became adept at cultivating popular support.[37] In 1681–82, civic radicals and parliamentary Whig leaders together transformed the Corporation into an alternative forum to Westminster. Convinced that the capital was reverting to the political pattern of 1641, the king, the ministry, and a Tory lord mayor responded in the long-remembered shrieval election of 1682. The ensuing confrontation between a Whig Common Hall majority and the mayoral prerogative propelled many London radicals from street theater towards the higher arts of popular coercion. Contemporary accounts of the accompanying disturbances emphasize both the bearing of arms by enraged citizens and the encouragement of agitation by prominent Whigs.[38]

Although some leading Whigs held back from open confrontation for fear of jeopardizing the city charter, other London radicals prepared to challenge the regime itself. Conclusive defense of this thesis would require a thorough analysis of London citizens involved in the Rye House plot and in Monmouth's rebellion.[39] A few general comments will suffice to characterize the resort by 1683 of some radicals to attempted regicide and revolution.

---

[36] The residences of 1680s' radicals have been derived from numerous sources, but especially from the assessments boxes for the 1680 parliamentary aid (CLRO). For this geographical division of the city, see De Krey, *A Fractured Society*, pp. 171–76. For this distribution of urban rate-payers, as indicated in the 1691 poll-tax returns, see De Krey, "Trade, Religion, and Politics in London in the Reign of William III," 2 vols., unpublished Ph.D. thesis, Princeton University, 1978, II, pp. 335–37.   [37] Harris, *London Crowds*, ch. 6.

[38] Library of Congress, London Newsletters Collection, 1665–85, VIII, fols. 79, 80–81, 91–92, 116; Cobbett, *Trials*, IX, pp. 219–26.

[39] For London Whigs and the Rye House plotting, see De Krey, "London Radicals," pp. 146–55. For London Whigs and Monmouth's Rebellion, see: BL, Add. Mss. 41,812; 41,813; 41,819 (Middleton Papers, vols. x, xi, xvii); BL, Landsdowne Ms. 1152A, fols. 227–311 (William Bridgeman's Papers); Richard Ashcraft, *Revolutionary Politics and Locke's "Two Treatises of Government"* (Princeton University Press, 1986), chs. 9–10.

Firstly, citizens active in the street politics of the Exclusion Crisis are quite noticeable among those tied to the Rye House conspiracy. Secondly, London plotters were almost unanimous both in dating their interest in revolution and regicide to the shrieval election of 1682 and in reciting civic grievances in justification of their behavior. Indeed, Monmouth's leading associates in 1685 astutely emphasized civic grievances in composing manifestos in defense of rebellion.[40] Thirdly, although artisan and plebeian radicals were especially notable in the plans for regicide, the revolutionary ends of the Rye House conspiracy apparently were known to well-to-do radicals. Lesser radicals bore the brunt of the government's retribution in these episodes, but the resort to rebellion, in deed and in thought, was again by no means restricted to individuals of humble social status.

These considerations support an assertion that many London Whigs of the early 1680s had become as revolutionary as the civic radicals of 1649. Devoted to the supremacy of the civic electorate, the London radicals were ready to defend that electorate through violence against the regime, if need be. Both the breadth of the Whig movement, as seen in the sociology of urban radicalism, and the depth of radical commitment, as seen in the Rye House conspiracy, made London a revolutionary capital in the early 1680s.

V

Radical citizens hoped the Revolution of 1688–89 would provide a resolution of constitutional issues that had troubled the Corporation for thirty years. The Revolution did indeed provide a resolution of these questions, but not the one the radicals expected. As the center of popular disturbances, public agitation, and extraconstitutional action, London was a revolutionary capital in 1688–89, perhaps even more so than it had been in 1648–49. However, the intentions of London radicals for the civic regime proved to match the intentions neither of William nor of parliament. The Revolution was more radical than some revisionist historians have suggested,[41] but the political principles of the London Whigs were more radical still. As the revolutionary crisis developed, discrepancies between the expectations of many city Whigs and those of many Westminster and country statesmen were at first unclear.

The autumn 1688 collapse of "popery and arbitrary government" seemed to promise the London Whigs a better opportunity to restore their revolutionary civic regime than the opportunities lost earlier in the decade. Their hopes probably were fed by awareness of the city's importance in the collapse of royal government. James II lost his capital even before he lost his nerve at Salisbury. Having returned the city's charter upon learning of William's

---

[40] BL, Harleian Ms, 6845, fols, 256–59.
[41] See, for instance: John Miller, *The Glorious Revolution* (London, Longman, 1983), chs. 3–4; J. C. D. Clark, *English Society 1688–1832* (Cambridge University Press, 1985), pp. 78–85, 119–41; J. P. Kenyon, *Stuart England*, 2nd edn. (Harmondsworth, Penguin, 1985), ch. 10.

invasion plans, James nevertheless failed to recover sufficient respect for himself or for the loyalist magistrates restored with the charter. London Whigs and London Tories alike were deeply distrustful of him. Indeed, Lord Chancellor Jeffreys was rebuffed in the streets in an October public progress intended to display both the restored charter and the king's generosity in restoring it.[42] Moreover, neither royal troops nor the trained bands proved capable of suppressing the extensive rioting which sporadically disturbed London for ten weeks and which contributed to the disintegration of authority in the capital and the nation.[43] Although these crowds focused their energies upon the Roman Catholic minority, their activities climaxed in a confrontation with Tory lord mayor, Sir John Chapman. He suffered a stroke, subsequently fatal, in defending mayoral authority against a crowd that broke down his doors.[44]

The extent to which radical London Whigs were involved in crowd disturbances in the autumn of 1688 is unknown; but their influence was apparent in city counsels by the time of James's initial flight. The common councilmen elected in late November included many "fit for the service now to be done," according to dissenting diarist Roger Morrice.[45] The enthusiasm of their address to William of December 11 far exceeded that of a simultaneous address from the provisional government of lords and privy councillors meeting at Guildhall.[46] Sir George Treby, reinstated as London's recorder, was the guiding hand behind the city address. An outspoken exponent of the authority of the electorate, especially as expressed in Common Hall, Treby officially greeted William upon his arrival at Westminster (plate 11), making the suggestion that he had been "called by the *Voice* of the People." Both as legal intermediary between the city and the new regime, and as chair of the first rights committee of the Convention, Treby would facilitate communications between civic and parliamentary radicals.[47]

---

[42] DWL, Roger Morrice, "Ent'ring Book, Being an Historical Registrar of occurrences from April, Anno, 1677 to April 1691," II, pp. 302–3.

[43] Tim Harris, "London Crowds and the Revolution of 1688," in Eveline Cruickshanks (ed.), *By Force or By Default? The Revolution of 1688–89* (Edinburgh, John Donald, 1989), pp. 44–64; Robert Beddard, "Anti-popery and the London Mob, 1688," *Hisory Today* 38 (1988), 36–39; William L. Sachse, "The Mob and the Revolution of 1688," *Journal of British Studies* 4 (1964), 23–40.

[44] DWL, Morrice, "Ent'ring Book," II, p. 355; *London Courant*, December 12–15, 1688; *Correspondence of the Family of Hatton*, ed. Edward M. Thompson (2 vols., Westminster, Camden Society, new series, vols. XXII–XXIII, 1878), II, p. 125; Sir John Bramston, *The Autobiography of Sir John Bramston*, ed. Richard G. Neville, Lord Braybrooke (London, Camden Society, old series, vol. XXXII, 1845), p. 339. This confrontation between one of the December 11 crowds and the Tory lord mayor is overlooked in both Harris, "London Crowds and the Revolution of 1688," and Beddard, "Anti-popery." Professor Harris's claim, subsequently qualified, that "there is no evidence of any hostility to James in London" (p. 55) is debatable. This assertion seems to have contributed to J. P. Kenyon's overstatement of Harris's argument in the Introduction to Cruickshanks (ed.), *By Force or By Default?*, p. 4. Kenyon's trivialization of the place of London and its citizenry in 1688–89 is tenable only within his own limited high political and constitutional framework.

[45] DWL, Morrice, "Ent'ring Book," II, p. 329.

[46] *To His Highness the Prince of Orange; the Humble Address of the Lord Mayor, Aldermen, and Commons of the City of London in Common-Council Assembled* (London, 1688); Robert Beddard, "The Guildhall Declaration of 11 December 1688 and the counter-revolution of the loyalists," *HJ* 11 (1968), 403–20.

[47] *The Speech of Sir George Treby, Kt. Recorder of the Honourable City of London, to His Highness the Prince of Orange, December the 20th. 1688* (London, 1688); Lois G. Schwoerer, *The Declaration of Rights, 1689* (Baltimore and London, Johns Hopkins University Press, 1981), pp. 43–47, 131.

The initial stages of the Revolution provoked little explicit reference to the civic constitution, but the increasing visibility of radical citizens in 1689 marked a revival of the movement for London's 1649 frame of government. As magistrates and common councilmen, as jurors and ward officers, as lieutenancy commissioners and parliamentary witnesses, civic radicals experienced in 1689 a gratifying return to office, power, and responsibility. For instance, Thomas Pilkington exchanged heavy fines, imprisonment, and political disgrace for the mayoralty, a knighthood, and membership in the Commons. Exile Sir Patience Ward returned to the Court of Aldermen, where he was joined by John Wildman and Sir William Ashurst, who reportedly saluted publicly "our Soveraigne ... Lords ye People."[48] Wildman and Ashurst were also elected to the Commons, where Wildman served on Treby's rights committee.[49] Altogether, about one-third of the Exclusion-era core radicals still alive in 1688–89 now assumed or returned to a civic or national office.

These civic radicals were active in encouraging the Convention to break from the past and in inaugurating the new regime with appropriate revolutionary *événements*. The year 1689 saw five popular London petitions concerning parliamentary affairs, the first an effort in February to encourage the Lords' concurrence with the declaration of a vacant throne.[50] The initial anniversary of revolution was marked with organized and spontaneous civic celebrations on October 29 (Pilkington's mayoral installation), on November 4–5, and on December 18 (date of William's arrival at Westminster). These revolutionary petitions and processions reflected the London Whigs' radical heritage in several ways.[51] They were organized, in part, through the renewed networking of civic Whigs with radical parliamentary figures like Charles Mordaunt (the Earl of Monmouth), Jack Howe, and Richard Hampden.[52] They enabled citizens to remember and to reassert the revolutionary civic principles of 1649 and of the early 1680s. And, they demonstrated anew the vertical appeal of Whig radicalism both through their social inclusiveness and through the large numbers of people involved.

Initially, the London Whigs' radical expectations about the meaning of the Revolution for the Corporation were supported by their interpretation of the work of the Convention and of its parliamentary successor. For instance, city radicals could find much language justifying their past political behavior in the Declaration of Rights. Some found vindication of their popular petitioning in Article 5, and others found sanction for their possession of arms for political self-defense in Article 7. Article 10 exonerated those Londoners, like Francis Jenks, Sir Thomas Pilkington, and Sir Samuel Barnardiston, who had suffered excessive fines and punishments for their political actions. Article 11

---

[48] BL, Sloane Ms. 203, fol. 60.   [49] Schwoerer, *Declaration of Rights*, pp. 304–5.

[50] DWL, Morrice, "Ent'ring Book," II, pp. 454–55, 524, 580; Grey, *Debates*, IX, pp. 45, 362–64; Schwoerer, *Declaration of Rights*, pp. 130, 196, 211, 284.

[51] See also De Krey, "Political Radicalism," pp. 597–600; De Krey, *A Fractured Society*, pp. 55–61.

[52] DWL, Morrice, "Ent'ring Book," II, pp. 566–67, and III, p. 58; Narcissus Luttrell, *A Brief Historical Relation of State Affairs* (6 vols., Oxford University Press, 1857), I, p. 541; De Krey, *A Fractured Society*, pp. 58, 61–62.

reasserted the independence of jurors like Edward Bushell and those citizens who had refused to indict Shaftesbury for treason.[53] Also, London radicals took encouragement from the 1689–90 parliamentary investigations of the civic disturbances of the early 1680s, of the London *quo warranto,* and of the remodeling of the livery.

However, the more the London Whigs spoke and acted in accordance with their radical antecedents, the more they provoked the suspicions of the "reluctant revolutionaries" who shaped the constitutional events of 1688–89. Chief among these was William, whose worries about "republicanism" were deepened by the course of events in his revolutionary capital. Church–Tory MPs who disliked the "strange" London petitions of early 1689 were concerned within the year about many more resemblances between the civic Whigs and Interregnum "commonwealthmen." As in the early 1680s, these critics were largely mistaken in believing that radicals in the city were republicans in the state; but they were not wrong to see striking religious, ideological, and family connections between the London Whigs of 1689 and the London revolutionaries of 1649.[54]

The leaders of the London Whigs of 1689 were, nevertheless, more discreet revolutionaries than their predecessors. Aware of the damaging potential of Tory charges about their political reliability, they were also much sobered by the political frustrations and fatigue of the past decade. Accordingly, the draft statute they prepared in 1690 for restoring civic government upon a parliamentary footing was devoid of ideological fanfare and rhetorical flourish.[55] It was clearly radical; and it clearly revived the revolutionary constitution of 1649, even going beyond that framework in certain respects. However, the document bypassed some matters likely to cause offense among civic and parliamentary Tories. It provided for the parallel emancipations of Common Council and Common Hall without speculation about the constitutional relationship between the two bodies. It thereby avoided the vexing questions of the ultimate authority in the Corporation and of the relationship between the liverymen and the freemen. Similarly, the draft mooted a widening of the ward franchise, but it did not emphasize the matter.

To suggest, however, that the leading London radicals of 1689 were already moderating their radicalism, any more than those of 1649 had done, would again be to pre-date the unexpected changes of the 1690s. The Tory author who described the London Whigs in 1690 as "State-Mountebanks" who wished to "spread . . . Contagion into all Corporations through the Kingdom" was reacting both to their principles and to their achievements in making London a revolutionary capital.[56] After the rejection of their draft

[53] Schwoerer, *Declaration of Rights*, ch. 4.

[54] Grey, *Debates,* IX, p. 362; X, p. 55; H. C. Foxcroft, *The Life and Letters of Sir George Savile, Bart.* (2 vols., London, Longman, Green, 1898), II, pp. 222, 224, 225, 226; W. A. Speck, *Reluctant Revolutionaries: Englishmen and the Revolution of 1688* (Oxford University Press, 1988), ch. 5; Harris, *London Crowds,* pp. 133–44.

[55] For membership of the drafting committee, see De Krey, "Political Radicalism," p. 594 n. 28. For the draft statute, see n. 4 above.

[56] *Reasons humbly offered, for the Lords ready Concurrence with the House of Commons in the Bill for reversing the Judgment in the Quo Warranto* (London, 1690).

statute in the House of Commons, many leading London Whigs did indeed moderate their erstwhile radical principles. However, this moderation occurred gradually and subtly. Some clarity was obtained only in 1695, when disillusioned liverymen embarrassed Whig magistrates by exposing discrepancies between their old libertarian rhetoric and their emerging oligarchic posture.[57]

Parliamentary opposition to civic revolution is, however, an inadequate explanation for the 1690s' demise of the radical tradition in seventeenth-century London politics. At least three effects of the Glorious Revolution account for the disintegration of Whig civic radicalism. Firstly, the Revolution weakened the connection in London between religious nonconformity and political opposition. Despite the loud attachment of eighteenth-century nonconformists to "revolution principles," the Dissenters of London lost interest in the democratic principles first expressed in the city's 1649 revolution. The Toleration Act of 1689 and the ease of occasional conformity combined to defuse the political militancy exhibited by urban nonconformists since the late 1660s. Satisfied Dissenters became complacent citizens; indeed, some satisfied Dissenters became active parishioners.

Secondly, the original Commonwealth disagreements among civic radicals about the manner of representation in the Corporation and about the relationship between Common Council and Common Hall resurfaced after 1689. These tensions within seventeenth-century civic radicalism had apparently been resolved by 1675. In the 1690s, however, those Whigs satisfied with the legislative emancipation of a representative Common Council again separated from those radicals still interested in direct democracy in the wards, the guilds, and Common Hall. In other words, those urban Whigs engaged in the defense of a Revolution now completed broke off from those urban Whigs still hoping for a revolution not yet accomplished. Just as John Locke may have intended to indict the cautious framers of the Revolution in his *Second Treatise*, so the radical liverymen of 1695 contrasted what the Exclusion-era London Whigs had promised in the Corporation with what the Revolution-era London Whigs had provided.[58] These dissatisfied voices were less articulate than before because of the intervening decease or superannuation of so many outspoken Restoration radicals, like Francis Jenks and Slingsby Bethel, who had once argued both for Common Council and for Common Hall.

Thirdly, the Revolution entailed the dissolution of the ideological *entente* among radical spokesmen of different occupational groups that had given the first urban Whigs both their distinguished leadership and their considerable popular appeal. This collapse in social dialogue is directly attributable to the war of William's reign, a war in defense of the Revolution with contrasting social consequences for merchants and for tradesmen. Some bourgeois families who had once pledged their consciences to radical principles now pledged their cash to the Bank of England and to the "funds." For other

---

[57] De Krey, *A Fractured Society*, esp. chs. 5–6.
[58] Ashcraft, *Revolutionary Politics*, pp. 572–89; De Krey, *A Fractured Society*, pp. 183–88.

families, action in the civic polity gave way to action in the wartime bureaucratic state that developed in defense of the Protestant succession. These families identified with the new political and financial apparatus of the Revolution regime and forgot their old civic suspicions about political oligarchy. Thus, the fortunes of many radical London families of the 1680s took unexpected turns after the Revolution. For instance, factor Henry Cornish, the elder, died a 1685 martyr to the Whig civic cause; but factor Henry Cornish, the younger, served William as Commissioner of Stamped Paper and as Million Bank director. Likewise, haberdasher John Jekyll was a leading radical civic organizer after the Oxford Parliament; but son Sir Joseph Jekyll served the crown as Chester Chief Justice and as King's Serjeant.[59]

As these and other wealthy Whig families braved the uncertainties of a wartime financial revolution in hopes of great reward, they embarked upon a contrasting quest for security in the Corporation. Their new philosophy of social control quickly distanced them from those artisans, many of them hard pressed by wartime taxation and dislocation, who still expressed political dissatisfaction with hierarchy and manipulation. Moreover, Sir George Treby, the recorder who had once championed the civic order of libertarian London freemen, was succeeded by functionaries determined to introduce a different legal order to a disorderly plebs. The radical bond that had transcended urban social divisions in the 1680s snapped in the face of the conflicting needs of different social elements. Within a few years, the social and political grievances of some artisans were expressed in a populist civic movement that also displayed high-church principles.[60]

If London remained a revolutionary capital, then, it was as the capital of the financial revolution and of a modernizing state. Perhaps especially through such unintended results, the Glorious Revolution, like some other revolutions, provided the sharpest departures from the past. Although political protests by the urban commons would remain part of eighteenth-century London life, something was very different after 1689: a distinctive London frame of mind – a civic, religious, and historical consciousness about 1649, and one that was socially inclusive rather than exclusive – began to weaken.

Finally, what does this account of the history of seventeenth-century London radicalism reveal about the nature of the Restoration that ended in 1688–89? Viewed from London, the Restoration cannot well be tied conceptually to the eighteenth century, considered as an *ancien régime* or otherwise.[61] From the perspective of London history, the Restoration appears intrinsically

---

[59] The post-Revolution wartime growth of the English state is examined in John Brewer, *The Sinews of Power; War, Money and the English State, 1688–1783* (New York, Knopf, 1989). For Henry Cornish, the elder, and Henry Cornish, the younger, see *BDBR*, I, pp. 177–78, Henry Horwitz, *Parliament, Policy and Politics in the Reign of William III* (Newark, University of Delaware Press, 1977), pp. 253, 361. For John Jekyll and Sir Joseph Jekyll, see *CSPD* 1683 (Jan.–July), p. 356; J. R. Woodhead, *The Rulers of London 1660–1689* (London Archaeological Society, 1965), p. 98; Romney Sedgwick, *The House of Commons 1715–1754* (2 vols., New York, Oxford University Press, 1970), II, pp. 174–76.

[60] Nicholas Rogers, "Popular Protest in early Hanoverian London," *Past and Present* 79 (1978), 70–100; De Krey, *A Fractured Society*, ch. 6.

[61] Clark, *Revolution and Rebellion*, pp. 7–8. See also the comments of Jonathan Scott in "Radicalism and Restoration: the Shape of the Stuart Experience," *HJ* 31 (1988), esp. 458–60.

more fragile than final; more of a piece with what preceded it than with what followed. The religious settlement was under open attack in London and elsewhere from the late 1660s. Intense parliamentary and civic disputes over unresolved issues had erupted by the mid-1670s; and by 1679, a "restoration crisis,"[62] accompanied by large-scale popular protest in the capital, showed how extensively these disputes could compromise political order. None of this made a collapse of the Restoration regime inevitable; but in London, those citizens hostile to the Restoration Settlement were numerous and were moved by political and religious ideas contrary to those officially established. Their understanding of the civic constitution naturally attracted them towards a view of the state as a "mixed" government, an understanding of sovereignty that had been proscribed in 1660. And their reflections upon history naturally connected them to revolutionary events that could not be obliterated as easily from civic experience as from law.

These urban critics of the Restoration are, for the most part, better described as radical than as republican. Some of them, or their friends and families, had once supported a republican regime in the state; but they believed their Restoration political beliefs were consistent with "English" monarchy. That the civic radicals of London looked backwards to 1649 to define their revolution is no argument against their radicalism. What had been done in the Corporation in 1649 marked a significant departure from the past; and although the radical Restoration Whigs talked about the recent and "ancient" past as normative, their success would have created a very different political order in the city. A circular understanding of the word "revolution" no more required them than other revolutionaries to repeat or to perpetuate the past. Neither the historical nor the civic vocabulary of these London radicals need obscure their assertion of democratic and libertarian principles that would be more universally expressed by the radicals of other revolutions.

---

[62] Jonathan Scott, *Algernon Sidney and the Restoration Crisis 1677–1683* (Cambridge University Press, forthcoming).

13

The cabinet and the management of death at Tyburn after the Revolution of 1688–1689

J. M. Beattie

In the generation after the Revolution of 1688–89 a number of significant changes took place in the English criminal law and its administration. Few of these resulted directly from the events of the Revolution itself. But they were all stimulated and made possible by the largely inadvertent changes that followed the Revolution: by the political and social consequences of the wars that the new regime led England into; by the anxious concern of successive governments about the threat posed by domestic as well as foreign enemies of the new political arrangements; and by the new relationship between parliament and the executive that the Revolution confirmed. As we will see, the Revolution was followed by a period of deepening anxiety about the threat of crime, particularly crime against property in London. But the political and institutional changes in William's reign and after also encouraged and made possible a variety of responses to the perceived crime problem that was to make this a period of considerable innovation in the law and the way it was administered.

Some of these changes were the result of legislation. The regularity of parliamentary sessions after 1689 made it possible for legislative initiatives to be pursued by interested MPs, and the reigns of William and Anne saw the introduction of about a hundred bills and the passage of a dozen statutes dealing in broad terms with the criminal law. The most important of these statutes aimed to strengthen the courts in their dealing with felonies, particularly with crime against property. On the one hand, several statutes extended capital punishment to a number of relatively minor property offenses; on the other, and equally important, this period also saw the first statutory authorization for the use of noncapital punishments for convicted felons, notably transportation to the American colonies. Transportation came to be widely employed by the courts and transformed the administration of the criminal law in the early decades of the eighteenth century.[1]

---

[1] For this legislation, see J. M. Beattie, "London Crime and the Making of the Criminal Law 1689–1718" (forthcoming); for the transformation of the penal system in the first half of the eighteenth century, see J. M. Beattie, *Crime and the Courts in England, 1660–1800* (Princeton and Oxford, Princeton University Press, 1986), ch. 9; and A. Roger Ekirch, *Bound for America. The Transportation of British Convicts to the Colonies, 1718–1775* (Oxford, Clarendon Press, 1987).

In addition to changes introduced directly by statute, a number of other important alterations in the way the criminal law was administered emerged in this period, largely unintended, from the political consequences of the Revolution. Particularly important in this respect was the more active engagement of the central government in the administration of the law. This can be seen, for example, in the government's sponsorship of some key pieces of legislation, and in their encouragement and support of criminal prosecutions, particularly after 1714. And it can be seen too in a development that is the subject of this essay: in the way in which the ministers of the crown came to control the administration of capital punishment in London. This significant development emerged without apparent forethought and planning from the circumstances of the reign of William and Mary, particularly the king's frequent absences from England. What began in the 1690s as a response to immediate needs continued thereafter as a useful device and settled habit. Well into the nineteenth century, the question of who among those convicted of capital offenses in London would be sent to the gallows at Tyburn, and who deserved to be pardoned and punished in some other way, was decided at a meeting of the cabinet.

The management of death at Tyburn became a regular item on the cabinet agenda and brought the business of crime and the working of criminal law within the purview of the king's ministers. It also encouraged the emergence of a more regular, more bureaucratic, yet more politically sensitive process by which pardons were granted to a large proportion of those convicted of capital crimes. The new procedures marshalled the pardoning power inherent in the royal prerogative to provide a flexible system that could manage the level of capital punishment in the metropolis. They were an important part of the broader discretionary machinery that made possible the administration of a criminal law increasingly overloaded with capital offenses. The more regular management of the pardon process lies at the heart of the administration of the law in the eighteenth century and – among many other things – helps to explain its successful resistance to change until the system was overwhelmed by the sheer numbers of cases it was called upon to process in the 1820s.[2]

The granting of mercy to condemned criminals had long been a prerogative of English monarchs, a fundamental attribute of kingship. Criminal cases were at the king's suit, and his control of the judicial system gave him alone the power of pardon. It was a power that served the essential function of correcting prejudiced convictions and of tempering the harshness of the law in particular cases. It also served the broad political purpose of presenting the king as a merciful and forgiving father, and constantly reforged the bonds that held the population in its allegiance.[3] But it was the necessity for such a power

---

[2] Douglas Hay, "Capital Punishment in England, 1750–1832," paper read at a conference of the American Society for Legal History, October 1986.

[3] Douglas Hay, "Property, Authority and the Criminal Law," in Douglas Hay, Peter Linebaugh, and E. P. Thompson (eds.), *Albion's Fatal Tree: Crime and Society in Eighteenth Century England* (London, Allen Lane, and New York, Pantheon, 1975), pp. 17–63.

in the judicial system – as in any judicial system – that underpinned this aspect of the royal prerogative. When the monarchy was abolished in 1649, the pardon power was lodged first in parliament, then in the Protector;[4] it reverted to the crown without question or limit when the innovations of the Interregnum were swept away in 1660. And it remained intact in the late seventeenth century and at the Revolution of 1689, even as other aspects of the prerogative came under suspicion. While the king's power of pardon was related in a broad sense to his much-disputed claim to be able to suspend particular statutes and to dispense individuals from the requirements of the law, the distinction between these forms of royal power was nonetheless clear: pardons simply relieved a convicted person from the consequences of his or her actions, whereas the dispensing and suspending powers attacked the basis of law by removing the illegal character of an action itself.[5] The broad power of pardon was never called into question in the way these more extreme claims were. The dispensing and suspending powers were to all intents abolished in the Bill of Rights.[6] The monarch's right to grant pardons in political cases was also limited after the Revolution – a limitation suggested in 1689 and embodied in the Act of Settlement in 1701.[7] But the pardoning power remained otherwise unquestioned. No limitations were imposed at the Revolution on the monarch's ability to pardon offenders convicted of ordinary criminal offenses. Indeed, these powers were to be exercised thereafter more vigorously than ever, and to be more essential than ever to the working of the judicial system. Lord Chancellor Finch was not alone in valuing the monarch as "the fountain of mercy, as well as of justice."[8]

Royal pardons could save convicted offenders from any sanction – from the death penalty of felony or treason, or from the fines or corporal punishment or a sentence to stand on the pillory imposed in misdemeanor cases. The concern of this essay is principally with pardons from the death penalty. They were granted in two ways. The most effective pardon from the point of view of the prisoner was issued specifically to the individual concerned under the Great

---

[4] *Acts and Ordinances of the Interregnum, 1642–1660*, ed. C. H. Firth and R. S. Rait (3 vols., London, HMSO, 1911), II, pp. 565–77; S. R. Gardiner, *The Constitutional Documents of the Puritan Revolution* (3rd edn., Oxford, Clarendon Press, 1906), p. 406 (Instrument of Government).

[5] This distinction was made by Mr. Justice Vaughan in 1674 in Thomas v. Sorrel (*Vaughan Reports*, p. 333, cited and discussed in Sir William Holdsworth, *A History of English Law* [17 vols., London, Methuen, 1903–72], VI, pp. 217–18).

[6] Lois G. Schwoerer, *The Declaration of Rights, 1689* (Baltimore and London, Johns Hopkins University Press, 1981), pp. 59–64; Howard Nenner, *By Colour of Law: Legal Culture and Constitutional Politics in England, 1660–1689* (University of Chicago Press, 1977), pp. 84–90; Corinne Comstock Weston and Janelle Renfrow Greenberg, *Subjects and Sovereigns: the Grand Controversy over Legal Sovereignty in Stuart England* (Cambridge University Press, 1981).

[7] The suggestion that the king be denied the right to pardon those impeached by parliament was made in the Heads of Grievances, which set out the first broad agenda from which the Declaration of Rights finally emerged (Schwoerer, *Declaration of Rights*, pp. 22–23, 299). It was not adopted on that occasion, but such a limitation on the royal prerogative was included in the Act of Settlement passed at the end of William's reign. Even that restriction came to be narrowly interpreted. It was thought in 1716 that the king would not be able to pardon the six Scottish peers impeached for their treasonable activities during the Rebellion of 1715, but he was assured by an address of the House of Lords that he would not be challenged if he did so after their conviction, and he did pardon three. (Mark A. Thomson, *A Constitutional History of England, 1642 to 1801* [London, Methuen, 1938], pp. 289–90).

[8] BL, Add. Ms. 36088, fol. 6.

Seal. Obtaining such a pardon was expensive; in addition, it required knowledge of the procedure, and if it did not absolutely require friends in the right places it was surely helped forward by such favor. In the late seventeenth century such individual pardons under the Great Seal seem to have been overwhelmingly sought by men in the middling and upper ranks of society who had been convicted of murder or manslaughter. Edward Matthews, convicted at the Old Bailey of the murder of Charles Trelawny in 1689, was granted a pardon by the king under the Great Seal when he brought evidence to show that "there appeared to be no premeditated malice in the case, but only a hasty blow with a stick."[9] Normally, in such cases the jury would have taken such evidence into account and found the defendant guilty of manslaughter. It may well have been that the Old Bailey jury in this case had not believed that evidence and that the king was responding to a judge's report on the case.

Most pardons of homicides in this period were granted in cases in which the defendant had been convicted not of murder but of manslaughter when the provocation and absence of premeditation was accepted by the jury. Manslaughter was a felony, but a felony within clergy (that is, a noncapital offense), and the pardon in this case was sought to save the convicted defendant from the burning in the hand that was the consequence of benefit of clergy and from the stigma of a felony conviction, and the possibility – remote though it was by the 1690s – that his goods would be forfeit to the crown and his heirs prevented from inheriting his estates.[10]

The second form of pardon was much less expensive and was indeed provided for "poor prisoners" who could not afford the fees that the individual pardon issued under the Great Seal required. This was often called a "general" or "circuit" pardon because it included the names of several offenders – as many as two dozen or more – from one jail or one assize circuit. The inclusion of an individual in such a pardon was more easily managed because the "circuit pardon" could simply be expanded to include any number of prisoners the king chose to add. Whether an individual was issued a separate pardon or was included in a general pardon turned entirely on ability to pay, rather than the character of the offense involved. In Lord Keeper Guilford's "Directions for drawing of circuit pardons," it is emphasized that "No person to be inserted [in a circuit pardon] that is able to bear the charge of a particular pardon."[11]

Pardons were central to the administration of the criminal law. They could be used to correct miscarriages of justice, when (in a judge's view) a jury insisted on wrongly convicting a defendant.[12] But pardons could also be used

---

[9] SP 44/338, p. 429.

[10] Individual pardons issued under the Great Seal freed the prisoner from "all indictments, convictions, pains, penalities, and forfeitures incurred by reason thereof." The possibility of forfeiture of goods was still apparently regarded as a serious threat in the late seventeenth century, but in fact that had entirely fallen into disuse and by the first decades of the eighteenth century those convicted of manslaughter ceased seeking a formal pardon.

[11] BL, Add. Ms. 32518, fol. 117v.

[12] John H. Langbein, "The Criminal Trial before the Lawyers," *University of Chicago Law Review* 45 (1978), 296–97.

to limit and control the level of capital punishment. Since so many offenses had been removed from clergy and made subject to capital punishment by the eighteenth century, a large number of convicted men and women faced the gallows after every session of the assize courts or of the Old Bailey in London. In the eyes of society and of the courts and king, some were much more deserving of death than others. But, in any case, it is clear that by the late seventeenth century there was some reluctance to see large numbers of convicted men and women being executed together. The management of death was a crucial aspect of the administration of the law – striking the right balance between the terror the gallows were intended to create by executing a sufficient number of offenders to discourage others at that particular time and place, and yet not risking feelings of disgust in the public by too bloody a display. The royal power of pardon made it possible for the judges, and the king and his ministers, to shape the punishments suffered by particular individuals, and to determine the number of prisoners who would be executed at any time and place. There is no doubt that the level of capital punishment was manipulated in these ways.[13]

Who was to be hanged and who pardoned following sessions of the assizes and the Old Bailey was determined in two ways. Perhaps the most common, certainly the most straightforward, was by the judge's immediate recommendation. Having sentenced a number of convicted felons to death, the judge could reprieve one or more and recommend them to the king for a pardon. In the seventeenth century, the judges sent these so-called "circuit pardons" containing the names of those they recommended directly to the Chancery.[14] At the conclusion of virtually every session of the assizes a number of convicted offenders were reprieved, and the rest "left to be hanged." Some of the condemned might still save themselves by petitioning the king either to be included in the general pardon, or, as we have seen, to be granted an individual pardon. Such special treatment would obviously be eased if the prisoner could find a patron to sponsor and forward his application. Certainly, if the pardon was to save the convicted offender from the gallows (rather than, say, from the consequences of benefit of clergy), his petition would have to be supported by the trial judge – or at least not vigorously opposed by him. A prisoner petitioning for his life would hope first to obtain a reprieve to forestall his execution and then to be included in the general pardon for the circuit (or, in the case of London, for Newgate) when one was issued.

There is a suggestion in the way records came to be kept in the office of the secretaries of state that the process by which pardon petitions were considered became increasingly regularized after the Revolution of 1688–89. Not a great deal is known about the way the process worked in the seventeenth century

---

[13] Beattie, *Crime and the Courts*, pp. 430–49. The anonymous author of *Hanging Not Punishment Enough* (London, 1701) recognized this instrumental use of the pardoning power – while complaining that it was not working – when he said that crimes were increasing sharply even though pardons were "but few" (p. 19).

[14] That at least is implied in a set of instructions for the issuing of pardons in the 1680s among the papers of Lord Keeper Guilford (BL, Add. Ms. 32518, fol. 117v.).

and I do not want to suggest too great a contrast here.[15] But it appears that rather more of the business of pardon was concentrated in the secretaries' office by the end of the seventeenth century than it had been earlier and that, as a result, greater oversight and regularity became possible. The series of "Entry Books" established by the under-secretaries in the first decade of the eighteenth century, some of which were specifically for "criminal" business, was itself an expression of a more orderly administration of the pardon procedures.[16] But that can be seen, too, in the secretaries' correspondence with the judges and in the systematic way in which the judges dealt with requests for reports on condemned prisoners. Certainly, by the first quarter of the eighteenth century correspondence between the secretaries' office and the judges over pardon matters was being recorded, circuit pardons were being copied, and the whole process had developed an air of routine. That did not perhaps change the process by which circuit pardons were issued, nor the grounds upon which condemned prisoners were pardoned, but it did clarify and regularize the procedure and perhaps made it easier for the secretaries' office to keep track of requests and decisions.

There *was*, however, one important change in this period in pardon pro-cedure that did make a significant difference to the decision-making process: that is the engagement of the Privy Council (or the cabinet council) in the business of deciding who would be hanged in London. In effect, the sentenc-ing of capital convicts at the Old Bailey was taken out of the hands of the judges who had presided at the trials and was assumed by the cabinet. The purpose initially must have been to shield the monarch from a large number of petitions for pardons from condemned prisoners. The new procedures were introduced early in the reign of William and Mary as a direct result of William's absences from the country. When the king left for Ireland in June 1690, Mary was empowered to govern in his name as well as her own. But she made it clear that she was not anxious to have the sole direction of affairs, and William set up a committee of nine privy councillors to take on the main burdens of government.[17] This pattern was also followed in subsequent years, when William went to the continent to direct the war against Louis XIV. Among its many other tasks, this committee of the council seems to have taken on the job of making pardon decisions, especially with respect to the offenders condemned at the Old Bailey where such decisions had to be made regularly eight times a year. Queen Mary did not remove herself from all pardon questions; she continued to deal with petitions from condemned offenders. But she clearly found this aspect of governance distasteful,[18] and it seems likely that it was her willingness to leave routine pardon decisions – and

---

[15] For pardon in the late sixteenth and early seventeenth centuries, see J. S. Cockburn, *Calendar of Assize Records. Home-Circuit Indictments. Elizabeth I and James I. Introduction* (London, HMSO, 1985). For a full account of pardon procedure before the Revolution we must await the work of Cynthia Herrup, who is engaged in a major study of the royal pardon under the Stuarts.

[16] SP 44/77 and following volumes.

[17] R. Doebner (ed.), *Memoirs of Mary, Queen of England, 1689–1693 Together With Her Letters And Those of Kings James II. and William III. To the Electress, Sophia of Hanover* (Leipzig, Veit, and London, D. Nutt, 1886), pp. 22–33; S. B. Baxter, *William III* (London, Longman, Green, 1966), pp. 262–63.

[18] Doebner (ed.), *Memoirs of Mary*, pp. 40–42.

hanging decisions – to her ministers that established the practice. It is not clear, however, why these ministers came to deal with *all* capital cases at the Old Bailey and not just with petitions for mercy from offenders left to be hanged by the judges – the cases, that is, that James II and earlier monarchs must have dealt with.[19] But they were doing so within a few years of the Revolution.

These changes in the way the death penalty was managed at the Old Bailey were almost certainly instituted because of William's absences and to spare Mary. But William clearly also found these new procedures a useful way of dealing with a constantly recurring problem, and with a task he did not himself perhaps relish. At any event, he continued to rely on the cabinet to give him advice on London cases even when he was in England. There is evidence of their doing so in January 1693, for example, before the king left for the campaigning season on the continent; and again in October 1695 when a secretary of state can be found organizing a meeting of members of the council on the king's order and after he had returned to England "to consider what persons under condemnation at the assizes in London [that is at the Old Bailey] might be fit objects of his mercy." That committee "called the Recorder of the city before them" and heard his report on the cases that had resulted in the death penalty.[20] What began as a practical response to the problems caused by William's regular and prolonged absences from England took root and developed a more permanent form because the king was also happy to assign this duty to others. There were, indeed, some suggestions in the 1690s that the cabinet might take on all the pardon cases arising in the country.[21] But as it worked out in practice, the cabinet's engagement in the sentencing process was to be confined to London cases. The assize judges continued to send in recommendations in writing at the conclusion of the provincial assize circuits of the condemned prisoners they thought deserved the royal mercy. After 1689 those recommendations were commonly sent via the secretaries of state's office rather than directly to the Chancery, and were thus more subject than they had been – and if anyone cared – to political scrutiny. But essentially the pardon process for offenders tried on the six assize circuits remained unchanged.

It was on London cases that the new system focused. This was in part, no doubt, because those cases accounted for a very large proportion of the capital

---

[19] This is still something of a presumption: that is, that before 1689 the judges at the Old Bailey, like the judges at the assizes, reprieved some of those they had sentenced to death, and included them in the equivalent of a "circuit pardon," and that the monarchs received pleas for mercy from some of those left to be hanged. There is certainly no obvious evidence – in the State Papers, Domestic, for example – that the king or the Privy Council dealt with the cases of *all* prisoners condemned to death in London before 1689 as they clearly were by 1693 at the latest.

[20] SP 44/99, p. 225; CLRO: Rep. 97, p. 100.

[21] There was some suggestion, at least, that the lords justices whom William left after Mary's death to govern in his absences might deal more broadly with pardon decisions. On at least one occasion in 1695, the judge who had held the assizes in Surrey and Sussex was also called in to report on those trials and to receive the lords justices' decisions about who among those convicted of capital offenses should be hanged and who pardoned. But that proved to be distinctly unusual, and the lords justices, like the cabinet when the king was in England, confined their deliberations thereafter to London cases. For the lords justices see below, p. 228.

offenses tried in the country and because they came up so regularly, since the Old Bailey met roughly every six weeks. But ministers could also deal with London cases more readily than those tried on the provincial assizes because Old Bailey business could be fitted easily into the cabinet's pattern of work. This was made possible, in part at least, by the easy availability of an official who could be called to meetings at short notice and who could speak authoritatively about the cases tried in the capital: the recorder of London. The recorder was the chief legal advisor to the city government, and a magistrate deeply involved in criminal administration in the city. He also played an important role at the Old Bailey sessions. He was the only lawyer who was a permanent member of the Old Bailey bench, for there was no certainty that the same high-court judges – three of whom were included in the jail delivery commission to deal with the prisoners in Newgate – would be assigned to the court every session. But in addition, the recorder was the sentencing officer of the court. The trials were heard by one or more of the judges, by the recorder himself or, occasionally, by the lord mayor or one of the London magistrates present.[22] But the recorder pronounced all the sentences at the conclusion of the session. It is possible that that meant he was, in fact, present on the bench for most of the trials; at the least, it meant that he had some knowledge of the capital cases, however that knowledge had been acquired. The recorder came to act as a link between the cabinet and the Old Bailey, presumably because he could speak with some authority about the cases. He could also be called quickly to cabinet meetings, whenever it was convenient for the king and his ministers to deal with this business. The procedure depended on the recorder – or his deputy – being readily available: they were often notified the day before they were to appear. It also depended on one other characteristic that made for speed and flexibility: the recorder gave his report to the cabinet orally. He was called into the cabinet room, stood at the end of the table,[23] and reported in turn on each of the men and women convicted of capital offenses at the previous Old Bailey session. He received an immediate decision in each case – that is, whether convicted offenders were to be hanged or pardoned, and, if pardoned, whether they were to be punished in some alternative way or simply allowed to go free.

It is unclear whether the recorder was the link between the cabinet and the Old Bailey from the beginning of the reign, but he certainly was by 1693, when there is evidence that the new system was established in its essentials. By January of that year there were complaints from other London magistrates that this new method of dealing with condemned offenders from the Old Bailey gave the recorder too much influence over the final outcome of London cases. They wanted to be consulted. The court of aldermen – several of whom were magistrates of the city[24] – ordered that "after every Sessions of Gaole

---

[22] On the possible collegial character of the Old Bailey bench, see John H. Langebein, "Shaping the Eighteenth-century Criminal Trial: a View from the Ryder Sources," *Chicago Law Review* 50 (1983), 31–36.

[23] This, at least, was the procedure when he appeared before the lords justices, for whom see below.

[24] J. M. Beattie, "London Jurors in the 1690s," in J. S. Cockburn and Thomas A. Green (eds.), *Twelve Good Men and True: the English Criminal Trial Jury, 1200–1800* (Princeton University Press, 1988), p. 216.

Delivery of Newgate, Mr. Recorder doe before he attend his Majestie with his Report come into this Court and take the Sence and Judgement of the same in what Character and Circumstance he shall Represent to his Majesty the several Condemned persons."[25] But that proved not to work effectively, perhaps because the recorder could be called to a cabinet meeting at short notice and before the next aldermanic court had met. By August 1693 a committee of aldermen had been appointed to find some other way of influencing the decisions that determined the level of capital punishment in London; and the recorder himself reported that "the present Method of reporting to their Majesties after every Sessions" had given rise to "great and intollerable troubles and many unjust Jealousies and Reflections." He recommended that the justices present at the Old Bailey decide before the session was concluded who deserved to be hanged and who spared, and he would take that advice to the cabinet.[26] That may have been done on occasion thereafter, but it was clearly not done routinely, and the arrangements for reporting Old Bailey cases to the adjudication of the cabinet continued to cause trouble from time to time, at least until 1700.[27] It seems certain that the recorder continued for the most part to give his own views to the cabinet. Certainly, his new role made him an even more influential figure in the administration of the criminal law in the city and at the Old Bailey than he had been before the Revolution.

After 1689, the recorder of London thus began to meet regularly with the cabinet council to manage the level of capital punishment in London. William or Mary may have been present at some of those meetings, but it is clear that that was not thought necessary. After Mary's death at the end of 1694 the same practice continued. The recorder reported to the cabinet when the king was in England; when he left the country for the continent, which he did in each of the next three years, William empowered the lords justices to whom he delegated some of the affairs of the country on these occasions to deal with the Old Bailey cases. The working of the new pardon system becomes even clearer during these years because the lords justices kept full minutes, which note the recorder's regular appearances "to give an account of the sessions."[28]

This system of dealing with the dozens of condemned convicts at the Old Bailey every year developed in William's reign because it suited him to give this duty to others. It continued and was confirmed by his successors. It had not resulted from restrictions on the king's prerogative powers of pardon at the Revolution of 1689. Neither Anne nor George I nor his son was any more willing than William had been to see the prerogative of the crown diminished. None relinquished final control over the pardon process; indeed, petitions to the monarch flowed in from the Old Bailey as well as the provincial assize

---

[25] Rep. 97, p. 100.

[26] *Ibid.* pp. 448, 465.

[27] See, for example, *CSPD*, 1696, p. 212. In 1700 the court of aldermen complained that the recorder was not keeping them informed of the advice he was giving the cabinet about London cases. At one point they withheld his annual gratuity of a hundred guineas and reaffirmed the rule that required him to consult the court. But there is no evidence that he ever did so. (Rep. 104, pp. 251–52, 290, 296).

[28] See for example, *CSPD*, 1694–95, p. 474; and *CSPD*, 1695, p. 12. For the discussion of pardon cases in the cabinet, see below, p. 228.

circuits in increasing numbers in the eighteenth century.[29] Nothing had changed in terms of the locus of the pardoning power itself. What had changed was the way that power was exercised with respect to an important group of cases. The judges at the Old Bailey no longer made the fundamental decision about who should be pardoned and therefore who should be hanged for capital offenses committed in London. Those decisions were now made by the cabinet. And while it was still possible for offenders sentenced to death by this process to make a personal appeal to the monarch, such petitions were likely to have been restricted by this new procedure. It was, indeed, suggested at one point that no further applications for mercy should be received after the recorder's report had been made and deliberations on those cases had been completed.[30] That came to naught; it proved impossible to prevent petitions being sent in or to refuse to deal with them once they had been. But, as important as such petitions were to individual prisoners, most London cases seem to have been settled by the early eighteenth century in the routine meetings between the recorder and the cabinet.[31] It was that body that managed the way the death penalty would be exercised in the capital.

The cabinet continued to deal with London cases after William's death. The practice of his reign established criminal business as an item of cabinet business, though we might presume that the accession of a queen followed by another prince unfamiliar with the English criminal-justice system reinforced for both monarchs the personal value of the new procedure. A "Report for her Majesty of the convicts in Newgate who received sentence of death" was prepared in December 1704, for example, for a meeting of the cabinet; and one can find petitioners asking to have their pleas "read in Council" and recommended to the queen.[32] And the same practices continued in George I's reign. In his early years in England, the king was invariably present at the cabinet meetings at which the recorder presented his report. In May 1715, the recorder was informed by an under-secretary of state that "the Cabinet Council being summoned to meet at St. James's tomorrow at noon, my Lord Townshend [secretary of state] has commanded me to acquaint you with it that you may attend to make your Report to his Majesty."[33] His summons in September 1717 to attend the cabinet council at Hampton Court and "Report to his Majesty as usual" makes it seem distinctly routine by that time. When the king went to Hanover (at least after the first occasion in 1716 when the Prince of Wales acted as regent), he left affairs in the hands of a group of lords

---

[29] Hay, "Property, Authority and the Criminal Law"; Peter King, "Decision-makers and Decision-making in the English Criminal Law, 1750–1820," *HJ* 27 (1984), 25–58; Beattie, *Crime and the Courts*, ch. 8.

[30] SP 44/279, pp. 22–24.

[31] Petitions for pardons from Old Bailey prisoners passed over by the cabinet continued to be received. But the new system of cabinet discussion and decision seems to have very significantly reduced their number. There is certainly a noticeable falling off in the number of secretaries' warrants dealing with individual Old Bailey cases over the first few years of the 1690s (SP 44/341–46: warrant books). I am as yet unclear whether such petitions for pardons from Old Bailey prisoners – the personal appeal to the king for his mercy – were routinely handled by the cabinet after 1689 or were passed on via the secretary of state to the monarch. The former may have been the pattern in the reigns of William and Mary, but George I dealt with some of them at least, and the recorder was then asked to make a further report on the case directly to the king. See, for example, SP 44/79A, pp. 248, 259, 262.

[32] SP 34/5/6; SP 34/35/49.   [33] SP 44/147: 3 May 1715.

justices, as William had done, and they too dealt regularly with the recorder's report. They made decisions about who should be reprieved and who left to be hanged, though the final decision on the ultimate fate of those they reprieved was left to the king.[34]

By the early eighteenth century, then, the recorder of London routinely took the list of condemned Old Bailey offenders to the cabinet or the lords justices, where their fates were decided.[35] Some were pardoned and either released or punished in some way short of death, generally by transportation; others were marked down to be hanged. The recorder brought an outline of each case, and no doubt a recommendation. It is unclear whether he came in any sense formally instructed by the Old Bailey bench in the way that some of the London magistrates had wanted him to be in the 1690s.[36] But the final decision was the cabinet's. They would also have received petitions on behalf of some of the prisoners, sources of additional evidence if they chose to use them. At any event, the cabinet appears to have discussed each case in turn. No doubt, most were passed over very quickly, since the recorder's report was fitted into a regular meeting of the cabinet or lords justices at which a wide range of subjects would be on the agenda. The fate of a group of convicted felons was not likely to be allowed to take a great deal of time away from affairs of state. And the recorder's recommendations in each case must normally have been persuasive. Nonetheless, the cabinet was no rubber stamp: cases were discussed. It was resolved at a meeting of the lords justices in May 1695, for example, that one man convicted of a capital offense at the Old Bailey should be pardoned and transported since the facts of the case showed him to be no more culpable than an accomplice already sentenced to be sent to America. And William Wake, convicted of burglary, was also saved from the gallows at this meeting and transported, "the evidence being that he did not make the bettey wherewith the house was broken open, but only procured it, and the smith who made it has run away." The lords justices also considered petitions from Wake's neighbors that he was a "quiet, industrious man."[37] At another meeting two months later, the lords justices received a series of petitions and the recorder's report on a murder case, reprieved the condemned offender for a week while they sought the views of the judges who

---

[34] The lords justices kept a separate set of minutes (a copy of which was sent to Hanover) which reveal the recorder's attendance. The minutes kept in 1719 and during subsequent visits to Hanover are at SP 44/279 and following volumes. The recorder's attendance on the lords justices is clearly revealed in the useful list of *Records relating to Ministerial Meetings in the Reign of George I, 1714–1727*, compiled by the List and Index Society, 214 (London, 1987). George I kept a close eye on the pardoning of criminal offenders while he was out of the country. Judges' recommendations for pardons were sent to Hanover for the king's approval, for example (SP 44/79A, p. 300). And the recorder was required in 1719 to hand in a written account of the cases that he reported on orally to the lords justices. This was marked with their decisions and sent to the king in Hanover so he could see why they had decided whom to reprieve and whom to leave to be hanged.

[35] The procedure seemed to be that the recorder had to request the meeting and an under-secretary of state informed him – generally at short notice – when he could be heard. In 1718 an under-secretary told the recorder that two Old Bailey sessions had gone by without his being summoned to make his report because "there was no application made, as usual, for such Summons." As he had now made application, "Orders will be given as you desire against the next Cabinet Council" (SP 44/147: 23 Oct. 1718).

[36] See above, p. 226.   [37] *CSPD*, 1694–95, p. 474.

had heard the case, and discussed the issues again at a second meeting before deciding to let the law take its course.[38]

Whether discussion of pardon questions in the cabinet and in the meetings of the lords justices resulted in fairer or harsher decisions may be impossible to establish. But several consequences of these regular discussions of London crime matters by the most powerful political body in the country seem clear. One is that the grounds on which pardons would be granted are likely to have been clarified. The pardon process always remained open to the play of influence in the eighteenth century. It remained an enormous advantage to have an influential patron to put one's case forward – an aristocrat, or a socially or politically important person – if only because such patronage would ensure the case was taken seriously. Pardons were sought and obtained as straightforward political transactions – as favors to the friends or relatives of an important MP or peer, to gratify voters, and so on.[39] But over the whole range of pardon decisions that had to be made every year, the play of such influence could only have been of marginal importance. Such large numbers of condemned men and women were dealt with so regularly – and in case after case in which no patron of any kind had any interest – that decisions could only have been made most of the time on grounds other than simple influence and patronage. What those grounds were to be in the eighteenth century is revealed in the patterns of pardons granted and denied, and in the correspondence of the judges and the secretaries of state on pardon questions: they arose from a consideration of the offense and the character of the offender, his or her age, disposition, previous life, and criminal record. Pardons granted over the century exhibit striking regularities, particularly a tendency for the authorities to come down hard on murder and on property offenses that threatened violence, especially by "old offenders," and to limit the number of lesser offenders sent to the gallows.[40] One of the ways in which such considerations emerged as grounds for the exercise of mercy seems to me likely to have been the regular discussion of pardon questions in the cabinet. And the recorder's reports on Old Bailey prisoners, brief and to the point as they no doubt were, must have helped to shape those pardon criteria. Having regularly to voice his opinion about capital cases and to make recommendations about the fate of condemned offenders, the recorder of London could only have made explicit to himself, and to those whose decision it was to make, the grounds upon which pardon might be granted or withheld.

Some sense of the considerations that shaped pardon decisions can be found in the minutes of cabinet meetings early in the century. On May 15, 1717, to take that simply as an example, the minutes record the following decisions on the prisoners convicted of capital offenses at the recent session at the Old Bailey:

---

[38] *Ibid.*, 1695, pp. 12, 19.
[39] Hay, "Property, Authority and the Criminal Law," pp. 40–49; Beattie, *Crime and the Courts*, pp. 444–45.
[40] For the pattern of pardons in the eighteenth century, and for varying points of view on the relative importance in the decision-making process of "influence," considerations of the character of the offender, and the nature of the offense, see the sources cited in note 29 above.

Sarah Panks for stealing 22s.2d. from her mistress; solicits for her transportation [i.e. she asked to be pardoned on condition of being sent to America]; first time [i.e. it is her first offence]; granted

William Collins, 16 years old; first time; enticed by ill company; to be transported

J. Fox for picking pockets, £3; first time; Mr Hampden desires he may be transported; the person robbed desires the same having received his money; as the Recorder proposes [transported].

Thomas Love, pick-pocket; 16 years old; transported

John Carrol, picking pockets, 8s. Very young. Transported.

W. Wells, notorious for house-breaking in the night. To be executed.

Francis Williams and Matthew Chersey, for robbing the Mail. The last once pardoned by H.M. October last. To be executed and hanged in chains.

Martha Pitrow, an old offender; house-robber; to be executed

Christopher Ward, John Lemmon, old offenders for Burglary in the night. To be executed. [41]

In addition, two other burglars, one pickpocket, and a man whose offense was simply described as stealing (and may have been shoplifting or theft from a house) had been convicted by the Old Bailey juries and sentenced to death: the execution of the two former was also confirmed by the cabinet; the latter two were pardoned.

Present at the meeting were the king, the two secretaries of state, the first lord of the treasury, the lord chancellor, and four other ministers or household officials. The Archbishop of Canterbury always withdrew when the fate of the convicts was to be discussed. The decisive issue at this cabinet meeting seemed to be the nature of the offense committed: all those convicted of burglary or housebreaking – offenses that threatened life as well as property – were left for execution and the pickpockets were pardoned and transported instead of being hanged. I do not want to argue that this tiny sample reveals the grounds on which pardons were granted in this period or any other, especially since what was thought to be the current level of crime was always likely to be an important consideration, as indeed were personal and political influences: this was, after all, a highly partisan body. Few of those considerations are revealed in these terse notes of cabinet decisions. It is also important to note that the cabinet minutes do not disclose all the evidence that the recorder might have presented about the ages of the prisoners, or their previous character and disposition, or other testimony that might have emerged at the trial. It notes such evidence as justificatory only when the offender was in fact pardoned. That is, of course, not insignificant, since it reveals the grounds on which it was thought pardons might be justified: those shown mercy were young or were thought to have committed few crimes; "old offenders" were hanged. But the fundamental consideration at work at this meeting – and indeed over the century – was the nature of the crime. Considerations of youth, character, previous behavior, and promise of good conduct provided broad justifications for showing mercy to those who had not

[41] SP 35/9, fols. 13–14.

committed the most damaging offenses. The youth of a burglar would not count for as much as that of a pickpocket, nor the recidivism of a shoplifter weigh as heavily against him as that of a housebreaker. In the end, by far the largest proportion of those executed under the "bloody code" had committed offenses which took or threatened life – murder, robbery, and burglary.[42]

The cabinet did not take the whole of the pardoning process into its hands: the recommendations of the high-court judges continued to determine who would be hanged on the assize circuit throughout the country; and the king continued to receive petitions for mercy from those condemned to death in London and the provinces and to act on those petitions in his closet, perhaps on the advice of ministers, perhaps not. But in dealing with the London cases, the cabinet was concerned with a large proportion of the prisoners in the country threatened with execution in any year. They had it directly in their power to manage the levels of execution in the capital as circumstances warranted in a much more immediate way than ever before. In determining who and how many and what kinds of offenders were hanged at Tyburn – at what was by far the busiest, most famous, most influential place of execution[43] – the cabinet controlled and shaped the public face of execution.

The fact that this mainstream criminal business became a routine matter for consideration at cabinet meetings seems to me important for one further reason. The discussion of capital punishment and pardon brought the cabinet in touch with one of the continuing problems that had faced the courts and to some extent the central government for fifty years or more: the need for a more effective noncapital punishment for felons. Crime and punishment became items on the political agenda. And this proved to be particularly important after 1714. The new Hanoverian regime saw itself beset by a variety of internal and external enemies, and the Whig administrations that George I established showed themselves to be willing to mobilize the political and financial resources of the government in the maintenance of social order and the security of the new dynasty. The accession of George I also took place in the midst of a serious escalation of violent property offenses in the capital – a postwar experience that was to become increasingly familiar over the next hundred years.[44] The dimensions of this crime problem in London – at least, of the levels of prosecutions – came regularly to the attention of the government at their meetings with the recorder. This accumulating knowledge, and the determination of governments after 1714 to use the resources of the state to maintain order, almost certainly explains the administration's support of legislation in 1718 and 1720 that established transportation to America as an effective punishment.

It was distinctly unusual for the government to play a role in the making of

---

[42] Beattie, *Crime and the Courts*, pp. 454, 501, 515, 536–37, 591; King, "Decision-makers and Decision-making."
[43] Peter Linebaugh, "The Tyburn Riot against the Surgeons," in Hay, Linebaugh, and Thompson (eds.), *Albion's Fatal Tree*, pp. 65–117.
[44] For the effect of war on the prosecution of offenses against property, see Beattie, *Crime and the Courts*, ch. 5.

criminal legislation in this period.[45] But the Transportation Act was introduced by the solicitor-general, and it was followed two years later by another statute that ensured the success of the new transportation system by committing public money to it. Transportation had been in sporadic use for more than a century by then, mainly as a condition of pardon granted to men and women sentenced to death. But it had not been available to the courts as a punishment that could be imposed on noncapital felons. Nor, indeed, had it worked at all well even for the few offenders ordered to be sent to the colonies, for it was constantly undermined by the difficulties of actually getting them across the Atlantic.[46] The regular transportation of convicts to America which the new legislation made possible (along with the government's dismissal of American objections) not only gave the courts the first noncapital punishment they could impose directly on felons; it also immensely facilitated the administration of the ever-enlarging capital code by providing an effective alternative punishment for those pardoned from capital sentences.

How much the king's ministers were conscious of that advantage when they put the government's support behind the new transportation system is impossible to say. But it is likely that their experience of dealing with long lists of convicted robbers and burglars and shoplifters was crucial to their decision. It was also surely important that the solicitor-general who introduced the Transportation Act into parliament, Sir William Thomson, was also the recorder of London. It seems reasonable to think that this most significant measure, a measure which transformed the penal system and the relationship of the government and the courts, resulted from a policy decision at the highest level of the administration and that it was at least encouraged by the cabinet's knowledge of the fluctuating state of crime in the capital.

The discussion of London cases in the cabinet and the bureaucratization of a large part of routine pardon procedure may also have resulted over time in a certain distancing of the king from the pardon process. The Hanoverian monarchs continued to make decisions on a large number of pardon petitions; and pardons were still, of course, issued in the king's name and could still be seen as the exercise of the king's mercy, proceeding from his fatherly concern for his people. But when the cabinet took responsibility for the exercise of the royal prerogative with respect to the large number of London cases arising at the Old Bailey, and when decisions became more routine and to some extent predictable, some of the arbitrary quality of pardoning and perhaps some of the personal identification of the king with the exercise of mercy were diminished. The pardon process that developed in the early eighteenth century thus reflected a style of governance more closely suited to the constitutional monarchy emerging after 1689 and signaled a change in the way power was exercised and managed. It was also a part of a broader pattern of the

[45] Several important criminal statutes – including some capital statutes – were passed in the reign of William and Mary and in Anne's reign, all without direct government involvement. See Beattie, "London Crime and the Making of the English Criminal Law, 1689–1718."

[46] For the difficulties that plagued efforts to establish transportation before 1718, see Beattie, *Crime and the Courts*, ch. 9.

central government's expanding involvement in the early eighteenth century with issues of crime and disaffection. That was particularly true after 1714, as I have suggested, when powerful political forces were brought to bear in the defense of the new dynasty, and Whig governments pushed through legislation – the Riot Act, the Transportation Act, the Black Act – that made for more effective prosecution and punishment of criminals and those who threatened public order and the stability of the government. At the same time, especially in the 1720s, the Walpole administration pursued such enemies energetically in the courts. John Brewer has recently revealed the ways in which the capacities of the English government to deal with external enemies were transformed after 1689.[47] Changes in criminal administration signal the emergence on a more modest scale of governments that were also more active with respect to domestic issues. Those changes too were the inadvertent consequences of the Revolution of 1688–89.

[47] John Brewer, *The Sinews of Power: War, Money and the English State, 1688–1783* (New York, Knopf, 1989).

14

The Glorious Revolution and Ireland

Karl S. Bottigheimer

In a reconsideration of the Glorious Revolution on its tercentenary, what should one say about Ireland? First of all, that the "revolution" was, like so much of Anglo-Irish history, an essentially English event with collateral Irish consequences. Unlike that other and earlier seventeenth-century revolution, sometimes called "Puritan," occurrences in Ireland were not causative. If rampant Catholophobia played a part in 1688, it was not because the Protestants of Ireland were believed to have been slaughtered as an appetizer on the way to a main course consisting of Protestant England. The unapologetic and aggressive Catholicism of James II eclipsed all contributory Irish causes. It was, rather, that the Glorious Revolution in England set in train a series of events which marked – one might better say scarred – Anglo-Irish relations for generations to come.

The late J. G. Simms of Trinity College, Dublin, remains the authoritative commentator on the subject, which, in his final summation, he termed "The War of the Two Kings, 1685–91."[1] Simms portrayed a Catholic Ireland whose great hopes of James were cruelly dashed. French assistance to the Jacobite cause was far less than expected or needed. Irish Catholics, as in the 1640s, remained divided between those who were willing to back an English king and those who were restrained by doubt. Simms concluded that the Catholics lost the war because "the securing of Ireland was a more important objective for William and his supporters than the buttressing of the Jacobite regime was for Louis."[2] He viewed James and William as equally indifferent to their partisans in Ireland, whom they saw as mere means to achieving the English throne.

If this remains the received view of what happened in Ireland between 1685 and 1691, where does it fit into the broad legacy of the Revolution? Simms's title for his chapter in *A New History of Ireland*, "The War of the Two Kings, 1685–91," gives a clue. It was not a "revolution" in Ireland at all. Revolu-

---

[1] In T. W. Moody, F. X. Martin, and F. J. Byrne (eds.), *A New History of Ireland* (9 vols., Oxford, Clarendon Press, 1976–89), III (1534–1691), pp. 478–508.

[2] *Ibid.*, p. 508. See also the same author's earlier monograph, *Jacobite Ireland, 1685–1691* (London, Routledge and Kegan Paul, 1969).

234

tions are transformations. They may leave, relatively speaking, winners and losers, but the very concept of revolution suggests a blurring of distinctions as a remodeling process occurs. It is "wars" in which elementals contend, and in which victories and defeats are the principal product. The "revolution" in Ireland left winners and losers, rather than transforming the society and its institutions. The "revolution" is remembered as a "war," and it is remembered very differently by those who regard it as a victory and by those who regard it as a defeat.

For the triumphalists the distinctive resonance of the event in 1689 is captured in a passage from the *Personal Sketches* of Sir Jonah Barrington (1760–1834), written over a hundred years later. Expatiating on an organization he encountered in the Dublin of his youth called "the Aldermen of Skinners' Alley," Barrington described its commemoration of the Protestants who had been purged from the Dublin Corporation in 1687. These aldermen, Barrington recounted, had

secreted some little articles of their paraphernalia and privately assembled in an alehouse in ... a very obscure part of the capital: here they continued to hold Anti-Jacobite meetings; elected their own lord mayor and officers; and got a marble bust of King William [after his accession], which they regarded as a sort of deity! These meetings were carried on till the battle of the Boyne put William in possession of Dublin, when James's aldermen were immediately cashiered, and the Aldermen of Skinners' Alley [were] reinvested with their mace and aldermanic glories.[3]

When Barrington joined this organization in the 1780s, it claimed to be nearly a hundred years old. Barrington called it "the first Orange association ever formed."[4] Whether it was or not – the formal "Orange Order" is usually dated from 1795 – the Aldermen of Skinners' Alley exhibited much of what came to be characteristic of the Orange tradition through the years. Barrington further explained the success of the group:

To make the general influence of his association the greater, the number of members was unlimited, and the mode of admission solely by the proposal and seconding of tried aldermen. For the same reason, no class, however humble, was excluded – equality reigning in its most perfect state at the assemblies. Generals and wig-makers – King's Counsel and hackney clerks, etc. all mingled without distinction as brother-aldermen: – a lord mayor was annually appointed; and regularity and decorum always prevailed – until, at least, towards the conclusion of the meetings, when the aldermen became more than usually noisy and exhilarated, – King William's bust being placed in the centre of the supper-table, to overlook their extreme loyalty.[5]

The meetings seemed to have been held in conjunction with a dinner which included sheep's trotters (an allusion to King James's running away from Dublin), and a good deal of strong drink. Everything on these ceremonial occasions led up to what Barrington called the "Grand Engine" of the "Charter Toast" when "every man unbuttoned the knees of his breeches, and drank the toast on his bare joints."[6] Barrington provides a garrulous version

[3] Hugh B. Staples (ed.), *The Ireland of Sir Jonah Barrington* (London, Owen, 1968), pp. 212–13.
[4] *Ibid.*   [5] *Ibid.*, p. 213.   [6] *Ibid.*, p. 214.

of what he terms "this most ancient and unparalleled sentiment" of the Orange Toast, but a more fastidious wording is found in the eleventh edition of the *Encyclopaedia Britannica* (*sub* Orangemen): "The glorious, pious and immortal memory of the great and good King William who saved us from popery, slavery, brass money, and wooden shoes" with (the editor comments) "grotesque or truculent additions according to the orator's taste." Should anyone doubt the usual flavor of these accretions, Barrington's toast includes the following:

May we never want a Williamite to kick the [arse] of a Jacobite! – and a f[art] for the Bishop of Cork! And he that won't drink this, whether he be priest, bishop, deacon, bellows-blower, grave-digger, or any other of the fraternity of the clergy; – may a north wind blow him to the south, and a west wind blow him to the east! May he have a dark night – a lee shore – a rank storm – and a leaky vessel to carry him over the river Styx! May the dog Cerberus make a meal of his r[um]p, and Pluto a snuff-box of his skull; and may the devil jump down his throat with a red-hot harrow, with every pin tear out a gut, and blow him with a clean carcase to hell![7]

All of this blasphemy ended solemnly, of course, with "Amen."

The implication of this inflamed rhetoric, which by no means characterized *all* Protestant opinion in post-"revolutionary" Ireland but, rather, the opinion of an enduring "Orange" element (plate 12), is that it imprisons the legacy of the Revolution in a mental strait-jacket. It reduces the Revolution to an uncomplicated struggle between nefarious ultra-montane Catholicism and heroic settler Protestantism. J. G. Simms devoted much of his scholarly career to challenging this parochialism, but in the popular culture of Ireland, both north and south, it remains firmly entrenched despite Simms's efforts.

The Catholic nationalist obverse of the Orange triumphalist view is equally uncomplicated. In it the Revolution provided merely the occasion for per-fidious Albion to perpetrate further crimes and betrayals on a prostrate – but still defiant – Irish Catholic population. The defeat at the Boyne, the slaughter at Aughrim, the evasion of the civil articles of the Treaty of Limerick, and the *sequelae* of confiscation and penal legislation are the principal chapters of that saga of iron-heeled oppression. It might be added that in both the Orange and Catholic nationalist versions the Revolution in Ireland was far from bloodless. On the contrary, Ireland was its sanguinary battle-ground, and "glorious" only to those who would celebrate a further effusion of Catholic blood.

What has all this to do with profound political and intellectual changes occurring in England in the 1690s? The temptation has always been to dis-miss the Irish parallel like some base relative, familiar in form but wholly contrary by nature; and never is that instinct stronger than on the occasion of a family feast when one wishes to recall what is most sustaining and noble in the past, rather than what is most sordid and dividing. But England *is* an island-nation, and it shares its archipelago with other peoples. As the author

[7] *Ibid.*

Plate 12 "Ballycraigy Temperance True Blues, L.O.L. No. 537" – William III on horseback. Images of William III are part of the living folk art of Ulster. This banner was produced by the Northern Ireland firm of Bridget Brothers shortly before it was borrowed and photographed by the Ulster Folk and Transport Museum in 1974.

of the guide to the Tercentenary Exhibition ("The Age of William III and Mary II") accurately observes, "Though the invasion and accession [of William] had been bloodless, 1690 was not . . . The Battle of the Boyne on July 1 routed [James II's] troops . . . and the aftermath opened religious wounds that still fester today." It did so because the issues which animated the Glorious Revolution in England were irrelevancies in Ireland. The only issue of consequence was whether the Protestant regime would endure.

We *expect* historical interpretation to change over time, and when we return to a series of dramatic events, like those which occurred in Ireland between 1685 and 1691, and find their interpretation virtually *un*changed, we are disappointed. But that is essentially the case with regard to Ireland and the Glorious Revolution. The humane, Protestant account published twenty years ago remains substantially unchallenged. In it both William and James are portrayed as lacking any specific interest in Ireland or in their enthusiastic supporters there. To be in Ireland under such circumstances was simply the two kings' bad luck.

The "history" of this episode is relentlessly narrative. It is a story of unfolding events and of personalities reacting to them. We hear little or nothing about communities, towns, provinces, or classes; only of amorphous, polar "interests," Protestants, Catholics, and their respective heroes. (These are subjects that await their historian.) Like the story of King Alfred and the cakes, the events of the Glorious Revolution in Ireland long ago assumed mythic proportions. Even very recent tellers of the tale, such as Patrick Macrory in *The Siege of Derry* (1988), are unapologetic about not being able to know (due to scant documentation) what actually happened, because, they contend, it is more important to know what people at the time (and ever since) *believed* had happened, of which there is abundant evidence. This is particularly true of the many alleged atrocities on both sides.

To sample the quality of the narrative, let us look at one of the stock characters in this celebrated drama: Richard Talbot (1630–91), Earl and titular Duke of Tyrconnell. Talbot is sometimes portrayed as a figure midway between a buffoon and a villain. Macaulay dismissed his ancestry as being "one of those degenerate families of the Pale which were popularly classed with the aboriginal population of Ireland." In fact, the "aboriginal population" – if that is a suitable term for Patrick Sarsfield and the Gaelic foes of William III – distrusted Talbot during the wars as too much a courtier and an Old English aristocrat. But Talbot, a great swearer of oaths, was the uncontested *bête noire* of the Protestant interest in his capacity as James II's Catholicizing agent in Ireland from 1685–88. Even a would-be rescuer of his reputation calls him "God's gift to wig-makers, being accustomed, when provoked, to throw his wig down on the floor and stamp on it, and in cases of extreme provocation to hurl it into the fire."[8]

Talbot's first interview in Dublin with the new Lord Lieutenant, the Protestant Henry Hyde, second Earl of Clarendon (James II's brother-in-law), is usually portrayed as an exhibition of his "insolent contempt" or outrageous bluster.[9] The appointment of Clarendon in early 1686 signified the continuation of the Cromwellian/Restoration land settlement which had expropriated virtually all Catholic land. Sensitive to the implications, at their meeting Tyrconnell reportedly told Clarendon:

My Lord, I am sent hither to view this army; and to give the King an account of it . . . You

---

[8] Patrick Macrory, *The Siege of Derry* (Oxford University Press, 1988), p. 111.   [9] *Ibid.*

must know, my Lord, the King, who is a Roman Catholic, is resolved to employ his subjects of that religion, as you will find by the letters I have brought you, and therefore some must be put out to make room for such as the King likes.[10]

Passing onto the land settlement, he observed, "By God, my Lord, these Acts of Settlement and this New Interest are damned things!" and when Clarendon replied that "neither you nor I are well informed of all the motives and inducements which carried on those affairs twenty-six years ago," Talbot spluttered in reply "Yes, we *do* know all those arts and damned roguery contrivances which procured those Acts." When Clarendon demurred further, Talbot stomped off (without, apparently, on this occasion jumping on his wig) with the parting words: "Well, I will say no more at present; but by God, my Lord, there have been foul damned things done here!"[11] Six months later Clarendon was recalled to England and Tyrconnell appointed in his place.

Even in the most sympathetic light, Talbot remains an unappealing hero – and the events of 1685–91 revealed him to be an ineffectual one as well – but on the merits of the land settlement his outrage was justified. "Foul damned things" *had* been done in Ireland and the land settlement rather than religion is the key to understanding the Irish role in 1689. To point this out is not, at this distance in time, so much to execrate the land settlement as to emphasize its disruptive, destabilizing effect. From an English Protestant point of view the massive Cromwellian expropriations, confirmed for the most part by Charles II, were no less than justice for the rebellion and associated atrocities committed by Irish Catholics in 1641 and after. But the atrocities were almost impossible to investigate until many years later, and in any case they were not exclusively the work of those expropriated, many of whom were quite innocent. As for the alleged act of "rebellion" at a moment (October 1641) when Charles I was facing the veritable insurrection of his House of Commons, it was partially actuated by feelings of loyalty to the crown. As Charles II confided to Clarendon at a Privy Council meeting in late 1661, "rebel for rebel, I had rather trust a papist rebel than a presbyterian one." Clarendon's somewhat trimming reply was, "The difference is that you have wiped out the memory of the rebellion of the one, whilst the other is liable to all the reproaches."[12]

Charles II and James II never entirely lost sight of this irony, and the new proprietary class could never forget that its title to Irish land required that the irony be overlooked. If Charles II declined to set matters right, it was simply that he feared to provoke the new Protestant proprietors who controlled Ireland in the late 1650s and facilitated the Restoration.[13] But James II rushed in where Charles had feared to tread. At least in prospect (although

---

[10] *Ibid.*   [11] *Ibid.*

[12] *Notes which Passed at Meetings of the Privy Council between Charles II and the Earl of Clarendon, 1660–7*, ed. W. D. Macray (London, Roxburgh Club, 1896), p. 498.

[13] See my article, "The Restoration Land Settlement in Ireland: a Structural View," *Irish Historical Studies* 18 (1972), 1–21.

after 1688 he changed his mind), he was willing to question the entire moral basis of the Cromwellian and Restoration land settlements. This put the new proprietary at risk of annihilation. In theory, it left the earlier Elizabethan and Jacobean proprietors unthreatened, but after the traumas of the 1640s, they were unlikely to view equably the return of their Catholic neighbors, and the removal of their Cromwellian co-religionists. James II's intended reopening of the land question thus threatened the continuing formation of a Protestant ascendancy and raised the specter of Catholic revenge.

That was the issue posed by the Glorious Revolution in Ireland. If William and James were fighting for the throne and possessed (as Simms insists) little intrinsic interest in Irish affairs, their Irish partisans were fighting for two antithetical notions of Ireland. One would set back the clock to at least 1640, and Protestant proprietors would be left with less than half of the profitable agricultural land of the island. The other would confirm the Cromwellian settlement, and extend the hegemony of Protestants over Catholics that it had established.

We cannot be sure of the form which a Jacobite triumph would have taken. Some have argued that it would have resulted in a more tolerant and less sectarian island than the Williamite victory produced. But it is only the victors who can be judged, and in the instance their success riveted, rather than reversed, the landed constitution of the 1650s and 1660s, and the expropriations which were at its heart. It is true that the Catholic tenantry were little better served by Catholic lords than by Protestant ones, and that the adjustment finally achieved by the land reform acts of the late nineteenth and early twentieth century did not, at a stroke, resolve the island's problems. But it remains appropriate to see the Williamite victory in Ireland as the charter of the "Protestant Nation," first, in its island-wide eighteenth-century incarnation; and since 1921 in its truncated six-county form of Northern Ireland. This may not have been what William necessarily intended, but it is his legacy nevertheless.

The Orange tradition then, however "grotesque or truculent" its embroidery upon the facts, is not at serious variance from them. Far from being a vulgar embarrassment, the Orangemen's beatification of William, the Derry apprentice-boys, and a host of lesser heroes is appropriate to the sense of the "Revolution" in Ireland as a "war" which was won by Protestants and lost by Catholics. The lines were drawn with extreme clarity; the outcome of the struggle was unambiguous.

An old Irish story tells of an Aer Lingus pilot who, on the London to Dublin route, came on the public-address system as the plane was beginning its descent into Dublin Airport and reminded the passengers that there was a change in time: would they please set back their watches 300 years. This may be both fanciful and unjust, but it captures the point that the Irish dynamic retains seventeenth-century elements which have died out almost everywhere else. Two "interests" have contended for possession and control of almost everything of value in Ireland. Although there were ethnic differences *between* these two interests, there were also ethnic differences *within* them. Half the old interest was Gaelic; the other half was "Old English." Half the new interest was English; the other half was Scottish. The denominator which most efficiently distinguished the two interests thus became religion rather than race or culture.

With an effort, we can imagine the sectarian passions of 1685–91. The period began not only with the accession of James II, but with the Revocation of the Edict of Nantes, and the flight of French Huguenots to many Protestant sanctuaries including, ironically, Ireland. The refugees brought a congenial (to their Protestant neighbors) Catholophobia based on often-bitter experience. The aggressive foreign and military policies of Louis XIV in the 1670s and 1680s lent renewed substance to what Hugh Trevor-Roper calls *Le Grand Peur*, a dread of Catholic subjection amounting very nearly to paranoia. It was not difficult to tar James II with this brush, to portray him as the knowing or witless agent of a French-driven imperialist Catholicism. In the event, after 1688 James was unwilling to support drastic revision of the Irish land settlement, because he feared it would alienate him from the English Protestant gentry whose support he required to recover his throne; but in the Orange tradition he is denied any redeeming credit for this pragmatism.

The Orangemen believe they (and their ancestors) were saved by Providence, and by their own exertions, as, most notably, at Derry. Nicholas Canny has suggested that their crisis in 1685–91 constituted a "Machiavellian Moment," a species of nation-forming trauma out of which emerged a commitment to "liberty."[14] But at the moment of their salvation – whether by Providence, King William, or their own valor – their dependence upon Protestant Britain was undeniable. When William King, later Church of Ireland Archbishop of Dublin, published in 1691 his now-classic *State of the Protestants of Ireland under the late King James Government*, he argued that Ireland was "a kingdom dependent on the crown of England and part of the inheritance thereof and therefore must follow its state which it cannot decline without much apparent ruin to the English interest in it."[15]

The subsequent eighteenth-century experiment with a semi-autonomous "Protestant Nation" foundered on this inconvenient fact. The political nation (from 1691–1800) was constituted of an Anglo-Scottish, Protestant landholding class whose title was based on conquest. The Union of 1800 was required to protect that hegemony of which the Williamite Settlement was the capstone. As Simms expressed it, "The Williamite confiscation reinforced the territorial predominance which Protestants had enjoyed since the Cromwellian settlement and which had been maintained, although in a diminished form, after the restoration."[16] Simms estimated that the Catholic share of

---

[14] See his *Kingdom and Colony: Ireland in the Atlantic World, 1560–1800* (Baltimore and London, Johns Hopkins University Press, 1988), p. 119.

[15] Cited in Canny, *Kingdom and Colony*, p. 120.

[16] *The Williamite Confiscation in Ireland, 1690–1703* (London, Faber, 1956), p. 162.

profitable land declined from 22 per cent in 1688 to 14 per cent in 1703; and by the operation of the penal laws it was further reduced in the first three-quarters of the eighteenth century. Thus was created the society described by the young Frenchman, Alexis de Tocqueville, on his visit to Ireland in 1835: "If you want to know what can be done by the spirit of conquest and religious hatred combined with the abuses of aristocracy, but without any of its advantages, go to Ireland."[17]

For the Catholics of Ireland, the "Revolution" of 1688 had thoroughly inglorious consequences. It completed, and sealed, their dispossession. If this affected at first hand a relatively small number of Catholic landowners, it nevertheless came to have for the broader Catholic population a symbolic significance which cannot be argued away. For the Protestants of Ireland, the glorious tunes of 1688–91 could be modulated from *sotto voce* all the way up to *fortissimo*. For the most secure and affluent, *sotto voce* was often sufficient. But for those whose station and livelihood visibly required keeping Catholics in their place, the Orange tradition of ostentatiously commemorating Williamite victories had enduring appeal.

We see the operation of this principle in Northern Ireland today. Whereas the Irish dimensions of the Glorious Revolution have been generally down-played during its tercentenary celebration in British portions of the United Kingdom, 1989–91 has seen in Ulster spirited commemorations and reenactments of the great Protestant victories of three centuries ago. The rituals and regalia do not have to be manufactured, but can simply be adapted from the elaborate annual celebrations which are an ingrained part of the province's Protestant culture. "King Billy" is not a distant, unknown figure – some dusty, ancient, foreign soldier – but a ubiquitous presence to whom praise is constantly due for the deliverance of the Protestant interest. The Orange Lodges and their incessant parades colorfully demonstrate the vitality of this version of a truly glorious revolution, and keep alive the watchwords of the Boyne, Aughrim, Londonderry, and their Protestant heroes. Unlike the annual celebrations of the fourth of July in the United States, these are not politically insignificant, or neutral, events which draw the population together. In the public life of the United States, the enemies of the Revolution – the American Tories and their British allies – are no longer a factor. The British have long since surrendered and gone home, to become in the twentieth century trusted allies. The Tories too have disappeared, so that celebrating their defeat affronts no constituents of the American Republic.

By contrast, the Williamite legacy remains a sectarian weapon in Northern Ireland. Its celebration does not unite the community as a whole, but only its Protestant majority against its substantial Catholic minority. It evokes, and is meant to evoke, that early-modern European world in which Catholics and Protestants feared and loathed one another; in which a Spanish Philip II or a French Louis XIV could be regarded by northern Protestants as a latter-day

---

[17] *Journeys to England and Ireland* (New York, Anchor Doubleday, 1968), p. 113.

Genghis Khan or Tamerlane. The legacy of the Glorious Revolution is in Ireland no innocent thing. Its philosophical and constitutional aspects are irrelevant, or rather, entirely eclipsed by its parochial significance. The problem is not so much how to keep alive the memory of the Glorious Revolution as how to neutralize and objectify it, how to remove it from the living, who have claimed it as their property and who are prepared to defend their private versions of it with guns, bombs, and decades of continuing violence.

The situation has been astutely described by K. T. Hoppen, who wrote, quite recently: "By the beginning of the present century both nationalists and unionists had each constructed a self-contained theatre of the past in which to play out current aspirations against backdrops painted to represent the triumphs of former times."[18] To replace those "backdrops" by a more objective and ecumenical version of the past remains the challenge for the historian of the seventeenth century in Ireland.

[18] *Ireland since 1800: Conflict and Conformity* (London and New York, Longman, 1989), pp. 2–3.

15

The poverty of political theory in the Scottish Revolution of 1688–1690

Bruce P. Lenman

One of the main thrusts of some of the best modern writing on the history of political thought has been a welcome emphasis on the social construction of political theory. The subject is no longer seen simply as a canon of great works which rise above time to eternal verity and all of which are written by quite exceptional minds. Rather do the best contemporary scholars in the field assume that it is their task to recreate the political and ideological context which at any given moment in time defined a range of issues as contentious and a corresponding range of questions as appropriate for debate. Seen from this perspective, any given tradition of political thought is the product of thousands of individual contributions, and the historian must, in the words of Quentin Skinner, one of the most brilliant of the exponents of this new approach, try "to write a history centred less on the classic texts and more on the history of ideologies," aiming at "general framework within which the writings of the more prominent theorists can then be situated."[1] Anyone writing about political theory in the Scottish Revolution of 1688–90 finds this approach at once imperative and sobering. The Scottish Revolution was, as were upheavals in the contemporary British world, dissimilar to the trigger Glorious Revolution in England, not least because it involved the shedding of blood and therefore cannot have the adjective "Glorious" added to its title. More disconcerting still is the ideological context in which it took place, for the role of political thought in 1688–90 was both limited and deeply ambiguous. The historian who sets out to probe the political theory of those who supported the Revolution has to explain that in the years preceding William III's spectacular descent on England, a student of Scottish political thought must reconstruct the deconstruction of an ideological context or, to put it more simply, explain why there was a dearth of recently articulated political theory amongst the declared opponents of James VII. Participants in the Scottish Revolution of 1688 already had a national heritage which embraced a spectrum of possible political ideologies. Not only did they shun the formulation of new paradigms, but they also deliberately reached back across the

[1] Quentin Skinner, *The Foundations of Modern Political Thought*, I: *The Renaissance* (2 vols., London and New York, Cambridge University Press, 1978), Preface, p. xi.

244

spectrum towards old, indeed almost antiquarian, and always conservative formulations to articulate their position. Instinctively, they were reluctant to be more articulate than was absolutely necessary. For this there are solid explanations.

It was extremely dangerous to be known as the writer of what the monarch deemed to be politically subversive literature in the late seventeenth century. Late Stuart absolutism was more sensitive to the ideological atmosphere of its realms than, for example, were the far more absolute prime ministers of the twentieth-century United Kingdom, and for obvious reasons. Lacking the elaborate, centralized bureaucratic, police and military power of modern rulers, Charles II and James II were much more dependent on their ability to control the minds of their subjects. Both monarchs went to very great lengths in the 1680s to enforce their legal monopoly of published political propaganda, through a licensing system, and through a relentless pursuit of deviationist publicists both at home and abroad.

Their methods can be demonstrated from a letter written from Anstruther in Fife in September 1685 by William, eighteenth Earl of Crawford, to two ministers, consulting them on the question of his emigrating. That he should have considered this option is hardly surprising, for he was a convinced Presbyterian with no sympathy with the existing regime in kirk and state, especially since the accession of the aggressively Roman Catholic James VII. The earl was to be an active member of early Williamite administration after the Revolution. He listed the reasons for departure, which included deep distress at having to witness "sad things that are coming to Scotland," to which was added, among other things, an apprehension that his ecclesiastical enemies might persuade the monarch to strip him of most of his honors and possessions, in order to give them to the senior branch of the Lindsay family to which the Earl of Crawford belonged. That senior branch, the Lindsays of Edzell, would no doubt have welcomed a transfer of assets from a cadet branch, for its financial affairs were already heading towards the bankruptcy which overwhelmed them in the early eighteenth century.

Against these considerations, Crawford set out the disadvantages of emigration for a person of his high social rank. The first point he stressed was that noblemen were not allowed to leave the country for any length of time without royal permission, for fear that they were going abroad to plot treason. Some sort of deal would have to be negotiated with the monarch if his leaving Scotland were not to be construed as a crime, with grave consequences for his family and estate. He had felt that the price which Charles would try to exact would probably be outrageous, and he suspected that the price demanded by King James would be worse. Then he knew that masters and skippers of ships were warned under severe penalties not to accept such passengers as him for transportation abroad without license. On top of strict checks at the point of departure for unauthorized passengers, he had to allow for the fact that, under James, the ships of the king's navy regularly patrolled the main sea routes with a view to stopping English and Scottish ships and searching them for illegal emigrants. The idea of a flight to America was clearly ruled out when the earl insisted that neither he nor his wife "has inclination for long voyages by sea, or a retreat far off from Scotland."

On the other hand, if he were to retire to some country in western Europe, which was obviously the only kind of retreat which he contemplated with any degree of enthusiasm, he faced another problem, for, as he said:

Besides the danger of rencountering on the seas with any of our King's ships, and the strict scrutiny that they make when they meet with any ships belonging to these three nations, to what place in the world could I retire to for more safety? It is informed (I know not how warrantably) that our King has signed a league defensive with Holland, Denmark, and some other states, upon this express condition, that they shall deliver up, without a call, all declared rebels belonging to either nation, and upon demand shall give up all such, however free of public censure, as he shall nominate to them.[2]

In fact, this was an excessively simple and misleading account of the situation with respect to extradition. Two points, however, have to be made about Crawford's letter. One is that it shows the extent to which James had psychologically turned his kingdoms into a prison camp for his subjects who belonged to the political nations and were not in good odor with him. The second is that the crude fears of Crawford about what the extradition situation was, reflected with absolute precision the crude views of King James as to what the position ought to be, and these positions were ones he was continually trying to force neighboring states to accept by a mixture of cajolery and threats. It is hardly surprising that Crawford, in the event, chose to stay in seclusion at home, keeping his own counsel until the Revolution enabled him to stand up and be counted, not as a victim of the arbitrary power of James Stuart, but an effective opponent of its pretensions.

There was nothing unusual about the worries expressed by the Earl of Crawford. These considerations loomed large in day-to-day life to the exiled Scots community which had been gathering round the court of the Prince of Orange in the Republic of the United Netherlands for some years before the Revolution. A good example is the Anglo-Scot Gilbert Burnet. He had retired to the continent because his relations with the Stuart court had reached a dangerously low ebb after he had attended his close friends, William, Lord Russell, and Algernon Sidney, on the scaffold where they suffered in 1683 for their part in the Rye House plot. Charles II had ordered the Master of the Rolls to dismiss Burnet from his incumbency of the Rolls Chapel, on grounds that the monarch could not tolerate a disaffected preacher in a chapel which he deemed peculiarly his, yet Burnet himself could certainly have passionately denied that he was in any legal or moral sense of the word disaffected. Though enormously impressed by the serene equanimity of Russell in the face of death, he had to the last tried to persuade Russell to denounce the doctrine of the right of resistance. Like most finer points, this one was largely wasted

---

[2] Alexander Crawford, Lord Lindsay, *Lives of the Lindsays: a Memoir of the House of Crawford and Balcarres,* 2nd edn. (3 vols., London, 1858), II, Appendix, p. xxxviii, "Letter from William eighteenth Earl of Crawford to two Ministers, consulting them on the question of Emigration."

on the mind of the then Duke of Albany and York, the future James VII and II, whose antipathy to Russell was personal and venomous. Burnet's discreet move abroad might have rendered him less positively obnoxious to the new King James after 1685, but the publication of the exiled divine's *Some Letters: containing an account of what seemed most remarkable in Switzerland, Italy, etc.* in Amsterdam in 1687 rubbed out whatever credit Burnet had accumulated in royal Stuart circles by going away. It was a brilliant work of propaganda which articulated one of the basic paradigms of the English-speaking world's political consciousness for the next 200 years: that popery and poverty go together, because popery goes with tyranny and tyranny is econocidal. In chapter after chapter, Burnet compared the relative prosperity and freedom from unreasonable burdens enjoyed by Protestant-ruled states even when, like the Dutch or the Protestant Swiss, their lands were inherently poor, with the miseries that afflicted the populations of Counter-Reformation absolutisms. The theme continued to resonate in the minds of the leaders of the English-speaking world from Burnet through political economists like Davenant to propagandists in word and image such as Fielding and Hogarth, and indeed right through the American Revolution until it can be found in the opinions of the rulers of the young American republic like Jefferson and John Quincy Adams.[3]

Needless to say, the only success Burnet's book enjoyed at the court of James VII and II was a *succès de scandale*. The sale of the book was banned in England and insofar as it could, the government tried to seize all copies circulating in the realm.[4] The predictable effect was to increase the demand for the volume in much the same way that the attempts of the government to suppress the publication of Peter Wright's *Spycatcher* in the 1980s boosted demand for that book. There was, however, one vital difference between the situation of King James and that of twentieth-century leaders. Though he could ban a book, he could not define the defiance of his will and views in print, especially abroad, as a criminal act, unless the publication contained incitement to treason or personal attacks on the monarch in a form that would be recognized as such by common law.

James did his best by transferring his pursuit of Burnet to the more compliant legal system of Burnet's native Scotland. Burnet had maintained an interest in Scottish politics, partly because he rightly suspected that James tried out ideas in his northern realm to see if they could be used as precedents for action in England, so it is hardly astonishing that he had penned and published *Reflections* on the proclamation of toleration which James had issued in Scotland on February 12, 1686/87. Burnet concentrated not so much on toleration, but on the obsessive references in the proclamation to the absolute power of the monarch. His theme was that the whole concept is a dangerous

<hr />

[3] Bruce P. Lenman, "Providence, Liberty and Prosperity: an Aspect of English Thought in the era of the Glorious Revolution," forthcoming in Dale Hoak (ed.), the proceedings of the World of William and Mary Conference, held at the College of William and Mary in Virginia, February 8–10, 1989.

[4] T. E. S. Clarke and H. C. Foxcroft, *A Life of Gilbert Burnet Bishop of Salisbury* (Cambridge University Press, 1907), p. 229.

innovation. Burnet was himself in favor of a large measure of religious toleration. Not for nothing was he a pupil of the ecumenically spirited Archbishop
Robert Leighton. Burnet's opening lines speak for themselves:[5]

The Preamble of a Proclamation is oft writ in haste and is the Flourish of some wanton
Pen: but one of such an Extraordinary nature as this is, was probably more severely
examined; there is a new Designation of his Majesty's Authority here set forth of his
Absolute Power, which is so often repeated, that it deserves to be a little searched into.
Prerogative Royal and Sovereign Authority, are Terms already received and known; but
for this Absolute Power, as it is a new Term, so those who have coined it may make of it
what they will.

He continues the argument, pointing out that the definition of this new
absolute power is in fact outrageously extreme, for it specifically extends
beyond mere externals to claim control over the wills of the subjects, who are,
in the words of the proclamation, obliged "to obey without Reserve." Though
the proclamation contained concessions which were attractive to many of the
king's subjects, there was no logical reason that the same claim to absolute
power should not be used in the future to impose the royal will, especially in
cases where that will was at odds with the opinions of the bulk of the subjects.
Although these statements were extremely unwelcome to King James, they
were not by the wildest construction of common law treasonable. Were
Burnet indicted before the Grand Jury of Middlesex, a body the Stuarts had
learned to dislike very much, the odds were that the charge would be thrown
out on the grounds that the statements of the accused were neither illegal nor
untrue. Such was the stubborn rage of James, however, that he ill-advisedly
had Burnet cited before the Privy Council of Scotland on the charge of high
treason. Even in Scots law, which was more flexible than English law, the
citation was bad law, and even though bolstered by patently untrue charges
such as of consorting with those plotting previous rebellions, it proved so
disreputable that it was allowed quietly to die.

It was extraordinarily injudicious even to issue the citation, because it
allowed, or rather compelled, Burnet to issue a devastating reply addressed to
Charles, second Earl of Middleton, the principal Scots politician in immediate attendance on James in London. Burnet pointed out that he was about to
marry in the Netherlands, and that he had been naturalized there (a wise
precaution under the circumstances), but his most important points are, in
fact, the ones which are often glossed over as mere rhetoric. Burnet stressed
that he was a born subject of King James, and that he was anxious to defend
both his loyalty and his integrity. He insisted that his original decision to
remain indefinitely abroad sprang from no disloyalty, but from the clear
indications he had received that King James preferred that he stay abroad.
The charges against him he solemnly swore were groundless. He had ever
preached that subjects had no inherent right of resistance in arms.

[5] "Some Reflections On His Majesty's Proclamation Of the Twelfth of February, 1686/7. for a Toleration in
Scotland: Together with the said Proclamation," printed in *A Collection Of Eighteen papers, Relating to the Affairs Of
Church and State, During the Reign of King James the Second. (Seventeen whereof written in Holland, and first printed there)*
(London, 1689; Scholarly Resources Reprint, Wilmington, Del., Scholarly Resources, 1973), pp. 10–24. Leighton
was first Bishop of Dunblane, later Archbishop of Glasgow.

All this was true, but perhaps the most significant single statement in Burnet's answer was the one in which he deplored being forced to answer a citation in the sacred name of his sovereign. This was no humbug. Conservative men like Burnet really had no desire to face basic and searching questions about the nature of sovereignty. As Burnet said in his answer to a second criminal citation, based on charges derived from his reply to the first, it was James who kept raising questions which all sensible monarchists would prefer not to see in the public domain, not least by his contempt for due legal process in his realms.

Having started the hare of high treason, James and his minions actually abandoned it in the second citation in the hope of catching Burnet on other charges, one of which, as Burnet pointed out, was both fatuous and an insult to all sovereigns, including James himself. Burnet's naturalization in the Netherlands was treated as a criminal offence despite the fact that naturalization was an attribute to sovereign majesty everywhere in Europe, including England, where James had not only naturalized the French Roman Catholic Louis Duras, but had made him Earl of Faversham and commander-in-chief of the army. It was not men like Burnet who were calling in question the viability of traditional monarchy and alienating its natural supporters; it was James Stuart. It was not necessary to have a radical political ideology to oppose this king: he was the radical.[6]

To say this is not to deny that there were members of the exiled Scottish and English community in the Netherlands prior to the Williamite invasion of England in 1688 who were radical. Indeed, Scotsmen like Robert Ferguson and James Johnston, who was Burnet's nephew, were disproportionately prominent in those exiled radical circles. Indeed, Johnston was to be rewarded by William for his outstanding services in England as an undercover agent before the invasion with a secretaryship of state in Scotland in 1688. Nor can it be denied that the origins of the debate and split within the Whig ranks over the objectives of the Glorious Revolution in England lie in the inner tensions within the exiled groups between 1685 and 1688. But the key word here is "inner." These men did not conduct a great public debate on political theory. They had enough trouble surviving the twofold offensive which James continually mounted against them. With one hand, James tried to split them with offers of toleration and selective pardon; with the other, he tried to seize them, either by bullying the States of Holland into extraditing them into his power or by simply ordering his envoy, Bevil Skelton, to kidnap them and ship them, in defiance of international and local law, to England to face execution.

The great English political thinker John Locke was in the Netherlands at this juncture, and there would seem to be a good case for Richard Ashcraft's charged, on unconvincing evidence, of complicity in the Rye House plot, and

---

[6] "The Citation Of Gilbert Burnet, D. D.," along with Burnet's "Answer" and the second and third letters to the Earl of Middleton provoked by further harassment, as well as the "Advertisement" in which Burnet insists that his cause is that of all European sovereigns (all of which works were published in the Hague in 1687) can be found in *ibid.*, pp. 145–71.

view that he there associated with and sympathized with the more radical amongst the exiled figures. Yet the fact remains that he did not stick his neck out and publish radical political tracts.[7] Peter Laslett's great insight, in his 1960 edition of Locke's *Two Treatises of Government*, remains valid, despite the valuable additional insights incorporated into the work of scholars like Richard Ashcraft: Locke's *Treatises* date from as early as 1679–80 and were the product of his association with Anthony Ashley Cooper, first Earl of Shaftesbury during the Exclusion Crisis. They were not a justification of the Glorious Revolution. They were old work, adapted without being radically changed. Locke remained even after 1688–89 an author who refused to acknowledge the authorship of his most significant book, who, indeed, in Laslett's words displayed "extraordinary furtiveness" about the work. It has been suggested that this may be due to his consciousness of the deep difficulty of reconciling the thought of the *Treatises* with that of his *Essay Concerning Human Understanding*, and one would not wish to rule this out as a factor,[8] but at the same time one might venture to suggest that Locke must have left his exile with an ingrained paranoia about the potential danger in an unstable world of being identified with contentious political views.

He was not the only one who chose discretion. Sir James Dalrymple, later Viscount Stair, the eminent Scots jurist, is a good example of the same phenomenon. He began his career as an advocate in the Scotland of Oliver Cromwell, joining with his fellow advocates in 1654 in refusing to take the Tender, an oath of allegiance to the Commonwealth which also involved a formal repudiation of monarchy. So successful was this united resistance that the government allowed the issue to drop. On the recommendation of General George Monck, Stair was appointed to the Cromwellian Council of State for Scotland in 1657. Monck's recommendation appears to have secured him the patronage of Charles II after the Restoration, for he became a Lord of Session in 1661 and in 1662 the vice-president of the Court of Session, Scotland's supreme court of civil cases. There was trouble when he later refused to take a loyalty test to the Stuarts in a form known as the Declaration, but Charles wisely allowed him to take it in qualified form, and helped by his close association with Charles's all-powerful Scottish minister, John Maitland, Duke of Lauderdale, he had become the lord president of the Court of Session by 1671. In 1681, he fell foul of the Duke of Albany and York by refusing to take the Test, which the heir to the throne had pushed through the Scots parliament and which demanded subscription to a formula that not only left no guarantee for the established kirk remaining Protestant, but also contrived to be hopelessly self-contradictory. Stair retired to his remote Galloway house to supervise the printing of his epoch-making *Institutions of the Law of Scotland*. Instead of leaving him in peace, James harassed him to the point at which he decided to retire to Leiden in the Netherlands. By 1684, he was being

---

[7] Richard Ashcraft, *Revolutionary Politics and Locke's "Two Treatises of Government"* (Princeton University Press, 1986), ch. 11, "A Radical Manifesto."

[8] John Locke, *Two Treatises Of Government*, ed. Peter Laslett (Cambridge University Press, 1960), pp. 64–66.

by 1685 he had been outlawed. Even when his eldest son, Sir John Dalrymple, who had risen by relentless subservience to be Lord Advocate of Scotland, secured a pardon for him in 1687, he did not deem it wise to return.[9]

Though he was to sail to England in William's flagship in 1688 and to serve as the main liaison between the Prince of Orange and the provisional Williamite government that seized power in Edinburgh, all he published in the Netherlands were two collections of the decisions of the Court of Session and a monograph on physics. He had, after all, left Scotland, like others, quite legally, and with the tacit approval of James. The wild charges of treason must have come as a shock. James was liable to encourage men to leave his dominions if he deemed them Whiggish. He encouraged, for example, the plans of Sir John Cochran of Ochiltree to set up a Scots settlement in the Carolinas, telling him to his face, as he later told Queensberry, "I was glad he and others of his persuasion thought of going there, because they would carry with them disaffected persons."[10] Then, of course, James was liable to turn round and regard residence abroad as proof of treason. Nobody who became the victim of these tactics could be sure that he would escape extradition or, if he did, he would also escape the efforts of Skelton to kidnap him, not to mention the facilities offered by Louis XIV for the spiriting of kidnapped persons to England across French territory.[11] Dealing with Louis de Bourbon and James Stuart, a man was wise to put nothing on paper that might assist his prosecution for treason.

Besides, there is no reason to think that if Stair had written an account of his political views in the years before the invasion of 1688, they would have been anything other than a collection of conservative monarchical truisms. In 1690, when he was goaded to reply in an *Apology* to attacks in print on his integrity which, though anonymous, were generally thought to be by Robert Ferguson, "the Plotter," he said that:

I have been ever perswaded, that it was both against the interest and duty of kings to use arbitrary government; that both king and subjects had their titles and rights, by law; and that an equal ballance of prerogative and liberty was necessar for the happiness of a commonwealth.

Stair added that these were views which he had always held and which he had never tried to conceal from the many kings he had served. They were views which even James would not have dared make the basis of criminal charges, not because he did not violently dislike their implications, but because he could see the damage he would do to his own cause by publicly challenging such a formulation. When he and Stair had first publicly clashed in Scotland in 1681 he had, in Stair's later words, instigated "hundreds of examinations, and reexaminations . . . even of my most intimate domestic servants, and my

---

[9] James Dalrymple, Viscount Stair, *The Institutions of the Law of Scotland*, ed. David M. Walker (Edinburgh, University Presses of Edinburgh and Yale, 1981), Introduction, pp. 1–10.
[10] George P. Insh, *Scottish Colonial Schemes 1620–1688* (Glasgow, Maclehose, Jackson, 1922), pp. 196–97.
[11] Clarke and Foxcroft, *Life of Burnet*, p. 236.

sisters-in-law," in what proved the vain hope of digging up some other grounds for charges of political disaffection.[12]

Another eminent jurist of the period, Sir John Lauder of Fountainhall, like Stair a senator of the College of Justice, ended the manuscript of his "Historical Observations" with the following note, to explain why the main series broke off:

> In April 1686, my two servants being imprisoned, and I threatened therewith also, that they would seize upon my papers, and search if they contained anything offensive to the party then prevailing, I was necessitat to hide this Manuscript and many others, and intermit my Historick Remarks till the Revolution in the end of 1688.[13]

Neither in his experience not in his underlying political preferences was Stair an unusual man. His views were probably shared by the vast majority of conservative Protestant nobles and lairds, a category that certainly included the vast majority of the Scottish ruling class. They had no interest in the ideas of the tiny minorities of millenarian Presbyterian radicals who had defied the Stuart regime from the moors and bogs of the west country, in the name of a religious culture which was unacceptable to the post-1660 nobility, with their determination to keep ecclesiastics in their place. At the same time, bitter experience of the absolutism of James Stuart, for an unlucky minority during his vice-regality in the early 1680s, for most during the traumatic years of his reign after 1685, had left the Scots political class with a deep determination, should the opportunity ever occur, to see an end of absolute sovereignty as defined by James, and above all as interpreted and manipulated by the Drummond brothers, Perth and Melfort, who had contrived to establish an unbreakable grip on the regime, by cleverly exploiting the prejudices and confusions of an absentee sovereign.

The fact is that even those who were to take a leading role in the first Jacobite episode in Scottish history, which took the form of a rebellion against the regime of the Estates who had taken up the reins of power after the flight of James, shared the two main assumptions of this consensus. Colin, Earl of Balcarres, who would have controlled the civil administration of a Jacobite Scotland, on the strength of a commission from the despairing King James issued just before that monarch's successful flight to France, was an old and bitter opponent of Perth and Melfort. Unlike those two leaders of the Roman Catholic convert interest, Balcarres was the staunchest of Protestant Episcopalians in 1688–90, and he was determined to overthrow the tiny Catholic clique that James had allowed to dominate the Scottish executive. Balcarres always said before the Revolution that "the King intended him to succeed Melfort, being even then convinced that men of that religion were incapable to serve him."[14]

---

[12] *An Apology For Sir James Dalrymple Of Stair, President Of The Session, By Himself* (Edinburgh, 1690; repr. Edinburgh, J. Ballantyne, 1825), pp. 8 and 5.

[13] *Historical Selections From The Manuscripts Of Sir John Lauder Of Fountainhall*, Volume First, "Historical Observations, 1680–1686" (Edinburgh, the Bannatyne Club, 1837), p. 249.

[14] Lindsay, *Lives of the Lindsays*, II, 156–58.

Even more interesting – and so misunderstood by the few historians who have noticed it – was the position of that other staunch Episcopalian, John Graham of Claverhouse, Viscount Dundee, the future military leader of the Jacobite rebellion of 1689. He sat as a member in the Convention of Estates of the Kingdom of Scotland which assembled in Edinburgh in March 1689 in response to circular letters issued by the Prince of Orange. Two days after it opened, the Convention passed an act declaring itself a free and lawful meeting of the Estates, on significant grounds:

> Forasmuch, as there is a letter from King James the seventh, presented to the Meeting of the Estates, they before opening thereof, Declare and Enact that, that notwithstanding of any thing that may be contained in that Letter for Dissolving them, or Impeding their Procedure; yet that they are a Free and Lawful Meeting of the Estates, and will continue undissolved, until they Settle and secure the Protestant Religion, the Government, Laws and Liberties of the Kingdom.

Peter Hume Brown, in the massive multivolume *History of Scotland*, with which he both established his own position as the leading historian of Scotland of his day, and established Scottish history as a legitimate academic study in the expanding history departments of early twentieth-century Scotland, noticing that even Dundee assented to this statement, described his act as "a stain on his scutcheon, which his own signature avouches."[15]

The inflated romantic language of Hume Brown is a clear warning that he is here the prisoner of a school of writing that propagated a tradition of chivalry and authority as an antidote to the seemingly endless social and political flux of nineteenth-century industrial society. Although his own Jacobite writings were notably well balanced, Sir Walter Scott was the founder of the school, and he was followed by many other men of the right in politics and religion who found the Jacobites suitable material from which to mold plaster saints. A glance at the list of signatures subscribed to the resolution of the Estates in question shows how unrealistic it is to berate Dundee for failing to live up to the expectation of his Victorian admirers. Three prelates of the still episcopal Kirk by Law Established signed it, and the bench of bishops was to prove Jacobite to a man.[16] Even if they kept him on his thrones, these conservative Episcopalians were determined to charge King James's conduct. After all, the resistance of the Seven Bishops and the threat of invasion from the Netherlands had earlier forced James to submit in England to an Anglican counter-revolution which had destroyed his power to subvert the Church of England. A parallel program in Scotland in 1689 was not unthinkable, merely implausible. It was most unlikely that James Stuart, if restored by a war in which he was already leaning heavily on support from French and Catholic Irish forces, would have been contrite towards his Protestant subjects or for that matter less autocratic in spirit. Dundee and Balcar-

---

[15] Peter Hume Brown, *History of Scotland* (3 vols., New York, Octagon, 1971), II, p. 442.

[16] "Act Declaring the Meeting of the Estates to be a free and lawful Meeting, March 16, 1689," printed in *The Acts and Orders of the Estates of the Kingdom of Scotland, Holden and begun at Edinburgh, the 14th Day of March 1689* (Edinburgh, Heirs and Successors of Andrew Anderson, 1690).

res left the Convention when it became clear that there would be no concessions to their views or ambitions, but it is significant that their attempt to organize a rival assembly in Stirling failed miserably. Nobody who mattered turned up, and the Edinburgh Convention had a point when it passed an Act summoning all the fencible men and militia of Scotland to be ready to resist the Jacobites in arms and added acidly that the Jacobite leaders had themselves concurred in the resolution "that the Estates would continue their Meeting undissolved, until they should Settle and Secure the Protestant Religion, the Government, Laws and Liberties of the Kingdom."[17]

Fortunately, Dundee proved incapable of plunging his country into a bloodbath on behalf of a political program which did not have much support. With his death and the subsequent rout of the Jacobite army, Scotland was spared the experience which James Grahame, Earl and later Marquis of Montrose, had contrived in the 1640s. Most members of the ruling class did very little in the crisis. It was passive disobedience, or just sheer passivity, which did more than anything else to ensure that James could not regain his Scottish crown. The Estates controlled the central government, while in the Highlands, where alone there was significant fighting, a small minority of active Jacobites were checkmated by an even smaller minority of active Williamites. The Williamites were eventually victorious, but they cannot be said to have fought under a very radical ideological banner. In his semi-official apologia for William's invasion of England, their leading intellectual, Burnet, had argued that it was designed to uphold the legal framework of monarchy. *The Enquiry Into the Measures of Submission To The Supream Authority* linked the existing law of property to the existing law of monarchy. It was easy, and convincing, to argue that both had to be defended from King James.

It is no accident that Burnet's rhetorical strategy, with its stress on the subversion of legal government by James, closely resembles that adopted by John Locke on a much larger scale in his *Two Treatises of Civil Government*. They came from the same exile circle and shared a perceived need to counter the known ability of King James to exploit the conservative instincts of the Scottish and English ruling classes after 1660 to paralyze their will to resist him. Thus Locke concludes his treatise, in sections he expected to leave a final impression on the reader, by leaning heavily on two early seventeenth-century royalist sources. One is His Late Sacred Majesty King James I, addressing the English parliaments of 1603 and 1609; the other is another Scot, much admired by King James I: William Barclay, civil lawyer, professor at French universities, and ardent apologist for absolute monarchy. Locke can point out that in his *De Regno et Regali Potestate*, published in Paris in 1600 and dedicated to Henry IV, Barclay admitted of rare circumstances where a king, by extreme behavior shattering the received legal frame, could unking himself and make resistance to his will legitimate. Just possibly, historians have overstressed Locke the systematic, if ambiguous, political thinker, and under-

---

[17] "Act for putting the Kingdom in a Posture of Defence. March, 19, 1689," *ibid.*, p. 5.

emphasized the fact that in the treatise he, like Burnet in his contemporary pamphlets, was a skilled political rhetorician trying to claw away from James that conservative constituency which abhorred radicalism, but which everyone knew had the power to make or break kings.

In the opening lines of their declaration of April 1689, which offered the crown of Scotland to William and Mary, the Estates of Scotland pointed out that James had assumed regal power without taking the usual coronation oath to uphold "the laudable laws," and had then used his absolutist pretensions to subvert due process of law in general. They concluded that he had "forefaulted" his right to the throne. This was not a radical but a conservative interpretation, drawn from technical feudal law. Fiefs were forefaulted, and God invested kings with their regal fiefs at their coronations, after they took appropriate oaths.[18] How, then, did the politics of post-Revolution Scotland become so bitter and polarized when the actual Revolution was marked by apathy on the part of the bulk of the political nation, and a cautious neo-feudalism on the part of the first apologists for the new regime? Obviously, both Burnet and the Estates were reaching out for a conservative consensus. Why did it fail to emerge?

Late seventeenth-century Scotland was like the early seventeenth-century England depicted by J. P. Somerville. It was a land where several different and conflicting political ideologists were available for use by different persons or, often enough, by the same person under different circumstances. Clergymen dependent on the king for placement and promotion tended to advocate and advance the king's absolutist views, and they found it difficult to abandon these views because their preaching and teaching publicly committed them.[19] The Episcopal clergy were to have a long and important career in Scotland as manufacturers and propagators of an ideology of indefeasible hereditary right, which helped nerve many an active rebel against the Hanoverian dynasty, but their views would not have mattered if a large section of the nobility and gentry had not been disaffected. The nobility of Restoration Scotland were deeply anticlerical. Even bishops were servants to be dismissed if their services ceased to give satisfaction.[20] Though the government of post-Revolution Scotland necessarily leaned heavily on an atypical group of returned Williamite exiles, they were able to rely on the tacit acquiescence of the bulk of the ruling class. Normally, political groups would slowly have increased their support of the regime as time sealed its success and saved their faces. To explain why this did not happen, it is essential to

---

[18] Gilbert Burnet, *An Enquiry Into the Measures of Submission to the Supream Authority And of the Grounds upon which it may be Lawful or necessary for Subjects, to defend their Religion, Lives, and Liberties.* (London, 1688); Locke, *Two Treatises,* pp. 417–18, and 437–43; "1689 Claim of Right," repr. in Gordon Donaldson (ed.), *Scottish Historical Documents* (Edinburgh, Scottish Academic Press, 1970), pp. 252–58; for the technical meaning of "forefault," see under "forfaultry" in *The Oxford English Dictionary,* 2nd edn. (Oxford University Press, 1989), VI, p. 66.

[19] J. P. Somerville, *Politics and Ideology in England, 1603–1640* (London and New York, Longman, 1986), esp. pp. 10–12.

[20] It will be clear that the author of the present essay would like to think that this constitutes a significant refinement rather than a repudiation of his contribution on "The Scottish Episcopal Clergy and the Ideology of Jacobitism" to Eveline Cruickshanks (ed.), *Ideology and Conspiracy: Aspects of Jacobitism, 1689–1759* (Edinburgh, John Donald, 1982), pp. 36–48.

grasp just how early disillusionment set in with William of Orange in Scotland and to understand that the core of the complaint was that his administration represented an attempt to preserve much that was most obnoxious about the absolutism associated with James VII. Major-General Hugh Mackay of Scourie, the shrewd but blunt soldier who commanded William's forces in Scotland during Dundee's rising, managed to get through the war on the simple assumption that William's was that of Protestantism and the liberties of Europe. General officers are not noted for subtle political views, but Mackay wrote to George Melville, first Earl of Melville, who effectively ran the Williamite government of Scotland, and said in July 1689 that he thought the Dalrymples, Lord Stair and his son Sir John, should voluntarily lay down the offices they had accepted from William, because their presence in office was incredibly offensive to most Scots who "are persuaded that the tyme of their full delyvrance from the slavery which was imposed upon them by the Ministers of State during the late reignes is cum, if his Majestie were rightly informed."[21]

As we have already seen, Stair himself indignantly answered this, asserting that few had suffered as much as he and survived during the reign of King James. However, he admitted in the same reply that he was disliked as much for his role in the high-handed, arrogant ministerial tyranny imposed on Scotland in the reign of Charles II by his associate and patron, the Duke of Lauderdale. English Whigs such as Russell has always feared and detested Lauderdale on the ground that his regime in Scotland was a precedent and warning to England. Lois Schwoerer is correct in suggesting that his English critics misunderstood the implications of some of Lauderdale's Scottish policies, and especially the legislation that he sponsored on the Scottish militia, but the critics were not at all misguided as to the spirit of administration in Scotland under the duke: it was an extreme example of what Mackay called "the slavery which was imposed upon them by the Ministers of State."[22]

William's retention in office of Stair's son, Sir John Dalrymple, was deeply offensive, and his role, as Master of Stair, in the Massacre of Glencoe in 1692, though beyond the scope of this essay, confirmed what staunch Revolution Whigs like Andrew Fletcher of Saltoun said at the time: nothing had changed, for this was the style of the ministers of James VII. More immediately relevant is the apparently baffling record of one of the most apparently committed Scots Revolution Whigs, Robert Ferguson, the likely author of the attacks that provoked Stair to reply in print. He was a Scot who had made an ecclesiastical career in England until expelled for nonconformity at the

---

[21] Major-General Hugh Mackay, *Memoirs of the War Carried on in Scotland and Ireland* (Edinburgh, 1833), *passim*. For Mackay's views on the damage done by the presence in office of the Dalrymples, see Mackay to Melville, July 24, 1689, printed in *ibid.*, pp. 246–48.

[22] Lois G. Schwoerer, *Lady Rachel Russell: "One of the Best of Women"* (Baltimore and London, Johns Hopkins University Press, 1988), pp. 74, 89; *No Standing Armies* (Baltimore and London, Johns Hopkins University Press, 1974), pp. 105, 109. That the militia systems of Restoration Scotland were designed to keep effective coercive power in Scotland in the hands of the nobility is the theme of a paper by Bruce P. Lenman, "Militia, Fencible Men and Home Defence" in Norman MacDougall (ed.), *Scotland and War* (Edinburgh, John Donald, 1991), pp. 170–92).

Restoration, after which he became a bitter foe of Stuart absolutism, a close friend of Lord Shaftesbury (he was with him when he died in exile in 1683), and a supporter of both Exclusion and assassination as answers to the impending accession of the Catholic James to the British thrones. After backing Monmouth's unsuccessful 1685 rising, in which he was alleged to have penned its very radical manifesto, he fled to the Netherlands, but returned with William in 1688. In 1689, he published two pamphlets which repay examination. One is devoted to the argument that in the immediate aftermath of the flight of James, the only practical solution is to put William on the English throne, in association with Mary. In it, this militant radical starts by saying that "The Consideration of Government in General, is none of my Province at this time." Though he obviously can, and does, make it clear that he regards doctrines of passive obedience and nonresistance as "Treason against the Constitution," his pamphlet is genuinely empirical, remarking that "it is impractical to establish . . . a Commonwealth where there is a numerous Nobility and Gentry, unless we should first destroy and extirpate them." From a man whose manifesto for Monmouth has been deemed the last trumpet call of the Good Old Cause of the Commonwealth, this was sober realism indeed.[23]

Ferguson's second pamphlet of that year is at first sight less interesting, for it is a violent blast on the No-Popery trumpet, clearly designed to rally all Protestants, and especially Dissenters, against King James. Insofar as he had a function in William's invasion, it was Ferguson's job to maintain contact with the Dissenting interest. Yet there runs through the text a recurring secular argument against absolutism as such. Ferguson remarks on the abuse of the legal system which was such a marked feature of the reign of James, adding almost casually that he thought Burnet rash to reply to his citation for treason, since any reply, however phrased, was bound to be twisted into further grounds for legal action by James and his minions. Ferguson was genuinely hostile to the whole doctrine and practice of absolutism. There are few more lapidary rejections of the ideas dearest to the heart of King James than the following:

> For though he be pleased to assume to himself an Absolute Power, which all are bound to obey without reserve, and in the virtue of which he suspends, stops and Disables what laws he pleaseth, yet I do not know . . . why we may not enter our plea and demur to the dictates of his Judgement.[24]

Yet, by the end of 1690, Ferguson was involved with a group of Scots politicians who, under the leadership of Sir James Montgomerie of Skelmorlie, were actively intriguing with the exiled Jacobite court in France.

---

[23] Robert Ferguson, *A Brief Justification Of The Prince Of Orange's Descent into England, And of the Kingdoms late Recourse to Arms. With a Modest Disquisition of what may Become the Wisdom and Justice of the Ensuing Convention in their Disposal of the Crown* (London, 1689), pp. 5, 9, 23.

[24] Robert Ferguson, *A Representation Of The Threatening Dangers, Impending Over Protestants in Great Britain, Before the Coming of His Highness the Prince of Orange* (London, 1689), Postscript, pp. 53–54.

It was a pattern that characterized Ferguson to the end of his ambiguous life. He was arrested on the eve of the possible Jacobite invasion of England in 1692; was suspected of involvement in the Lancashire plot of 1694; was certainly somehow involved with his fellow-countryman Sir George Barclay, who masterminded the unsuccessful bid to assassinate William in 1696; and at the very end of his career clashed with another devious individual, Simon Fraser, Lord Lovat, when the latter tried to slander leading Scots Whigs as crypto-Jacobites in the opening years of the eighteenth century in the episode known as the "Scotch Plot." The sort of adjectives which seemed to fly around this much arrested, never convicted man were "false, scandalous, and seditious." Historians find him an enigma,[25] as they do Montgomerie.

They need not, for the key has been in their hands since James Halliday published his excellent article in 1966, explaining what Montgomerie and his political associates, known as "the Club," were trying to achieve in 1689–90. It is regrettable that more recent and more massively documented work has failed to develop Halliday's insights, indeed has tried to bury them under the charge that all late seventeenth-century Scottish politics demonstrate is rampant faction. By 1689, William had made it clear that he positively liked the main features of Stuart government in Scotland. He was reluctant to repeal the Act of Supremacy, which even Archbishop Leighton saw reduced the kirk to a degraded royal footstool. The lay patronage that went with the Act seemed equally desirable to William, as did the Committee of the Articles that the Stuarts had used to control and manipulate the Scots Estates or parliament. He meant to continue the tradition of governing Scotland with ministers chosen with scant attention to the feelings of the lieges, and in the persons of the Dalrymples, tried and tested tools of tyranny, he had made choices that left nobody in doubt as to the temper of his rule.[26]

There was little hope of salvation in the structures of contemporary political theories. When he addressed the Lords of Justiciary, Scotland's supreme central criminal court, in January 1690, Justice-General Robert Kirk, fourth Earl and first Marquess of Lothian, more or less said so, dismissing first the idea that climate or fertility determined the fate of nations, arguing that some of the most fortunate countries in these respects were profoundly susceptible to "Misery, Slavery, and Bondage." Lord Lothian also deprecated too much stress on "the goodness of the Laws" on the ground that even pagans could claim to have excelled in this respect. To his lawyer's mind the important task was to establish confidence in the existence of a spirit of equity in the administration of the laws, but to do so it was essential to keep that

---

[25] There is a useful account of Ferguson in *DNB*. See also James Ferguson, *Robert Ferguson the Plotter; or, the Secret of the Rye-House Conspiracy and the Story of a Strange Career* (Edinburgh, D. Douglas, 1887).

[26] James Halliday, "The Club and the Revolution in Scotland 1689–90," *Scottish Historical Review* 45 (1966), 143–59. Most unfortunately, the formidable scholarship of P. W. J. Riley in *King William and the Scottish Politicians* (Edinburgh, John Donald, 1979), it organized around the blackest of legends regarding the Scots nobility. Similar criteria applied to English politicians of this period would presumably compel Dr. Riley to conclude that England would have been well rid of its representative institutions.

administration out of the hands of those whom "Luxury, Pride, and Covetousness have rendered such fit Tools for Tyrannical and Arbitrary Men."[27]

Lothian somewhat underestimated the potential of specific laws, but his distrust of theory was shrewd. What dedicated Whig enemies of executive tyranny like Montgomerie and Ferguson did when faced by the intransigence of William was to recreate, by a heroic display of tactical and intellectual flexibility, the nonideological or transideological consensus that had destroyed the tyranny of James Stuart's ministers in Scotland, and turn it against the unacceptable face of the regime of Dutch William. To destroy "the Club" William had to accept its program. Just as the English Bill of Rights was a watered-down version of a radical Whig program swallowed reluctantly by William at a time when it was clear his regime was dangerously unpopular in England,[28] so were the great concessions that dismantled Stuart absolutism in Scotland reluctant concessions to stark necessity. William was able to turn Montgomerie and other conspirators into hunted fugitives, for the tactical alliance that gave them political victory was necessarily treasonable, and, of course, he made the consessions partly because he hoped to take them all back by means of an incorporating union that would deprive the Scots nation of any serious control over its government. It is no accident that incorporating union was both the first and the last theme William harped on in his dealings with Scotland. Still, even a temporary reversal of the sustained attempt by the British government to deprive the events of 1688 of any long-term significance was a remarkable achievement. In the Roman mode, which they would have appreciated, a Scots historian may be forgiven for concluding that men like Montgomerie and Ferguson deserved well of the republic.

[27] "The Earl of Lothian, Justice-General of the Kingdom of Scotland, his Discourse to the Lords of the Justiciary, at the opening of the Court at Edinburgh, January the 27th 1690," printed in E. W. M. Balfour-Melville (ed.), *An Account Of The Proceedings Of The Estates in Scotland 1689–90* (Scottish History Society, 3rd series, vol. XLVII, Edinburgh, 1955), II, 97–99.
[28] Lois G. Schwoerer, *The Declaration of Rights, 1689* (Baltimore and London, Johns Hopkins University Press, 1981), pp. 275–85.

16

The Glorious Revolution and the British Empire 1688–1783

Jack P. Greene

Any examination of the meaning of the Glorious Revolution for the newest and most distant members of the vast extended polity that comprised the English Empire at the end of the seventeenth century must confront three related questions. First is the question that, in one way or another, is being addressed by all of the essays in this volume: what precisely was the Glorious Revolution? Second is the question of the immediate context and impact of the Glorious Revolution in the colonies. Third is the question of the long-range significance of the Revolution for the extending anglophone or, after 1707, British Empire.[1]

Few historians of metropolitan Britain – the core areas of England, Wales, and Scotland – have much concerned themselves with either the second or the third of these questions, and most colonial historians who have interested themselves in the meaning of the Glorious Revolution for the colonies have concentrated upon the years immediately surrounding it, upon the contemporary uprisings in Massachusetts, New York, and Maryland, and on relationships between metropolis and colonies during the decades immediately before and after. In the process, they have neither sought to refine nor to extend definitions of the Revolution borrowed from historians of the metropolis nor shown much interest in exploring the long-term implications of the Revolution and the revolutionary settlement for the proliferating polities of colonial British America. In the interest of trying to achieve some broader perspective on the Glorious Revolution and its meaning for the larger anglophone world, this essay will focus primarily upon those long-term implications. In the process, it will examine how the consensual basis of governance within the extended polity of the British Empire contributed to produce and sustain in the distant polities in America and Ireland interpretations of the significance of the Glorious Revolution that diverged sharply from those that emerged in metropolitan Britain.

Before launching into this extensive subject, however, it will be useful to

---

[1] The argument and materials presented here are largely drawn from the author's recent book, *Peripheries and Center: Constitutional Development in the Extended Polities of the British Empire and the United States, 1607–1788* (Athens, University of Georgia Press, 1986).

explore some of the ramifications of the rather complex recent historiography on the immediate context and impact of the Glorious Revolution in the colonies. The view that seems to be emerging from this historiography is, for the most part, a success story – for the metropolis. In this interpretation, the Glorious Revolution was little more than a stage in the successful effort, begun under Charles II, to consolidate the authority of the metropolitan government in the colonies.

The experiences of the two principal continental colonies have been cited to illustrate the wider dimensions and essential features of such an interpretation. Whereas Virginia, the oldest American colony, had already been forced fifteen years earlier in the wake of Bacon's Rebellion in 1676 to come to terms with post-Restoration English imperialism, Massachusetts, the most populous New England colony, was compelled in the immediate wake of the Revolution to accept a charter that made the governor, who drew his authority from England, far more powerful than the elected House of Representatives, which drew its authority from the towns, a revolutionary development that significantly altered both the spiritual and the secular worlds of Massachusetts. Nor in either colony did the centralizing impulse stop at the colonial capitals. In Massachusetts, as a result of the new charter, the town ostensibly lost authority to the provincial government. In Virginia, the elected House of Burgesses and the localities its members represented apparently lost power to the royally appointed council.[2]

Still other developments seem to provide support for this emerging view. In the wake of 1688–89, New York, New Jersey, Pennsylvania, and Maryland, all formerly private colonies, came under the immediate control of the crown, albeit Pennsylvania rather quickly and Maryland within a generation reverted to their proprietary owners. A new Navigation Act in 1696 broadly extended central control over the external trade of the colonies, and London officials proved generally and often successfully resistant to most efforts by colonial legislatures to secure for their constituents the principles of limited executive authority usually associated with the Glorious Revolution in England. Only where metropolitan representatives had obviously acted in outrageously arbitrary ways, as was the case in Jamaica with the Duke of Albemarle in 1688, did the crown show much concern for disciplining its agents for behavior that appeared to locals to violate the rights usually thought to have been confirmed to metropolitan English people by the Glorious Revolution. Moreover, what the Revolution and the Revolutionary settlement left undone in this centralizing process, the wars of the next quarter century apparently accomplished, several scholars having emphasized how the intercolonial wars of 1689–1713 heightened colonial dependence on the center.[3]

[2] These developments are treated most extensively in Stephen Saunders Webb, *1676: the End of American Independence* (New York, Knopf, 1984); and Richard R. Johnson, *Adjustment to Empire: the New England Colonies, 1675–1715* (New Brunswick, N.J., Rutgers University Press, 1981).
[3] David S. Lovejoy, *The Glorious Revolution in America* (New York, Harper and Row, 1972); J. M. Sosin, *English America and the Revolution of 1688: Royal Administration and the Structure of Provincial Government* (Lincoln, University of

From studies of these subjects as well as from a variety of analyses of other aspects of metropolitan–colonial relations during earlier and later periods can be constructed a broad interpretive framework that seems to be gaining considerable scholarly support. According to this framework, an extraordinary devolution of authority outwards to the new colonial peripheries during the first half of the seventeenth century was followed by a gradual resumption of that authority between the Restoration and the middle decades of the eighteenth century as a result of several related developments: the imposition of the Navigation Acts; the royalization of many private colonies; the establishment of successful patronage networks running between the metropolis and the colonies; the expansion of the royal bureaucracy; growing colonial dependence upon the metropolis for defense; and what one scholar has referred to as the "gradual and grudging adjustment [on the part of colonists] to imperial membership and monarchical rule." What had been a loose congeries of political entities before 1660 slowly during the century thereafter became integrated into a large imperial framework with London at its center and the metropolitan political nation as its presiding force in a worldwide conflict of political empires.[4]

Although much can be said in favor of this line of interpretation, an examination of the long-range effects of the Glorious Revolution upon the wider British Empire suggests that it had been carried vastly too far. Such an examination will first require a general consideration of those domestic features of the Revolution that seem to have had particular saliency for the wider imperial polity.

For English people, at least for those of a Whig persuasion, the Glorious Revolution more than anything else represented a victory for law and liberty, for limited *and* representative government. As a result of the Revolution, the king's power within England was circumscribed and the principle of coordination, the idea of the king as one of three branches of parliament, each with coordinate authority, was enshrined as the new orthodoxy. As Jennifer Carter has observed, England now "had a monarch depending on a parliamentary title, and a constitution based on law." The "two salient features of the post-Revolution constitution were, first, that however much it was disguised a parliamentary monarchy had replaced a divine right

Nebraska Press, 1982); and I. K. Steele, *Politics of Colonial Policy: the Board of Trade in Colonial Administration 1696–1720* (Oxford, Clarendon Press, 1968).

    [4] On these developments, see, in addition to the works cited in note 3, A. P. Thornton, *West-India Policy under the Restoration* (Oxford, Clarendon Press, 1956); Philip Haffenden, "The Crown and the Colonial Charters, 1675–1688," *William and Mary Quarterly*, 3rd series, 14 (1958), 297–311, 452–66; Michael G. Hall, *Edward Randolph and the American Colonies, 1676–1703* (Chapel Hill, University of North Carolina Press, 1960); Richard S. Dunn, "Imperial Pressures on Massachusetts and Jamaica, 1675–1700," in Alison Gilbert Olson and Richard Maxwell Brown (eds.), *Anglo-American Political Relations, 1675–1775* (New Brunswick, N.J., Rutgers University Press, 1970), pp. 50–75; and James M. Henretta, *"Salutory Neglect": Colonial Administration under the Duke of Newcastle* (Princeton University Press, 1972). The quotation is from Richard R. Johnson, "The Glorious Revolution in the Context of the Search for Atlantic Empire: the Example of John Nelson," unpublished paper presented at a conference on "The Glorious Revolution in America – three hundred years after," April 30, 1988, p. 13.

monarchy; and, secondly, [that] since 1689 the monarch had somehow learned to live with Parliament."[5]

Of course, as many scholars have emphasized, these developments were by no means a "foregone conclusion" at the time of the Glorious Revolution. Only gradually over the next half century did parliament grow from what Burke subsequently called "a mere representative of the people, and a guardian of popular privileges for its own immediate constituents ... into a mighty sovereign," from a body that was not simply "a control on the crown on its own behalf" to one that, as Burke put it, "communicated a sort of strength to the royal authority." As several historians have recently stressed, the "concept of a sovereign parliament" had not been "reasonably foreseeable in 1689," was largely "a development of the mid-eighteenth century," and was only just "hardening into an orthodoxy" during the 1760s. By the latter date, however, this great constitutional change was virtually complete, and one of its primary effects, as Harry Dickinson has noted, was to transform the ancient "doctrine of non-resistance from a buttress of divine right monarchy into the strongest defence of an existing constitution, whatever form it might take."[6]

But the historians' conventional preoccupation with national events and central institutions and their focus upon the ascendancy of parliament within Britain and the eventual triumph of the doctrine of parliamentary omnipotence during the mid-eighteenth century has perhaps tended to obscure a second important result of the Glorious Revolution and the broad political and constitutional settlement that came in its wake, a result that had particularly important implications for the governance of the most distant portions of the empire.

The rise of parliament may have been the most important result of that Revolution, but it was by no means the only one. Within Britain, as Carter has pointed out, another consequence of the Revolution was "a distinct, though not complete, withdrawal of central authority from local affairs." Earlier in the seventeenth century, Charles I had undertaken an extensive effort to exert the authority of the central government over county and local affairs in both the civil and religious realms. Although this effort had been interrupted during the Civil War, the later Stuarts resumed it after the Restoration. "Perhaps nothing done in the 1680s by Charles II and James II," Carter has noted, "caused so much reaction against them as their inter-ference with local privilege and the accustomed pattern of existing hierarchies – in counties, in corporations, or in university colleges."[7]

[5] Jennifer Carter, "The Revolution and the Constitution," in Geoffrey Holmes (ed.), *Britain after the Glorious Revolution, 1689–1715* (London and New York, Macmillan and St. Martin's Press, 1969), pp. 40, 47.

[6] *Ibid.*, p. 55; Edmund Burke, "Letter to the Sheriffs of Bristol," in *The Works of Edmund Burke* (16 vols., London, F. C. J. Rivington, 1815–27), III, p. 188; H. T. Dickinson, "The Eighteenth-century Debate on the Sovereignty of Parliament," *Transactions of the Royal Historical Society*, 5th series, 26 (1976), 189, and "The eighteenth-century debate on the "Glorious Revolution," *History* 61 (1976), 33, 39; Barbara A. Black, "The Constitution of the Empire: the Case for the Colonists," *University of Pennsylvania Law Review* 124 (1976), 1210–11; John Phillip Reid, *In Defiance of the Law: the Standing-Army Controversy, the Two Constitutions, and the Coming of the American Revolution* (Chapel Hill, University of North Carolina Press, 1981).

[7] Carter, "The Revolution and the Constitution," p. 53.

At least in the short run, the Glorious Revolution effectively put a brake upon this centralizing effort and thereby created the conditions necessary for "the typical eighteenth-century situation of gentry and aristocratic independence in the localities." Within Britain, the localities, along with the people who dominated them, enjoyed much less interference from the central government during the first half of the eighteenth century than they had at any time under the Stuart monarchy. Especially under the Hanoverians, the establishment and cultivation of extensive patronage networks by the center helped to mitigate the centrifugal tendencies that flowed out of this situation and to enhance the power of London. But during the eighty years following the Glorious Revolution, Britain may very well have experienced a significant redistribution of power – a devolution of authority – to the localities, as English, Welsh, and (after 1707) Scottish counties came close to resembling what the sociologist Edward Shils in another context has referred to as "pockets of approximate independence."[8]

To what extent and in what ways these two broad domestic results of the Glorious Revolution affected the many outlying polities that composed the empire is not a subject that has received much attention from historians. Recent literature on the immediate effects of the Revolution would seem to imply that they were by no means powerfully evident outside the home islands. If the Glorious Revolution had guaranteed that Britain would thenceforth have a constitution of principled limitation and government by consent, if it had made it clear that English kings would thereafter, as the Massachusetts lawyer James Otis later declared, be "made for the good of the people, and not the people for them," the same apparently was not true for the king's American polities.[9]

That the Revolution did little to stem the activities of an aggressive metropolitan government bent upon consolidating English authority in the New World seems to be confirmed by that government's continuing insistence upon asserting a level of prerogative power in the colonies that, in the wake of the Revolution, had been much eroded in England, where parliament effectively acted to impose explicit restrictions upon royal authority. But metropolitan administrators never consented to extend those restrictions to the colonies. With parliament taking no role in the internal governance of the colonies, crown officials were free to continue to claim wide prerogative powers there. Thus, long after the crown had stopped vetoing laws and given up its rights to prorogue and dissolve legislative bodies and determine the

[8] *Ibid.*, T. H. Breen, *Puritans and Adventurers: Change and Persistence in Early America* (New York, Oxford University Press, 1980), pp. 4–24; Edward Shils, *Center and Periphery: Essays in Macrosociology* (University of Chicago Press, 1975), p. 10. See also Norma Landau, *Justices of the Peace, 1679–1760* (Berkeley and Los Angeles, University of California Press, 1984), on the continuing independence of county elites in regard to the internal affairs of the counties; and E. P. Thompson, "The Grid of Inheritance: a Comment," in Jack Goody, Joan Thirsk, and E. P. Thompson (eds.), *Family and Inheritance: Rural Society in Western Europe, 1200–1800* (Cambridge University Press, 1976), pp. 328–360, on the "tenacity and force of local custom" in determining patterns of social and legal relations in English local society.

[9] James Otis, *A Vindication of the Conduct of the House of Representatives of the Province of Massachusetts-Bay* (Boston, 1762), p. 18.

frequency of their meetings, to dismiss judges at pleasure, and to create courts in Britain itself, it continued to claim and in many cases actually to exercise such authority for its governors in the colonies.[10]

Yet the argument that the achievements of the Glorious Revolution did not apply to the colonies can be sustained only by ignoring a mass of evidence from the colonies. In 1688–89, the Revolution was widely, if by no means exclusively, interpreted in the colonies as a victory for the security of the rights of Englishmen not just in the metropolis but throughout the English-speaking world, a victory, moreover, that some colonists, at least in Maryland, New York, and Massachusetts, had helped to gain through a common struggle against oppressive royal officials who, no less than their Stuart masters at home, appeared to have been agents of arbitrary government. Indeed, the Revolution seems to have supplied a new intensity to efforts by colonial legislatures, previously stimulated by the centralizing efforts of the later Stuarts, to secure explicit written guarantees of their constituents' rights to English liberties and privileges. Between 1688 and 1696, the legislatures of at least seven colonies tried to pass measures in imitation of parliament's 1689 Declaration of Rights.[11]

Notwithstanding the continuing resistance of crown officials to any efforts to limit the royal prerogative in the colonies, their behavior following the Glorious Revolution made it clear that the events of 1688–89 had effectively settled the question of representative government in the colonies in favor of the colonists. Although representative institutions had been an integral part of colonial governance since 1619, metropolitan officials under James II had moved strongly in the mid-1680s in the direction of abolishing them altogether by bringing all of the New England colonies together in the unrepresentative Dominion of New England. But the New Englanders had overthrown the Dominion in 1689, and neither William III nor his advisors showed any disposition to revive it or to govern the colonies without representative assemblies. Not, in fact, until the nature of the empire changed in the nineteenth century did the home government again think of trying to govern settler colonies without representative institutions.

Other developments had similar results. Although the new Massachusetts charter of 1691 placed significant limitations upon the colony's traditional self-governing powers, it also provided the colony with greater self-governing privileges than were then enjoyed by any royal colony, and the return of Pennsylvania to William Penn in 1694 revealed both the new government's more respectful attitude towards charters and the limits of the metropolitan movement to royalize proprietary and corporate colonies. Following the Glorious Revolution, in fact, the campaign for a consolidated empire, for the

---

[10] See Bernard Bailyn, *The Origins of American Politics* (New York, Knopf, 1968), pp. 66–71.

[11] See Jack P. Greene, *Great Britain and the American Colonies, 1606–1763* (Columbia, University of South Carolina Press, 1970), pp. xiii–xli; A. Berriedale Keith, *Constitutional History of the First British Empire* (Oxford, Clarendon Press, 1930), pp. 141–42; Lovejoy, *Glorious Revolution*; Nuala Zahadieh, "The Glorious Revolution in Jamaica," unpublished paper presented at a conference on "The Glorious Revolution in America – three hundred years after," April 30, 1988.

retrenchment of local authority in the colonies through the elimination of private colonies, securing permanent revenues, and restricting the authority of colonial legislatures was desultory, sporadic, unsustained, and, at best, only modestly successful.

Why this campaign was not more sustained and successful is a question that has a direct bearing upon the larger problem of the meaning of the Glorious Revolution for the peripheries of the empire. This question can be explained partly in terms of ideology and partly in terms of the necessary structure of governance within the empire. Within the metropolitan political establishment, the ideological commitment to limited governance and to the sanctity of private and corporate rights, a commitment that was reinforced by the conception of the British polity confirmed by the Glorious Revolution, obviously served as a powerful restraint upon metropolitan behavior towards the colonies.

Probably even more important were the nature and sources of metropolitan authority in those portions of the empire that lay outside the home islands. In the early 1720s, in a passage in *Cato's Letters* that many writers on the colonies later found appropriate for quotation, John Trenchard and Thomas Gordon remarked that distant colonies could be kept dependent upon their parent states either "by Force" or by "using them well."[12] Unlike most later and ostensibly similar political entities, however, the early modern British Empire was emphatically not held together by force. The few military units stationed in America before the mid-1750s were intended not to police but to defend the colonies, and British political society was strongly averse to paying for expeditionary forces to intervene in the colonies' domestic affairs. Bacon's Rebellion in 1676 was the last – and the only – time before the late 1760s that London authorities employed such an expedient. At least to some extent, British political society following the Glorious Revolution also found the use of force to intervene in local affairs ideologically uncongenial.

Without a much larger force that they either had or could afford to have in the colonies, the British government thus had no choice in its efforts to maintain its authority there than, in Trenchard's and Gordon's words, to use them (the colonies) well. That "public opinion sets bounds to every government," that no government could function, as Burke put it, "without regard to the general opinion of those who were to be governed," was a truism among early modern political theorists; and although those people who were most closely involved in colonial administration in London often demanded tighter controls over the colonies, the metropolitan government never during the seven decades following the Glorious Revolution made a concerted effort to govern the colonies in ways that were at serious variance with colonial opinion.[13]

Just as the lack of troops in the colonies meant that metropolitan authority

---

[12] John Trenchard and Thomas Gordon, *Cato's Letters* (4 vols., London, 1724), III, p. 286.

[13] James Madison, "Public Opinion," December 19, 1791, in Gaillard Hunt (ed.), *The Writings of James Madison*, (9 vols., New York, G. P. Putnam's Sons, 1900–10), VI, p. 70; Burke, "Letter to the Sheriffs," in *Works*, III, p. 179.

was heavily dependent upon provincial opinion in its relations with the colonies, so the absence of elaborate and effective law-enforcement agencies within the colonies, as well as the widespread distribution of the franchise, meant that provincial polities had to adopt a similarly consensual mode of governance towards the localities, a mode that was necessarily highly sensitive to local interests and opinions. Except in those few places where local governing functions were handled by the provincial governments, as was the case only in the smaller island colonies and in low-country South Carolina before the 1770s, enormous political responsibility – and authority – thus devolved upon local governing institutions. To a not insignificant degree, then, effective government in the empire resided not in London, and not even in the colonial capitals, but in local communities – just as it did in England itself. In the early modern British Empire, imperial government was thus very largely provincial and local government.

Moreover, the small size of the public realm in the colonies and the powerful resistance to taxation to pay for expanding that realm meant that leadership and office holding were primarily voluntary rather than professional. In contrast to the situation in metropolitan Britain, the demands of war nowhere led either to the proliferation of civil and military offices nor to the development of elaborate systems of public credit presided over by an extensive and entrenched bureaucracy. For those reasons, the metropolitan patronage system in the colonies was not anywhere nearly so large as would seem to be suggested by the attention modern scholars have lavished upon it. There were fewer than 100 offices in the gift of the crown in the colonies in 1752 and, despite the creation of more than ten colonies during the intervening period, fewer than 200 in 1775. Failure to establish the sort of deep patronage networks that enabled London authorities to exert some degree of central control over localities in the home islands during the eighteenth century greatly inhibited a parallel development in the colonies.[14]

The scantiness of metropolitan coercive and utilitarian resources in the colonies necessarily meant that governance in the early modern British Empire was consensual and that metropolitan authority was heavily dependent upon whatever normative resources in the form of loyalty and patriotic attachment the crown could command. The intense British patriotism of the colonists thoughout the American sections of the empire in the decades immediately before the American Revolution has been well documented. What has been much less studied is the great extent to which the strength of that patriotism in the colonies depended upon the continuing

---

[14] List of Offices in the American Colonies, the nomination to which was vested in the Board of Trade by Order in Council of March 11, 1752, Chatham Papers, PRO 30/8/95, PRO, London; a List of Offices in the North American and West Indian Colonies, 1775, William L. Clements Library, Ann Arbor, Michigan. Among scholars who have stressed the importance of patronage in colonial political life are Alison Gilbert Olson, *Anglo-American Politics 1660–1775: the Relationship Between Parties in England and Colonial America* (London and New York, Oxford University Press, 1973); Stanley Nider Katz, *Newcastle's New York: Anglo-American Politics, 1732–1753* (Cambridge, Mass., Belknap Press of Harvard University Press, 1968); John A. Schutz, *William Shirley: King's Governor of Massachusetts* (Chapel Hill, University of North Carolina Press, 1961); and Henretta, "*Salutary Neglect.*"

credibility of the colonists' belief that they shared in the legacy of the Glorious Revolution. Epitomized by the enjoyment of limited and representative government, by a high degree of local control over local affairs, and by a respect for the customary rights and privileges of corporate entities like the colonies, that legacy was chiefly what throughout the eighteenth century made English liberty not only the envy of much of the western world but also the pride of Englishmen wherever they resided within the vast extended polity of the British Empire.[15]

If the maintenance of this pride among colonists was the main source of strength for metropolitan authority in the colonies, then that authority depended very heavily upon the restraint of metropolitan officials in trying to exert it. To a significant degree, London officials following the Glorious Revolution managed to retain, probably even to enhance, the authority of the center in the peripheries of the empire by acquiescing in the devolution of considerable power to provincial governments. Like the central government in Britain itself during the same period, those governments in turn exercised that power in cooperation with, and often in deference to, the opinions of strategic elites within the localities.

Notwithstanding the undeniable preference among metropolitan officials for a more centralized imperial system, then, their commitment to revolution principles – to limited government, government by consent, and local control – and their weak resources of control dictated that the same flow of authority from the center to the localities that took place in England following the Glorious Revolution would also occur in the empire at large. At least over the long haul, the devolution of authority that had begun with colonization in the early seventeenth century was not seriously arrested before the American Revolution, and the extraordinary localization of authority that occurred in Ireland, the West Indies, and the North American colonies after 1688 insured that it, in contrast to contemporary continental monarchies, Britain's expand-ing nation-state and overseas empire would emphatically *not* be founded on "methods of centralization and absolutism."[16]

In both Ireland and the American colonies, the wide and highly selective application of English common law by provincial and local courts and the growth of parliamentary institutions during the eighteenth century sym-bolized this development. Before the Glorious Revolution, the Irish Parlia-ment had convened only rarely. Though it met somewhat more frequently under Charles I, there were only three Irish Parliaments under Elizabeth and only one each under James I and Charles II. Between 1666 and 1692, it did not meet at all. Hence, as J. C. Beckett has noted, "The Irish parliament as we know it in the eighteenth century begins in 1692," when the ascendancy of the Protestant population as a result of the Revolution enabled it "to take a

---

[15] See Max Savelle, "Nationalism and other Loyalties in the American Revolution," *American Historical Review* 67 (1962), 901–23; Paul A. Varg, "The Advent of Nationalism, 1758–1776," *American Quarterly* 17 (1964), 160–81.
[16] Carter, "The Revolution and the Constitution," p. 56.

more independent line than formerly," while the insufficiency of the crown's hereditary revenues to meet the usual costs of government provided it with an opportunity "to assert its rights, even against England," in exchange for granting funds to make up the difference. As a result of these developments, the Irish parliament beginning in 1692 both met regularly and developed a vigorous "spirit of independence." Comparable developments took place throughout the colonies in America. Just as was the case in Ireland with the Irish Parliament during these years, the local legislatures in the colonies became more and more essential to – and more and more the centerpieces of – provincial governance in every established colony.[17]

For the development of the British Empire as a whole, then, perhaps the most important results of the Glorious Revolution were the localization of power, the growth of parliamentary institutions, and the entrenchment of the associated traditions of principled limitation and government by consent, not just within Britain but also in Ireland and the American colonies. Notwithstanding important distinctions between the British and Irish parliaments, on the one hand, and the colonial assemblies, on the other, the growth in the power of all these bodies during the eighteenth century depended upon the same circumstances: the crown's inability to cover either the normal costs of government or extraordinary wartime expenses without formal grants from local legislative bodies.[18]

Contrary to recent historiography, moreover, war may have functioned to hasten this process, not to retard it. Although the involvement of Massachusetts in the Seven Years War was probably more extensive than that of any colony, local government there, as the legal historian John Philip Reid has shown so forcefully, remained so strong that local authorities were repeatedly able to frustrate the designs of metropolitan officials during the 1760s and 1770s. To a very important extent, then, the British Empire in the 1760s and 1770s was still a loose congeries of political entities, each of which enjoyed such extensive authority over local affairs as to be, practically speaking, almost self-governing states.[19]

The colonists' experience over the long period from 1688 to the 1760s had thus taught them that, as one Marylander put it in the late 1740s, "since the Settlement made at the *Revolution*," the constitutions of the colonies, no less than that of Britain itself, had entered "*a new Aera*" in which "the main strong lines" of "the people's rights (including Americans)" had "been more particularly pointed out and established." In recent years, several scholars have suggested that in resisting parliamentary authority during the 1760s and

[17] J. C. Beckett, "The Irish Parliament in the Eighteenth Century," *Belfast National History and Philosophical Society Proceedings*, 2nd series, 4 (1955), 18–20.

[18] See Jack P. Greene, *The Quest for Power: the Lower Houses of Assembly in the Southern Royal Colonies, 1689–1776* (Chapel Hill, University of North Carolina Press, 1963).

[19] Alan Rogers, *Empire and Liberty: American Resistance to British Authority 1755–1763* (Berkeley and Los Angeles, University of California Press, 1974); John Phillip Reid, *In a Defiant Stance; the Conditions of Law in Massachusetts Bay, the Irish Comparison, and the Coming of the American Revolution* (University Park, Pennsylvania State University Press, 1977).

1770s, the American colonies were "reject[ing] the results of" the Glorious Revolution. Far from rejecting the results of the Glorious Revolution, the colonists simply assumed that they were entitled to *all* its benefits. As a result of the Revolution, they felt, their "Liberties & Constitution[s]" had been "secur'd & establish'd upon [just as] firm and lasting [a] foundation" as had been those of Britain, and, in their view, an important foundation for that establishment had been the significant devolution of authority to provincial governments throughout the empire.[20]

Historians have often and accurately described the anglophone world following the Glorious Revolution as an age of oligarchy. While this characterization is appropriate for all but the newest socio-polities in that world, it may well be misleading to the extent that it implies a cohesiveness or a centralization of authority within the larger extended polity of the empire. Even within Britain itself, and certainly within each of the many polities in the periphery of the empire, oligarchies were segmented by space and identified powerfully with specific places and with the structures and customs of authority and privilege appertaining to those places. Perhaps as much as the familiar association of liberty with Englishness, this identification among locality, authority, and liberty had, in the wake of the Glorious Revolution, been encouraged and sustained in the outermost polities of the wider anglophone world by the devolution process that did so much both to shape the separate polities in that world and to determine the character of relations among them.

To appreciate the deepest significance of this process in the era after the Glorious Revolution, it is useful, I would suggest, to understand that, in a fundamentally important sense, it extended well beyond the mere devolution of political authority from metropolis to provinces and from provinces to localities. By permitting individuals to exercise only lightly regulated control over their own lives and fortunes, it extended as well to individual freeholds and estates, even to individuals themselves, a development exemplified by the fetish for personal independence that was so powerful in eighteenth-century Britain and British America. It might even be suggested that this devolution of authority to the individual self went far deeper among the free population of America because of the much broader achievement of *independence* as a result of the wider dispersion of property among free people and the widespread diffusion of *dependence* through the proliferating institution of chattel slavery.

Not surprisingly, in view of these developments, the metropolitan assertion of the doctrine of parliamentary supremacy as it was newly articulated in reference to the colonies in 1764–65 seemed, to many colonials, to represent "a total contradiction to every principle laid down at the time of the

---

[20] A Freeholder, *Maryland Gazette* (Annapolis), March 16, 1748; Alison Gilbert Olson, "Parliament, Empire, and Parliamentary Law, 1776" in J. G. A. Pocock (ed.), *Three British Revolutions: 1641, 1688, 1776* (Princeton University Press, 1980), p. 289; C[hristopher] G[adsden], *South Carolina Gazette* (Charleston), December 17, 1764; *New York Gazette* (New York), October 21, 1734.

[Glorious] Revolution, as the rules by which the rights and privileges of every branch of our legislature were to be governed for ever." Indeed, by its insistence upon exerting a "*supreme* jurisdiction" over the colonies, parliament seemed, to colonial spokesmen, not merely to be violating the most essential principles of the Glorious Revolution but actually to have assumed and to be acting upon precisely the same "high prerogative doctrine[s]" against which that Revolution had been undertaken. Thus, the colonists believed, if, by resisting parliament, they had become rebels, they were "rebels in the same way, and for the same reasons that the people of Britain were rebels, for supporting the [Glorious] Revolution."[21]

That is, they were merely acting to defend the rights they had long enjoyed as a result of the same devolution of authority to the localities, the same expansion of legislative power, and the same elaboration of customary legal traditions and institutions that had occurred in Britain itself following the Glorious Revolution. For the colonists, then, the Glorious Revolution signaled the rise not just of the British parliament but of provincial parliament*s* in every polity within the empire. If, as the colonists and many people in the metropolis believed, the most important legacy of the Glorious Revolution was freedom from arbitrary government, then the metropolitan efforts of the 1760s and early 1770s seemed to be nothing less than an attempt to deprive the colonists of any share in that legacy.

Unrestrained by domestic and international circumstances that made island colonies in the Atlantic and the Caribbean, Nova Scotia, Quebec, and the Floridas dependent upon the metropolis for defense, the leaders of the thirteen rebellious colonies in 1776 could thus without the slightest logical legerdemain undertake an American Revolution in the conviction that it was necessary to secure for their inhabitants the guarantees of the Glorious Revolution, guarantees that were seen to be under assault from a British parliament and an aggressive ministry bent upon governing the colonies in the arbitrary high-prerogative mode associated with the later Stuarts. In the historical circumstances that sustained this conviction, perhaps, lies the deepest meaning of the Glorious Revolution for the early modern British Empire, and especially for those colonies that seceded from that empire in 1776.

[21] John Dickinson, *An Essay on the Constitutional Power of Great Britain over the Colonies in America* (Philadelphia, 1774), repr. in Samuel Hazard (ed.), *Pennsylvania Archives* (138 vols., Philadelphia, Harrisburg, Pa., 1852–), 2nd series, III, p. 565; *An Argument in Defence of the Exclusive Right Claimed by the Colonies to Tax Themselves* (London, 1774), p. 104; "An Apology for the late Conduct in America," *London Gazeteer*, April 7, 1774, in Peter Force (ed.), *American Archives* (9 vols., Washington D.C., 1837–53), 4th series, I, p. 242; "To the Freemen of America," May 18, 1774, in *ibid.*, p. 336; (Hugh Baillie), *Some Observations on a Pamphlet Lately Published* (London, 1776), pp. 2–3.

Selected readings

Amussen, Susan D., *An Ordered Society: Gender and Class in Early Modern England*, Oxford, Basil Blackwell, 1988.

An Account of the Proceedings of the Estates in Scotland 1689–90, ed. E. W. M. Balfour-Melville, 2 vols., Scottish History Society, 3rd series, XLVI–XLVII, Edinburgh, T. and A. Constable, 1954–55.

Ashcraft, Richard, *Revolutionary Politics and Locke's Two Treaties of Government*, Princeton University Press, 1986.

Bailyn, Bernard, *The Origins of American Politics*, New York, Knopf, 1968.

Baxter, Stephen B., *William III*, London, Longman, Green, 1966.

Beattie, J. M., *Crime and the Courts in England, 1660–1800*, Princeton and Oxford, Oxford University Press, 1986.

Beddard, Robert, "Anti-popery and the London Mob, 1688," *History Today* 38 (1988), 36–39.

  (ed.), *A Kingdom without a King: the Journal of the Provisional Government in the Revolution of 1688*, Oxford, Phaidon, 1988.

Black, Barbara A., "The Constitution of the Empire: the Case for the Colonists," *University of Pennsylvania Law Review* 124 (1976), 1157–1211.

Buckroyd, Julia, *Church and State in Scotland 1660–1681*, Edinburgh, John Donald, 1980.

Cannadine, David, *Rituals of Royalty*, Cambridge University Press, 1987.

Canny, Nicholas, *Kingdom and Colony: Ireland in the Atlantic World, 1560–1800*, Baltimore and London, Johns Hopkins University Press, 1988.

Carswell, J., *The Descent on England. A Study of the English Revolution of 1688 in its European Background*, London, Cresset Press, 1969.

Childs, John C. R., *The Army, James II and the Glorious Revolution*, Manchester University Press, 1980.

  The British Army of William III, 1689–1702, Manchester University Press, and New York, St. Martin's Press, 1987.

Clarke, G. N., *The Dutch Alliance and the War against Trade, 1688–1697*, Manchester University Press, 1923.

Cockburn, J. S., *Calendar of Assize Records. Home Circuit Indictments, Elizabeth I and James I. Introduction*, London, HMSO, 1985.

Corvisier, André, *Louvois*, Paris, Fayard, 1983.

Cruickshanks, Eveline (ed.), *By Force or By Default? The Revolution of 1688–89*, Edinburgh, John Donald, 1989.

Cruickshanks, Eveline and Jeremy Black (eds.), *The Jacobite Challenge*, Edinburgh, John Donald, 1988.

D'Avaux, Jean Antoine de Mesmes, comte, *Négociations de Monsieur le Comte d'Avaux en Hollande*, 6 vols., Paris, 1752–54.

De Krey, Gary S., "London Radicals and Revolutionary Politics, 1675–1683," in Tim Harris, Paul Seaward, and Mark Goldie (eds.), *the Politics of Religion in Restoration England*, Oxford, Basil Blackwell, 1990, pp. 133–62.

A Fractured Society: the Politics of London in the First Age of Party, 1688–1715, Oxford, Clarendon Press, 1985.

Doebner, R. (ed.), *Memoirs of Mary, Queen of England (1689–1693), Together With Her Letters And Those Of Kings James II. and William III. To The Electress, Sophia of Hanover*, Leipzig, Veit, and London, D. Nutt, 1886.

Dunn, John, *The Political Thought of John Locke: an Historical Account of the Argument of the Two Treatises of Government*, Cambridge University Press, 1969.

Ekirch, A. Roger, *Bound for America. The Transportation of British Convicts to the Colonies, 1718–1775*, Oxford, Clarendon Press, 1987.

Ezell, Margaret J. M., *The Patriarch's Wife: Literary Evidence and the History of the Family*, Chapel Hill, University of North Carolina Press, 1987.

Ferguson, William, *Scotland 1689 to the Present*, The Edinburgh History of Scotland, 4 vols., Edinburgh and London, Oliver and Boyd, 1968, IV.

Fitzpatrick, Brendan, *Seventeenth Century Ireland: the Wars of Religion*, Dublin, Gill and Macmillan, 1988.

Fletcher, Andrew, of Saltoun, *Selected Political Writings and Speeches*, ed. David Daiches, Edinburgh, Scottish Academic Press, 1979.

Foster, R. F., *Modern Ireland, 1600–1972*, London, A. Lane, 1988.

Frankle, Robert J., "The Formulation of the Declaration of Rights," *HJ* 17 (1974), 265–79.

Geyl, P., *The Netherlands in the Seventeenth Century, Part II, 1648–1715*, London, Benn, and New York, Barnes and Noble, 1964.

Goldie, Mark, "The Roots of True Whiggism, 1688–1694," *History of Political Thought* 1 (1980), 195–236.

Greaves, Richard L., *Saints and Rebels: Seven Nonconformists in Stuart England*, Macon, Ga., Mercer University Press, 1985.

Greenberg, Janelle, "The Confessor's Laws and the Radical Face of the Ancient Constitution," *EHR* 104 (1989), 611–37.

Greene, Jack P., *Peripheries and Center: Constitutional Development in the Extended Polities of the British Empire and the United States, 1607–1788*, Athens, University of Georgia Press, 1986.

The Quest for Power: the Lower Houses of Assembly in the Southern Royal Colonies, 1689–1776, Chapel Hill, University of North Carolina Press, 1963.

Haley, K. H. D., "William III" (in English) in A. G. H. Bachrach, J. P. Sigmond, and A. J. Veenendael, Jr. (eds.), *Willem III: de stadhouder-koning en zijn tijd*, Amsterdam, De Bataafsche Leeuw, 1988, pp. 31–50.

The First Earl of Shaftesbury, Oxford University Press, 1968.

Harris, Tim, *London Crowds in the Reign of Charles II: Propaganda and Politics from the Restoration until the Exclusion Crisis*, Cambridge University Press, 1987.

Hatton, Ragnhild, *George I, Elector and King*, Cambridge, Mass., Harvard University Press, 1978.

(ed.), *Louis XIV and Europe*, London, Macmillan, and Columbus, Ohio State University, 1976.

Hay, Douglas, Peter Linebaugh, and E. P. Thompson, (eds.), *Albion's Fatal Tree: Crime and Society in Eighteenth Century England*, London, Allen Lane, and New York, Pantheon, 1975.

Henretta, James M., *"Salutary Neglect": Colonial Administration under the Duke of Newcastle*, Princeton University Press, 1972.

Herrup, Cynthia, *Participation and the Criminal Law in Seventeenth-Century England*, Cambridge University Press, 1987.

Hobsbawm, E. and T. Ranger (eds.), *The Invention of Tradition*, Cambridge University Press, 1983.

Holmes, Geoffrey (ed.), *Britain after the Glorious Revolution, 1689–1714*, London, Macmillan and New York, St. Martin's Press, 1969.

Hopkins, Paul, *Glencoe and the End of the Highland War*, Edinburgh, John Donald, 1986.

Horwitz, Henry, *Parliament, Policy, and Politics in the Reign of William III*, Manchester University Press, 1977.

  Revolution Politicks: the Career of Daniel Finch, Second Earl of Nottingham, 1647–1730, London, Cambridge University Press, 1968.

  "1689 (and All That)," *Parliamentary History* 6 (1987), 23–32.

  "Parliament and the Glorious Revolution," *BIHR* 47 (1974), 36–52.

Israel, Jonathan I., *Dutch Primacy in World Trade, 1585–1740*, Oxford, Clarendon Press, 1989.

  "The Dutch Republic and Glorious Revolution of 1688/89 in England," in Charles Wilson and David Proctor (eds.), *1688: the Seaborne Alliance and the Diplomatic Revolution*, Greenwich, National Maritime Museum, 1989, pp. 31–44.

Johnson, Richard R., *Adjustment to Empire: the New England Colonies, 1675–1715*, New Brunswick, N.J., Rutgers University Press, 1981.

Jones, David Lewis, *A Parliamentary History of the Glorious Revolution*, London, HMSO, 1988.

Jones, George Hilton, "The Irish Fright of 1688: Real Violence and Imagined Massacres," *BIHR* 55 (1982), 148–53.

Jones, J. R., *The Revolution of 1688 in England*, London, Weidenfeld and Nicolson, 1972.

Kenyon, J. P., "The Revolution of 1688: Resistance and Contract," in Neil McKendrick (ed.), *Historical Perspectives: Studies in English Thought and Society in Honour of J. H. Plumb*, London, Europa 1974, pp. 43–70.

  Revolution Principles. The Politics of Party 1689–1720, Cambridge University Press, 1977.

Lacey, Douglas R., *Dissent and Parliamentary Politics in England, 1661–1689: a Study in the Perpetuation and Tempering of Parliament*, New Brunswick, N.J., Rutgers University Press, 1969.

Legg, L. G. Wickham, *English Coronation Records*, Westminster, A. Constable, 1901.

Linklater, Magnus and Christian Hesketh, *For King and Conscience: John Graham of Claverhouse, Viscount Dundee*, London, Weidenfeld and Nicolson, 1989.

Loftis, John, *The Politics of Drama in Augustan England*, Oxford, Clarendon Press, 1963.

Lord, George DeF. (ed.), *Poems on Affairs of State*, 7 vols., New Haven and London, Yale University Press, 1963–75.

Lovejoy, David S., *The Glorious Revolution in America*, New York, Harper and Row, 1972.

Macaulay, T. B., *A History of England from the Accession of James II*, ed. C. H. Firth, 6 vols., London, Macmillan, 1913–15.

Maccubbin, R. P. and Martha Hamilton-Phillips (eds.), *The Age of William III and Mary II. Power, Politics and Patronage 1688–1702*, Williamsburg, Va., The College of William and Mary, 1989.

McInnes, A., "When was the English Revolution?," *History* 67 (1982), 377–92.

Macrory, Patrick, *The Siege of Derry*, Oxford University Press, 1988.

Miller, John, "The Glorious Revolution: 'Contract' and 'Abdication' Reconsidered," *HJ* 25 (1982), 541–55.

  James II. A Study in Kingship, London, Wayland, 1977; repr. London, Methuen, 1989.

Mitchison, Rosalind, *Lordship to Patronage: Scotland 1603–1745*, The New History of Scotland, v, London, E. Arnold, 1983.

Nenner, Howard, "Constitutional Uncertainty and the Declaration of Rights," in bara C. Malament (ed.), *After the Reformation: Essays in Honor of J. H. Hexter*, Philadelphia, University of Pennsylvania Press, 1980, pp. 291–308.

By Colour of Law: Legal Culture and Constitutional Politics in England, 1660–1689, University of Chicago Press, 1977.

Neveu, Bruno (ed.), *Correspondence du nonce en France: Angelo Ranuzzi (1683–1689)*, 2 vols., Paris, Ecole française de Rome, Université pontificale grégorienne, Rome, 1973.

O'Connor, John T., *Negotiator out of Season: the Career of Wilhelm Egon von Fürstenberg 1629 to 1704*, Athens, University of Georgia Press, 1978.

Olson, Alison Gilbert, *Anglo-American Politics 1660–1775: the Relationship Between Parties in England and Colonial America*, London and New York, Oxford University Press, 1973.

Orcibal, Jean, *Louis XIV contre Innocent XI. Les appels au futur concile de 1688 et l'opinion française*, Paris, J. Vrin, 1949.

Parks, Stephen, *John Dunton and the English Book Trade, a Study of His Career with a Checklist of His Publications*, New York and London, Garland, 1976.

Pateman, Carole, *The Sexual Contract: Aspects of Patriarchal Liberalism*, Stanford University Press, 1988.

Plomer, Henry R. and H. G. Aldis, *A Dictionary of the Printers and Booksellers Who Were At Work in England, Scotland, and Ireland from 1668 to 1725*, ed. Arundell Esdaile, London, Bibliographical Society, Oxford University Press, 1922.

Pocock, J. G. A., *The Ancient Constitution and the Feudal Law: a Study of English Historical Thought in the Seventeenth Century, A Reissue with a Retrospect*, Cambridge University Press, 1987.

(ed.), *Three British Revolutions: 1641, 1688, 1776*, Princeton University Press, 1980.

(ed.), *Virtue, Commerce and History. Essays on Political Thought and History, Chiefly in the Eighteenth Century*, Cambridge University Press, 1985.

Poems on the Reign of William III, introduced and selected by Earl Miner, Augustan Reprint Society Publication, no. 166, Los Angeles, University of California Press, 1974.

Reid, John Philip, *In Defiance of the Law: the Standing-Army Controversy, the Two Constitutions, and the Coming of the American Revolution*, Chapel Hill, University of North Carolina Press, 1981.

Riley, P. W. J., *King William and the Scottish Politicians*, Edinburgh, John Donald, 1979.

Roberts, Michael, *Essays in Swedish History*, London, Weidenfeld and Nicolson, 1967.

Rosenfeld, Sybil, *The Theatre of the London Fairs in the Eighteenth Century*, Cambridge University Press, 1960.

Rousset, Camille, *Histoire de Louvois et de son administration politique et militaire*, 4 vols., Paris, Dédier et Cie, 1861–64.

Rule, John C. (ed.), *Louis XIV and the Craft of Kingship*, Columbus, Ohio State University Press, 1970.

Schochet, Gordon J., *Patriarchalism in Political Thought*, New York, Basic Books, 1975; 2nd edn. 1988.

Schwoerer, Lois G., "Celebrating the Glorious Revolution, 1689–1989," *Albion* 22 (1990), 1–19.

"Images of Queen Mary II, 1689–1695," *Renaissance Quarterly* 42 (1989), 717–48.

"Women and the Glorious Revolution," *Albion* 18 (1986), 195–218.

The Declaration of Rights, 1689, Baltimore and London, Johns Hopkins University Press, 1981.

Lady Rachel Russell. "One of the Best of Women," Baltimore and London, Johns Hopkins University Press, 1981.

Scott, Jonathan, *Algernon Sidney and the Restoration Crisis 1677–83*, Cambridge University Press, 1989.

Senior, Hereward, *Orangeism in Ireland and Britain, 1795–1836*, London, Routledge and Kegan Paul, and Toronto, Ryerson, 1966.

Shanley, Mary L., "Marriage Contract and Social Contract in Seventeenth Century English Political Thought," *Western Political Quarterly* 32 (1979), 79–91.

Shapiro, Barbara J., *Probability and Certainty in Seventeenth-Century England: a Study of the Relationships between Natural Science, Religion, History, Law, and Literature*, Princeton University Press, 1983.

Sharpe, J. A., *Crime in Early Modern England, 1550–1750*, London, Longman, 1984.

Simms, J. G., "The War of the Two Kings, 1685–91," in T. W. Moody, F. X. Martin, and F. J. Byrne (eds.), *A New History of Ireland*, 8 vols., Oxford, Clarendon Press, 1976, III, pp. 478–508.

  Jacobite Ireland, 1685–91, London, Routledge and Kegan Paul, 1969.

  The Williamite Confiscation in Ireland, 1690–1703, London, Faber and Faber, 1956.

Slaughter, Thomas P., "'Abdicate' and 'Contract' in the Glorious Revolution," *HJ* 24 (1981), 323–37.

  "'Abdicate' and 'Contract' Restored," *HJ* 28 (1985), 399–403.

Speck, W. A., "The Orangist Conspiracy against James II," *HJ* 30 (1987), 453–62.

  Reluctant Revolutionaries: Englishmen and the Revolution of 1688, Oxford and New York, Oxford University Press, 1988.

Spurr, John, "The Church of England, Comprehension, and the Toleration Act of 1689," *EHR* 104 (1989), 927–46.

Stone, Lawrence, *The Family, Sex, and Marriage in England, 1500–1800*, New York, Harper and Row, 1977.

Straka, G. M., *Anglican Reaction to the Revolution of 1688* (Madison, University of Wisconsin Press, 1962.

Sutherland, James, *English Literature of the Late Seventeenth Century*, Oxford History of English Literature, VI, Oxford University Press, 1969.

Sykes, Norman, *From Sheldon to Secker: Aspects of English Church History, 1660–1768*, Cambridge University Press, 1959.

Thomas, Roger, "Comprehension and Indulgence," in Geoffrey F. Nutall and Owen Chadwick (eds.), *From Uniformity to Unity, 1662–1962*, London, Society for the Promotion of Christian Knowledge, 1962, ch. 4.

van der Zee, Henri and Barbara van der Zee, *William and Mary*, London, Macmillan, 1973.

Weston, C. C. and J. R. Greenberg, *Subjects and Sovereigns*, Cambridge University Press, 1981.

Wilson, Charles, *Anglo-Dutch Commerce and Finance in the Eighteenth Century*, Cambridge University Press, 1941; repr. 1966.

Winn, James, *John Dryden and His World*, New Haven and London, Yale University Press, 1987.

Wood, Neal, *The Politics of Locke's Philosophy: A Social Study of "An Essay concerning Human Understanding,"* Berkeley and Los Angeles, University of California Press, 1983.

The Works of John Dryden, ed. Edward Niles Hooker and H. T. Swedenberg, Jr., 20 vols., Berkeley, Los Angeles, and London, University of California Press, 1956–89, XV, *Albion and Albanius, Don Sebastian, Amphitryon*, ed. Earl Miner, 1976.

Zwicker, Steven N., *Politics and Language in Dryden's Poetry: the Arts of Disguise*, Princeton University Press, 1984.

Index